PENN

University of Pennsylvania Press

Philadelphia

Radclyffe Hall

Radclyffe Hall

A Life in the Writing

Richard Dellamora

A volume in the Haney Foundation Series, established in 1961 with the generous support of Dr. John Louis Haney.

Published by
University of Pennsylvania Press
Philadelphia, Pennsylvania 19104-4112
www.upenn.edu/pennpress

Printed in the United States of America
on acid-free paper

10 9 8 7 6 5 4 3 2 1

Library of Congress Cataloging-in-Publication Data
Dellamora, Richard.
 Radclyffe Hall : a life in the writing / Richard Dellamora.
p. cm. — (Haney Foundation series)
Includes bibliographical references and index.
ISBN: 978-0-8122-4346-8 (hardcover : alk. paper)
 1. Hall, Radclyffe—Criticism and interpretation.   2. Lesbianism in literature.   3. Spiritualism in literature.
PR6015.A33 Z635   2011
823'.912 B 22   2011010285

Overleaf: Radclyffe Hall and Una Troubridge, 1927.
Hulton Getty/Liaison Agency.

I never write my own life—,
I could not.

  —Radclyffe Hall

CONTENTS

ILLUSTRATIONS

PREFACE

Since the 1970s, the memory of Radclyffe Hall has depended for the most part upon one novel and its place in her work as an activist on behalf of the social rights of women with sexual and emotional ties to other women. The effects of near exclusive focus on *The Well of Loneliness* (1928) and related court cases has been to impose upon Hall a biographical trajectory in which the single overriding feature of her life is her emergence as an early leader in the struggle for gay and lesbian rights. Hall herself, however, rejected this view and attempted in subsequent writing to recapture the less specialized readership of her earlier fiction. My interest is to consider the factors in relation to which this particular trajectory arose. In recent years, the development of the field of queer theory has made possible a view of Hall that gives due emphasis to three concerns that primarily engaged her: namely, female same-sex desire, engenderment, and spirituality.

A study of the five short books of poetry with which she began her literary career indicates that her signature from the start carried with it the affirmation of sexual and emotional ties between women. For Hall, this impulse was married to an equally strong desire to define herself as an artist and to mark out the contours of her personal life, directly and indirectly, in her published and unpublished poetry, fiction, essays, and lectures. Equally, all the metaphysical turns in Hall's life are related to her ties with female partners or lovers: namely, her conversion to Roman Catholicism in 1912;[1] the six years she devoted to psychical research following the death of her first long-term partner, Mabel Veronica Batten; the adherence to Spiritualism implicit in the years of séances with Mrs. Gladys Osborne

Leonard, a prominent British medium; the theosophical narrative structure of *A Saturday Life* (1925); and the desire for interpersonal fusion that characterizes the letters to Evguenia Souline in the final decade. In this context, the traditional view of the primary significance of Hall's sexual interests may appear to be confirmed. It remains the case, however, that whether one begins with Hall's desire for other women or with her concern with cross gender or with mystical states, each leads to the others.

Hall was a charismatic figure with a complex affective and sexual life. This reality, combined with her courting of scandal and the exclusive attention directed by critics to *The Well of Loneliness,* accounts for the fact that almost all of the books published about her have taken the form of biography or biographical memoir. Hall became a celebrity as part of the enterprise of developing a lesbian public culture in the early twentieth century, but this apparently straightforward statement masks complexities. For instance, I know of no instance where Hall uses the word *lesbian* to designate a member of a particular sexual minority. Rather, she seems to have written at almost the last possible moment in the twentieth century in which the public affirmation of sexual and emotional ties between women could be made without using that word. Hall uses three other terms instead, each drawn from a different history in the development of discourses about female same-sex desire. In the course of this book, the reader will find Hall's interest in desire between women frequently characterized in terms of Sapphic culture, derived from French Aestheticism, as that culture came to exist in male and female lives and writing of the late nineteenth century in France and England. Equally important is the highly developed Sapphic culture—complete with rituals, a sacramental life, mythography, sacred texts, heroes, and martyrs—that Natalie Barney built around herself in a high-profile experiment in Paris after 1900. In the fiction of the 1920s, Hall participated in and reported on this Parisian scene. By this means, she joined Barney's venture; but, as I have mentioned, from the early years of the new century, Hall was already conducting her own experiments in Sapphic culture.

Second, Hall associated herself with modern sexual science in its efforts to define what later came to be called the lesbian subject. Well versed in popular accounts of Freud,[2] she chose in her writing to use the more established terminology of sexual inversion. While this choice may seem to suggest that Hall lagged in familiarity with modern psychology, Freud's oedipal account of female-female sexual desire in the 1920s did not definitively separate itself from sexological discourse.[3] Moreover, the language of female sexual inversion, which characterized female-female sexual desire as "masculine," offered the only scientific terminology available for exploring the topic of cross gender.[4] The female invert, in Hall's telling, was less a modern "lesbian" than a crossgendered subject. As a result, *The Well of Loneliness* has become an important way marker for contemporary theorists of transgendered and what in the LGBT community are referred to as stone-butch identities.[5]

Third, as Ruth Vanita and others have observed, there is a long tradition in which Marian and Christic references signal both female-female and crossgendered female-female desire. In recent years, Frederick S. Roden, Ellis Hanson, and other writers have made important contributions to the analysis of this discourse.[6] All three modes of address—Sapphic, sexological, and Catholic—contributed to articulating a complex understanding of sexual and emotional ties between women. And all three characterize Hall's approach at specific moments.

As author and individual, Hall's life was an exercise in new ways of being in the world. Unfortunately, the genre of biography is not well suited to experiment. Biographies, at least marketable ones, depend upon novelistic narratives, well-defined characters, and familiar emotions and moral views. The ideological effect of biographies is to reinforce these views by repeating them. Facts and situations may be novel but not the ideas, affects, and emotions with which they are presented. As a result, it has been necessary to write this book *against* the genre of Hall biography. On occasion, I take explicit exception to how the rules of the genre operate in a particular biography. Nonetheless, because Hall's experiment is one in life *and* writing, I am in debt to the writers of her biographies, especially to Michael Baker, whose work is often paraphrased in later biographies, and Sally Cline, whose 1997 biography for the first time locates Hall's start as a writer within the context of an accomplished and adventurous group of female artists, Sapphists, and feminists.

Cline makes clear the collaborative character of Hall's art from the outset. Collaboration too is not well suited to conventional biography. Biographies of writers usually focus on one or at most two individuals. Moreover, Hall and her second long-term partner, Una Troubridge, invested in the ideology of singular artistic genius. Despite the apparent contradiction, however, without Troubridge, Hall is unlikely to have produced the chain of literary successes that she enjoyed in the 1920s. Moreover,

Troubridge shares responsibility for the outspoken activism of *The Well of Loneliness*. Hall's output depended intimately upon Batten, Troubridge, and a later lover, Evguenia Souline, plus additional abettors, such as Barney and Colette. Strongly individualistic herself, Hall yearned for partnership and community, desires that drove her intellectually and emotionally to question conventional notions of selfhood.

In the most recent biography, Diana Souhami has added the important discovery that Hall was very likely dyslexic, a disability that poses challenges to those who choose to write on her in future. In part for this reason and in part because of parental neglect, Hall's formal education was limited. Admitted to King's College, London, she spent little time there.[7] Hall was not an intellectual and did not have an intellectual's interest in ideas and the language in which they are expressed. But she had a keen interest in human psychology, particularly in the boundaries of the self: between human and nonhuman, between conscious and unconscious, between I and the other. She explored this interest by means of the speculative psychologies available to her, including psychoanalysis. In entertaining vernacular modes of speculative and religious belief, Hall was less interested in arriving at dogmatic conviction than in finding popularly accessible ways of overcoming the limits of the individual ego, particularly as posited in English eighteenth-century empiricist psychology and political economy. In her life and in her writing, Hall continually returns to the task of exploring selfhood in other terms than those of ego-centered calculation. Her experience as a crossgendered subject contributed to this interest as did her attraction to mysticism. Crossgendered existence and mystical experience are both phenomena that depend upon a shattering of the self. The attempt to recuperate such extremity within the routines of conventional "life and writings" biography contradicts the inevitable discontinuities and contradictions entailed in such ways of being.

Current commentators on Hall tend to deplore her conservative politics, and, at times, her views were deplorable, though for the most part they were typical of the social circles in which she moved. The frequently reactionary ideology of political conservatism in England and the United States since the late 1970s, moreover, has tended to block awareness of progressive tendencies within conservatism. Hall's critique of the market economy, her repeated explorations of isolated communities of working- or lower-class inhabitants, her participation in the pastoral turn in modern English poetic and musical culture, her interest in queer affinities between different orders of organic and inorganic existence, all register a critical response to modernity. While critical, however, Hall remained a modern, not a reactionary. For example, in choosing to define female same-sex desire in *The Well of Loneliness* in terms of the sexological concept of sexual inversion, she attempted to base her polemic in scientific modernism. Likewise, she accepted the key axioms of Freudian thought: the power of unconscious motivation in human life; the unconscious play of symbolic action in dreams and other aspects of everyday experience; the mechanisms of repression, sublimation, and desublimation in subjectivity and culture; the erotic bases of human motives; and the primary function of incestuous desire within subject-formation. Both Hall and Freud also believed that the mind-body relation is internalized to the bodily ego. Within limits, Hall accepted even Freud's insistence on the Oedipus complex as the basis of human psychic development. What she disagreed with was his decision to use the male Oedipus complex as the basis from which to theorize about female sexuality. And she rejected his insistence on psychoanalysis as the only valid mode of speculative psychology. Rather, Hall could be persuaded by Freudian concepts without relinquishing ones derived from Roman Catholic practice and from her experience of Theosophy, Spiritualism, and psychical research.

Given the limits of biography as genre, how is one to approach it? I have done so in three ways. First, at times I have pointed out obvious shortcomings. Second, I have focused on complex situations and symbolic relations, often in unpublished and incomplete texts. For example, the scene of classroom instruction in *Michael West* that I discuss in the Introduction brings together the sensation and affect of shame in relation to the difficulties that Hall experienced in writing and reading as a result of her dyslexia plus the attendant gaze of a desired female other, whose acceptance and encouragement are necessary if the anxieties generated within the scene are to be surmounted. The incident brings together a complex of elements that Hall reprises later in both autobiographical and fictional contexts. In Hall, writing and desire are codependent. Similarly, the climax of this unfinished novel, in which the young male protagonist, who stands in for young Hall, simultaneously experiences ecstasy, acceptance as a lover, and transfiguration as a figure of exquisite, crucifixial sacrifice, likewise brings together elements in a recurring complex. Third, I examine the ways in which Hall's novels continually play with combinations of biographical, autobiographical, and fictive material as part of their appeal to their original readers.

In the Introduction, I consider how Hall's incomplete drafts of an auto-biographical essay graphically demonstrate that the failure of mother love in her early experience left her without a necessary genealogical basis for writing herself into time and space. In Chapter 1, I discuss how Hall's poetry explores various modes of sexual and emotional interaction between women. This effort is situated in poems of the English countryside, neo-Hellenistic pastoral, and, in *The Forgotten Island* (1915), an imitation of Sappho. In the poetry, Hall writes as both a modern and an antimodern, a feminist and an aesthete and a decadent, a follower of Pan and Dionysus and a Christian believer. One of her most important points of reference exists in the aestheticist, homophile, and antimodernist poetry of A. E. Housman. Even more significant is A. C. Swinburne, a founder of Aestheti-cism and the Decadence in England. By her own account, it is through Swinburne's imitations of Sappho in his early poetry that Hall accessed Sapphic tradition. Swinburne is equally important in shaping the moder-nity of her work. In "Ode to Swinburne" (1909), she affirms a carefully considered, coherent statement of Swinburne's late Victorian secular hu-manism. The poem demonstrates that, despite the fact that Hall was bap-tized as a Roman Catholic shortly thereafter, her poetry is written from a humanist stance. The final section of the chapter shifts attention to Hall's spectacular if unanticipated success as the author of a lyric, "The Blind Ploughman." The poem, in the voice of a male agricultural laborer, com-bines religious faith with moral earnestness and a capacity for visionary experience. Set to music, "The Blind Ploughman" became an anthem of popular patriotic and religious sentiment during World War I. Its impact demonstrated to Hall her connection with cultivated British middle-class taste.

After Batten's death in 1916 following a stroke, Hall turned to psychical research for a period of six years in search of an objective means of proving the survival of individual personality after death. The result is a long ac-count of her researches that appeared in the *Proceedings of the Society for Psychical Research* in 1919. In preparing the manuscript, Hall both gained a collaborator in Batten's cousin, Troubridge, and learned how to research and write a long piece of prose narrative. In Chapter 2, I analyze Hall's account of her sittings with Mrs. Leonard. Hall's experience illustrates how the technology of mediumship operated at the time of World War I so as to enable the subject in mourning to come to terms with loss by incorporat-ing the beloved object through a particular kind of physical enactment proper to the séance. The sessions reassured her of Batten's continuing existence and love as well as of her approval of Troubridge as Hall's new partner. There is reason to doubt, however, whether the sittings enabled Hall to come to terms with her responsibility for the estrangement that existed between the two women at the time of Batten's fatal stroke.

The psychical research marks an important turn in Hall's engagement with the creation of a public lesbian culture since both the essay and the public lectures on which it was based converted the Sapphic triangle in which Hall was involved into publicity. The combination of personal, even private, experience with the public performance of sensational material leads to Chapter 3, an account of how Hall achieved notoriety in the English mass media by filing a suit for slander against a founding member of the Society who, on the basis of the publication of her research, had accused her of being "a grossly immoral woman."[8]

Chapter 4 deals with *The Unlit Lamp* (1924), the first novel completed for publication by Hall but the second to appear in print. Possibly Hall's best work, it focuses on psychological and social blocks to sexual and emotional ties between women that existed in the years between 1870 and 1920. On the psychological side is the unresolved incestuous tension of the protagonist, Joan Ogden's, relationship with her mother. On the social side, Hall takes aim at the late Victorian institution of friendship between well-educated single women. Hall is particularly skeptical of the rule of celibacy that attended love between women in female same-sex institutions, such as the newly founded colleges for women at Cambridge University.[9] In both emphases on female relationships, Hall's novel provides illustrations of what was missing from Freud's contemporaneous effort to explain female (homo)sexuality.

Chapter 5 focuses on *The Forge* (1924), Hall's first published novel. It has a double protagonist in a married couple: Hilary Brent, a young, independently wealthy husband suffering from writer's block, and his wife, Susan, who has chosen not to pursue her early promise as a painter. Readers who, directly or indirectly, were aware of Hall and Troubridge's life together in London early in the decade had no difficulty in noting resemblances between the real and the fictional pairs. Indeed, the autobiographical linkage was part of the appeal of the novel. The novel further capitalized on Hall and Troubridge's familiarity with Sapphic high and low culture in Paris in the mid-1920s. In this respect, *The Forge* is the novel by Hall that engages most directly with the creation of a cosmopolitan lesbian public culture. With the publication of this novel, Hall began building a double readership composed of Sapphic readers and others, middle class and mainly female.

In *A Saturday Life* (1925), Hall is preoccupied with the psychological and social challenges faced by individual women in integrating the desire to find fulfilling adult work with traditional middle-class gender roles. An experiment in gender performativity, the novel draws the reader's attention to the question of whether sexual and gendered self-fashioning results from choice or from psychic compulsion. Based on correspondence that Hall received from her readers, it appears that Frances Reide, the novel's stable pivot, enjoyed great appeal to both sets of Hall's readers, while Sidonia Shore, the attractive, mercurial, and boyish young female protagonist, provided a way to explore the construction of gender in new ways. Framed in terms of theosophical mythmaking, the outline of Shore's life suggests that gender-formation is unconsciously driven, including the extent to which masculinity forms a component within it. As usual, female masculinity is pertinent as is the possibility of sexual and emotional intimacy between women, though, for both Shore and Reide, the opportunity remains unrealized as it had for Jane Ogden and Susan Brent in the two previous novels. Nonetheless, and drawing upon Troubridge's unpublished autobiographical essays, Hall emphasizes the multiplicity of Sidonia's selves and the self-consciousness of her performance of female gender, both with regard to her choice of marriage and childbirth at the end of the novel and in her persistent, albeit short-lived, artistic enthusiasms.

Hall's next three novels are very different. Long, serious works, with harrowing endings and strongly naturalist in character, all three are also explicitly religious, indeed Roman Catholic. Their protagonists are shaped along Christological and, in the case of *The Well of Loneliness*, Marian lines. Chapter 7 begins with a general discussion of the place of Catholicism in Hall's thinking and ends with a discussion of psychological extremity in the final pages of *The Well of Loneliness*. Catholicism offered a more intellectually and emotionally developed framework in which Hall could articulate her intuitions about the porous boundaries that she believed to exist between nonhuman and human existence, individual and intersubjective experience, and the consciousness of the living and the dead. Previously, she had expressed her sense of these connections in terms of psychical research, Spiritualism, and Theosophy; but these formations did not permit her to address the more abstract philosophical and theological question of theodicy, that is, why and how God, if there is a God, permits the existence of evil in individual and social existence. For Hall, this question was entangled with her awareness of the seemingly gratuitous suffering of subjects of same-sex desire. Writing in the psychoanalytically attuned cultural environment of England in the 1920s, moreover, she also perceived the problem to be lodged in the psychological structure of the nuclear family and, in particular, in destructive aspects of mother-daughter relations. Hall, Batten, and Troubridge were converts to Roman Catholicism. As women involved in sexual relationships with other women, they stood in anomalous relation to the orthodox teaching of the Catholic Church, which condemns all sexual activity outside marriage. In choosing to be baptized as a Roman Catholic while in effect living with Batten, Hall chose to enter the Church as a witness to the sacramental character of love between women. The pair intended in this way to contribute to the Church Militant by force of example.

The central portion of the chapter concentrates on *Adam's Breed* (1926), the first of the religious novels. Although in form a bildungsroman tracing the life of its male protagonist, Gian-Luca, the novel offers something of a cultural anthropology of the Roman Catholic, working-class Italian immigrant colony in Soho in which he is born and raised. As one might expect from a writer who came to Catholicism from an English Protestant background, Hall perceives the religious practice of Gian-Luca's family and neighbors to be credulous, superstitious, and highly materialistic. Moreover, she shows how the moralizing character of day-to-day existence in a tightly knit Catholic community provides ample opportunity for the self-righteous policing of other people's behavior. Hall's sense of the thoughtlessness, ignorance, and indeed blind moral cruelty of self-preening members of the laity was intensified by her experience while traveling in Italy in the 1920s with Troubridge, who had relatives there. Hall uses the Italian section of the novel to demonstrate the extent to which rural Italians made perverse use of their religion to excuse everyday acts of sadism toward pets, farmyard animals, and outsiders, such as Gian-Luca. But Hall's is an insider's criticism. She frames her strictures in terms of Catholic notions of blasphemy, infidelity, and idolatry. Finally, the portrayal of Gian-Luca himself as a heroic, self-sacrificial figure draws on Catholic feeling and belief, supplemented late in the novel with theosophical hints that the young

Anglo-Italian may be a latter-day materialization of a Self of which the historical Christ is another exponent.

The commercial and critical success of *Adam's Breed* established Hall's reputation as a serious novelist. Taking advantage of her new position, Hall moved quickly in her next novel to address the question of the psychological and social position of subjects of same-sex desire. Although she chose to do so within the genre of the social problem novel, in the final section of Chapter 7, I consider how the novel also builds upon and in a sense repeats the structure of *Adam's Breed* by converting Stephen Gordon, the gendercrossing novelist and protagonist of *The Well of Loneliness*, into another figure of self-sacrificing love modeled upon both Christ and, in this case, his mother, Mary.

Chapter 8 takes a secular perspective in focusing on *The Well of Loneliness* as an activist text. In this respect, the key question that arises is that of the spatial and temporal forms of dissident existence. In other words, what social forms might the expression of male and female same-sex desire appropriately take? Hall answers by emphasizing the need to develop institutions of same-sex marriage. This demand for legal and other changes became a focus for attacks upon the novel during the trials of its publisher on charges of obscenity. If Hall's position offended moral and religious conservatives, it also offended sexually experimental bohemians, to whom it seemed both outdated and irrelevant. Hall's stance, however, was neither idiosyncratic nor out of touch since the question of the durability of same-sex pairings was a live topic in both private and public discourse of the 1920s and 1930s.

The final portion of the chapter considers the recently published private contract of marriage that Natalie Barney wrote in 1918 for herself and her lifelong lover, Elisabeth de Gramont, Duchesse de Clermont-Tonnerre. In the face of the affairs with other women that both had already embarked upon and that might engage them in future, Barney wrote: "Since the danger of affairs is ever present and impossible to foresee, one will just have to bring the other back, neither out of revenge, nor to limit the other, but because the union demands it. . . . No other union shall be so strong as this union, nor another joining so tender—nor relationship so lasting."[10] In the mid-1930s, Noël Coward put the same argument in the mouth of a newlywed speaking to his wife in *Shadow Play*, in which Coward starred opposite Gertrude Lawrence: "If I'm bad or foolish or unkind, or even unfaithful—just remember this, because this is what really matters—this lovely understanding of each other—it may be a jumping-off place for many future journeys—but however long the journey one's got to come back some time."[11]

In "Miss Ogilvy Finds Herself," a short story drafted in 1926 before Hall began writing *The Well of Loneliness* but not published until afterward, Hall develops a relational model of crossgendered identity, that is, one in which the masculine woman is understood to be unable fully to come into her double engenderment until she is recognized and passionately loved as such by a womanly woman. Chapter 9 explores both concepts in the context of an allegory of sexual becoming, part realist fiction, part theosophical fantasy.

Chapter 10 focuses on "The Rest Cure—1932," one of the most highly reflexive of Hall's fictions. In this story, Hall's self-conscious analysis of the failure of the "I" as an avatar of selfhood prompts her to re-reengage with the Buddhist-influenced pantheism of her friend, May Sinclair, an important experimenter in modernist fiction, a pioneering feminist philosopher, and a pre–World War I proponent of psychoanalysis. In "The Rest Cure—1932," Charles Duffell, an English industrialist, experiences a breakdown following the loss of his firm after the stock-market crash of 1929. A catastrophic rupture in the experience to which his family, citizenship, gender, and status had sentenced him drives him—like Miss Ogilvy—to a rural retreat. Unable to surmount the limits of the ego even in fantasy, however, he regresses to a primitive state of gender dysphoria, which results in his incarceration in a mental institution. Duffell's success is limited to refusing the options afforded him. Unlike Miss Ogilvy's ecstatic fantasy of integrated dual gender, Duffell's access to mystical experience is confined for the most part in the via negativa.

Because of the sexual indeterminacy of feminine women, the sexual-inversion model remains highly unstable. Moreover, for Hall, crossgendered existence did not necessarily imply homosexual object choice. In her final published novel, *The Sixth Beatitude*, Hall fashions a protagonist in Hannah Bullen, a virile young woman who is strongly attracted to males. In Chapter 11, I consider this novel along with two other sets of material: the draft manuscripts of *Emblem Hurlstone*, an incomplete novel undertaken by Hall in the first months of her absorption in Souline; and the letters to Souline, not published until 1997, which were to be a major preoccupation for Hall from 1934 until her death in 1943. In addition to offering a self-conscious exploration of the meaning of Sapphic desire, the letters provide a reflexive commentary on both novels as well as on Hall's general understanding of the play of biography, autobiography, and fiction in writing.

In "The Rest Cure—1932" as in other stories and novels beginning with *Adam's Breed*, Hall offered not solutions but invitations to extremity, couched in harsh circumstances. In the letters and fiction of her late autobiographical writing, she lived similarly but with an ever-renewed commitment to the passional self and with a mystic's openness to the human and natural environments to which she bore witness. Hall did so in the form of an open series of meditations on the continual reentwining of the polarities of gendered experience.

Writing Radclyffe Hall Writing

The position of social and economic privilege occupied by Hall and Troubridge, their Tory sympathies, Roman Catholicism, and eugenicist views are
not factors calculated to endear them to members of contemporary lesbian
and queer counterpublics.[1] In recent years, Hall's self-identification as a
masculine woman drew even more criticism. To some second-generation
feminists, Hall was felt to have misled generations of young women into
believing that, if they desired sexual intimacy with other women, then they
must be psychically male. In 1975, for example, Jane Rule, complaining
about the reputation of *The Well of Loneliness* as "the Lesbian bible,"
quoted two leading young lesbian feminists who argued that "unfortunately, to the uninitiated the book perpetuated the myth of the Lesbian as
a pseudomale, and many young women . . . emulated the heroine, Stephen
Gordon."[2] Hall and her novel were regarded as a source of contagion, pol-
luting female difference with masculine traits, style, affects, and emotion.

The view of Hall as a "pseudomale" is the most damning allegation that
lesbian feminists laid against her. Hall, however, did not view herself as
male nor did she desire to be one. Rather, from an early age she understood
herself to be gendered as a masculine female. This sense, based in what
Freud refers to as "the bodily ego,"[3] makes her queer in the sense that, as
Jay Prosser has reminded readers, Eve Kosofsky Sedgwick takes as her point
of departure in *Tendencies* (1993): "Queer is a continuing moment, movement, motive—recurrent, eddying, *troublant*. The word 'queer' itself means

across—it comes from the Indo-European root *-twerkw*, which also yields the German *quer* (transverse), Latin *torquere* (to twist), English *athwart*."[4] Using the term in this sense, I will frequently refer to desire in Hall as queer even though it is more often referred to as lesbian. In his discussion, Prosser further associates the sense of crossing with the term *transgender* (22). Queer existence is premised on bodily and psychic unease with fixed gender identification. Queers always exist athwart their assigned gender identities. Such crossing is crucial both to Hall's sense of self and to her writing. The development of transgender discourse in the writing of Prosser and others in recent years has enabled a less defensive, more accurate awareness of Hall's sense of embodied selfhood. She has found favor among dyke and butch readers as well as among transgendered and transsexual subjects, who find in Stephen Gordon's struggles a mirror of their own.

The vicissitudes of Hall's reception testify to one of the strengths of her writing, namely, its enticement of the reader to take part in a play of identification and counter-identification with the author and characters that depends on the actively crossgendered character of Hall's writing.[5] Hall did not think of female masculinity as a ticket to male privilege, nor did she think of it as a state of being. Rather, she thought of it as an action, at once intransitive, transitive, and self-reflexive. Her uncanny capacity to inhabit gender-crossing gender positions complicates the tendency of her work, particularly in *The Well of Loneliness*, to invest in the concept of sexual inversion.

Activists lend themselves as hostages to posterity. Powerful mutual identifications exist between them and those on whose behalf they venture to speak. As a result, the lives of activists are expected to conform to the goals and ideology of movement politics. It is expected that leaders will conform to the ways of life of those who identify as members of a particular minority. However, the lives of activists often look very different lived forward rather than backward from the destinations at which they eventually arrive. Individuals are crossing points of many interests, conditions, motives, and desires, conscious and unconscious. As Benjamin Harshav remarks, "In principle, it would be more appropriate to see the individual [and her writing] as an open semantic field through which various tendencies crisscross: some of them are involuntary and some [s]he herself embraced and helped formulate, some become dominant and others merely hover in the field of consciousness. . . . Individuals, even highly articulate ones, are often undecided on various matters, inconsistent, compromising between opposite ideas, changing their position with time."[6] Individuals' interests and views may take very different forms at different times, and this fact was particularly so for members of a number of emergent groups at the turn of the twentieth century. Harshav has in mind the Central and Eastern European Jews who founded and led the Zionist movement. For this generation of Jews newly emerging into civil society, many choices in life and thought were possible; hence he emphasizes the highly experimental character of their lives.

In Western Europe, a similar process occurred among those called homosexual. Simultaneously with the emergence of male and female homosexuality as a serious topic in medical literature, subjects of same-sex desire who began to think of their desires as linked with social and cultural typology entered a period of individual and social inventiveness.[7] Oscar Wilde, for example, became involved in the 1890s with young men at Oxford University who were engaged in what they referred to as "the Cause."[8] Although Wilde did not define himself as an activist on their behalf, he encouraged their talent and ambition and entered into friendships, collaborations, and, at times, sexual intimacies with them. In his professional life, he increasingly found himself fashioning the persona of a sexually nonconformist theatrical celebrity. Wilde's self-fashioning was in itself a form of activism that drew upon a developing tradition in the private and public lives of such actresses as the American Charlotte Cushman and the Jewish Parisian Sarah Bernhardt.[9] It is as though, having met and admired Bernhardt, Wilde decided to open a London shop of the Paris firm with himself in a double role as playwright and star.[10] In the circle of Natalie Barney in Paris, a similar process unfolded. Hall fashioned herself along comparable lines. The emphasis here is on personal, cultural, and social innovation.

Cultures of sexual dissidence come into existence in multiple discursive contexts. It would be a mistake to consider turn-of-the-century sexual politics exclusively in relation to attempts to reform criminal law or to challenge bias within the developing social sciences. Christianity, especially forms of Catholicism, provided a rich resource for imagining sexual difference. Whether individuals retained, converted to, or abandoned traditional religious beliefs, same-sex desire was often articulated within Catholic rhetoric. For example, Charles Ives, the leader of "the Cause" at Oxford and later, transferred to his own autobiographical narrative the terms of Incarnational devotion, ecstasis, self-mortification, martyrdom, and even crucifixion associated with the life of Christ.[11] Hall, who found her way to

Roman Catholicism under the guidance of a female partner, at times merged her identity with that of the historical figure of Christ. Gender and sexuality studies have much to gain from exploring the structuring of the subjectivity of subjects of same-sex desire in heterodox religious terms.[12]

The turn to Catholicism in Hall registers her recoil from the definition of the individual as a subject of rational calculation. This shift characterizes her as a modernist. In the words of Cathy Gere, "When we turn to the history of the human sciences . . . , a consensus seems to have emerged that modernism denotes a distinctive and often self-conscious sense of generational crisis, beginning around 1870 and persisting until just before the Second World War. This was distinguished, above all, by a profound loss of confidence in the Enlightenment legacy of rationalism."[13] While Hall's concern is less with reason than with the ideology of acquisitive individualism, she, like many other late Victorian and early twentieth-century writers, including many women, sought ways to express her awareness that personal existence is not limited to individual consciousness or even to human consciousness. For Hall, spirituality and sexuality both needed to find a place within a wider, more diffused sense of conscious and unconscious experience. The crossgendered experience of her fictional protagonists figures as one aspect within this larger challenge to the limits of species-centric thinking.

Hall's life was shaped as much by the ambition to become a novelist as by the desire to improve the condition of subjects of female same-sex desire. Her activist and literary concerns came mutually to reinforce one another. In turn, the desire to become an author may have had less to do in the first instance with a talent for writing than with a desire for distinction. To a young woman of means but little intellectual culture and limited education, the writing of popular fiction may have seemed, as it had for English-speaking women in the nineteenth century, to offer the most likely chance of success. In a self-reinforcing loop, moreover, for Hall the desire for literary distinction was fed by the myth of queer exceptionalism—that is, by the view expressed by Ives, John Addington Symonds, Edward Carpenter, and the Sapphic circle in Paris, among others, that the modern homosexual enjoyed a privileged insight into the human condition as a result of being double gendered.

Hall looked to writing to justify her continuing existence. If one wishes to consider Hall as an author, one needs to consider not only the range of her published fiction but the unpublished work as well. When one does so, one begins to see her less as an author than as a writer and, indeed, as a writer for whom writing was a necessary but perilous task, hence the title of this book. Hall continually attempted to write her way to a secure sense of selfhood. For the protagonists of a number of her novels, moreover, becoming paradoxically requires an undoing of the self and along with it the objects of everyday existence. Because Hall has most often figured as the author of a single novel, books about her tend to define her more in biographical than in literary terms. Including Troubridge's memoir, five of the six books devoted to Hall are biographies. The narrative of her complicated love life—the early sexual experimentation, followed by an extended relationship with Mabel Batten; the second long relationship, with Una Troubridge as partner and literary collaborator; and the *ménage à trois* with Troubridge and Evguenia Souline during the final decade—are more familiar to readers of the biographies than are her literary works. This history poses a challenge to anyone attempting a new book: how can one possibly structure it in ways that will not already be predetermined by the novelistic narratives of the biographies, with their familiar cast of characters and the banal moral inferences that they invite?[14]

In addition, in her fiction, Hall continually invokes the genres of memoir, biography, and autobiography. The engagement of her fiction with these genres constitutes the self-reflexive aspect of her work. This sort of self-consciousness, moreover, was already codified as a standard feature of realist fiction at the time she wrote. As Philippe Lejeune, a leading theorist of autobiography, observes, one of the main features linking nineteenth-century with modernist writing is the emphasis on the autobiographical character of the novel, a tendency exacerbated in Hall's case by her preference for the subgenre of the bildungsroman. Lejeune characterizes the genre of autobiography in terms of an "autobiographical pact," in which the author assures her reader of "the identity of the proper name shared by author, narrator, and protagonist."[15] Autobiography proper, however, was an impossible genre for Hall. She recoiled from writing a text in which she coincides with her signature—a signature, by the way, that frequently changes in her early writing, sloping at times to the left, at times to the right.[16] In writing autobiographically, she adopts the fictional genres of the novel and the short story. But, as we shall see, she often experiences difficulty in accepting the normal operation of the author-function—that is, the representation and self-representation of the writer of a text as being its authoritative source and the guarantor of whatever truth it may have to communicate.

Lejeune further distinguishes autobiography from the genre of autobiographical fiction in terms of what he refers to as "the phantasmatic pact." In this genre, it is the reader who is responsible for affirming that the characterization of the fictional protagonist "makes . . . accessible . . . the personal, individual, intimate truth of the author."[17] As the phrase indicates, this approach frankly acknowledges the phantasmatic relation between reader, protagonist, and author since the genre functions successfully only if the reader is convinced that her imaginary projection of an identification between author and protagonist is correct. At the same time, the reader is structurally positioned so as to be invited to identify herself with the place of the signature of the author, which, in autobiography proper, attests to the authenticity of the genre. In Hall's autobiographical fiction, it is the reader who establishes the authenticity of Hall's representation.

Since the leading protagonists of Hall's novels usually occupy a crossgendered subject position as masculine women or feminine men, the phantasmatic subject-position of the reader becomes yet more variable as herself, as author-function, and as crossgendered subject. This overdetermined position works in a number of different directions: on the one hand, it provides a necessary support for Hall in her roles as celebrity and authorfunction. But the position can also threaten fictional protagonists and the reader with a vertiginous sense of loss of selfhood as occurs in the final pages of *The Well of Loneliness*. This last effect has in turn a strong ideological basis in Hall since, like other female writers of the late Victorian and early modernist periods, such as Michael Field, Vernon Lee, May Sinclair, and Virginia Woolf, Hall believed the ego to be permeable to alterity. Through her religious beliefs, mysticism, and interest in both vernacular and scientific psychology, Hall sought means to explore selfhood beyond the limits of individual subjectivity. The dissolution of the self that awaits her protagonists at the end of a number of her novels further complicates the pressing sense in Hall's work of the double identification of author and reader with these same figures.

As a member of the culture of Sapphic celebrity in the 1920s, Hall repeatedly references not only herself in her fiction but her partner and her social circles in Paris and London as well.[18] The deliberate play with autobiographical reference in her writing constitutes it as partly a personal archive. I have usually drawn upon this aspect of her writing as a source of revealing discrepancies vis-à-vis the facts as these can be ascertained in the biographies and archives. Recognizing the fiction to be an autobiographical archive may help one understand Hall's response to the situation of being a masculine woman who affirms desire between women by entering the public sphere. Likewise, when one turns to unpublished writing by Hall in public archives, one can see Hall at work *before* she assumes the position of author-function. This material enables one to bring to bear a dimension of personal development that Harshav, for all his flexibility, ignores: namely, the play of the unconscious in the formation of conscious life. Hall's unpublished manuscripts permit one to see her not as an author but in the process of personal and aesthetic becoming that we call writing. *Radclyffe Hall, A Life in the Writing* is in part an archival study that considers how Hall writes her way toward and at times halts painfully short of the author-function.

After publication of *The Well*, Hall found herself to be the author of a sensational novel, widely read outside of England, and notorious as a result of the 1928 obscenity trials. This situation had a double effect. On the one hand, Hall and her partner found themselves withdrawing from café society in London, from friends and acquaintances, into a self-imposed exile abroad that became increasingly extended in the period of economic depression and growing political instability of the 1930s. On the other hand, Hall entered into a voluminous correspondence prompted by the novel. And there were frequent invitations to speak as a writer respected for exercising freedom of speech and claiming tolerance for subjects of same-sex desire. The unfinished drafts of some of these lectures still exist. At times, Hall's grasp of who her potential listeners are seems to slip from her in the course of writing—so that the text finally breaks off as an utterance by and to oneself that is both interminable and incapable of public delivery.

One of these incomplete essays, "Forebears and Infancy," exists in draft in a number of different manuscripts at the Harry Ransom Humanities Research Center at the University of Texas at Austin. Hall begins the first draft of what she refers to as this "autobiography" by speaking in her function as the author of *The Well of Loneliness*. She assures her listeners that those who think that *The Well* is "my own life story" will be disappointed. Negating both the sense of autobiographical intimacy she creates in the novel as well as the chronological line of the essay, she remarks that she did not spend her youth "in a gracious house of Georgian red brick" nor did she have parents like Stephen's.[19] She then proceeds to attempt to establish her genealogy as author. En route, she encounters a major obstacle, in relation to her mother, which eventually brings the essay to an abrupt halt. In the third and most-finished version of the essay, she contrasts Stephen's childhood to her own. "Let me begin by saying at once that my home was entirely unsatisfactory; it had neither dignity nor repose, and, moreover, was deplorably lacking in beauty."[20]

In recent years, subjects of same-sex desire have been dissociated from what Lee Edelman refers to as the "reproductive futurism" of heterosexual chronology.[21] I refer to this form of narrative as genealogical time: namely, the familiar familial narrative of origin, progeny, planning for old age, legacy, and inheritance that Edelman identifies with heterosexual temporality. In the incomplete drafts of this essay, Hall struggles unsuccessfully to fashion a genealogy of her own existence. Her inability to do so bespeaks both an unassuaged sense of exclusion from heterosexual (read human) temporality and the consequent conscious revolt that she associates with the authorship of *The Well of Loneliness*.[22] As the prosecution of the publisher of *The Well* indicates, in publishing the novel, Hall succeeded in literally exploding the continuity of conventional genealogy. Comparing her action with that of her father as a young man when he left his hometown and then returned, to the shame of *his* father, as an actor in a touring company, Hall remarks: "My father had suddenly torpedoed the ark, as a witty American woman said of me when I wrote *The Well of Loneliness*, and naturally an explosion followed" (Version 3).

In leaving incomplete this autobiographical essay, Hall indicates her inability to devise a new genealogy of sexual dissidence, whose effect would be successfully to locate her in time and place. Unable to establish a loving connection with her mother as point of origin, Hall recognizes herself to exist outside the realm of the human. She literalizes this maternal threat to her existence in Version 3, where she claims that her mother deliberately attempted to miscarry her. At the time of her birth, Hall experienced a near miss, precipitated, in her telling, by her eagerness to escape the emotional turmoil of her parents' continual fights: "As for me, I rushed headlong into the world several hours before my advent was expected. The nurse had gone out to get something from the chemist, my father was out and so was the Doctor; but fortunately the nurse returned just in time to sever the navel cord, so all was well, my mother survived and I lived to write *The Well of Loneliness* and to find myself standing in the police court."[23]

Earlier I spoke of Hall as economically and socially privileged. This description, however, leaves out of account the social isolation in which she grew up. As Hall reports, again in Version 3, her American mother quickly estranged her new husband's family. Divorcing him shortly after her daughter's birth and having won both custody of her daughter and a handsome allowance, Hall's mother subsequently refused to permit Hall to have anything to do with her paternal relations. In effect, Hall was raised in England as an exile. The essay functions as an effort to repair this estrangement. The Georgian house that Stephen Gordon is forced to quit by his mother in *The Well of Loneliness* is the metaphorical equivalent of the upper-middle-class paternal genealogy of which Hall's mother deprived her daughter. The self-styled bomb thrower and criminal defendant—identified in the very telling with the artistic and bohemian revolt of her father—experienced lifelong regret over this exclusion from an English Eden. The fact that Hall later chose American cousins met while traveling in the United States to be among her first lovers and long-lasting friends is one sign of how atopical she found her situation in England to be. Hall also reports that she had an older stepsister, Florence, by her mother's first marriage, who died shortly after birth. This brief reference suggests a possible reason for the rejection of Hall by her mother, who may have found in her second daughter an inauthentic substitute for the one already lost. In this respect, Hall's childhood tomboyishness may have expressed tacit rejection of her mother's devotion to a lost domestic futurity. In the essay, however, her mother's narcissism serves as the primary reason for her emotional neglect and physical abuse of her surviving daughter: "Always my mother, violent and brainless, a fool but a terribly cruel fool, a terribly crafty and cruel fool, for whom life had early become a mirror in which she saw only her own reflection" (Version 3).

Hall's earliest and most important relation was a failed one. Her mother did not love her. In the person of Michael West, an early fictional persona, Hall hints that the rejection was mutual: as early as his fifth year, we are told, Michael "did not love his mother, of this he was quite certain."[24] The threat posed to autobiography by a failed primary relationship, however, does not reside only in mutual estrangement between mother and child. Writing to the point at which she must begin speaking of her mother, in the earlier drafts Hall finds herself unable to do so. Instead, she swerves into imaginary idealizations of the mother she never knew. Hall is aware of the unconsciously driven character of this turn. She writes: "Some devilish, and possibly misplaced sense of humour, makes me want to write my ideal of a mother . . ." (Version 1). The breaking off of the draft at this point suggests that if her mother's behavior poses a major obstacle to Hall in fashioning a genealogy, the obsessive need to project an imaginary opposite can be equally devastating.

The difficulty continues even when Hall discusses her maternal grandmother, who provided the unconditional love that Hall would have liked to receive from her mother. Hall describes her grandmother Diehl as embodying the ideal of motherhood: "To her I owe all the tenderness that was ever given me in my childhood, what she lacked in brains she made up for in heart. On her ample and unfailingly welcoming bosom, I would many a time lay my troubled head while she called me foolish, endearing names— Suggie-plum, for example, which I turned into Tuggie; to her I was Tuggie to the day of her death. She never understood me, of course,[25] but she loved me" (Version 3). In Hall's experience, however, a primary love relationship was liable to be compromised by its opposite. In any event, grandmother Diehl, dominated by her daughter, failed to protect Hall from maternal abuse. "The influence of my mother was so potent that it held my grandmother perpetually in chains; she who so firmly believed in God, and in prayer, and in me, her beloved grandchild, could yet never free herself from those chains."[26]

As I mentioned, the first draft of the essay breaks off at the point where Hall's mother is introduced. This version is more complete and more consecutively written than Version 2, "Anticedance [sic] & Infancy," which repeats the same material, less well, in fragmentary fashion. This attempt begins as Version 3 does with the fourth commandment: "Thou shalt honour thy father and thy mother," followed immediately by Hall's assertion that she is unable to do so through no fault of her own. To begin in this way is to acknowledge that the autobiographical project itself is unrealizable. In Version 2, Hall finds herself again drawing a portrait of her fantasized maternal ideal, this time sentimentally portrayed in old age and so forth. And once again, the essay can't move past the impossible task of describing Hall's relation with her actual mother. In the incoherent attempt at a second start, a further reason for this blockage is disclosed. Suddenly, Hall finds herself thinking about herself as a sexually queer subject and imagining the consequences for her mother of recognizing this fact about her daughter. In a new paragraph, surrounded by blank space, Hall asks:

Does she know me for what I am? I wonder. If she does she must often be bewildered, must be at a loss to understand—

for

But

and they two

In Version 3, Hall focuses on the genealogy of her father's side of the family. If it is impossible to trace a female genealogy, perhaps it will be possible to trace an oedipal one, although, as I mentioned earlier, because she scarcely knew her father and was not permitted ever to meet her paternal grandparents, the effort lacks a basis in relational experience. Hall identifies her work with her great-grandfather John Hall's medical practice: "He became a healer of bodies, not of souls"; in her poetry and fiction, Hall attended to both.[27] Likewise, Hall identifies with her grandfather, a highly successful medical specialist in the town of Torquay. "My grandfather was a man of strong emotions, I am practically certain of this if his portrait, which is in my possession, was a faithful likeness. The face in the portrait is sensitive and marked by much mental suffering." Hall was particularly struck by his inability to overcome the grief occasioned by the death of his youngest stepdaughter.

Hall scarcely knew her father. But he had shown his love by making her the heir to his fortune, while protecting her capital from the depredations of her mother and stepfather, Alberto Visetti, a music teacher with a roving eye. In her good-looking, rebellious, charming, and highly sexed father, Hall found much to admire and much that reminded her of herself. Out of his traits, she fashioned a bohemian, decadent, even degenerate genealogy for herself. Both alienated themselves from their families: "Alas," she writes, "that it should have been my father and I who were destined to subject . . . [the members of his extended family] to the first breath of scandal." Hall associates with herself her father's idleness and wildness as a young man, his abilities as a horseman, his love of hunting, his sexual and romantic entanglements with women, his interest in the arts, his abilities as a composer and songwriter, his success as a dog breeder, his affinity with animals, even possibly his skill at conjuring. Hall also felt an affinity with her father's loneliness, depression, and inability to sustain intimate relationships. As she found also in her own experience, "my father must have been a man of vast discontents during the latter part of his life. He was never content with any one place for long, especially if he was in it." When Hall published her first novel, she dropped Marguerite, her baptismal name, and adopted Radclyffe, her father's first name as well as the first half of his hyphenated surname. On the Radclyffe side, she also crossed paternal with female genealogy, associating herself by means of an inherited portrait with a woman named Sarah Radclyffe.

Version 3 of the essay ends with Hall's change of first name: "My mother had me christened Marguerite; she could not have chosen a more inappropriate name, I detest it, and kindly note that I have dropped it." Beginning with a fated revolt against the decalogue and ending with a revolt against *both* her mother and her Christian name, Hall outlines a genealogy of revolt that honors the wayward example of her father's life. Hall observes that, like herself, he was the victim of parental injustice. In an instance that mirrors hers mother's rejection of Hall after the death of her infant sister, Hall's grandfather became estranged from his son after the death of a step-daughter on whom he doted. Hall's grandfather plunged his household into an unending state of mourning, against which Hall's father eventually rebelled. As a result, Radclyffe was cast out of the family for a time in the 1870s, according to Hall "the most hypocritical age in our history." Selecting the daughter of a fisherman for "his mistress," he provoked a local scandal, then compounded the offense after leaving home by returning to town as an actor in the role of Charles Surface.[28] His father was angered to find that his son had arranged to have photographs of himself placed in the windows of local stationers' shops.

To this point, I have emphasized Hall's frustration over her inability to live within genealogical time as well as the difficulty she found in developing a sense of living in time and place consistent with her awareness of herself as a gender-crossing woman whose sexual and emotional life focused on other women. Sexologists took the view that female same-sex attraction was congenital and therefore, although a statistical anomaly, by no means unnatural. On this basis, they called for tolerance of male and female homosexuality. Within the authoritative discourses of religion, the law, and medicine, this structure of belief best suited Hall's purpose. Nonetheless, the exclusion of Hall from the ideological construction of heterosexual genealogy posed continuing difficulties for her.

During the 1920s, it was commonplace to refer to love between women as "sterile." Compton Mackenzie, for example, routinely uses this word in referring to the Sapphic lovers whom he mocks in *Extraordinary Women* (1928). In *The Well of Loneliness*, Stephen Gordon repeatedly refers to herself as sterile. When, in the second half of the novel, she finally finds in Mary Llewellyn a woman who loves her passionately, Stephen maneuvers her into marrying a male friend since Stephen cannot offer Mary marriage, a respectable home, a place in society, and children. Again, genealogy is bound up with a maternally defined origin, present, and future.

It is important to bear in mind that Hall was well aware that Sapphic lovers were not inevitably doomed to be caught within this maternity-centered double bind. In one of the most important passages in the novel, Stephen's best friend, Valérie Seymour, urges Stephen to continue her relationship with Mary. Like Natalie Barney, Seymour argues that women with emotional and sexual ties with other women need to build their own institutions and modes of interpersonal relationship. Against the backdrop of Hall's continuing difficulties in imagining queer temporalities and spaces, the effort by such artists and intellectuals in France between 1900 and 1930 as Barney, Renée Vivien, Romaine Brooks, Colette, Gertrude Stein, Djuna Barnes, Claude Cahun and Marcel Moore, and Suzy Solidor to create a Sapphic mythology, models of individual and collective heroism, new modes of intersubjectivity, and both avant-garde and commercial modes of cultural expression take on even greater importance.[29] The heroic tendency in Sapphic culture in the early twentieth century was a requisite counter to the institutional negation of the lives and desires of female subjects of same-sex desire.

If Hall was troubled by her exclusion from genealogy defined in terms of maternal origins, she was also troubled by a sense of outlawed status in relation to the printed word.[30] Hall's difficulty with the symbolic order involved not only the legal suppression of the publication and sale of *The Well of Loneliness* in England. She had long been engaged in a more basic struggle regarding access to and mastery of the English language. In the most recent biography of Hall, published in 1999, Diana Souhami discloses for the first time that Hall was dyslexic.[31] The term *dyslexia* was coined in 1887 by Rudolf Berlin. An important article on the disorder appeared in the *British Medical Journal* in 1896, but the most significant British researcher of the condition was James Hinshelwood, a British ophthalmologist, who in the 1890s and early 1900s published a series of articles in medical journals describing similar cases of word blindness, which he defined as "a congenital defect occurring in children with otherwise normal and undamaged brains characterised by a difficulty in learning to read."[32]

Batten and Troubridge were aware of Hall's difficulties in reading and writing; but none of the three seems to have connected this weakness with a physical condition—despite the fact that in 1917 Hinshelwood published a book, *Congenital Word Blindness*, in which Hall could have found her own situation described. The opportunity recurred in the 1920s as a result of the work of the American neurologist Samuel T. Orton, who pioneered the study and remediation of this reading disability. Had Hall and her partners been familiar with this research, it is possible that she would have inferred a connection between being dyslexic and her potential as an artist—just as she did in connection with being crossgendered.[33]

In Hall's unpublished manuscripts, there are two extended passages in which she discloses the shame that she experienced in the schoolroom. In yet another draft of "Forebears and Intimacy," she revisits a recurring scene of trauma in her childhood. The passage is heavily scored, and Hall crosses out wording in which she lays the blame for her shortcomings on her own moral failings:

> In those days I entirely lacked consentration ~~I was not a good student being careless and lazy~~, also my spelling would put me shame, and greatly irritate the [word crossed out] professors—one of them in particular made a point of reading out ~~a~~ my mistakes in class: "Now I wonder what this word can be . . . [,]" he would drawl, & then he would spell it letter by letter as I had ~~spelt~~ spelled it—a terrible moment. Nor has my spelling improved to this day—I spell badly at all times, but when in the throughs of ~~inspiration it becomes~~ inspiration [inclusion of this word is indicated by a row of dots penciled underneath the cancelled word] I spell so oddly [insert from facing page] that I cannot always read my own script and must try to help myself out by the context ~~odd that I cannot always decide myself, when~~ {additional words crossed out} ~~re-reading, what~~ {words} ~~I was~~ {trying} ~~meaning to write and must carefully study the context~~.[34]

In fictional form in her early, unpublished autobiographical novel, *Michael West*, Hall returns to the same site.[35] This fictional recasting is of special significance for the way in which it suggests how the shaming that resulted from the condition entered into the psychic structure of Hall's sexuality. Hall was to find passage by way of love out of the blockages imposed both

this bullying gentleman — A noble life and many settled books

this copy

by the hour — she read Dickens to me from cover to cover. A good woman, upright, devoted and kind — originally sprung from Quaker stock. I look back upon her with gratitude; she did what she could and gave all she could in circumstances that were none too easy.

My school, that was kept by Mrs Cole, had been attended from time to time by people who afterwards became well known: Violet and Irene Vanbrugh, for instance; Edith Craig, the daughter of Dame Ellen Terry; and later, in my day, by a dark, pretty child who was always talking about her mother — Stella, Mrs Patrick Campbell's daughter. From this school I went for a time to King's College where my career was far from distinguished — I was not a good student being careless & lazy, also my spelling would put me ... and greatly irritate the professors — one in particular made a point of reading out a mistake in class: "how I wonder what this word can be...." he would drawl, & then he would spell it letter by letter as I had

1. "Forebears and Infancy." Holograph ms., untitled. Radclyffe Hall collection, 22.5. Harry Ransom Humanities Research Center, University of Texas, Austin, Texas. (Version 2)

2. "Forebears and Infancy." Holograph ms., untitled. Radclyffe Hall collection, 22.5. Harry Ransom Humanities Research Center, University of Texas, Austin, Texas. (Version 2)

spelled

spelt it — a terrible moment. Nor has my spelling improved to this day — I spell badly at all times, but oddly in the throughes of inspiration it becomes so odd that I cannot always decide myself, then, that word I was trying madly to write re-reading, to what word I was meaning to write and most carefully study the context.

From King's I went on to Germany, and finished my education in Dresden. There was much to be said for the Germany of those days — but all that is too long for my limited space, suffice it to say that I was happy, and as foolish, and as given to Schwärmerei as were most of my fellow students. So much then for my education; as for degrees I never took any.

When and under what circumstances did I begin my writing? I am told by my mother that at three years old I suddenly composed the following poem: "No wonder the birdies love you,

No wonder the butterflies love you,
No wonder the roses grow above you,
No wonder the birdies love you, dear!"

by the failure of matrilineal genealogy and her difficulties with the written and printed word.

When it comes time for young Michael to enter "Miss Pelham's select day-school,"[36] he is at first enraptured. At Whiteleys, his nurse helps him choose pencil boxes, pencils, a penknife, a satchel, penholders, and an eraser for school. He is also outfitted with clothes and new shoes. Michael's excitement with his new gear shows how, for Hall, the attraction to the appurtenances of writing was both markedly physical and associated as well with the male sex, masculine dress, and a masculine rite of passage. It is significant too that the mediator of Michael's exchange is not his mother but rather another significant female other, his nurse.

Michael's first day at school results in a traumatic scene that at the same time suggests a way out of the dilemma posed by his disability. In the room where new students are to be tested for placement, Michael takes a place next to a young girl named Daisy, to whom he is immediately attracted. When Michael is tested orally for reading and other skills, he fails miserably. Miss Pelham then asks a four-year-old to read. "Michell who was very backward in reading listened to his performance in wonder." The young reader, however, finds himself unable to identify the word spelled "B-O-S-O-M." Michael also fails to do so. Daisy, however, provides the correct answer. Interestingly, the word that Michael does not know is a genteel signifier of a female sexual body part. Daisy's familiarity with the word suggests her access not only to a female knowledge but to a *jouissance* that Michael will later come to associate with the women with whom he falls in love. Daisy signifies both the source of and the bridge to this pleasure.

The passage continues:

One by one the children read aloud, Michel sweated with terror as his turn drew nearer. & when ~~it~~ at last it came ~~at last~~ he forgat even the little he already knew. ~~Painfully, &~~ Slowly, in an agony he faltered and hesitated. Even simple words presented insurmountable difficulties. He was terribly conscious of Daisey's ~~curious~~ inquisitive eyes ~~fixed on him, with an amused~~ there was amusement in their scrutiny. He lost his place, found it & began all over again—only to become still more deeply involved in a tangle of indeciphorable ~~words~~ sentences.

"Dear dear" murmured Miss Pelham in a shocked voice. "Why you cant read at all Michell I'm afraid—try this simple reader please—now then begin[."]

"The Cat and the mouse ran round the house ~~faltered Michell~~ go on please thats ~~better~~ a little better."

Michell spelt out the foolish words in a swelter of shame and misery. The other pupils ~~eyed each~~ looked at [each] other with smiles & nudges—Michell could just see them out of the corner of an eye. His heart was beating painfully, tears dimmed his sight—but he remembered that at school ~~apparently~~ one apparently did not cry—so he struggled on ~~manfully~~ as best he could[.]

It came to an end at last—& now it was Daisys turn ~~had~~. She glanced at Michell as who should say "This is the way in which *I* do it." And proceeded to read aloud in a calm—unruffled voice—She read well for a child of ~~seven~~ 7, & she knew it.

"Very nicely done" remarked Miss Pelham approvingly.—"excellent."

Daisy preened. ~~You~~

"You never learned to read I suppose" she whispered in Michells ear"

Michell shook his head miserably—he turned a beseaching eye on Daisy—it was a humble eye, & Daiseys heart was touched.

"You'll soon learn" she murmured under her breath[.] "Its as easy as nothing at all. You'll see if it isn't."

But Michell was dispondant—he felt ~~humiliated in Daisys ey~~ that he had dropped ~~miles~~ fathoms in ~~Daiseys~~ her estimation.[37]

To this scene of instruction, Daisy adds a third element, namely, a young girl who witnesses the scene and to whom Michael is immediately drawn. In this way, Michael's shaming is eroticized. At the same time, the female figure acquires a redemptive charge: her acceptance of Michael over the course of the year enables him to overcome the debilitating effects of that first day. "Michells school days became less distressing as ~~time~~ the weeks went on. He learnt quickly—making up for lost time with ~~marvelous~~ great rapidity. Daisy too had ceased to be distant and superior. She liked Michell, she championed him."[38] Michael soon catches up, later moves on to St. Paul's School, and is destined for Oxford.

In the passages considered here, Hall links writing with masculinity and a conventionally coded masculine ability to draw support from a desirable female. The work of reading and writing is envisaged as possible with the practical support of a loving female partner—a pairing that Hall herself accomplished with Batten and Troubridge. Hall's career as a writer of fiction contributes to the extensive rewriting of the mid-Victorian script according to which the success of the professional man of letters was seen as dependent upon his ability to fashion a successful bourgeois marriage.[39] Failure of belief in this model characterizes the work of late Victorian and early twentieth-century writers, such as Walter Pater, Thomas Hardy, George Gissing, May Sinclair, Virginia Woolf, James Joyce, and D. H. Lawrence. All of these writers, however, retain a belief in the necessary linkage between writing, relationship, and desire. Hall's contribution is to emphasize elements of cross gender and female same-sex desire.

At the outset, I mentioned economic, political, gendered, and sexed terms in which Hall and Troubridge can be read. The reading of character in terms of these typologies, however, leaves invisible the dynamic processes in which psyche and world interact. As Hall's inability to write herself into history in the autobiographical essays suggests, ontological categories were a difficult matter where she was concerned.[40] And the passages from *Michael West* indicate how not only narrative but the very access to language, read and written, stood in Hall's way. Nonetheless, it will be evident to many readers that the story I have told could easily be recast in familiar psychoanalytical terms: namely, of Hall's difficulty in overcoming a pre-oedipal bond of love and hate with her mother, a difficulty that impeded her in proceeding to the oedipal phase, whether that be understood in terms of arriving at heterosexual sexuation, in Sedgwick's term, or a good-enough mastery of the symbolic order. However, to read Hall in these terms would be to rob her of the significance that is unique to the person and project that she named "Radclyffe Hall." Second, to do so could be to fall into the slur, often lodged by psychoanalysts against female subjects of same-sex desire, that their affective and sexual choices signify a failure to achieve a normal oedipal development.[41]

Hall emerged as a writer simultaneously with the vogue in England of the work of Sigmund Freud.[42] She was familiar with the leading concepts associated with his name. To subsume her experience within Freudian theory, however, would be to ignore the challenges that her work poses to Freud's thinking about both female sexuality and gender nonconformity. The exploration of female sexuality in Hall's fiction needs to be read as tacitly contesting the views of Freud and Ernest Jones, the leading proponent of Freudian psychoanalysis in England. As I argue in Chapter

4, it was in the 1920s that male and female psychoanalysts first seriously dealt with the question of the character of female sexuality, which both men approached through the topic of female homosexuality. Their efforts, however, suffer from a primary liability in being modeled on Freud's theory of the male Oedipus complex. Freud's theory of psychic development is unisexual, in the first instance male and with subsequent awkward adaptations in light of female anatomy and subjectivity. The addition by Ruth Mack Brunswick, Melanie Klein, and others of a theorization of a pre-oedipal psychical phase complicates this situation without overcoming the original limitation.[43] Since Hall's best and most psychoanalytic study of female psychology in *The Unlit Lamp* (1924) is contemporaneous with efforts within psychoanalysis to theorize about female sexuality, the best way to think of her approach is as a parallel, responsive, and critical set of reflections in relation to widespread contemporary interest in this subject.

A model of childhood development that Freud suggested before he theorized the Oedipus complex is more apropos of Hall's thinking in *Michael West* than is Freud's later approach. In a passage from his unpublished *Project for a Scientific Psychology* (1885), which he sent in draft to Wilhelm Fliess, Freud imagines a young child's first contact with another young child. Freud refers to this other as the *Nebenmensch*, "an unusual German word meaning something like 'the next-man' or 'adjoining-person.' "[44] Freud is interested in how this young stranger is converted into a neighbor. The subject experiences the meeting first as one of somatic identification with a similar other, based on memories of the subject's own embodiment. Simultaneously, however, the subject perceives the other *as* other, as not being a part of the subject itself. Kenneth Reinhard has observed that it is in this encounter with a child from outside the home that the subject first becomes able to overcome its psychic identification with its primary caregiver(s) sufficiently to recognize another that has an existence like but independent of its own. This encounter marks a momentous moment in the development of human intersubjectivity. Freud further regards it as opening the possibility of recognizing actuality, of becoming capable, in Freud's formulation, of learning (*erkennen*).[45]

Working independently of this unpublished material, in *Michael West*, Hall imagines an experience in which a child becomes what Reinhard calls "the subject of cognition" by recognizing the existence of another whose crucial characteristic is that it exists outside of the maternal dyad or the nuclear triad (Reinhard, 26, 29). More expressly than Freud, she also recognizes that a scene of this sort is a love scene, albeit not sexualized. Since Hall loves other women and the character Michael functions in part as the protagonist of a fictional autobiography, his first real other is a girl. As Hall's surrogate, moreover, Michael is a boy-girl. The composite figure, Michael/Hall stands yet again in an illicit relation to the world of masculine-identified reading and writing. His/her desire for access to that world is marked both by strong masculine identification and by shame at his/her inadequate mastery of literacy. The relation with Daisy as the other has a competitive aspect that is necessary if Daisy is to help Michael overcome what the reader recognizes to be an undiagnosed disability. Finally, by cross gendering Michael and turning the young girl whom he desires into an authoritative source of book learning, Hall as feminist exposes the lie of the view that the work of cognition belongs to boys and men.

Hall further recognizes that love between a crossgendered woman and another female can help the subject overcome a debilitating inability to individuate from one's mother. Here it is important to point out that Hall is not thinking of the normal identification of mother and child of either sex in a pre-oedipal phase. In the novel, Michael experiences an intensified sense of psychic vulnerability, imposed by the predatory narcissism of his mother. Daisy plays the role of the stranger whose advent opens for Michael the possibility of recovery. At the same time, and this is a point on which Freud and Hall are at one, both recognize that first love in childhood can open a world to the child beyond the constraints of the love-hate tensions of the nuclear family. For Hall, this opening, despite Michael's literal gendering, is not into a paternal or phallic symbolic order but rather into one not structured in terms of the conventional gender binary. In this early rendition of crossgendered existence, the gender coding of literacy is perceived to be not intrinsic but cultural.

The opening to the world that Hall envisages in love between Michael and Daisy remains precarious. Family drama again impinges, this time insofar as Daisy was a pet name given to Hall by her father on his rare visits.[46] Giving this name to the first schoolmate with whom Michael falls in love casts an oedipal shadow over the passage—as though Hall imagines Michael's love-object by reflecting something that her father had found desirable in herself as a youngster. Hall's experience with her loving grandmother suggests another danger implicit in this first love. Hall ends one of her autobiographical accounts by observing how her grandmother, unable to protect her from her mother's abusive behavior, betrayed that love. In so doing, the beloved grandmother collapses back into the hateful mother. Implicit in *Michael West* is the danger that Michael will recoil from Daisy on the basis of some failure of sympathy, real or imagined, on her part. In this way, Daisy could be transformed from an actual point of contact with the outside world into a screen onto which internalized bad relations can be projected.

Hall signals this possibility within the novel. The scene of instruction cited above is not the first time that a Daisy turns up in *Michael West*. In chapter 2, on Michael's daily visits with his nurse to Kensington Gardens, he is not permitted to play with children of another class for fear that he may contract "infectious diseases" from them.[47] The lonely boy retaliates by inventing a playmate of his own, named Daisy, whom he uses as a pretext to engage in naughty, that is, normal, unrepressed child's behavior. When his nurse and mother insist that he admit that Daisy does not exist, he refuses to do so. As a result, he receives the first of many whippings at the hands of his mother. "Daisy," then, has a prior existence in the novel as a purely imaginary other. The fact that Hall gives the same name to the first girl with whom Michael falls in love indicates Hall's awareness that here too actuality could give way to fantasy. However, her choice of this name for Michael's love-object suggests that in some circumstances projective fantasy may in actuality be surmounted.

Hall betrayed all three of the women with whom she became most intimate. This fact suggests that, as in her autobiographical account of her loving grandmother, at some level Hall was liable to find a woman's loving commitment to her bound to fail. Disappointed by her grandmother's inability to protect her, Hall may have spurned other love objects in anticipation of such failure. In this way too, Hall may have continued in unregulated fashion to play out anger against her mother. Freud's account of one's first love-object outside the nuclear triad posits this possibility.[48] But the step that he takes toward a theory of the *Nebenmensch* suggests something else as well—namely, the possibility that love of one's first significant other outside the family may enable not only cognition but in particular an ability to recognize a world of others, so to speak, as autonomous yet comparable with oneself. Hall took the step from loving other women in her personal life to advocating for the civil and social rights of female subjects of same-sex desire across lines of class, outlook, and nationality. There is no necessary or automatic link between these two kinds of commitment. Love may be transient or it may be constrained within the dyad. But Hall's scene of instruction proposes a way of thinking an originary scene of love outside the family that takes into account both unconventional engenderment and female same-sex desire. She imagines ways that enlarge and enable one's engagement with the world, including the possibility of moving toward love of those who might otherwise remain unrecognizable.

1

Reading the Poetry

Some echoes of her simple lay will reach the farthest future.
— *Sussex Daily News*, March 22, 1913

Desires

In view of Hall's uncertainty about the durability of close ties between women, it is not surprising that one finds in her early volumes of verse not only poems that celebrate a singular relationship with another woman but also those that imagine sexual and emotional ties as fleeting. Hall's personal life during her twenties and early thirties resembles the High Victorian Bohemianism exemplified by Charlotte Cushman (1816–1876), an actor celebrated for her performance in Shakespearean trouser roles. With the wealth that she earned on the stage, Cushman retired to Rome, where she supported various American relatives and Emma Stebbins, the female sculptor whom Cushman chose to be her long-term partner.[1] Cushman also supported other female artists, friends, and lovers, including at times their husbands. She spoke of the members of this entourage as her "belongings," a colloquial term that suggests the degree to which Victorian bourgeois life fell within the traditional terms of domestic alliance as described by Michel

Foucault.[2] One's relations belonged to one by virtue of blood and/or legal connection—and one belonged to them too. For a financially self-supporting woman such as Cushman, one's female lovers were also "belongings," to be retained if possible as friends once an affair played itself out. Transient desires implied longer-term claims. This practice evokes a second meaning of belonging—that of longing, yearning, desire.

When Hall entered into her majority, she used her newfound wealth to move out of her mother's house and into one of her own. She took her grandmother Diehl with her, and she surrounded herself with women she met while traveling in the United States: Jane Randolph, a widowed cousin with children, and, after a second trip, another cousin, Dorothy Diehl. Both women became Hall's lovers, then friends, and Hall supported them in England. Jane eventually returned to the States and married a rich man. Diehl married Robert Coningsby Clarke, a promising young composer, who set a number of Hall's poems to music.[3] For Hall, as for Cushman, these complex arrangements implied a capability and interest in both enduring and short-term relationships.

Hall's lyric poetry focuses on both brief and lasting attractions. The doubling, which can seem contradictory, is especially marked in her third volume, *Poems of the Past & Present* (1910).[4] Shortly after publication of the book, abrupt changes occurred in the lives of Mabel Batten and Hall—namely, the deaths of Hall's grandmother and of Batten's much older husband, George. These events freed the pair to live together in a de facto female marriage until Batten's sudden death six years later. *Poems of the Past & Present* memorializes the romance, which is signified in the title and arrangement of the volume. The collection is framed with a dedication and with poems of the present that celebrate the couple's mutual devotion as well as Batten's collaboration in preparing the poems for publication.[5] *Poems of the Past* refers most specifically to a sequence of Sapphic verses called the "Fruit of the Nispero." This group, written earlier, celebrates a playful, sometimes painful and fleeting, pagan love; the framing poems affirm long-term commitment.

Hall dedicated the book "to Mrs. George Batten." The "Mrs." and the "George" are diplomatic touches. Marriage offered financial and emotional security to Batten as well as useful cover for extramarital affairs.[6] The opening poem, entitled "A Dedication," sets out the book as inspired by—and written in gratitude for—Batten's love. Book-ending the volume, "Postscript" acknowledges her role in revising, editing, and compiling the poems:

Your hands have touched the cover of my book,
              Beloved hands!
Your eyes have read each page and found it good,
              Beloved eyes!
What can my verses now attain? Your look
Has given immortality, your wise
Sweet thoughts upon mine own, have surely crowned
These words with laurels Love himself has wound. (125)

Despite the flattery, already in the volume's second poem Hall discloses an irrepressibly cheeky, seductive side. She drops the persona of faithful lover almost as soon as she has assumed it. In this poem, the lyric voice belongs to Pan's piper, who plays a "wayward melody." The poem ends in "love's delight."

With Batten on board, Hall began crafting a persona as author. *Poems of the Past & Present* is the first of her books to include photographs of the author. Opening to the title page, one finds pasted into the book a passport-sized photograph with a three-quarter profile of the head of the author. The semiotics of the image is masculine-feminine.[7] Hall's hair is pulled back tightly from her forehead, but she sports the spit curl that appears characteristically in publicity photos of the following decade. She also wears an earring in her ear. Most of the image is given over to her costume of expensive woolen frock coat, tailored jacket, skirt, and cravat. Facing the table of contents is another photo of Hall, with a flawless complexion, portrayed as a sensitive, thoughtful, independent-minded young woman. Again, the hair is pulled back tightly. She wears a stiff, upturned shirt collar, checked bow tie, and tailored jacket.

The dedication of the volume to Batten and the masculine coding of the author's photographs are ploys inviting readers to receive the poetry as autobiographical. Hall does so again in the dedication of her final book of poetry, *The Forgotten Island*, a volume of erotic verse that recalls Sappho's Lesbos. By this time, the relationship with Batten was strained. Hall declares in the dedication that her inspiration has been prompted by the advent of a new "FRIEND," "Mrs. Gordon Woodhouse" (5), the talented harpsichordist to whom Batten had introduced Hall several years earlier.[8] A high Bohemian, Woodhouse's *mariage blanc* left space for long-held ties with several male lovers at the same time that she cultivated the admiration of Sapphists, such as the composer Ethyl Smyth.[9] In 1914, Hall embarked on a flirtation

POEMS OF THE PAST & PRESENT

BY
MARGUERITE RADCLYFFE-HALL

LONDON
CHAPMAN AND HALL
1910

3. Marguerite Radclyffe Hall [*sic*]. *Poems of the Past & Present* (1910). Title page. Stanford University Library, Stanford, California.

4. Marguerite Radclyffe Hall [*sic*]. *Poems of the Past & Present* (1910). Facing table of contents. Stanford University Library, Stanford, California.

with Woodhouse that likely ended in bed.[10] The account that Hall provided of the book suggests that it may chart the trajectory of an affair. In Baker's words, her "idea was that the poems represented someone's recollection of a previous incarnation on a mythical island like Lesbos and, taken as a whole, they told the story of a love affair which runs from the heights of passion to the dull yearning for new pastures" (57).

In contrast to the newly discovered relationship announced in *Poems of the Past & Present*, in her final book of poetry, Hall is filled with "eager, sweet longing," a phrase that brings to mind the "sweetbitter" character of desire in Sappho.[11]

XLVII

A ship is a lovely thing, great with adventure.
I cannot behold the white sails of a vessel
But lo! I am stirred with an eager sweet longing
For that which may wait on the hour of my coming.

E'en thou, my belovèd, when thou art beside me,
The spell of thy presence restrains not my spirit;
My spirit goes out with the wind to the masthead—
Mine eyes turn away to the ship that is passing![12]

Teasers of this sort help account for the fact that almost all the attention directed to the poetry to date has been biographical in character. The invitation to read the poems in this way, however, can lead to error. Baker, for example, believes that *A Sheaf of Verses*, Hall's second book, grows out of the early days of her sexual intimacy with Batten: Hall "dedicated the collection to 'Sad Days and Glad Days.' In spirit the poetry reflected the latter: 'Believe me, the world is a place full of joy, / And happiness stretches afar.' The technique and the emotion revealed a growing maturity. The love poems suggested greater confidence. John's homosexuality received an oblique mention" in poems in which "she alluded to her abnormality as a thing of symbolic beauty, a cause of pride not shame, 'a path to gained respect'" (36). *A Sheaf of Verses*, however, was published in fall 1908, only a short time after the two women first became lovers, in August 1908 (Baker, 36).[13] Much of the book must already have been written by that date. Accordingly, the connection with Batten is not responsible for what Baker regards as Hall's coming out as homosexual in the book.

Constructing the poetry in terms of sexual identity misses more complex views that Hall takes of human relationality and selfhood. Consider, for instance, the poem "Re-Incarnation." In it, she writes:

Meeting you I felt a thrill,
　　Strangely sad, and strangely sweet!
Some compelling force of will,
　　Sprung from sympathies complete,

Sympathies, that rose again
After death's ennobling pain. (35)

These lines express a troubling double awareness of the power of sexual attraction. On the one hand is a telepathic ideal of spontaneous and complete affective sharing—an ideal that has haunted twentieth-century affirmations of lesbian sexual identity.[14] On the other hand, the speaker experiences psychical fusion as a potentially threatening subjection to the "will" of another. In the case of the poem, this other is not only or possibly not even primarily the person referred to as other; it is also a spectral visitant.[15] The twosome may and will be several, and that several will consist of women and likely men as well who lived in other times and places. Hall does not always sustain this view of multiple selfhood, but the apprehension shapes her work.

The concept of reincarnation in the early twentieth century is most familiar within the context of Theosophy. Whether Hall believed in theosophical doctrine is an open question. What is definite is that the idea of reincarnation familiar within Theosophy provided a frame within which Hall could explore aspects of speculative psychology, in particular, the multiplicity of human selfhood. Spiritualist belief functions similarly for Hall as a vernacular mode in which to pursue questions being worked on in very different ways in the new science of psychoanalysis. Because of the limiting effects of dyslexia on Hall's education and reading, little information exists about the intellectual grounding of her thought. It is known, however, that in part through Batten, a talented singer and sponsor of contemporary music,[16] Hall was thoroughly familiar with musical culture at a time that has been referred to as the "English musical renaissance."[17] Similarly, although it was not until after Batten's death that Hall became immersed in the work of the Society for Psychical Research, from the first book of poetry onward, she shows a keen interest in speculative psychology.

New English music at the turn of the twentieth century was strongly antimodernist in character, a trend within modernity that Hall embraced. In *Songs of Three Counties and Other Poems* (1913), she emphasizes this aspect of her outlook in poems modeled on those of the Classicist and homophile poet A. E. Housman. Poems from *A Shropshire Lad* were frequently set to music by the new generation of composers. Hall's relation to Aestheticism and the Decadence in late Victorian culture shows not only in the Sapphism of her verse but more broadly as well in her participation in another renaissance, namely, the Hellenistic Revival in English poetry at the turn of the century.[18] From her first book onward, she frequently writes in the genre of Theocritean pastoral, with intimations of same-sex desire cloaked in gender-neutral or sexually conventional terms. In an early poem, "Ode to Sappho," and in *The Forgotten Island*, she elects for herself the lyric tone of Sappho, a founding voice of Greek poetry that through the genre of pastoral and such figures as Catullus, comes to have strong late antique associations. Hellenistic too—and in congruence with the poetry of Michael Field (Katherine Bradley and Edith Cooper) and the feminist anthropology of Jane Harrison—is Hall's conflation of pagan with Christian sentiment in her poetry.

The most significant of Hall's poems from an intellectual point of view is her "Ode to Swinburne." In it, she offers a convincing account of Swinburne's secular humanism that is all the more impressive in view of the fact that she converted to Roman Catholicism not long after publishing the poem. As with other neo-Hellenistic poets, such as Field and the Alexandrian Greek poet C. P. Cavafy, who received his early schooling in England, Hall was capable of holding more than one idea in her mind at a time. This openness to possibility, complexity, and contradiction are important to bear in mind in view of the tendency, evinced by Baker, to narrow Hall's position to that of a writer preoccupied above all with questions of sexual identity. Hall was deeply religious. But as her sympathy with Swinburne's radical humanism suggests, her faith was heterodox. This combination of faith and self-consciously modern thought is characteristic of the Hellenistic Revival.

In her poetry, Hall's spirituality is most powerfully expressed in "The Blind Ploughman," the final poem in the sequence entitled "Rustic Courting" in *Songs of Three Counties*. In the final section of this chapter, I consider how the poem unexpectedly took on a second life as a populist hymn during World War I. In contrast to Ivor Novello's "Keep the Home Fires Burning," another wartime anthem written by a subject of same-sex desire, Hall's poem emphasizes not domestic sentiment but the solitary encounter of the individual with God. This lyric poem, with whose male protagonist Hall was strongly to identify, figures in a set of circumstances that brought forcibly home to her the disadvantages that she faced as a female writer in the music publishing industry.[19]

Aesthetic Desire

Hall desired to make art and to become known for doing so. In the writing of Frederic Myers, the leading psychological theorist among the founders of psychical research, she found persuasively combined an interest in artistic genius, conscious and unconscious mental processes, and dissident desire. In his posthumously published work, *Human Personality* (1903), Myers writes:

> Genius—if that vaguely used word is to receive anything like a psychological definition—should rather be regarded as a power of utilising a wider range than other men can utilise of faculties in some degree innate in all;—a power of appropriating the results of subliminal mentation to subserve the supraliminal stream of thought;—so that an "inspiration of Genius" will be in truth a *subliminal uprush*, an emergence into the current of ideas which the man [sic] is consciously manipulating of other ideas which he has not consciously originated, but which have shaped themselves beyond his will, in profounder regions of his being. I shall urge that there is here no real departure from normality; no abnormality, at least in the sense of degeneration; but rather a fulfilment of the true norm of man, with suggestions, it may be, of something *supernormal*; of something which transcends existing normality as an advanced stage of evolutionary progress transcends an earlier stage.[20]

With slight changes in terminology, Myers's emphasis on mental processes outside consciousness is close enough to Freud to help explain the dialogue that he entered into with leading members of the Society for Psychical Research after 1910.[21] In 1912, he responded to an invitation from the Society to submit a paper to its *Proceedings*.[22] As Ernest Jones warned Freud, however, Myers's and, later, Hall's recognition of unconscious mental processes was compatible with vernacular belief systems rejected by Freud, such as Spiritualism and Theosophy.[23]

As the discussion continues, Myers suggests the possibility that genius is not restricted to a play of rational and unconscious elements in the mind of the individual. Creative thinking also depends in part upon one's being permeable to a selfhood capable of existing outside of time and space.

"Sometimes," he writes, "we seem to see our subliminal perceptions and faculties acting truly in unity, truly as a Self;—co-ordinated into some harmonious 'inspiration of genius,' or some profound and reasonable hypnotic self-reformation, or some far-reaching supernormal achievement of clairvoyant vision or of self-projection into a spiritual world. Whatever of subliminal personality is thus acting corresponds with the highest-level centres of supraliminal life. At such moments the *subliminal* represents (as I believe) most nearly what will become the *surviving* Self" (73). In the early years of the twentieth century, the primary object of the Society was to demonstrate by means of objective experiments whether there was good evidence to believe in the survival of human personality after death. Some members of the Society, however, already harbored this belief. In the preceding quotation, Myers indicates that he is one of these. He does so first by use of the phrase "a spiritual world," which is drawn from spiritualist rhetoric where it refers to the spirit world. Second, at the end of the paragraph, he openly states his faith in survival after death. Myers further combines spiritualist axioms with theosophical ones. Theosophy distinguishes between the individual soul, referred to by Myers as the "Self," and its manifestations in selves that exist in time and space. Through recollection, these material selves could momentarily access the embodied experience of prior selves with all their differences of sex and gender. These beliefs could be used to explain why a woman felt masculine or a man felt feminine.

The scientific rhetoric within which Myers's discussion of genius occurs is that of anthropology, evolutionary biology, and, more specifically, degeneration theory. The aesthetic rhetoric is that of the Decadence. Two major tropes within decadent writing are those of the decay of reason and the contamination of enlightenment thought by an upsurge of primitive instinct and feeling. Myers uses both, although, as often happens within decadent thought, access to primitive emotion and affect is seen as necessary in order dialectically to surmount the deleterious effects of modern civilization. In this way, the resurgence of primitive psychic material is seen as necessary to evolutionary progress. The modernist artist functions as an exemplary figure of individual and, in due course, general improvement. Her exemplarity may also include sexual and gender nonconformity. This fact is signaled in the defensive tone that Myers takes in rejecting the contemporary view of the "degeneration" of artists and philosophers, such as Richard Wagner, Friedrich Nietzsche, and Oscar Wilde. Myers insists to the contrary that in vanguard work there is "no real departure from normality."[24]

For Myers, genius is not a condition peculiar to great artists; it exists to a degree in all human beings. Moreover, rather than assuming it to be confined to male artists or to a universal "man," as Myers's rhetoric has it, one might argue that both womanly women and manly women with sexual and emotional ties to other women enjoy a similar ability to coordinate conscious with unconscious mental processes in the production of ideas. Seen in this way, the self-development of both sorts of Sapphists could be recognized as free of "abnormality." Likewise, the achievements of such women might well be regarded as "transcend[ing] existing normality as an advanced stage of evolutionary progress transcends an earlier stage." Hall effects precisely this translation of Myers's theory into her own politics of gender.

She formulates this line of thought in a programmatic statement in *The Well of Loneliness* that occurs immediately after the protagonist, Stephen Gordon, has discovered that she belongs to the category of those whom the sexologist Richard von Krafft-Ebing defines as female sexual inverts. Puddle, Stephen's companion and former teacher, choosing this moment to come out to Stephen, offers her the following words of consolation: "You've got work to do—come and do it! Why, just because you are what you are, you may actually find that you've got an advantage. You may write with a curious double insight—write both men and women from a personal knowledge. Nothing's completely misplaced or wasted, I'm sure of that— and we're all part of nature. Some day the world will recognize this, but meanwhile there's plenty of work that's waiting. For the sake of all the others who are like you, but less strong and less gifted perhaps, many of them, it's up to you to have the courage to make good, and I'm here to help you to do it, Stephen."[25]

Hall and Antimodernism

At the beginning of this chapter, I cited the confident view of one of Hall's contemporary readers that her poetry would reach "the farthest future." That confidence stemmed from Hall's ability, both canny and spontaneous, to tap a vein of English antimodernist sentiment. This reaction began before World War I but became a major cultural factor during and after the war. In the music of two generations of English composers, the turn in

contemporary music-making, both pastoral and rustic, enabled a specifically localized reaction against the brutalizing effects associated with modern life in the northern industrial towns and the East End of London but
most pointedly against the mechanized slaughter of trench warfare. It is
easy to mistake this music as nostalgic, and at times it is. But as Jackson
Lears writes, "The antimodern impulse was both more socially and more
intellectually important than historians have supposed. Antimodernism was
not simply escapism; it was ambivalent, often coexisting with enthusiasm
for material progress. And it was part of a much broader quest for intense
experience which ranged from militarism and 'Progressive' social reform to
popular occultism and the early fascination with depth psychology. Far
from being the nostalgic flutterings of a 'dying elite,' as historians have
claimed, antimodernism was a complex blend of accommodation and protest which tells us a great deal about the beginnings of present-day values
and attitudes."[26] Antimodernism is best understood, in dialectical relation
to early twentieth-century Modernism, as a series of moments of internal
critique. The clearest point of difference occurs in the rejection of the notion that aesthetic Modernism is to be regarded as identical to formal experimentation.[27]

Hall's embrace of Violet Gordon Woodhouse says a good deal about
Hall's attitude toward publicity at this time. Artistic sexual nonconformity
was an open secret to be courted in the course of building a reputation for
"genius." Along with the today better-known Wanda Landowska, Wood-
bridge was one of the two most important performers on the harpsichord
in England in the first half of the twentieth century. By invoking Woodhouse, Hall summoned the ideal of a serious, female, amateur but accomplished and original engaged in contemporary musical culture.[28] Moreover,
Woodhouse's daily regimen of practice at the keyboards of early musical
instruments betokened a professionalism that Hall looked to emulate as her
career developed.

An important point of departure for the national movement in modern
English music occurred with the publication by Ralph Vaughan Williams
of "a small book on English folk song" in 1911. Already in 1910, when
Woodhouse heard Thomas Beecham conduct Vaughan Williams's *Fantasia
on a Theme of Thomas Tallis*, she recognized that like herself the composer
had observed "the manner in which Elizabethan and Stuart music—with
its freedom of rhythm and suppleness of phrasing—had evolved from folk
tunes." When Cecil Sharp, the most important collector of folk song and

dance in England, heard Woodhouse perform folk music in 1912, he immediately perceived the affinity between her approach and that of Vaughan Williams. Sharp introduced the pair to one another, and, in autumn 1912, the threesome "assembled a programme for an afternoon concert to be held in Stratford on 24 April the following year, . . . when Vaughan Williams was due to take up the position of musical director at the Memorial Theatre in Stratford. . . . The concert consisted mainly of English folk tunes collected by Sharp and arranged by Violet for the harpsichord as well as a number of early English pieces, in one of which she played the virginals."[29]

This concatenation of events offers a vivid example of Antimodernism in the ways in which Woodhouse and the others drew on new modes of engagement with early music, instruments, performance practice, and genres in creating a national school of modern musical composition. Such novelty changed the meaning of English national culture by means of invented traditions, which also included entrenched ideological elements.[30] Hall was eager to attach herself to these developments in music, sociality, and lyric. She does so both in the title of her next volume of poetry, *Songs of Three Counties and Other Poems*, and in choosing to dedicate the 1915 volume to Woodhouse.

In his biography of Lord Berners, the most formally modernist of early twentieth-century British composers, Mark Amory remarks: "There was, and had been for some time, an English musical renaissance. . . . The English set themselves against copying foreigners, instead looked for inspiration in English literature, English countryside, earlier English music, [often viewed through a Greek pastoral or Roman Catholic lens]. . . . Many had a sense of mission, an almost political wish to bring music to the masses. In 1904 Elgar had been knighted, . . . and in 1905, in a series of lectures, expressed his faith in the seriousness, earnestness and sincerity of the younger men."[31] When the work of such composers as Vaughan Williams or George Butterworth succeeds, antimodernist elements function primarily as form not content. That is to say, the thematic of rustic courtship, the ballad form in poetry, and elements of folk, medieval Catholic, and Elizabethan and Stuart music operate as modes of rhetoric to enable a critical response to the malaise of contemporary existence.[32]

Hall's Antimodernism is most evident in her fourth volume, *Songs of Three Counties*, published to good reviews in 1913 (Souhami, 58). The two-part structure of the book marks the continuing development of her relation with Batten as they entered what one might call the White Cottage, or marital, phase of their relationship. Falling between the death of Batten's husband in October 1910 and the commencement of Hall's affair with Phoebe Hoare,[33] summers during this period were passed at the "perfectly darling big cottage" (Souhami, 54) that Batten and Hall purchased at Malvern in 1911. Part one of the volume is Christian, English, and chaste; the second is for the most part pagan, Mediterranean, and given to sensuous abandon. Like the preceding book, *Songs of Three Counties*, as its title suggests, is directed toward the market for middle-class domestic music-making. The book advertises three of the poems as already set to music.

The first and better-known section of *Songs of Three Counties* is entitled "Rustic Courting," a cycle of love poems set in the voice of country lads that connotes the idyll of rural life that Hall and Batten enjoyed at the time. The most obvious antecedent of the collection is Housman's popular classic, *A Shropshire Lad* (1896).[34] Housman writes in a rural, vernacular mold but uses familiar folk and church idiom, form, and thematic to communicate the modern, aestheticist, and decadent meanings of his and Swinburne's naturalist faith. Not only a naturalist, Housman is also an Epicurean in the ancient philosophical sense. The only constant is material flux. Metaphysical pretensions—and moral doxa—are just that, destructive, self-destructive illusions.

Like Walter Pater, Housman believed the purpose of humanistic education to be personal transformation, though, like Pater, he was also aware that such transformation is ethically equivocal in its effects.[35] As a young professor at the University of London in the early 1890s, Housman was critical of the focus of education in the public schools and the universities on Classical philology. At the same time, he affirmed the Greek value of self-development based on the appreciation of beauty.[36] Self-culture depends on aesthetic taste. In pursuit of this goal, Housman encourages his young men to refuse the path of work, career, marriage, and material gain:

Existence is not itself a good thing, that we should spend a lifetime securing its necessaries: a life spent, however victoriously, in securing the necessaries of life is no more than an elaborate furnishing and decoration of apartments for the reception of a guest who is never to come. Our business here is not to live, but to live happily. We may seem to be occupied, as Mr[. Herbert] Spencer says, in the production, preparation and distribution of commodities; but our true occupation is to manufacture from the raw materials of life the fabric of happiness; and if we are ever to set about our work we must make up our minds to risk something.[37]

Housman's aesthetic-ethical ideal is well expressed in the second poem of *A Shropshire Lad*, a favorite for musical settings during the period:

Loveliest of trees, the cherry now
Is hung with bloom along the bough,
And stands about the woodland ride
Wearing white for Eastertide.

Now, of my threescore years and ten,
Twenty will not come again,
And take from seventy springs a score,
It only leaves me fifty more.

And since to look at things in bloom
Fifty springs are little room,
About the woodlands I will go
To see the cherry hung with snow.[38]

In the poem, Housman concedes to the beauty of a tree in bloom in spring the power of individual transformation that is promised to Christians by the miracle of Easter. It is the significance of this change that validates the young, implicitly male speaker's aesthetic choice of visual sensation in preference to the sort of goal-directed behavior, including the choice of a wedding partner, that young men were expected to make. The speaker of the poem instead values sensation, contemplation, and being in the moment.

Hall too opposes rural values to commercial ones in "Rustic Courting," where she associates the threat of absorption in the race for money with heterosexuality—that is, with avaricious young women seeking to seduce a young man into abandoning the countryside. In "In the City," the male speaker recoils:

Oh! City girls are pale-like,
And proud-like, and cold-like,
And nineteen out of twenty
Have never been our way.
I tells them of the tall hills,

The green hills, the old hills,
Where hawthorns are a-blossoming,
And thrushes call all day.[39]

The debate continues in "The Call to London," the one poem in the sequence of which the speaker is female:

Oh! come to London, fine lad,
Here's where the money flows.
But he said: "There's gold in plenty,
Gold enough and more for twenty,
Where the kingcup grows."

Oh! come to London, strong lad,
I am wanting you.
But he said: "It be a grand sight,
When the stars at midnight
Stretch along the blue."

Oh! come to London, dear lad,
I am fair to see!
But he said: "Along of our way
Trees are thick with white may,
Wonderful they be!" (*Songs of Three Counties*, 25–26)

Hall's Housman is not the collector of nineteenth-century male pornography and Victorian sexology, later donated by his brother Laurence to Cambridge University Library.[40] Nor is he the poet perhaps best known today for the imitation of a broadside ballad, written in 1895, in which he satirizes Wilde's imprisonment by telling of the similar fate that befell a "young sinner" imprisoned because of "the colour of his hair."[41]

Now 'tis oakum for his fingers and the treadmill for his feet,
And the quarry-gang on Portland in the cold and in the heat,
And between his spells of labour in the time he has to spare
He can curse the God that made him for the colour of his hair.[42]

Instead, Housman's poems in *A Shropshire Lad* celebrate yeomanlike ladship from the distanced vantage of a celibate, bachelor don.[43] The suffusion of the text with a chaste same-sex desire focused on young rural men was likely part of its appeal to Hall. Housman traced one direction in which same-sex desire could be expressed. Moreover, in "In the City" and "The Call to London," one catches a glimpse of another basis for Hall's identification with vigorous rural lads: namely, her elision of conventional femininity with a grasping egoism. While Hall shares Housman's negative reaction to the world of modern marriage and money, however, "Rustic Courting" is absent the vein of anti-imperial critique of *A Shropshire Lad,* with its repeated reminders that Housman's beloved young men were all too likely to meet an early death in the service of Britain overseas.

In the first poem of "Rustic Courting," Hall responds to "'Loveliest of Trees'" in a way that discloses another part of the appeal for her of the male-female love lyric. In the private space of "walking out," aesthetic taste, physical touch, and visuality shift from the cherry tree to Hall's favored erotic object, an attractive young lass:

> Walking Out
> Upon a Sunday afternoon,
> > When no one else was by,
> The little girl from Hanley way,
> > She came and walked with I.
>
> We climbed nigh to the Beacon top,
> > And never word spoke we,
> But oh! We heard the thrushes sing
> > Within the cherry tree.
>
> The cherry tree was all a-bloom,
> > And Malvern lay below,
> And far away the Severn wound—
> > 'Twas like a silver bow.
>
> She took my arm, I took her hand,
> > And never word we said,
> But oh! I knew her eyes were brown,
> > Her lips were sweet and red. (*Songs of Three Counties* 1)

Sapphic Resurgence

Hall's Antimodernism functions as a specific articulation of modernist culture, one that defines itself for Hall in terms of desire. Batten set to music three lyrics from *Poems of the Past and Present*. Two are poems, one of them phallicized, in which a male figure (the wind in one, a pipe player in the other) makes music for his beloved, who sings a lyric in response. Batten clearly enjoyed playing the female beloved to the male wooer. One of the poems is from the "Fruit of the Nispero" series.[44] The song of most note, however, is the third, "To a Child." Late Victorian Sapphic verse often focuses on female chastity, by which is meant a body and spirit reserved from phallic sexuality.[45] "To a Child" exists in the moment before waking to sexual experience. Nominally addressed to a prepubescent girl, as sung by Batten, the poem's "Belovéd child" might refer to the much younger Hall, possibly a "child" in the mind of Batten; in this case, though, the child would be a boy-girl because Batten gave Hall the pet names of Johnnie (for use in the domestic circle) and John (in social settings), a name further implying David (as in the biblical pair of Jonathan and David). Batten styled herself Jonathan to Hall's David. John/David implied something both martial and heroic about Batten's young lover as well as their mutual commitment to a lifelong bond (Cline, 66).[46] In this context, "child" recalls *childe*, a term denoting a young candidate for knighthood. As directed by Hall to Batten, however, the poem's "Belovéd child" might be Batten herself, who enjoyed playing the role of the beautiful woman cared and provided for by her husband and lovers. In either case, the virginal chastity referred to is female.

Recontextualized as a public love exchange between an older and a younger woman, this poem of childhood takes on a scandalous, even perverse edge. Moreover, gender becomes scrambled in a maternal love that fondly observes a masculinity intrinsic to the embodiment of the young girl. This masculinity, moreover, is sexualized as characteristic of the embodied psyche of the virgin, like the "stain" of the hair that "Lies dark and splendid" over the child's unguarded "bosom's whiteness."

> Belovéd child, I would not have you wake:
> > Stay closed sweet eyes, stay folded languid lips,
> And let Love go a beggar for your sake.
>
> Not even pausing once to kiss your hair,
> > That on your bosom's whiteness like a stain
> Lies dark and splendid where the skin is fair.

Soft lotus lily, float upon the stream
    Of happy innocence to isles of peace,
And let no lover wake you from your dream;

Nor part that mouth with kisses: 'tis too sweet
    To mate with any other. Ah! those lips!
Love could but make their beauty less complete. (24)

Cherishing a moment before the advent of conscious sexuality, the poem is premised nonetheless on acknowledgment that such "innocence" cannot continue. It will be—as for Hall and Batten it already has been—imaginatively broken by a female "mate."

Understood in this light, "To a Child" provides a complex view of the female psyche and of intimacy between women. The implicitly relational emphasis of the poem is notably different from the emphasis of Hall's self-absorbed earlier signature poem published in 1908, "The Scar." The castrating gesture at the end of the poem signifies in part the social and psychological construction of femininity and the female body within a phallocentric economy, in part the physical and emotional isolation of the speaker, whose "secret needs / Quenched by the bleeding of that fountain are."

Upon my life I bear one precious scar:
Each night I kiss it, till anew it bleeds,
And tell each drop of blood, as hallowed beads
Are told by those dear few who faithful are.
To me it seems to beautify, nor mar,
My inner self, for from that deep wound leads
A path to gained respect, my secret needs
Quenched by the bleeding of that fountain are.

The fiery contest when that wound was won,
    Still burns within my brain, and robs of life,
And terror, every lesser hurt that's done
    To heart or spirit; let all harm run rife.
I shall not fear again to look upon
    The gleaming edges of Fate's sharpest knife.[47]

"The Scar" is the utterance of a seasoned warrior, not a squire or childe; and its *amor* seems both sexual and blasphemously religious. The "precious scar" that bleeds again nightly calls to mind the wound in the side of Christ, here a male-female one,[48] a reference bolstered by the comparison between the drops of blood that flow from the scar "as hallowed beads / Are told by those dear few who faithful are." The poem is intensely inward-looking, its emphasis on how the scar beautifies "My inner self." Despite the poem's seeming solipsism, however, communication with others is also indicated. The speaker's "tell"ing (i.e., counting) of "each drop of blood" connotes as well her telling (i.e., speaking) in verse, whose rhyme words form "beads" that tell the "bleeds." "Those dear few" who tell their beads suggest the elect group of poets who, in "Ode to Sappho," another signature poem published in the same volume, are linked to the Greek poet by beads that in this poem are not drops of blood but tears.

> Oh! Sappho . . .
> Not thy deep pleasures, nor thy swiftest joys,
>   Have made thee thus, immortal and yet dear
> To mortal hearts, but that which naught destroys,
> The sacred image of thy falling tear.
>
> Beloved Lesbian! We would dare to claim
>   By that same tear fond union with thy lot.[49]

I have emphasized "The Scar" to be the poem of an *isolato*. However, it may also be read in relational terms, although in this case in terms of st(r)ains of pain. The vaginal scar nightly kissed by the speaker might be that of her lovers, who, "faithful," worship in turn at the shrine of her wound, which bleeds *cyprine*. From the kisses of these lovers, the champion gains the "respect" necessary to overcome "The gleaming edges of Fate's sharpest knife." In "The Scar," however, relationality is fraught with pain for both lover and beloved.

Hall's poetry can be parsed within female poetic tradition in Victorian England. Emily Brontë and Elizabeth Barrett are important precursors, and *The Forgotten Island* is an imitation of Michael Field's *Long Ago* (1889). Both books fashion Sappho's island home of Lesbos as a landscape of desire, and the lyric personae of both works are often double-voiced as that of Sappho, who pursues the love of young maidens, and an ambiguously gendered poetic piper engaged in a similar quest. Important points of convergence also exist between Hall's neo-Hellenistic version of Roman Catholicism and the Dionysiac Christianity of the devotional verse that the couple wrote after their conversion to Roman Catholicism. In the programmatic "Prayer," from Part 2 of *Songs of Three Counties*, Hall combines pantheistic, Christian, and pagan associations in affirming sexual love between women. The lyric voice apostrophizes "the Poet-God" responsible for all creation:

> Whose image is revealed to all
> Great lovers in the loved one's face,
> Whose passion mystical and deep
> Kindles the holy fires that sleep
> Within the heart's most secret place.
> Whose breath is incense on the shrine
> Of earthly love, burning divine
> And changeless, through all time and space![50]

The English poet most significant to Hall's Sapphic poetry, however, is a male, A. C. Swinburne. "Ode to Swinburne" revisits female masculinity in a new light: it sutures Hall's Sapphism with the tradition of male Aestheticism and the Decadence. Echoing the rhetoric of "The Scar" and "Ode to Sappho," Hall sees Sapphic subjectivity as channeled through Swinburne's "Anactoria" and other Sapphic poems. Swinburne has "wakened" women to their identification with female same-sex desire, shameful in the eyes of Victorian propriety but a badge of "worth" to those prepared to claim their love. As usual in Hall's work, this worth is accessed through "deep manhood," both that of the male poet and that of the female lover. Finally, just as Myers defends genius against charges of abnormality and degeneration, Hall defends Swinburne against the notorious attacks on his "sterility."[51] Far from being sterile, Swinburne has generated a Sapphic progeny:

> Round thy head
> The laurels of men's thoughts, and tears that bled
> From souls thou wakened to their shame or worth.
> In thee was nothing sterile, and no dearth
> Was known to thy deep manhood, strong and fed
> Upon vast musings.[52]

The "Ode to Swinburne" connects the emergence of Sapphic existence with the progress of the human race in the face of Swinburne's usual gang of antagonists in conventional morality, the police power of the state, and the crippling authority of institutional religion. This linkage motivates Hall's willingness to think the thought, so to speak, of human existence as a work of self-invention that constitutes *the* ethical project of the life of the species.

> . . . Thou all gods did'st look
> Between the eyes, didst smite with thy swift breath
> Until they crumbled into less than death,
> And in thy hands their dim white ashes took
> And cast aside. . . .
> Though gav'st to man himself, eternity
> Of life in death, all things in one, that one
> A million millions, since time was begun
> A vast harmonious whole, less than a breath,
> And more than the great fires of earth or sun.[53]

Popular Success and Lessons Learned

In closing this chapter, I turn to the single poem by Hall that, even before the outbreak of World War I, made the greatest impact on the British public, namely, "The Blind Ploughman." In addition to aspects mentioned in the first section of the chapter, "The Blind Ploughman" includes an element of vernacular religious mysticism that proved both adaptable and highly communicative. Hall would reprise key tropes of this work until the end of her career.

> Set my hands upon the plough,
>   My feet upon the sod;
> Turn my face towards the east,
>   And praise be to God!
>
> Every year the rains do fall,
>   The seeds they stir and spring;
> Every year the spreading trees
>   Shelter birds that sing.

From the shelter of your heart,
    Brother—drive out sin,
Let the little birds of faith
    Come and nest therein.

God has made his sun to shine
    On both you and me;
God, who took away my eyes,
    That my *soul* might see![54]

A dramatic lyric that introduces a Wordsworthian natural man to the reader, the ploughman speaks for the first time in the final stanza. As aesthetic statement, however, the lyric may be regarded as the words of the poet telepathically gaining entry to the countryman's subjectivity, then translating their communion into familiar diction and an accessible rhetoric. In this way, the poem becomes a collaboration between a fictional male subject and the poet. The final stanza can be read triply, as expressing the ploughman's sentiment, as the reader's should s/he make the choice of reading the poem with the necessary degree of sympathy, and/or as that of the poet/author. If the reader or the poet claims the stanza for themselves, literal blindness becomes metaphoric blindness; and the visionary capability that arises from affliction becomes a possibility for both reader and author.

At the time of publication of *Songs of Three Counties*, Hall was better known as a lyricist of drawing-room songs than as a poet. It is likely that "The Blind Ploughman" had already been set to music by Clarke before its publication, and it quickly became "one of the most famous ballads of the day" (Cline, 48, 88). On November 23, 1913, Hall accompanied Batten, her cousin Dorothy Diehl, and Phoebe Hoare to an evening concert at the Queen's Hall to hear the musical setting of the poem sung by Charles Tree (88). Appearing in public with her domestic partner plus one former and one current lover, Hall piqued the curiosity of members of the audience who might know or guess the details of her tangled private life. She also made a political point by tacitly claiming the countryman's experience for herself and for women like her. Hall had already explored the notion of a sexual disability that gives rise to higher powers in "The Scar." In attending the performance as she did, she implicitly claimed the spiritual, even visionary, capabilities of what a condescending onlooker might have regarded as a regrettable deviation from propriety. Sapphic readers or observers and others in the know might listen to the song or read the poem as affirming the creative possibilities of Sapphic desire.

Earlier I suggested that the third stanza opens the possibility for the reader to claim the lines as expressing his or her own personal condition. In this respect, the poem may function not only as the utterance of a male rustic or a Sapphic writer; it can serve many other purposes as well. During World War I, "The Blind Ploughman" served the need described by Rosa Bracco for middlebrow literary texts that could sublimate the devastating effects of the war on combatants and noncombatants alike. Bracco argues that authors who produced such texts were committed to "a didactic literature of social communication . . . based on the assumption of values and experience shared with their readers."[55] This middlebrow character helps explain the tension in the poem between the simplicity of form and diction, which recalls one of William Blake's *Songs of Experience*, and the thoroughly conventional view of God proposed, which Blake rejected.

Combining English poetic tradition with populism and conventional religiosity, the song was perfectly suited to its use in a historic performance at Usher Hall in Edinburgh. The popular, ideological function of the piece, moreover, did not undercut other meanings it held for Hall. Into the 1930s, she continued to identify herself and other Sapphists with the image of the ploughman as a stricken but blessed worker/activist. In a bitter, unfinished public address to sexual inverts who were also World War I veterans, Hall's manuscript breaks off, somewhat incoherently, as follows: "But I say & you say that we must be better. More faithful, more patient, more honest, more courageous. For we have a harder furrow to hoe—a hard, long grewelling [sic] furrow to hoe. And we dare not take our hands from the plough till the furrow is driven home straight & true—We dare not to relax our grip for a moment."[56]

In 1918, however, Hall's sense of desperate, isolated mission lay in the future. At Usher Hall, "The Blind Ploughman" was sung by a blinded military officer, Captain MacRobert, before an audience of three thousand listeners. Confirming once again the intimacy of the world of song recitals, Hall's new partner, Una Troubridge, was acquainted with MacRobert, whom both she and the American diva Mignon Nevada knew as "Laddie." Nevada sent Hall and Troubridge a copy of a letter from MacRobert in which he discusses his experience of singing the song. The letter also contains a notice of a sighting at the concert experienced by "a great clairvoyant."[57]

Both the clairvoyant's vision and MacRobert's experience of singing the song are couched in the terms of contemporary spiritualist belief. In his letter, MacRobert uses the language of mediumship to describe the experience of singing the song: "I felt that I was just an instrument," he writes; "my friends . . . felt I was conveying a message." The song provides a means of linking audience, singer, the entire musical ensemble, composer, and lyricist in an experience of communal consolation. MacRobert continues: "I do wish to dedicate my voice to uplift and bring joy to humanity and I feel that I can and shall with that song. Of course foolishly, the audience thinks it was myself and my voice, they are not developped [*sic*] enough to see beyond the material side, whereas I know there was 'Someone' of the higher Angelic order that was really there and just used my vehicle!" At this point, his attention shifts to Hall, to his connection with her, and to her role in this psychical experience of channeling the "message" of those who have been sacrificed in war. "How I should love to meet Miss Hall. What a happiness it must be to her to feel & to know what a wonderful gift she has made to the world by her great, soul uplifting poem."[58]

Experiences like this one corroborated Hall's initial conviction as a writer of the dependence of her poetry upon "inspiration." But the wartime success of "The Blind Ploughman" also shaped her sense of her role as the impersonal medium through which the experience of the suffering of some could be communicated to the public at large. The vehicles of belief for these exchanges were vernacular notions of Catholicism, Theosophy, and Spiritualism. This approach to communication was wedded to mass spectacle as in the Usher Hall concert and the dissemination of feeling and belief through the mass media. At Usher Hall, Hall's salon writing crossed over into the media of modern entertainment. A good example of how this process worked is afforded by the news clipping inserted in Nevada's letter, which reports on the concert as the occasion of a mass telepathic experience. During the late 1910s and 1920s, group experiences of this sort were frequently reported in the media, and spiritualists produced photographs, later debunked, of the faces of young men lost in battle hovering over the crowd at home. "Over the people's heads a grey haze [appeared,] that as it ascended higher gradually went from blue to violet and finally from pink to a dazzling yellow-white which seemed to be full of moving forms. Some looked like spirits, others like stars with 5 or 7 points to them, that were constantly vibrating and over the whole building there seemed a wonderful feeling of Peace and Harmony."[59] In this account too, the social aggregate is conciliated in the face of mass catastrophe.

I have spoken of the lyricist's role in this social production as that of an impersonal point of transfer of the significance of collective loss. One might describe this function as existing outside the terms of ego-driven aspiration or intention. But the context of the circulation of Hall's lyrics as mass entertainment also necessarily involves celebrity. In this way as well as through the networking of the small community of those involved in the private world of salon-music making, Hall's orphic utterances are marked with the author's signature as well as, more generally, by Sapphic cultural politics.

News of the response to "The Blind Ploughman" must have been unusually welcome to Hall in early June 1918, since there is evidence that she and Troubridge were highly disturbed by the outcome of a trial a month earlier involving Maud Allan, a dancer with sexual and emotional ties to other women. Allan had gained notoriety for her performance in the role of Salomé in Wilde's play of the same name. She lost the libel suit that she launched against extreme right-wing politicians and polemicists who condemned her attempt to mount a private production of *Salomé* in spring 1918, when a major German offensive put the outcome of the war in doubt. The Allan trial opened on May 29, 1918, at a time when war weariness and hysteria were at their high point. Troubridge had been a house guest at Nevada's home in Edinburgh in March 1917. Nevada added to her letter some gossipy questions as to "some rather queer things" that may have motivated the right-wing campaign against Allan. Of these efforts by Allan's antagonists, one of whom was a relative of Una's estranged husband, Nevada asked: "I wonder if Troubridge knew too much?? And if the explanation of his persecution won't be found ultimately to lie at the bottom of all this muck heap?" By Troubridge she means Admiral Troubridge, from whom Una, who was living with Hall in spring 1918, was seeking a separation.[60] This web of connections demonstrates the tight interweaving of private and public politics and the barely submerged development of a lesbian public politics, one to which Nevada was sympathetic and which involved Troubridge and Hall as well.[61]

For a number of years, Hall had been pleased to see her lyrics set to music by a number of different composers. The extraordinary success of "The Blind Ploughman" prompted her to begin thinking about the possibility of earning money from sales of sheet music for this and other of her songs published by Chappell and Company. Accordingly, she wrote to Chappell to raise the question of royalties for the lyrics of "The Blind Ploughman." The reply that she received indicates how exploitative of lyricists music publishers were prepared to be. In a letter dated June 13, 1918, a representative of the company wrote Hall: "Unfortunately, we cannot afford to pay royalties to lyric writers. One or two other publishers may, but if we were to once introduce the principle, there would be no end to it. Many lyrics are merely a repetition of the same words in a different order and almost always with the same ideas. Hardly any of them, frankly, are worth a royalty, although once in a way [sic] they may be. It is difficult to differentiate, however. What I do feel is that you are quite entitled to have an extra payment for these particular words, and I have much pleasure in enclosing you, from Messrs. Chappell, a cheque for twenty guineas."[62]

In contrast, young Ivor Novello had a very different experience with a wartime hit. Born in 1893, Novello was just beginning his career in 1914, at the outset of World War I. He would become a dominant figure as the composer, lyricist, and star of West End vehicles by the end of the 1920s.[63] Like Hall, Novello did not conceal his affectional and sexual preference for members of his own sex. Like Hall too, Novello socially was an outsider who came from a musical background. He, however, earned a great deal of money as a result of the success of his tune "Keep the Home Fires Burning," which became a sort of popular anthem for both soldiers at the front and civilians back home in England.

Unlike Hall's undertaking as poet and lyricist, which focused on prestige, Novello's was frankly commercial. In 1914, his mother urged him to write a hit song in support of the war effort. After initially resisting the injunction, Novello one day had an idea. In his biographer's somewhat mythologized retelling, "Without hesitation [Novello] sat at the keyboard and played verse and chorus straight off. He felt immediately that this was the music he sought: a sturdy march rhythm that led to an eight-bar melody once repeated." Novello then asked an American friend and collaborator, Lena Guilbert Ford, to write the lyrics, providing her with the lines, "Keep the home fires burning, while your hearts are yearning" (Harding, 28). When the song was complete, Novello arranged for its introduction at a music-hall performance. The occasion shares some features with the impact of Hall's song on a mass audience at Usher Hall. After the singer, Sybil Vane,[64] began repeating the chorus, the audience, which was hearing the song for the first time, joined in; and the band of the Grenadier Guards, who were also appearing, improvised an accompaniment. "The audience stamped their feet vigorously. In all they played and sang the piece half a dozen times" (29).

The music publishers Ascherberg, Hopwood and Crewe offered Novello a contract that included an annual retainer of £25 plus a royalty of three-pence on each copy of the sheet music. In all, Novello cleared £15,000–£18,000 on the song, a huge sum at the time. Like Hall, Ford did not fare as well: "She had little business sense and failed to insist on royalties for the words she contributed" (30). The similarities and contrasts between Novello's experience, Ford's, and Hall's indicate the limits that Hall now encountered as a poet and lyricist working within a genteel, feminine context. Her humiliating dismissal by Chappell prompted her to start seeing herself differently as a writer. As she shifted her interest in writing from poetry to fiction, she thenceforth worked hard to control the financial terms on which her work was published. Inspiration was fine, but writing was a profession.

I began this chapter by asking what contexts are appropriate for reading Hall's poetry. In discussing this early work, I have shown that Hall was already self-consciously playing with autobiographical reference in her work, pursuing celebrity, and attempting to establish a career as a writer.[65] Considered as an extended self-performance, her flagging of her sexual and emotional interest in other women plus the Sapphic program that she fashions in various ways in the volumes as they proceed, belong both to the history of the renewal of English music in the early years of the twentieth century and to the formation of mass and specialty listening and reading publics.

2

Psychic Incorporation

War, Mourning, and the Technology of Mediumship

With the onset of World War I and the traumatic death of her first long-term partner in 1916, the relaxed view of the possibilities of desire between women evinced in Hall's poetry came to an end. In the following years, she lost contact with many of the artistic and often feminist women that her connection with Mabel Batten had opened to her. Instead, the next six years were anxious ones, dominated by guilt over the circumstances attending Batten's death and by Hall's attempt to repair the loss. During this period, Hall turned to members of another group, the Society for Psychical Research, in part to build a new set of friends, acquaintances, and supporters, and in part as the next phase of her effort to build a position for herself in the public eye, an effort connected in turn with her ambition, fostered and in that sense now consecrated by Batten, to become a successful novelist. Along the way, Hall found herself drawn into the second and most important of her long-term relationships, namely, that with Una Troubridge.

The Society for Psychical Research was a socially and intellectually elite group, founded at Cambridge University in 1882 to engage in the scientific study of what today are referred to as paranormal phenomena. Entry into the Society provided Hall with a new source of cultural prestige as well as a way of potentially reconnecting with Batten, especially because the high number of war dead had resulted in a sharp increase in interest in séances, a principal area of research for the Society. At the same time, the Society's reputation was ambiguous. Popularly and in the mass circulation press, its members were regarded as upper-class eccentrics with a tenuous claim to intellectual seriousness. In terms of the Society's project, moreover, it was unclear whether its purpose was to prove or to disprove the hypothesis that individual human existence continues after death. At any rate, Hall's turn to the Society after Batten's death is symptomatic both of her loneliness and of the continuing marginality of her social position.

Hall's main piece of writing during these years is an extended report on the psychical research she undertook after Batten's death. The article appeared in the *Proceedings of the Society* in 1919. Batten figures largely in the research, while Troubridge is also a significant player. Accordingly and despite the attempt to provide an objective framework for the material in the idiom and structure of the psychical research essay, the study is inescapably autobiographical. This double aspect of the work—on the one hand, dry, jargon laden, wordy, and detached, and on the other, intensely personal, private, even scandalous—precisely matched Hall's psychic needs at the time. In this chapter, I analyze the essay in terms of its autobiographical performativity. The essay served to provide a narrative of Hall's recent and ongoing life and to define her most significant personal ties for the following decade and a half. This narrative structure is a double one: first a narrative occurs that accomplishes Hall's reconciliation with Batten. Accompanying this narrative is another in which Batten arranges for the love and care that she provided Hall during their relationship to be continued by Troubridge. During the sessions, however, Troubridge is constituted not merely as an assistant recorder and substitute caregiver. As the sittings continue, a narrative is fashioned that establishes her as an individual with her own psychic wounds and agency. The completed narrative tells the tale of three lives, henceforward to be permanently entwined, that of Batten, living beyond death; Hall; and Troubridge as her new partner.

The essay is also performative in relation to Hall's fashioning as a novelist. In the process of researching and writing the essay, Hall, with crucial assistance from Troubridge, transformed herself into a writer of prose narrative. Hall learned how to conduct research and work it into publishable shape. She also found one of the major preoccupations of her work as a writer of fiction: namely, the fashioning of the genres of the short story and novel into instruments for conveying an embodied experience of trauma between text and reader. In these ways, the essay is doubly autobiographical. Autobiographical in recording the genesis of a committed personal relationship, the project of the essay actualizes Hall's function as a writer.

One obvious direction in which to read the essay is as a piece of motherwriting. In it, Hall successfully reclaims the love and attention of the much older Batten. Hall was convinced that Batten had provided her with the love refused her by her biological mother. As she wrote to Sir Oliver Lodge in 1918 in a letter apropos Batten's daughter, Mrs. Austin Harris, "I never expect to know again such grief as I experienced at the sudden death of Mrs. Harris's mother, who represented to me all the affection and sympathy and complete understanding which had been absent from my early life."[1] At the same time, the circumstances of Batten's fatal stroke bear witness to Hall's unconsciously motivated rejection of this sort of acceptance and love. In this situation, Hall acts out the role of "bad boy," which, in her unpublished autobiographical essays and incomplete novel, *Michael West*, she contends that her mother had early projected onto her. Already at the time of publication of *The Forgotten Island*, she was involved with other women.[2] And at the time of Batten's death, Hall was having an open affair with Troubridge.

The tendency to read the material as motivated by fantasies of the fusion of female psyches can easily be supported in terms of current interpretations of the psychology of the séance. Stephen Connor, for example, writing about the popularity of séances during and after World War I, argues that one of the attractions of the practice was that it created an intensively feminine cultural space. Associating the darkened, often all-female space of the spiritualist sitting with Julia Kristeva's concept of the semiotic, Connor argues that women in séances were recalled by the experience of female voice in a darkened room to a pre-oedipal state, in other words, to a fantasy of fusion with a lost maternal other. And Jenny Hazelgrove, in her excellent history of the Spiritualist movement in England in the first half of the twentieth century, sees the double attitude of the Society toward paranormal phenomena as symptomatic of an unconscious play of attraction to and repulsion from a maternal other. Hazelgrove finds ambivalence to be key to the objectives of psychical research. On the one hand, there was the tendency, epitomized in the writing of Frederic Myers, to see psychical research as a way of accessing aspects of human experience, intrapsychic, interpsychic, and even between the living and the deceased, which the methods of the modern physical sciences were unable to chart.[3] On the other hand, another early leader, the Cambridge philosopher Henry Sidgwick, emphasized the need for dispassionate scientific inquiry: "We must remember that our raison d'être is the extension of the scientific method, of intellectual virtues."[4] Hazelgrove argues that psychical researchers (defined usually as male) were attracted to the phenomena associated with mediums as occasions of psychic fusion between those involved in a sitting. At the same time, however, psychical researchers anxiously recoiled against the potential loss of their own individuality.

In Hall's case, one may wonder whether the dual role of (feminine) participant–(masculine) observer sufficiently met her masculine psychic needs, a point to which I return at the end of the chapter. Notwithstanding this question, Hall's situation demands a rather different reading of the séances than that provided by Connor and Hazelgrove. In the sittings, Hall assumed the role of scientific investigator, or, in other words, a connotatively male subject-position. At the same time, the object of her interest in the sittings was to reconcile herself with her deceased lover. In other words, Hall's re-performance of the pre-oedipal tie posited by some commentators depends upon her occupying a masculine position within the sitting. In this way, both aspects of Hall's sense of self, both her masculinity and her femininity, are affirmed in the séance. This affirmation takes place as a result of her crossgendered performativity within the situation. Cross gender both enables and limits the possibility of fusion. Moreover, the technology of mediumship continually reminds sitters of the distance that exists between themselves and the spirits with whom they try to communicate. Records of sessions are full of what might be called interference effects, that is, of interruptions or distortions of communication that emphasize the "thickness" of these modes, their obliquity, and their propensity to produce errors in interpretation.

The technology of mediumship requires a medium, a sitter, a recorder (in the case of the Society's tests), a control, and a communicating voice. Hall worked with a medium named Mrs. Gladys Osborne Leonard. At the beginning of a session, Leonard would usually go into a trance. Communication would then be initiated by Feda, her "Control," or the spirit who guided Leonard's work as a medium and who had chosen her as a passive medium of communication. Early in her development as a psychic, Leonard learned that Feda was the spirit of an Indian girl, married to Leonard's great-great-grandfather. Feda reported that she herself had died in child-birth at the age of thirteen.[5] When communicating, Feda speaks in a foreign accent, with imperfect English and the vocabulary of a child. She lacks words to convey concepts or complex emotions or states of mind. Often, she does not know the particular word or words that a spirit is trying to send to the listening sitters, and much time is consumed as the sitters work with Feda to try to communicate what the spirit is trying to say. These difficulties are continual reminders that the sitters exist on a different plane of consciousness from that of Feda and other spirits. The difficulties, inter-ruptions, relays, blanks, and occasional failures all inhibit the likelihood of psychic fusion. Moreover, the language that controls do use is so simplified in character as to be generic. In other words, a sitter who prepared for a sitting by reading accounts of other sittings would already be familiar with the vocabulary and content of the messages that they were likely to receive from "the other side."

In addition to the control are the communicating voices, "spirits" in Spiritualist rhetoric, "purported communicators" in the awkward usage of the Society for Psychical Research. Here too problems of translation arise since spirits usually communicate by conveying psychical messages to the control, who then must translate the messages into her own words for the benefit of the sitters. At times in the sittings with Leonard, Batten seemingly assumes the role of control herself and speaks in something like her own voice. These more direct attempts to communicate tend to produce highly emotional responses in sitters.

Leonard's unconscious body served as means for physical communica-tion by the control or spirit. Feda often moves the body of Leonard as she tries to convey a point physically. At times, the motions are characteristic gestures of Batten herself. In other words, the technology of mediumship demonstrates the possibility that the body of one person can convey the bodily movements, affective signs, and sensations of another. I call this process enactment, and it seems to me to qualify Hall's experience of her deceased lover in a particular way.[6] Rather than speaking of fusion as the object of the séance, it is better to think in terms of identification by means of incorporation of the other through enactment. Again, the process is per-formative rather than merely one of assimilation or absorption of a fanta-sized other. When Feda moves Leonard's body to make a point of her own, to touch Hall, or to demonstrate a habitual gesture of Batten, she demonstrates that the body of one person can enact the experiences of the body of another. As a result of the demonstration, Feda conveys the idea that the sitter herself can embody the experience of the loved one. Communicating this idea is the primary epistemological objective of the sittings, and it makes possible what I describe later in the chapter as the payoff of the séances that Hall arranged. By participating in the series, Hall was able to reenact within her own body the experience of her lover in extremity. Instead of losing her identity in that of the other, she experienced within herself the embodied experience of another.

Hall's report on the sittings appeared in the *Proceedings of the Society for Psychical Research* in 1919. The article was a longer version of a two-part paper that she delivered to members of the Society and the public in London in January and March 1918. Presented as a serious piece of speculative psychology, the essay is based on sittings that Hall and Troubridge conducted between August 1916 and August 1917 with Mrs. Leonard, who had come to attention soon after the onset of World War I. In her autobiography published in 1931, she saw her entire career as predicated on the need for her services occasioned by the war. Leonard had begun working as a medium with Feda's guidance in 1913. In March 1914, Feda instructed her to "begin work as a professional medium as soon as possible." By a variety of means, Feda repeatedly communicated: "Something big and terrible is going to happen to the world. Feda must help many people through you."[7] In these words, Feda makes clear the therapeutic function of mediumship within a social context of widespread trauma.

Troubridge closely collaborated with Hall in taking and recording notes on these sessions, and in the journal she is credited with Hall as coauthor of the essay. This acknowledgment is important since it establishes the fact of collaboration from the outset of Hall's work as an author of prose. In part, this feature of Hall's work was an effect of the disability of dyslexia, which limited her ability to read and write.[8] To compensate for the disability, Hall had become a very good listener. In the sittings, information was communicated principally through hearing, sight, and touch. She may have found very welcome a mode of transmission that did not depend upon the written or printed word. In addition, the practice of taking notes and carefully transcribing them later may have helped her overcome anxiety in relation to the written word. However, organizing the research continued to be a major focus of anxiety.

Hazelgrove's approach ignores the serious interest of Society researchers, both male and female, in paranormal phenomena. The Society's work was not driven simply by its members' unconscious motives. In the late nineteenth century, both in England and the United States, an interest in aspects of the self outside the limits of the conscious ego fascinated psychologists and philosophers. Much of their interest focused not on the discursive content of the information thereby communicated but rather on the insights into human psychology that the phenomena might generate. In an article on automatic writing, for example, William James remarks that "the great theoretic interest of these automatic performances, whether speech or writing, consists in the questions they awaken as to the boundaries of individuality."[9] Sidgwick was a distinguished Utilitarian philosopher. Those who joined this and other such groups as the Theosophical Society examined the phenomena of mental telepathy, automatic writing, accounts of ghosts and haunting, and Spiritualism. In doing so, they attempted to bring an open-minded but objective spirit, what they referred to as "an evidential point of view," to their studies.[10] At times, they produce careful and lucid analyses, as, for example, when one investigator, Alice Johnson, attempts to distinguish "subliminal" and "supraliminal" awareness from evidence that she believes her correspondent can definitely not already have known at the time it was produced in the form of automatic writing (177).

In retrospect, the evidence produced by psychical researchers proved much less convincing than they had hoped. Since the evidence communicated in séances, for example, was usually already known to at least one of the sitters, the possibility of telepathic communication was readily available as an explanation. (The existence of mental telepathy was a phenomenon that members of the Society believed had been scientifically demonstrated in an early series of experiments conducted under the Society's auspices.)[11] Moreover, since the experiments were not controlled and reproducible, the evidence produced failed to meet the basic requirements of experimental research. In addition, the evidence provided by the controls is often trivial in character. And when voices from "the other side" attempt to communicate something of substance, the message is usually trite. For example, in Johnson's study of the automatic writing of the pseudonymous Mrs. Holland (in actuality, Alice Kipling),[12] the following bit of doggerel is communicated: "Believe in what thou canst not see, / Until the vision come to thee" (171). All of these factors reflect negatively on mediumship as a mode of epistemology.

One of the chief objectives of psychical research is to prove the continuing existence of the personality after death, but descriptions of life on "the astral plane" are likely to appear inconsequential to those not directly concerned in the sitting. At one sitting, for example, Batten reports that she now enjoys horseback riding, that she has acquired a new pet, and that she has a swimming pool reserved for her private use. When Hall, in another session, becomes absorbed in the control's laborious description of the interior of White Cottage, the intensity of her excitement in receiving this information is disproportionate to the actual content of the communication. Of much more interest is the psychological mechanism, called "dissociation of consciousness" by psychical researchers, that might account for this supposed communication from Batten through the control.[13] Hall herself is so intent on being convinced of Batten's survival after death that she does not analyze this possibility, but other psychical investigators do. Johnson, for example, suggests that "controls" may be "aided and abetted by the subliminal self (of which they may, indeed, be fragmentary manifestations)" (179).

Approaches to psychical research were strongly marked by gender. In the Theosophical Society, as Joy Dixon has shown, male members tended to emphasize the experimental, rational, and scientific character of their investigations.[14] On the other hand, most mediums were women. Feminists have argued that this division of labor permitted women to make claims to spiritual knowledge and authority that would not have been tolerated in the churches, universities, or marital households of the day. Male members of the Society tended to be skeptical about such wisdom. For its part, Hall's essay is written within the genre of scientific studies of spiritualist phenomena. In the essay, she presents herself as "an impartial judge of evidence."[15] This approach is consistent with her self-identification with mental qualities coded as masculine. But, as I have suggested, Hall is noticeably less intellectual in her approach than, say, Alice Johnson. And the dramatis personae of the sittings—with Mrs. Leonard as medium, Hall and Troubridge as sitters, and two female controls, Feda and Batten—are all women. The essay itself then, despite its framing in terms of "masculine" objectivity, is very much female-centered. This focus, moreover, takes the surprising, and at the time scandalous, form of what today might be referred to as a lesbian coming-out story. The narrative of the essay, in one line, is the cumulative revelation of two important sexual and emotional relationships in Hall's life. This revelation helps explain why Hall's lectures prompted a public scandal and efforts to force her to resign from the Society.

Mediumship can be regarded as a modern technology of the psyche, which gained prominence simultaneously with the invention of psychoanalysis. Both of these technologies focus on subjects in need of therapeutic attention. And both depend for their success on personal interactions, in one case, in spiritualist sittings and, in the other, in psychoanalytic sessions. In both settings, the relations involve processes of identification that psychoanalysts refer to with the terms *transference* and *counter-transference*.[16] In psychoanalysis, however, these processes are supplemented with other elements in order to help the analysand recognize the operation of this unconscious dynamic.

Hall's extended period of psychical research proved remarkably productive both in shaping her sense of self as a public person and a writer and in enabling her to commit herself to a long-term relationship with Troubridge. Her investment in psychical research, however, still left her very much in need. Unexamined aspects of her role as a participant, in particular the degree of her responsibility, directly or indirectly, for having provoked Batten's fatal seizure, limited Hall's ability to understand and evaluate the sessions. She entered into the sittings and pursued them with total absorption in a transparent effort to come to terms with the trauma prompted by Batten's death. The essay plots the narrative trajectory of the sittings that permitted her to act out this trauma. But no analysis of the trauma takes place. Hall's experience leaves open the question as to whether the technology of mediumship affords opportunities for this sort of self-reflection or not. There is, for example, a similar lack of self-reflection in the sessions, discussed later in this chapter, that Oliver Lodge undertook in attempting to communicate with his son Raymond, who was killed in action during the war. Instead, through the introduction of "Billy," Hall and Troubridge shift the focus of the second part of the essay to the third member of the romantic triangle.

Hall and Mabel Batten met in 1907, when Hall was twenty-seven and Batten was fifty-one and married to a much older man, George Batten. Hall fell in love with Mabel, developed a close friendship with the couple, and, after George's death, shared a flat with Batten in London and the White Cottage in Malvern Wells. They remained partners until Batten's death in May 1916. The later years of their relationship were, however, troubled by sexual infidelities on the part of Hall. On August 1, 1915, Troubridge, then twenty-eight, was introduced to Hall at a tea given by Batten's sister, Lady Clarendon. Eight years earlier, young Una had married Ernest Troubridge, a much older man with excellent prospects in the British Navy. However, both discontent with serving overseas on Malta as the wife of an officer and problems with her husband's sisters and children by a former marriage ensued. Early in 1913, she returned to England to enter psychotherapy with

Dr. Hugh Crichton-Miller. During the course of analysis and with his sympathetic support, she became aware that she might be bisexual or even primarily lesbian in orientation.[17] Shortly after war broke out in August 1914, her husband was recalled to London and was court-martialed as a result of a botched naval expedition he had commanded. Although he was acquitted, his reputation was damaged, and his career in the navy effectively shelved (Ormrod, 60–62). In May 1915, he was posted to Belgrade, and his wife found herself the mother of a young child and living "deeply distressed and intensely lonely in a tiny house in Bryanston Street."[18]

Troubridge had been introduced to Hall at an earlier date, but, at the time, Hall did not make an impression. Now, however, Troubridge was ready for a change. She found it in Hall's charm, high spirits, and boyish good looks. In her memoir of Hall, Troubridge says that she was immediately entranced (Ormrod, 46–47). The three women—Batten, Hall, and Troubridge—grew close and traveled together, and the younger pair began an affair. The seriousness of Troubridge's interest made this new connection a real threat to Batten and Hall's life together. Batten understandably became jealous, and her resentment came to the fore on the evening of May 14, 1916. Earlier that day, Hall and Troubridge had visited Maidenhead to look at a bulldog puppy for Troubridge (Ormrod, 72ff). After debating whether to stay overnight, the pair returned by train to London. Hall arrived home late, and an argument over the younger pair's involvement broke out. At its height, "Ladye, intending to make a dignified exit to show her disapproval, rose from the table and suffered an apoplectic seizure" (Ormrod, 74). Batten fell unconscious and remained in that state until her death eleven days later, on May 25.

Batten never spoke to Hall again, and, during the last days, Hall could not know for sure whether Batten could hear her words of love and repentance. After Batten's death, Hall, overcome with remorse, was driven in her extremity to attempt to make contact with her through mediums. In August, she attended her first sitting with Leonard. In October, Hall and Troubridge began visiting her together, one to sit while the other took notes. Their psychical research had begun. It was to continue on a twice-weekly basis for the next six years and intermittently thereafter for many more.

The first order of domestic business in the sittings was to decide what was to become of the ménage à trois now that one of its members was deceased. In effect, if the shock of Batten's death was not to drive Hall to break off with Troubridge, responsibility for Hall needed to be transferred from Batten to Troubridge. This problem takes pride of place early in the essay. For example, the sitting of October 13, 1916, ends with the following exchange between Troubridge, who takes the sitting on this occasion, and Batten, who communicates through the control, Feda:

U.V.T. [Troubridge] Tell Ladye she's got to help me take care of Twonnie [Hall].
F. [Feda] She says, yes, she wants that, she puts her in your charge.
U.V.T. Tell her I will do my best.
F. She says she's afraid you hardly appreciate the magnitude of your task. It will be perfectly awful sometimes, terrible. (365)

Batten, responding through Feda, obligingly entrusts to Troubridge the "task" of caring for Hall. It is exactly in these terms that Troubridge in her memoir of Hall characterizes their relationship (39). The brief exchange is telling in other ways as well. The use of the name "Twonnie," Feda's mispronunciation of Batten's nickname for Hall, has a humorous but infantilizing effect.[19] At the same time, the message includes a shrewd assessment of Hall's character. She did in fact cause Troubridge great pain in future years.

The second performative effect of the sittings is to reassure Hall of Batten's continued existence and unqualified love (Ormrod, 97). In order to assuage Hall's guilt, it is also necessary that Batten, at times at Troubridge's prompting (418), assure Hall that she experiences no suffering in the afterlife. This assurance contradicts other accounts of communication with the deceased, such as Johnson's, which emphasize the frustration felt by the deceased in attempting to communicate through mediums and controls. In Hall's case, the comparative ease of transmission correlates with her desire to be absolved of responsibility for having shortened Batten's life. Instead, both Hall in the psychical research and Troubridge in her memoir claim that Batten's stroke was the delayed effect of a serious automobile accident that took place in September 1914.

Hall writes of Batten's communications on this topic: "She certainly links up her death with her accident. This is a distinctly good point; because although to all appearances A. V. B. made a good recovery from that accident, there can be no doubt that she really never recovered from the shock, and several doctors have told me that it very probably hastened her end. It is undoubted that the consequences of the accident accentuated her tendency to lead the sedentary life most favourable to the development of the high blood-pressure which was the ultimate cause of her death" (426).[20] An automobile accident, leading to life as a semi-invalid, leading to high blood pressure, leading to a stroke is a long, indirect route toward Batten's seizure on the night of her argument with Hall.

In *The Life and Death of Radclyffe Hall*, Troubridge suppresses the fact that an argument occurred that evening. While I do not want to deny the possibility that a physiological link exists between Batten's stroke and the earlier accident, Troubridge's assertion that such a connection exists is even more definite—and more open to question—than Hall's. Troubridge writes that Batten "was an invalid for . . . many months; she never, I think, completely recovered, and moreover, when she died of a stroke less than two years later, the doctors were of opinion that she had suffered the first seizure at the time of the accident" (44). Both Troubridge and Hall appeal to authority, "the doctors," to displace the cause of Batten's death from May 1916 to the auto accident of September 1914.[21]

Communications about the auto accident dominate the first half of Hall's essay. Within the scientific frame of the essay, these messages receive attention as "Evidence of Memory Retained by the Communicator" (361). In terms of emotional motivation, this material is important in relieving the traumatic effects of the circumstances of Batten's death. Through Feda's relay, Hall's experience of loss is displaced to the scene of an earlier traumatic event in which Batten had been seriously injured in Hall's presence. In Hall's account of the auto accident, the later trauma is registered in a real-life incident that in Hall's telling has the force of a dream allegory. Here is her account: "Now the circumstances of the accident were these: A. V. B. and I were passing the Cross Roads at Burford, in our Limousine car, when suddenly a smaller car dashed into the side of our motor with great violence; the lady who was driving the smaller car mistook, in her panic, the accelerator for the brake; consequently the force of the impact was enormous, and our heavy car was jerked backwards and forwards several times before it finally fell over on to a stone wall, which it partly demolished, and then our car partially rebounded on to the road" (425).

At the time of the accident, Hall appeared to be unhurt. When the limousine driver broke down hysterically, she took charge of removing the unconscious Batten from the wreck and moved her with the help of local people to a nearby house. Hall appears not to have recognized that she herself was in shock nor to have received counseling or treatment afterward. Under the impact of Batten's death two years later, Hall is drawn back to the scene of the earlier crack-up, a scene for Hall of continuing, unrecognized trauma, exacerbated by the circumstances of Batten's sudden death a year and a half later.

Hall's return to the site of the accident bears the marks of the later crisis. The details of the incident, in which a panicky female driver blindsides the couple in their limousine and nearly kills one of them, allegorizes the crisis in Hall and Batten's partnership brought about by Troubridge's reckless disregard of the effect of her behavior on Batten's well-being and happiness.[22] In May 1916, Hall and Batten's relationship indeed was at a "Cross Roads," and the description of the accident indicates both that Troubridge was the major instigator and that her insistence was unconsciously motivated. After all, the lady driver did know better than to keep stepping on the accelerator.

The irrationality of Troubridge's behavior is underlined in her account of the accident. Mistaking the date of the accident by several months, she writes:

> During the early summer of that same year as their car (a heavy limousine) was passing the crossroads at Burford on the way to the White Cottage at Malvern Wells, it was literally charged from the near side by a small open car driven by a lady who met the emergency by mistaking the accelerator for the brake. The violence of the first impact was such that it flung the heavy car over against a stone wall which it demolished, while the aggressor proceeded to pound it repeatedly before her engine stalled. The big car ended up on its side, terribly shattered (the bodymakers subsequently expressed surprised that anyone had come out of it alive). (43)

In Troubridge's account, the lady driver is "the aggressor." Troubridge emphasizes the unconscious, repeated character of the other woman's action. In the memoir, Troubridge also takes responsibility for pursuing Hall: "As for me, I thought little and felt a great deal. I was swept along on a spate of feeling, of learning the endless aspects of this strange personality, and all I knew or cared about was that I could not, once having come to know her, imagine life without her. I had, at twenty-eight, as much consideration for Ladye or for anyone else as a child of six" (46–47). Despite her candor here, Troubridge destroyed her diaries for 1915 and 1916 in order to efface evidence of her sexual intimacy with Hall before the time of Batten's death (Ormrod, 71). Troubridge had her own reasons for regretting the impact of her entanglement on Batten, a cousin known to her since childhood, who befriended her both at the time of her marriage and again later when it began to break down. Uncannily enough, the other driver, a Mrs. Lakin, resembled Troubridge in other ways as well. Although it is not usually mentioned, the trial proceedings of Hall's suit against Lakin reveal that Lakin was accompanied in the car by both her sister and her young daughter.[23] Troubridge, who also had a sister, was encumbered with her own young daughter during the anxious months of 1916.

During the sittings, Batten relives the experience of the crash. Hall's narration of Batten's experience permits an indirect acknowledgment of Troubridge's role. Hall writes:

> And now we come to what I feel is one of the best points in the whole description. It is this: A.V.B. says through Feda that when she was jerked there was something at the side which frightened her, something which only caught her eye; according to Feda, A.V.B's own words are: "It was like a sudden flash." At the time of the collision I did not think that A.V.B. who, as I have said, was turning towards me, had seen the approaching motor; I questioned her about this afterwards, and many were the arguments, which invariably ended with the assertion on her part that she knew perfectly well that she had seen something; she used to say: "I tell you I did see something, what I saw was like a sudden flash."
>
> After getting the evidential words regarding the "sudden flash," through Feda, I feel quite sure that I allowed a certain amount of excitement to come into my voice when I said "good!" At all events I recorded in my notes, as a fact against myself, that I had spoken excitedly. (427)

This passage is one of the few times in the transcript of the sessions when Hall acknowledges that she and Batten had "arguments" or disagreements, which, if my sense of the allegorical character of this narrative is correct, refer to the "sudden flash" with which Batten at some point in 1915 realized that her young cousin's ties with Hall posed a major threat. Losing her composure as an observer, Hall for her part reads the moment as one confirming that Batten continues to exist, to communicate with, and thereby to sustain Hall herself.

Batten's communication concerning the car crash begins with bodily movements. During the sitting of December 30, 1916, with Troubridge sitting and Hall taking notes, "Feda showed signs of being uncomfortable, moving about restlessly" (417). She then proceeded to hold the back of her neck and to twist her head slowly from side to side while grimacing. Troubridge and Hall identify this and other movements as one that Batten often made after the accident. Troubridge then asks Feda whether the control can "tell us what caused these feelings" (420). Batten responds by describing the sensation of being unconscious and gradually becoming aware of Hall's presence. Eventually, Batten indicates that this is the moment when she was coming to after the auto accident. Hall follows her account word for word, corroborating Batten's evidence with her own recollection of events.

Hall's involvement in psychical research occurred at a time when it was potentially of large and public significance. The massive scale of Allied casualties in World War I and the fact that these losses occurred across the divides of social class prompted widespread participation in spiritualist sittings. In this context, spiritualist practices focused on alleviating the traumatic experience of the loss of a loved one. Accounts of these sittings tend to have a narrative structure, one of whose climactic moments occurs when the immediate occasion of the loved one's death is dramatized for sitters who usually were hundreds of miles away from the site of injury or death at the time it occurred.

The leading model of the psychical archive in this mode is Sir Oliver Lodge's best-selling book of 1916, *Raymond or Life and Death,* subtitled *With Examples of the Evidence for Survival of Memory and Affection After Death.*[24] The book went through many editions over the following decade. In it, the control re-experiences the trauma that caused the death of Lodge's son Raymond, who was killed on the western front. The moment is very different from the customary archiving of loss. For example, the account of Raymond's death that appeared in *The Times* reads in part as follows: "At the time of his death, [he] was in command of a Company engaged in some early episode of an attack or attempted advance which was then beginning. He was struck by a fragment of shell in the attack on Hooge Hill on the 14th of September 1915, and died in a few hours" (Lodge, 3). An account such as this one was liable to leave members of Raymond's family in an acute state of anxiety over the intensity and duration of his suffering. The description of the action, moreover, is vague to the point of irony, implicitly suggesting that his casualty occurred for no effective purpose.

The reenactment of this injury in a spiritualist setting is much different. During Lodge's first sitting with Leonard, Raymond's fatal injury is reenacted in Feda's voice and her control of the movement of the unconscious medium's body. The demonstration of the transfer of Raymond's trauma to Feda is crucial if the sitter is to be able to enact in his own body the experience of Raymond's extremity.

> Feda feels like a string around her head; a tight feeling in the head, and also an empty sort of feeling in the chest, empty, as if sort of something gone. A feeling like a sort of vacant feeling there; also a bursting sensation in the head. But he [Raymond] does not know he is giving this. He has not done it on purpose, they [the other spirits who appear with him] have tried to make him forget all that, but Feda gets it from him. There is a noise with it too, an awful noise and a rushing noise.
>
> He has lost all that now, but he does not seem to know why Feda feels it now. (127)

Feda speaks in the body in this passage. And yet her body is just as invisible to the sitter as is Raymond's. What the sitter sees and hears are bodily signs of what is happening to two "persons," neither of whose body is physically present. In short then, the bodily reenactment of the moment of the shell burst is a figure of a figure. This bodily figuration provides a mimetic example that can function as a model of the bodily reenactment the sitter is to experience.

Within a month of the publication of *Raymond*, Hall experienced the single most important moment of her psychical investigations. During the sitting of December 30, 1916, she experiences, again through Feda's simulation, her deceased partner's experience during the automobile accident. Hall associated Batten's injuries on this occasion with the blood clot that eventually caused her stroke, an association corroborated by a number of doctors. For both reasons, the accident acquired for Hall the kind of significance that Lodge and his readers found in Raymond's injury. On December 30, Feda began to make movements that Hall and Troubridge associated with Batten's characteristic gestures when she was in discomfort during the years following the accident (Hall, 417). When questioned, Batten indicates that she is re-experiencing the moment when she was coming to after the auto accident. Hall follows her account word for word, corroborating Batten's evidence with her own recollection of events. Six months later, in another sitting,

> Feda said suddenly: "Now she's going back to this," and began a stroking movement of the face, saying, at the same time, that all this had more to do with me than with "Mrs. Una." I, wishing to get a still clearer description, said that I did not quite understand; whereupon Feda said that is was not my face but A.V.B.'s, but that I knew about it. She said that this had not happened "only just a little time" before A.V.B. passed on, and that A.V.B. was most anxious to get it through. A.V.B. then endeavoured apparently to describe, through Feda, the sensations caused by a violent blow on the head, she spoke of a sensation of falling, a giddy feeling, that made you feel as if you must fall to the ground, she also impressed Feda with the feeling that everything was going black, as if one were becoming unconscious, as if, as Feda said, "you were going down, sinking, sinking." She then added, "This has nothing to do with her passing on, it was before." There followed a little more description regarding the blackness, a humming noise in A.V.B.'s head, etc., and then came these words spoken by Feda: "This happened a good time before she passed on, but she says that from that time everything that happened tended towards her passing on. What she's just described seemed like the first definite step towards her passing, yet she says she had an interval of time in between, when it seemed as if that condition had not contributed towards her passing on." (433–34)

The passage indicates how powerfully mechanisms of identification can operate within the technology of mediumship. The unconscious medium, Mrs. Leonard, becomes the vehicle of transmission of her control, Feda, who in turn demonstrates the capability of one human body to experience the sensations of another. Hall, witnessing this exhibition, unconsciously mimics it, producing in herself a vivid experience of what her deceased lover is undergoing. In this reenactment, Hall internally experiences the embodied memory of another.

Earlier, I mentioned that psychical research foregrounds the impediments that exist to unmediated access to the consciousness of another.

These interference effects frustrate the desire to access the past as "sponta-neous, alive and internal experience."[25] At the same time, Spiritualism feeds this desire since the sitter is invited to experience a new memory in a partic-ular way: namely, as an auditory and visual enactment whereby, through a psychic mirroring, the sitter is able to experience in her or his own body what the deceased has experienced. The bodily reenactment of another's trauma is a key demand, conscious or unconscious, of the sitting. Insofar as the sitter approaches this experience, she or he experiences something on the verge of a psychotic episode.[26] One becomes embodied both as an-other and as another who is deceased. In this way, limitations of time, space, mortality, and otherness are surmounted. This experience may be regarded as the payoff both promised by and feared from the séance. None-theless, this fantasy is by no means the only conceivable end point of spirit-ualist practice since the fantasy of experiencing within one's own body the embodied experience of another is momentary. Moreover, the experience of becoming other might be read in various ways, for example, as a religious or near-religious act, in which the mourner takes upon him- or herself the burden of suffering experienced by the deceased and in that way is united with them.

The enactment within her own body of Batten's experience is the psy-chological goal of Hall's study. At this point, it might seem that her essay could end. Were the process to end here, however, "Mrs. Una" would be left outside the circuit of identifications; and the function of these sittings in mediating the relationship between the three women would remain un-accomplished. The need to achieve this objective implicitly shapes the sec-ond half of the essay and helps explain what otherwise might seem to be a massive digression, namely, a discussion, thirty pages in length, of "Billy," a dog that attached itself to Batten in the afterlife. Again within the investi-gative framework, Batten's communications regarding Billy take on great interest insofar as, for Hall, they demonstrate "Knowledge . . . of Matters Entirely Unknown to the Sitters" (487). In her view, material dealing with Billy shows that, at least in this case, Batten's message cannot have been produced telepathically by the sitters themselves.

In the sitting of December 6, 1916, Batten communicates news of this pet to Troubridge and Hall. After a hint directed toward Troubridge, she recognizes the pet to be none other than Billy, a wire-haired terrier that had once been a pet of hers but which had died about eight months before her cousin's death (489). Troubridge had not seen the dog, which her mother boarded in the country, for the last eleven years. At another sitting a week later, Batten assures Troubridge: "He's very well, and will be in a very good condition for you when you come over" (490). (Batten antici- pated that Troubridge would die in the near future.) Batten provides infor- mation about the dog's recent medical condition, of which Troubridge was unaware. Contacting a local veterinarian and others, Hall was later able to confirm the accuracy of these descriptions.

Since Batten had good reason to be disaffected from Troubridge, it is not immediately evident why she would be caring for her pet in the afterlife. This question occurred to Hall, who asked it "on March 9th, 1917, at a sitting taken by me, acting as my own recorder" (504). As usual, the ques- tion is situated within scientific terms as a question about why Batten had decided to use Billy as an evidential "test" (504). Batten responds by reaf- firming her continuing investment in the "link" that exists between the three women even while she professes no awareness of the intimate charac- ter of the linkage. Hall continues questioning:

> M.R.H. How could you have known that Billy was Billy?
> F. She says: "That is difficult to explain. . . . I suppose, in this case, there must have been some sort of link between Billy and Una and you and myself, if only from the point of view of something that would be of interest. I don't know how those things come to one, but they do, and I found myself somehow automatically in touch with Billy. We have a far fuller knowledge of things here than I can ever hope to explain to you through Feda, it's much too big a thing to get through one brain."
> M.R.H. Have you actually got Billy, then?
> F. She says: "Yes, I have, and you may ask why I have. I think because Billy was a link and it was extremely useful to have Billy, in order to get that test through." (505)

Batten's evidence concerning Billy has to do with a number of injuries or ailments that he experienced at various times and particularly in his final years. One traumatic incident occurred shortly before his death. Miss Col- lis, who boarded Billy, confirmed that "a few weeks before the end, he had a bite from another dog on his back, which we were afraid would not heal" (497). Hall and Troubridge also interviewed the veterinary surgeon who had attended Billy. She reported that "far from healing, . . . [the wound] had been in a very bad condition from the first, having rapidly become mortified; and she went on to say that the smell of the wound had been so offensive that it was unpleasant having to dress it, which she had done daily" (502). This mishap was the immediate occasion of Miss Collis's decision to have the dog put down.

The attack on Billy provides Troubridge, by way of proxy, with an accident comparable in seriousness with the one experienced by the other two women. Batten too had experienced open wounds, in this case on her scalp, at the time of the crash. Just as the earlier sittings permit Hall to feel Batten's pain, so to speak, through the mediation of Billy's experience, Batten is able to feel Troubridge's. In this way, Troubridge is united with the other women in suffering. The element of feminine sharing in this pain is underscored by the fact that Billy experiences it as a victim of aggression. Troubridge regarded herself to be the victim of her estranged husband, from whom she believed herself to have contracted venereal disease.[27]

How is one to understand the apparent ability of the dramatis personae of the sittings to enter into one another's consciousness? Psychical researchers suggested that the phenomenon can be understood in terms of processes of identification whereby aspects of subliminal consciousness or the unconscious are projected onto other human beings. The relationship between the control and the medium vividly enacts this possibility, which the sitter first psychically mirrors, then reads back as evidence of the presence of a deceased other. Hall and Troubridge, however, had another means of understanding psychic interfusion through contemporary theosophical beliefs. Indeed, the belief in a selfhood shared between these three women that I explore in the remaining pages of this chapter makes better sense in theosophical than in spiritualist terms. The key point of spiritualist conviction is belief in the survival of individual personality after death. Theosophists, however, are much more interested in the possibility that the self may inhabit different personalities living in different times and places.

In theosophical myth, individuals consist in part of a soul, which exists outside time and space, and a number of finite personalities. The latter are regarded to be incarnations of the soul at different times and places. This teaching provides a way of imagining the self as not constrained within the limits of the individual ego. Theosophy offered an alternative way of thinking about the self. Troubridge exploited this aspect of theosophical teaching in her own view of the sittings. To her, they indicated that the personalities of the three women were interfused. Hall writes: "UVT has recently evolved a theory that several people might form part of the same ego, which would account for the occasionally strong ties that sometimes seem inexplicable" (July 6, 1918; Ormrod, 100–101). Hall's later practice of dedicating her novels "To Our Three Selves" indicates that she came to accept this belief.

In Theosophy, the personalities of the self may vary in sex and gender. Theosophists thought of male-female gender polarity in terms of an infinite series of gradations.[28] They also thought of gender as a male-female dynamic that existed as an aspect of the soul itself. In this view, gender was a bipolar psychical principle structuring all existence. Theosophists, then, have a double view of gender. On the one hand, it is material, a sign of the locking of the self into a particular body with the constraints that bodies carry in different times and places. On the other hand, gender is psychic, an aspect of the soul and of life itself. There is a strong Manichean tendency within both Theosophy and Spiritualism. Spiritualists tend to talk about the self as imprisoned in a corruptible body before being released from "the earth plane" by death. But there likewise exists a countertendency to view material existence as necessary to the development of the faculties of the soul. Lodge, who endorsed the objective character of Hall's investigations, writes:

> It may be claimed as legitimate to assume that the association between life and matter here on the planet has a real and vital significance, that without such an episode of earth life we should be less than we are, and that the relation is typical of something real and permanent. . . .
>
> *Why* matter should be thus useful to spirit and even to life it is not easy to say. It may be that by the interaction of two things better and newer results can always be obtained than was possible for one alone. . . . Do we not find, [for example,] that genius seems to require the obstruction or the aid of matter for its full development? (320)

This double view is consonant with a number of views in other modes of early twentieth-century speculative psychology: for example, with the concept of sexual inversion in sexology, in terms of which a male homosexual is defined as a person with "a female soul in a male body."[29] This view is question-begging insofar as the sexologists who put it forward usually were materialists. Whence then appeared the idea of the "soul"? With its metaphysical belief in an undying soul structured by both male and female principles, Theosophy offered other, potentially attractive ways of understanding what sexologists called sexual inversion. The double view within

Theosophy of the interaction of spiritual and material realities in the development of selfhood also has something in common with Freud's concept of the bodily ego. Freud argues that the ego is an embodied, which means also an engendered, entity: "The ego is first and foremost a bodily ego; it is not merely a surface entity, but is itself the projection of a surface. . . . A person's own body, and above all its surface, is a place from which both external and internal perceptions may spring."[30] Hall was a woman whose bodily ego was defined in terms of her perception that she existed across lines of gender. Theosophy's view of gender as doubly male and female, psychic and material, provided Hall with a way of understanding her embodied self as continually activated in relation to gender difference. Finally, since the concept of crossing gender is crucial to foundational formulations of queer theory in the work of Eve Kosofsky Sedgwick and Judith Butler, Hall's theosophical understanding of herself also makes her queer.[31] This characterization is accurate insofar as one can understand Hall by rereading her through the categories of later theoretical understanding. But I also mean that Hall reads herself as queer in terms of late Victorian and Edwardian understandings of the word. For example, when Vernon Lee, to whom Hall likely had been introduced, speaks of "the queer comradeship of outlawed thought," she is referring to a shared sense of sexual and cultural dissidence that Hall experienced as bred in the bone.[32]

Given the foregoing, one anticipates that Hall's essay will give evidence to a sense of the play of gender within the individual. Sally Cline, however, reads this period of Hall's life as one of lesbian acculturation and affirmation (59–90). And, as I suggested earlier, the essay has a strongly, at the time scandalously, feminine air. Masculinity appears only twice, once in the figure of Billy, "a rover by nature" (489) who enjoyed solitary forays into the city. The affectionate portrait of Billy and the strong sense of the dog as a personality in his own right is presumably collaborative since Hall did not know the dog directly. As a metaphor of Troubridge herself, moreover, Billy suggests that rather than being simply the "femme" as described by Cline (67), Troubridge too regarded herself as, in part, a masculine woman, albeit not as masculine as Hall. In the memoir, Troubridge refers to herself as an invert, in Vernon Lee's phrase, as one of those "women" who "seem to be born to have been men, or at least not to have been women."[33] In dreams, a particular figure may refer to more than one object or person. The same holds true for "Billy," whose roving nature belongs to Hall. The most obvious "link" between, in Batten's words, "you and myself" and

"Billy and Una" is Billy/Hall himself. Troubridge was strongly attracted to Hall's masculine good looks and "engaging and rather raffish smile." "It was," she writes, "not the countenance of a young woman but of a very handsome young man" (46).

There is one male figure whose brief appearance troubles the essay. Hall strongly identified with British men wounded or killed in service during World War I. At her first sitting with Leonard, one of these men immediately made himself known. Given the times, it was customary for séances to begin this way: "I addressed no conversation to Mrs. Leonard prior to my sitting, beyond thanking her for the appointment, and she went quietly into trance. Her control, Feda, began by describing a young soldier; I did not recognise him, and said so, asking if there were no other communicators wishing to speak. It seemed there were, for I very soon got the description of a great friend of mine who had died some months previously" (340).

If the figure of the young man is a projection of an aspect of Hall herself, then her failure to recognize him may be significant, and the sittings may begin with an act of self-estrangement or betrayal. It is possible that the drama of reunification between the three women that is accomplished in the course of the sittings occurs at the expense of the suppression of a key aspect of Hall herself, Billy notwithstanding.

When Hall died during World War II, after a long, debilitating illness, Troubridge found her body transformed:

"At one moment it was my beloved . . . wasted, drawn, lividly pale and at times distorted—the next, a stranger lay there on the bed. Very handsome, very peaceful, very calm, but with scarcely a traceable resemblance to my John." So strong was this sense of strangeness that when she had been laid out, Una and the nurse "stood looking down at her and I said: 'Poor boy; he must have suffered a lot before he died. . . .' It seemed a young airman or soldier who perhaps had died of wounds after much suffering. . . . Not a trace of femininity; no one in their senses could have suspected that anything but a young man had died." (Ormrod, 281)

These lines suggest a Manichean perspective on Troubridge's part, with female corporeality identified with the mortal body, while male embodiment, even in the body with stigmata, is associated with physical integrity, beauty, and, in the suggestion of flight, transcendence. At the beginning of her psychical research, Hall had to turn away the "young soldier" (Hall, 340) with whom she so strongly identified herself and desired connection. This figure had to be set aside if Hall was to be able to overcome both self-division and the differences that existed between herself, Batten, and Troubridge. The price of multiple feminine identifications, however, was the suppression of Hall's sense of embodiment as a masculine woman. And that price was one that she would be unable to sustain.

3

Symbiosis of Publicity and Privacy

The Slander Trial of 1920

Hall's insistence on making the private public brought her into court in 1920. While biographers have mentioned the action for sexual slander that she brought at this time, none have recognized its importance.[1] The case established the preconditions both for her emergence as a successful novelist and for her decision to write the first novel in English to take female sexual inversion as its focal point. As in the case of the 1928 trial, which resulted in the suppression of *The Well of Loneliness*, the earlier trial was a contest over the permissible limits of the representation of desire between women. In 1920, however, Hall won her case. The victory was a confidence builder that brought her renewed attention from Batten's Sapphic friends while at the same time ensuring a much wider notoriety.[2]

In January 1919, Hall purchased a home at Datchet outside London for herself and Troubridge. In December, Troubridge had informed her husband that she was leaving him. Promoted to the rank of full admiral with seniority, he returned home to London at the beginning of February. On February 3, he paid his wife an unannounced visit in a final but unsuccessful bid to save his marriage and avoid the scandal of a divorce. Instead, while avoiding a court action, he was forced to settle for a legal separation with a financial settlement on his wife and child's behalf. The separation was finalized on February 10. Shortly after the publication of the results of Hall's psychical research in December 1919, St. George Lane Fox-Pitt, a longtime member of the Society, showed the article to the admiral at the Travellers' Club. The admiral, who had formerly tolerated his wife's involvement in psychical research with a degree of amusement, was incensed. He complained to Fox-Pitt that his wife's absorption in this activity had permitted Hall to exercise an immoral "influence," which resulted in the break-up of his marriage.[3]

The setting of Fox-Pitt's exchange with Troubridge, inside a private members' club, calls to mind the situation that Wilde had faced twenty-five years earlier, when the Marquess of Queensberry left an insulting card at Wilde's club. The incident pressured him into filing a suit for libel against Queensberry that, in an unhappy sequence of events, resulted in Wilde's arrest and successful prosecution on grounds of gross obscenity. The clubs, limited to male members, functioned as both supplements and alternatives to domestic life. Markers of social status and respectability and institutions at once private and public, they offered privileged sites for the circulation of gossip, which in turn functioned so as to police the limits of acceptable social behavior. Troubridge was now ready to use his club contacts to curb Hall's extroverted sexual interest in other women. As a result of the conversation, Fox-Pitt decided to block Hall from being coopted for membership of the Council of the Society. To this end, he approached two women who played important roles in the Society: Isobel Newton, the secretary, and Mrs. Helen Salter, editor of the *Proceedings of the Society*. Both women, who later appeared as witnesses at the trial, responded by making use of the offices of the Society to protect both it and its unorthodox female members from scandal. Their success in doing so indicates how late nineteenth-century changes in the status of middle-class women had made it possible for well-positioned women to use the levers of institutional power to protect other women from the effects of male cabals.

Both during discussions with members of the Society at this time and later at trial, Fox-Pitt claimed that the charge of immorality that he made against Hall referred not to her private conduct but to the results of her psychical research. Subsequent commentators, assuming this defense to be specious, have argued that Fox-Pitt was attempting to shield the admiral's name from scandal; but Fox-Pitt did find both the article and the lectures that it was based upon to be immoral. First of all, he had long been opposed to the direction in which the research of Society members, such as Sir Oliver Lodge, was moving. Fox-Pitt held that psychical research was the objective study of paranormal phenomena. It was not directed toward drawing inferences—as Lodge did in *Raymond*—about such topics as whether or not individual personality survived death, much less the self-consciously modern system of religious beliefs that Lodge built up around this topic in the book. From Fox-Pitt's point of view, the case of Hall demonstrated the delusive and demoralizing effects that followed from spiritualist excesses. At the trial, he would portray Una Troubridge as a hysteric.[4]

The *Times* covered the trial on the same inside page on which it daily recorded the peccadilloes of the rich and famous. The article "Psychical Research: Spirits of the Dead" and other notices dealing with such items as divorce cases and jewelry thefts functioned in the first instance as forms of entertainment in a democratic, leveling age. But gossip and domestic scandal also served as touch points in setting off moral panics and prompting calls to order by elite males. Emphasizing Hall's social status, the article identified her as "a member of the council of the Society for Psychical Research," an upper-middle-class group with strong ties to men's and women's colleges at Cambridge University (4).[5] Her counsel introduced her as "a woman of independent means" and opened his remarks by detailing her relations with the admiral and his wife. In the course of these, he mentioned that a year earlier the admiral had "suggested" that "for the future, Lady Troubridge should make her home with the plaintiff, whose means were much larger than those of the Admiral" (4).

Hall doubtless enjoyed the put-down. But much though the case was another example of an upper-middle-class domestic dispute and much though Hall disliked having herself and her lovers characterized by Fox-Pitt as "immoral," she resented as much or more the onslaught against her intellectual credibility. Expressed in terms of gender, the attempt by Fox-Pitt to demonstrate the silliness and credulity of Hall's account of spirit life had larger implications for the disallowing of female speech on serious matters—especially at a time when women had for the first time won the right to cast ballots in parliamentary elections. It was extremely important to Hall to affirm that she was qualified to speak in public on paranormal phenomena. Cross-examined by Fox-Pitt, who chose to defend himself in the suit, she stated that she spoke not *in propria persona* but as a "scientific investigator" in the field of "psychology" ("Psychical Research," 4). This claim was consonant with Lodge's description of psychical research as "a genuine [if new] branch of psychological science."[6] Fox-Pitt was having none of it. He retorted, "This paper of yours is scientific rubbish, quite unworthy of the society, and its publication is extremely harmful. It has produced a condition of mind which I consider immoral" ("Psychical Research" 4).

In addition to its focus on Hall, the trial had wider implications. For one thing, it figured in an ongoing conflict among different factions within upper-middle-class and upper-class English society. This struggle resulted in a number of courtroom battles fought out before and during World War I, and it is the significance of the Hall trial in this sequence that is the object of my inquiry. The first of the cases in question was a libel suit brought against Arthur Ransome by Lord Alfred Douglas after the publication of Ransome's biography of Oscar Wilde in 1912. A critical and commercial success, the biography did much to rehabilitate Wilde's reputation at the expense of Douglas, his lover at the time of the trials, who was portrayed as the cause of Wilde's downfall.[7] With the assistance of Robbie Ross, Wilde's friend, former lover, and legal executor, Ransome's defense produced previously unpublished sections of Wilde's *De Profundis* that made clear the intimate character of his connection with Douglas. As a result of the revelations, Douglas lost the suit, his wife, and legal custody of his son.[8] In effect, he had sacrificed his efforts to normalize his life to his greater need to attempt to relieve himself of responsibility for Wilde's debacle.

The case makes clear the symbiotic relationship between publicity and privacy in emergent mass-media culture. In the courtroom and in the press, the realm and meanings of privacy were defined through the struggle over the publication of sensitive material. The case was also significant insofar as Ransome's biography helped resuscitate Wilde's legacy. In the positive reception of the book and in Ransome's success at trial, aestheticist culture, including its feminist and male homosexual implications, began to find a respectable place within the more orthodox and northern strain of Liberalism that grew out of Philosophical Radicalism and Protestant Nonconformity. A leading figure in this rapprochement was Margot Asquith, wife of Liberal Prime Minister Henry Asquith, Earl of Oxford.

Turning against both Wilde and Ross following the first trial, Douglas determined to destroy both men, in part by publishing his own memoirs, *Oscar Wilde and Myself* (1914), and in part by accusing Ross, in a letter sent to top government officials, of gross indecency. The address of the letter to leading politicians indicates how aware Douglas was of the cultural-political implications of the rehabilitation of Wilde. By forcing Ross to sue him, Douglas hoped to undo the conciliation of utilitarian progressivism with aestheticist culture that I describe above. In response to his attack, Ross felt obliged to sue Douglas for libel. Before the action went to trial, Ross was able to demonstrate that Douglas had been involved in a conspiracy to trump up charges of pedophilia against him. Unfortunately, however, Ross chose not to withdraw the suit at this point, and in the trial that followed in November 1914, Douglas was able to produce witnesses to testify to Ross's involvement in male homosexual circles. As a result, he was forced to drop the action and resign his posts as Valuer of Pictures and Drawings for the Inland Revenue as well as the London directorship of the Johannes-burg Art Gallery.[9]

The third suit was brought by the modern dancer Maud Allan, under the aggravated circumstances of right-wing moral panic in the final months of World War I. Allan lost, and her reputation also suffered. Again, the legacy of Wilde was implicated since the action arose out of an attempt to mount a private production of his play *Salomé*, which had been banned from public performance in England since 1892. The Allan trial opened on May 29, 1918, at a time when war weariness and hysteria were at their high point. Hall, in preparing her case, chose to hire Ellis Hume-Williams, the same lawyer who had represented Allan (Medd, 89).

Although the trials focused on particular people, individual rights and cultural innovation were at stake. The defendants in the trials were strongly opposed to the experimental approach to living one's life that Wilde had advocated with wit, elegance, and seductive charm in the 1890s. In the years immediately before World War I, an alliance between Bohemians and leading members of society had resulted in a cultural moment in which both Wilde and his stance were revalidated. Briefly, it looked as though the climate of reaction following the trials of 1895 might be dispersed. The advent of World War I, however, provided an opportunity for men on the far right, such as Douglas, to attack successfully such people as Ross and Allan. Wilde was once again turned into a symbol of all that was corrupt in modern life. By early 1918, with the war in stalemate, casualties high, and the Germans about to begin a major offensive on the Western Front, right-wing ideologues were able to inflame an atmosphere of moral panic that led political moderates to fear the outbreak of a popular insurrection fol-lowing the verdict in the Allan trial (Hoare, 185). In this series of trials, Hall's suit was the first to break the pattern of right-wing success. And although Douglas and his allies were not finally defeated until he himself was successfully sued by Winston Churchill and briefly imprisoned in 1923, Hall's success in 1920 marked a turning point.

The tactic pursued by Douglas and his associates was to maneuver their targets into suing them for libel. The resulting trials, widely covered in the press, were used by the defendants as occasions for arguing that moral corruption on the home front served the purposes of the German enemy. Sexual and cultural dissidence were linked as disguised forms of treason and subversion. Hall's 1920 action began in a similar way. Fox-Pitt, Douglas's former brother-in-law, laid accusations with the Society that Hall was "a grossly immoral woman."[10] Hall had little recourse except to challenge these allegations or to resign from the Society. Earlier, when she had reported on the results of her psychical research to the members of the Society in two public lectures delivered early in 1918, Fox-Pitt had taken alarm. When late in 1919 he learned she had been nominated for membership to the Council of the Society, he intervened to protest the nomination on grounds of her bad character. He also slandered Batten, Hall's deceased, former lover, as "a most objectionable person." And, for good measure, he complained that Hall, who exercised "a great influence" on Una Troubridge, had contributed to her mental instability and destroyed her marriage.[11] After attempting unsuccessfully through her lawyer to persuade Fox-Pitt to retract the allegation, Hall felt compelled to sue. In a trial held on November 18 and 19, 1920, the jury reached a verdict in Hall's favor, awarding her £500 in damages.[12]

Fox-Pitt's charges were, of course, personal, and they referred to private behavior. But their significance is public. Fox-Pitt claimed that Hall's approach to psychical research had in effect demoralized the Society and lowered standards of public decency. In the case, what is personal is in effect also public. For Fox-Pitt the transfer is automatic, and, despite the efforts of the trial judge to maintain a separation between individual character, scientific investigation, and the public presentation of self, psychical research as practiced by Lodge and Hall merged all three. The practice of Spiritualism had already been made public as a part of the wartime mobilization of the civilian population, in particular of women and especially the mothers of participants. Not surprisingly, the representation of women in this mobilization was conservative. Women were characterized in private, domestic terms, as "mother and house prop," as one medium put it (Lodge, 130). These were the loving women on whose behalf young men sacrificed their lives. In this highly charged context, Hall's appropriation of Spiritualism to affirm loving friendship between women was a startling affront both to the scientific pretensions of psychical research and to the politics of mass mobilization.

Hall's turn to psychical research took place under the influence of Lodge, a respected physicist and former president of the Society, who was also a pioneer of wireless telegraphy.[13] The association of his metaphysical speculations with advances in technology lent psychical research an aura of contemporary innovation. In *Raymond*, Lodge detailed the experience of his family in attempting to communicate with his son Raymond, who had been killed in action in France in September 1915.[14] Lodge sets the tone of the book in the dedication of the volume, in which he thanks Raymond's "Mother and Family . . . for Permission to Use Private Material for Public Ends" (v). The sudden and unanticipated loss of thousands of young men of the middle and upper classes in the opening year of the war had proven extremely disruptive on the home front. Spiritualism offered an opportunity for widows and bereaved mothers to find solace; at the same time, it offered them a way to contribute to the war effort by lending support to others who mourned, both in and outside the family. Speaking of the private information disclosed in the book, Lodge says, "I should not have [published this information] . . . were it not that the amount of premature and unnatural bereavement at the present time is so appalling that the pain caused by exposing one's own sorrow and its alleviation, to possible scoffers, becomes almost negligible in view of the service which it is legitimate to hope may thus be rendered to mourners, if they can derive comfort by learning that communication across the gulf is possible" (vii–viii). Making the patriotism of the effort clear, he says, "I have endeavoured to state the evidence fully and frankly for the persistent existence of one of the multitude of youths who have sacrificed their lives at the call of their Country when endangered by an aggressor of calculated ruthlessness" (85).

Lodge's reports of sittings communicate something of the scale of loss. At times, Feda, the medium Mrs. Leonard's control, says that she can see hundreds of spirits. And after contact is made with Raymond, he speaks of his role in offering solace to the newly deceased. Feda reports, "He seems to know what the work is. The first work he will have to do, will be helping at the Front; not the wounded so much, but helping those who are passing over in the war. He knows that when they pass on and wake up, they still feel a certain fear. . . . Some even go on fighting; at least they want to; they don't believe they have passed on. So that many are wanted where he is now, to explain to them and help them, and soothe them. They do not know where they are, nor why they are there" (126–27). Appeals are also directed to civilians. Participating in séances is part of their contribution to the war effort. If they do not do so, they will be letting down those who have died on their behalf. A deceased adolescent, for example, after speaking to Raymond, reports to his mother: "If you people only knew how we long to come, they would all call us" (120).

Lodge specifies three aspects of *Raymond*. First is the personal imperative, "the demand of affection" which requires that one make every effort to assure oneself both of the continued existence of a lost beloved and of their continuing well-being. Second is the component of "scientific interest" (83). Most of Part II of the book is given over to showing how the sittings produce evidence that Raymond continues to exist. He and other communicators are reported to be eager, even desperate, to prove the point.[15] The third component is "missionary zeal" (83). Psychical research offers an opportunity to prove that personality persists after death and that it is possible to communicate across the boundary that separates "the earth plane" from "the astral plane." Interlocutors from beyond the grave emphasize the immense value of the work that Lodge is doing, and Feda is reassuring: "Raymond really is happy now. He doesn't say this to make you feel satisfied. He is really happy now. He says this [i.e., psychical research] is most interesting, and is going to be fifty times more interesting than on the earth plane. There is such a big field to work in. Father and he are going to do such a lot together. He says, 'I am going to help for all I am worth'" (159–60).

Hall's preoccupation with psychical research after Batten's death had a place in efforts by members of the Society to promote Spiritualism as a means of bolstering civilian morale. Before Batten's death, Hall resented the fact that her partner's precarious state of health prevented her from volunteering for medical service on the Continent. Afterward, however, attempts to communicate with Batten became a way of fulfilling a civic duty.[16] Hall and Troubridge also helped Lodge reply to the many letters that he received from mourning survivors after the publication of *Raymond*.

Expression of extreme, barely suppressed feeling was part of the generic structure of the sittings. In *Raymond*, for example, the evidential portion of the volume reaches a climax when a medium in trance grasps the hand of

Raymond's brother, Alec, and speaks to him in the voice of Raymond (167). At such moments, the scientific aspect of psychical research is suspended. Sitters are unable to continue taking notes, and commentators draw the veil over what is described as privileged private communication. It is important to remember that these sublime private moments are fashioned by means of the genres of the research essay, lecture, and book. Public discourse in effect constructs private. After these intervals, moreover, bourgeois decorum is restored. And again it is femininity that is the carrier of order and restraint. At the end of the session with Alec, for instance, Lodge describes his wife, who was also present at the sitting: "Lady Lodge impressed me considerably with the genuine and deeply affecting character of the above episode of personal control. It was evidently difficult to get over for the rest of the day. I doubt if the bare record conveys much though it may to people of like experience" (170).

When Lodge speaks of the "missionary zeal" that animates Raymond, he has in mind Part III of the volume, which explicates the ideology and religious mythology of Spiritualism. Although Hall and Troubridge came to disagree with Lodge on both scores (Baker, 117), the tripartite structure of psychical research in *Raymond* informs their published paper. Hall and Troubridge's innovation is to direct this structure to a new end: namely, that of affirming emotional and, implicitly, sexual ties between women. This turn to the private, the domestic, the affectional, and the sexual, in a world of exclusively female relations, in effect perverts the special functions that Spiritualism had assumed during the war. In this respect, when Fox-Pitt claimed both before and during the trial that Hall's research was "immoral," he was correct. It is important to recognize how bold Hall and Troubridge's redirection of psychical research was. For both women, involvement in the work of the Society provided ways of making public their newly established partnership with the moral support of Society members and with its prestige behind them. The public delivery and subsequent appearance in print of the results of their research lent them a measure at once of celebrity and intellectual seriousness. From his perspective, Fox-Pitt perceived quite accurately the heretical, even blasphemous uses to which they put spiritualist ideology.

To this point, I have emphasized the woman-centered character of Hall's research. Hall's public presentation of self during the trial, however, puts this focus in a new light. When called to testify, she appeared "soberly dressed in a long dark jacket and skirt with a pale stock and high stiff collar" (Baker, 128). This presumably is how Hall thought a serious psychical researcher should look.[17] But the masculine objectivity thereby connoted is doubled by masculine suggestion of another sort. Hall's garb places her study of female love and friendship in the context of the interest of a person who resists conventional categorization as a woman. This particular woman's commitment to love between women issues from a gender-crossing stance. The stance may in turn connote the more active sexual interest that was usually associated at the time with men. The implicit gender transgression of Hall's costume connotes scientific detachment in one register and sexual nonconformity in another.

Hall's masculine style and the flirtatious attention that she showed to other women at Society meetings are sometimes regarded as eccentricities deemed permissible to a wealthy, upper-middle-class woman in her day. Hall's "lordly" or "mannish" manners can also be seen as drawing upon a long tradition of aristocratic, libertine behavior. In both cases, her performance of sexual dissidence is inconceivable without the simultaneous assertion of class privilege. This assertion, however, rested, as she well knew, on a shaky foundation since Hall, like some of the other American interlopers in England, had money but not class. Equally important, she lacked family connections in England that could shield her against allegations of license and immorality. This singularity contributes to the social isolation with which she characterizes the crossgendered heroines of her fiction. Her growing absorption in both psychical research and Troubridge accented this isolation, cutting her off from her American relatives, from Batten's family, and from some members of the feminist and Sapphic artistic and social circles to which Batten had introduced her.

Rather than being seen as a privilege bestowed by class then, Hall's gender-crossing ways are better understood as the expression of a self-consciously modern, female dandyism. Hall is a creative refashioner of the dandyism that Vernon Lee in *Miss Brown* (1884) associates with the Aesthetic movement and that Wilde epitomized in English commercial, artistic, and social life of the 1880s and 1890s. And, as in Wilde and in the writing of Charles Baudelaire, Hall's dandyism is best seen as an aspect of the emergence of democratic culture, a culture that also gave unprecedented importance to celebrity and the politics of scandal. As Jodie Medd has suggested in another context, Hall's self-invention helps define literary and cultural Modernism. This effect is as definitive in the 1920s as the affirmation of sexual and emotional ties between men was in the late Victorian period among a disparate group, including such men as Wilde, Walt Whitman, John Addington Symonds, Edward Carpenter, and young "Bosie" Douglas. Wildean dandyism was likewise reinvented in the style and craft of Noël Coward and Ivor Novello in the 1920s, but the specifically female appropriation is more central.[18]

Hall and Troubridge invested a great deal of time, energy, and money in psychical research from the autumn of 1916 onward. While Batten's death had threatened to bring their affair to an end, their investigative efforts put their relationship on a new footing. When they visited Lodge's family as house guests in 1917, they did so "openly as a 'couple' renewed by love" (Cline, 134). By January 1918, Troubridge was able to record: "J.s.I've m.L and I've m.y" [John said I have married Ladye and I have married you] (Cline, 137). This gain was, however, accompanied by a sharp narrowing of Hall's circle of intimates. Hall initially attended sittings with Dorothy Clarke, her cousin and former lover, whose husband had recently been killed in action. Troubridge soon displaced her. And after Hall's lectures, Cara Harris, Batten's daughter, protested to the Society that Hall had excluded her from the sessions (Baker, 106). Both exclusions were necessary if the psychic union of Batten, Hall, and Troubridge was to be achieved.

Hall and Troubridge needed a setting in which to play out their new status. As the visit with the Lodges suggests, the Society provided them with a new circle of respected friends and acquaintances in which to do so. As I have mentioned, Lodge's work and that of other Society members has its conservative aspects, but the Society also offered a positive environment for such nonconformists as Hall and Troubridge. One of their friends and collaborators in the Society, for example, was Mrs. Eleanor Sidgwick, widow of Henry Sidgwick and second president of Newnham College. Sidgwick's husband, a lifelong friend of Symonds and a cofounder of the Society, was a celibate whose strongest erotic attachments were to the male friends of his youth. Symonds was his most important friend.[19] Faced with the crisis of conscience experienced by Symonds in face of his same-sex desires, Sidgwick developed a theory of ethical reserve, which validated an experimental approach to personal morality on the part of a small vanguard of individuals. This position validated sexual nonconformity on the grounds that lives such as Symonds's would provide new knowledge that could be put to general use.[20] The position provided a philosophical, scientific rationale for sexually dissident behavior.

Hall and her partner responded to the new setting in a spirit of mischievous provocation. Years later, a former member recalled, "Radclyffe Hall was extremely aggressive in manner, and always had an eye for the ladies!" On another occasion, Troubridge startled the chairman by recounting a dream of hers, beginning, "Last night I had a most strange dream so I turned to John and said, 'Darling, I've just had such a dream.'"[21] Sidgwick's theory provided a philosophical basis for leading a double life, and his theory of "esoteric morality" (Schultz, 26) helped create the climate of opinion that Hall found within the Society. For their part, however, Hall and Troubridge were neither secretive nor discreet. In the preceding chapter, I argued that they were drawn to psychical research by converging personal agendas. Through it, Hall was able to reconcile herself with the deceased partner whom she had betrayed. Troubridge for her part was able to reestablish her connection with Hall on a new basis, to put her marriage behind her, and to enter a partnership that would continue until Hall's death in 1943. But how did the two women understand love between women? What was the basis on which Hall and Troubridge affirmed that love in their essay? And what was at stake in their defense of it?

In the first place, Hall was unwilling to relinquish to Fox-Pitt the right to characterize her relations with other women. Characterizing Hall and Batten as immoral, implicitly he identified them as lesbian, in the senses that were attached to that word during the war. Expanded employment opportunities for women, new political rights, and a soaring divorce rate provoked strong male anxieties about women at this time. In the Allan sensation, these anxieties attached both to the primary sexual characteristics of the female body and to the possibilities of desire between women. Because of the difficulty that men experienced in describing sexual practices between women and because of the public silence that usually surrounded this topic, female-female desire tended to be peculiarly nameless.[22] This fact made it especially useful as a phantasm to which could be attached public fear, rage, and ignorance about the state of the Allied war effort in the difficult early months of 1918.[23]

In 1921, members of Parliament attempted to criminalize sexual intimacies between women for the first time. One member named, curiously enough, Sir Ernest Wild, introduced a clause to extend the amendment to the Criminal Law Amendment Act under which Wilde had been tried and found guilty so as to include "gross indecency" between women.[24] Passed in the House of Commons, the bill failed in the House of Lords. Fox-Pitt's allegations against Hall followed the pattern already set in the Allan trial. In both cases, women were chastised for subverting institutions to immoral ends—in one instance, the theater club, and in the other, the Society for Psychical Research. These are institutions of a particular sort. Theater clubs and the Society were institutions composed of private members some of whose events were open to the public. These points of crossover permitted the circulation of material to which the public might otherwise be denied access on the legal ground that it was obscene. Both Fox-Pitt and Noel Pemberton Billing, in the Allan trial, condemn these settings as sites of lesbian contagion.[25]

Fox-Pitt described Hall as a "vulgar climber" and Batten as "a woman who was a most objectionable person."[26] These epithets suggest a specific context for anti-lesbian moral panic in English class politics. Earlier, I observed that the trial attempts to police the limits of the representation of desire between women. Fox-Pitt and others like him were, however, equally concerned about policing entry to the worlds of the arts, Society, and national politics. The targets of men like Douglas, Fox-Pitt, and Billing were also, not coincidentally, un-English. For example, although the son of a leading professional, Wilde was born and raised in Ireland and took his first undergraduate degree there. Allan was born in Canada and lived in the United States. Her brother was convicted of murder in the double homicide of two young women.[27] Hall's mother was an American widow, considered "vulgar" by her English in-laws at the time when she married Hall's father (Baker, 10). In the parlance of Wilde's drawing-room comic melodramas, to them she was an adventuress. For her part, Hall lacked school ties in England and was excluded from her father's family after her parents' early divorce. As a young woman, Hall hunted, ate at fashionable restaurants, and visited European spas; but she remained socially ungrounded, a position offset only in part by her reputation as a writer of poetry and songs.[28]

Mabel Batten offended in a different way. The daughter of a high-ranking Anglo-Indian official and a leading figure within London's musical salon culture, Batten signaled the survival into Edwardian society of the alliance of aesthetic with aristocratic culture. Batten enjoyed cordial relations with her much older husband, who had served as private secretary to the British viceroy of India, Robert, Earl of Lytton. She also engaged in affairs with Edward Prince of Wales, with other men, and with women as well. Her reputation as a woman of "quite depraved" (Cline, 62) sexual tastes together with her access to artistic circles, to society, and to the Court identified Batten both with what some saw as the moral turpitude of the 1890s and with the easygoing mores of Edward's circle. Since the late 1880s, moral conservatives, both on the left and the right, had attempted to curb the flamboyance of members of this group and to enforce upon them at least the appearance of moral and social conformity.[29]

This struggle was also political. The resuscitation of Wilde's name was associated with Asquith's Liberal premiership and with his wife, Margot, both of whom were sponsors of Ross. During the war, Margot, who was also a friend and benefactor of Allan, was accused of having sexual and emotional ties with other women.[30] Billing's right-wing newspaper, the *Vigilante*, for example, published Douglas's satirical attack:

> Out there in Flanders all the trampled ground
> Is red with English blood, our children pass
> Through fire to Moloch. Who will count the loss
> Since here "at home" sits merry Margot, bound
> With lesbian fillets, while in front of her brass
> "Old Squiffy" hands the purse to Robert Ross?[31]

Members of the circle who attacked Asquith were also anti-Semites. And, once the war began, he suffered from the liability of having as close friends a number of wealthy German Jews.[32] For Fox-Pitt, the point of bringing up the fact that Batten was a "most objectionable person" was to link the "incipient dementia" of Hall's essay to a social world very much on the defensive. Batten's alleged behavior characterized that world as both cause and effect of contemporary degeneracy—or "lunacy," as Fox-Pitt put it.[33]

Anti-lesbian homophobia peaked in the Maud Allan controversy of 1918. At the same time at which Hall was lecturing to members of the Society and the general public, Billing, an Independent member of Parliament with connections to the proto-fascist, new National Party, published an attack on a production of *Salomé* scheduled for presentation by Allan and others at a private theater club. Admiral Troubridge had links to the National Party, as did his sister, Laura Hope. His son by his first marriage, moreover, served as Billing's political agent. Billing was well informed about Hall and Troubridge's relationship.[34]

The Allan scandal began with the following item, placed by Billing in the *Vigilante* on February 16:

THE CULT OF THE CLITORIS

To be a member of Maud Allan's private performance in Oscar Wilde's *Salome* one has to apply to a Miss Valetta, of 9, Duke Street, Adelphi, WC. If Scotland Yard were to seize the list of these members I have no doubt they would secure the names of several of the first 47,000. (Hoare, 91)

"The first 47,000" was Billing's code for a list of names of compromised English subjects in the possession of German intelligence. As Billing's newspaper had reported in January 1918, in its earlier incarnation as the *Imperialist*,

> There exists in the Cabinet Noir of a certain German Prince a book compiled by the Secret Service from reports of German agents who have infested this country for the past 20 years. . . . In the beginning of the book is a precis [*sic*] of general instructions regarding the propagation of evils which all decent men thought had perished in Sodom and Lesbia. . . . There are the names of 47,000 English men and women . . ., [*sic*] Privy Councillors, wives of Cabinet Ministers, even Cabinet ministers themselves, diplomats, poets, bankers, editors, newspaper proprietors, and members of His Majesty's Household . . . [*sic*] prevented from putting their full strength into the war by corruption and blackmail and fear of exposure. (Hoare, 1)

Billing's sensational allegations about the subversion of national security were based in a fantasy of sexual contagion emanating from the primary sexual characteristics of the female body ("the Clitoris"). Fantasies about the oversexed female body were provoked by the rapid increase in marital breakdown during and after the war. Between 1913 and 1921, the divorce rate increased sixfold (Medd, 97). While unleashed female desire might move in any of a number of directions, Dr. Serell Cooke and other witnesses labeled it as lesbian. This desire, imputed to Allan, was understood to subsume the entire range of sexual perversions that witnesses found in Wilde's play, including "incestuous lust" (Hoare, 116), sadism, male homosexual desire, and necrophilia. In testimony on behalf of the defense during the trial, one witness identified the clitoris as "a superficial organ that, when unduly excited or over-developed, possessed the most dreadful influence on any woman, that she would do the most extraordinary things if she was over-developed in a superficial sense" (Hoare, 126). Dr. Cooke explained that the presentation of Wilde's play could set off an orgiastic scene: a "person of perverted instincts . . . would take extreme delight in the whole play. . . . It would appeal to them immensely, they would probably have sexual excitation, and even orgasm, watching the play" (Hoare, 146–47).

Lesbian desire as the trope of individual and social monstrosity posed a difficulty for Hall. The term's traditional Sapphic connections were overwhelmed by its association with individual and group degeneration (Hoare, 142). Under the circumstances, Hall needed to look elsewhere for language to refer to sexual and emotional ties between women. Earlier, in her published poetry, she had written ardent, sun-kissed Sapphic lyrics. Suitable vehicles for passionate expression, they did not invoke long-term commitments between two women. Another alternative was the rhetoric of female devotion familiar within female social purity, a language that regularly blurred the line between shared affection among anti-sex women who nonetheless were married and bore children and that which existed between single women firmly committed to emotional and at times sexual ties with other women.[35] More generally, the rhetoric of female friendship might refer either in conformist directions, as Sharon Marcus argues in *Between Women*, or might figure, as Martha Vicinus demonstrates, in emotional and sexual relationships that drew freely upon the language and passions of evangelical Christianity.[36] A fourth alternative existed among Roman Catholics who accepted the sexological argument that homosexual desire, while abnormal, was not unnatural. Attempting to square the circle between scientific tolerance and Roman Catholic moral teaching, Marc André Raffalovich in *Uranisme et Unisexualité* (1896) had called not for the suppression of homosexual difference but for the choice of celibacy by homosexual Catholics. Raffalovich went so far as to argue that, precisely because of their willingness to sacrifice sexual intimacy during their lifetimes, male homosexuals might be especially suited to the demands of the Roman Catholic priesthood.[37] Finally, there was the language of science, which described female same-sex desire in terms of sexual inversion, terminology that Hall would turn to in *The Well of Loneliness*.

In 1920, Hall's preferred choice and that of her lovers was a language of female love and friendship, often crossed with the rhetoric of male friendship tradition. Both Hall and Troubridge understood intimacy between women in these terms. For example, at the time of Hall's death,

Troubridge memorialized their relationship within the terms of a separatist female friendship tradition. In a letter posthumously written to "John," she confided: "I feel I must leave an unequivocal record of our life and love, just as the Ladies [i.e., of Llangollen] did, to cheer and encourage those who come after us" (Ormrod, 285). But Troubridge also understood her commitment to Hall as existing within the terms of male friendship writing that I have explored in *Friendship's Bonds*. To her literary executor, Troubridge remarked that the relationship had been a "marriage of true minds" (Ormrod, 114). This reference to Shakespeare's sonnet 116 inserts her union into a specifically male homoerotic literary tradition: in the first instance, referring to William Shakespeare's idealized friendship with a young man, whom many have identified with William Herbert, third Earl of Pembroke. In the second instance, the allusion calls to mind Wilde's fictional recasting of the debate over the identity of this friend in his short story "The Portrait of Mr. W. H." (1889).[38] The phrase links the best-known twentieth-century relationship between two women and the years at the end of the nineteenth century when the tradition of male friendship writing was actively adapted to the purposes of homophile apology.

For her part, Batten had called upon male friendship tradition when she gave Hall the nickname John, after David and Jonathan, the heroic pair of friends in the Hebrew Bible, who "in their death . . . were not divided" (II Samuel 1:23; Cline, 66). On October 2, 1916, in the first joint sitting taken by Hall and Troubridge, Batten communicated through Feda: "There is more in our love than there has ever been between two women before. . . . I am sure we feel more like married people do to each other" (Ormrod, 99). The linking of friendship with marriage was not customary within male friendship tradition, in which the perfect friendship of two men was contrasted to the secondary sort of friendship that could exist within marriage. In addition, given the failure of Troubridge's marriage, neither she nor Hall had much reason to recommend marriage. But all three women were among others, such as the lovers Vita Sackville-West and Virginia Woolf, who valued marriage not as it was normally understood but as it might become. In June 1929, in a joint BBC radio interview with Vita and her husband, Harold Nicolson, the latter comments to the Director of Talks, Hilda Matheson, that marriage is "a plant, not a piece of furniture. It grows; it changes; it develops."[39] Nicolson and Sackville-West had an open marriage, in which both engaged in affairs with same-sex partners. Sackville-West's sexual flamboyance was well known, and Matheson herself was a Sapphist. In this context, marriage means something quite different. Both Sackville-West and Woolf project it as a metaphor of the stability that they sought in a long-term relationship, "like a sunny harbour to me," as Sackville-West put it.[40] For the trio of Batten, Hall, and Troubridge, this safe space was a location to be worked toward.

Hall was fortunate in the outcome of the trial. The jury accepted Fox-Pitt's contention that his accusations of immorality were directed against spiritualist practice rather than toward the practice of "unnatural vice" (Baker, 130). When the judge advised them that Fox-Pitt's intentions were immaterial, however, the jury found in her favor and assessed £500 against the defendant. The latter decided to appeal, and in March 1921 a new trial was ordered. Hall, however, at the advice of her lawyer, decided to declare victory and desist. As for the Society, its prestige took a heavy hit.[41]

Hall and Troubridge continued to attend sittings twice weekly for two hours until 1922, and Troubridge published a carefully researched and considered psychological analysis of mediumship in the journal of the Society that year.[42] Hall was elected to the Council of the Society annually between 1921 and 1924. Significantly, when she resigned that year, she gave as the reason "the demands of professional writing" (Ormrod, 102). The intensive, extended period of psychical research had served an additional purpose in enabling her to make the transition to full-time writer of prose fiction. When Hall fell seriously ill in the 1940s, both agreed that, should she and Troubridge predecease the other, the remaining partner would not attempt communication through a medium (Ormrod, 273).

Already before the trial, the pair distanced themselves from the metaphysical doctrines that Lodge had attached to psychical research. After he visited them in July 1919, for example, Troubridge wrote: "He seems weak & odd in his head I think, . . . & rabid against all scientific criticism of spiritism—alas—we very distressed [sic]" (Baker, 117). If Hall rejected Lodge's new religion, however, she adapted important aspects of it to her emerging view of her own future as a writer. At the end of one sitting, a control said to Lodge: "Your heart's been bleeding. You never thought you could love so deep. There must be more or less suffering. Even though you are crucified, you will arise the stronger, bigger, better man. But out of this suffering and crucifixion, oh, how you are going to help humanity! This is a big work. It has been prophesied. It is through the sufferings of humanity that humanity is reached. It must be through pain" (Lodge, 177). The control continues by emphasizing the evangelical character of the work entrusted to Lodge and by assuring him that the salvation that his suffering will win for humanity is of the same sort as that which Christ preached. In the meantime, *Raymond* will bring joy to many (Lodge, 178).

As commodities, books are public. But they are usually written and read in private. Crucifixion is a form of homicide in which what is personal and private acquires its significance through and as public spectacle. In both instances, to use Roland Barthes's phrase, "the publicity of the private" comes into existence as "a new social value."[43] From *Raymond*, Hall derived a pattern that she adapted to her own writing and to her persona as author. Although highly critical of traditional Christian beliefs, Lodge's Spiritualism conserved the idea of Christ's crucifixion by referring it to Lodge himself and the gospel of psychical research. Likewise, Hall, even before beginning to publish as a writer of fiction, saw herself as a Christlike, sacrificial figure. In terms of gender, she was attracted both to the masculinist temper of the passage cited above as well as to the androgynous character of conventional representations of Christ. The ground of her evangel, however, would be found in the female same-sex desire that motivated her turn to Spiritualism in the first place. The sacrificial ideal was not a new one in homosexual apology of the late Victorian and early modernist periods. But no one else would pose the view as provocatively, and no one else would focus the assertion on desire between women.

4

The Unlit Lamp

A Feminist Experiment

The first novel completed by Hall and the second to be published, *The Unlit Lamp* (1924), is a feminist work that focuses on the impossibility of lesbian desire. To say impossible is to speak paradoxically because during the postwar decade Hall lived in an open same-sex relationship while contributing to the construction of a lesbian public culture in England. The impossibility to which the novel refers then is theoretical, specifically in the difficulty that psychoanalytic theory in the 1920s and early 1930s, whether practiced by men or women, had in articulating and grounding adult female sexuality.[1] As Hall indicates, however, the difficulty was also practical since the development of lesbian existence depended upon financial independence for women, which depended in turn upon their access to intellectually stimulating, well-compensated work. In a departure from the psychoanalysis of the day, Hall locates the becoming-possible of lesbian existence in women's entry into areas of life, such as the medical profession, that were largely restricted to male practitioners. Moreover, she posits this possibility without basing female agency in envy, rivalry, or disaffection from men as psychoanalytic theorists, both male and female, did. To say as much is not to deny Hall's competitive attitude toward men. She recognized, however, that envy was not a good basis on which to construct female psychological and professional autonomy. Nonetheless, it was precisely on envy—envy of the missing penis—that psychoanalysts based what they referred to as the female masculinity complex.[2]

The novel shows Hall to have been equally aware of the dangers of inhabiting the sort of pre-oedipal sexuality that leading female psychoanalysts began theorizing in the 1920s and that Freud would attempt to integrate within his theoretical work early in the following decade. Instead, she looked to the possibility of a female virility disabled neither by absorption in a maternal dyad, on the one hand, nor by masculine ambition and aggression against males on the other. Hall locates this possibility fictionally in the potential of Joan Ogden, the protagonist of the novel. While this promise remains unfulfilled, it constitutes the novel's desire, propelling the reader forward with increasing frustration and chagrin as Joan's attempts to attain autonomy are repeatedly blocked by conditions both external and internal.

This pattern of repetition is ultimately disclosed to be the book's real subject. In order to trace this process, Hall adapts to her purpose the genre of the bildungsroman, the novel of individual self-development in the first or the third person, familiar in both nineteenth-century and early modernist fiction.[3] While writing the novel, she read an important piece of feminist experimental fiction in this genre: May Sinclair's *Mary Olivier* (1919).[4] Sinclair's novel is preoccupied with the struggle of its protagonist to escape her mother's love and conventional expectations.[5] In addition to reading this and other works of fiction concerned with the im/possibility of female autonomy and same-sex intimacy, such as Virginia Woolf's *The Voyage Out* (1915),[6] Hall's approach to the genre drew upon her experience in psychical research, which had required careful attention both to circumstantial detail and to unconscious mental operations.[7] Within a naturalist style, Hall explores the entanglement of socioeconomic with unconscious factors in individual development.[8] For Hall, the active connection between early childhood relationships and later ones is shaped equally by sociological and psychological factors. Psychologically, the operation of the mother-daughter relationship at the unconscious level is determinative. Leading sociological factors are limited access to professions for women and the unintended consequences of social-purity female friendship among New Women.

Joan's mother, Mrs. Ogden, occupies a failed marriage to Colonel Ogden, a martinet, who is forced to retire on a reduced income from his post in India as a result of a weak heart. Ogden compensates for this failure of phallic potency by continually bullying his wife. In reaction, Joan from the outset rejects the possibility of marriage and, implicitly, any other long-term partnership with another human being. She also reacts against the gender-based authority that entitles men to subject women. In oedipal terms, she becomes an early and alas too successful rival for her mother's emotional and physical attentions. On the mother's side, desire for her daughter arises in the context of a phobic reaction against sex with her husband. Mrs. Ogden "remembered her wedding night; it had not been at all like her slightly guilty dreams; it had been—she shuddered. Thinking back now she knew that she herself, that part of her that was composed of spirit, had been rudely shaken free, leaving behind but a part of the whole. It had not been her night, but all James's, a blurred and horrible experience filled with astonished repugnance."[9] Mrs. Ogden's disappointed desire attaches to her daughter, who enjoys her own illicit pleasure as her mother's companion. In the opening chapter, after Mrs. Ogden has spent a miserable morning over the grocery accounts with her husband, she comforts herself with her twelve-year-old daughter's embraces. At such moments, "Joan's strong, young arms would comfort and soothe, and her firm lips grope until they found her mother's; and Mrs. Ogden would feel mean and ashamed but guiltily happy, as if a lover held her" (13).

Joan is the sort of coltish young girl whom Hall frequently chose to put at the center of her novels: she "was large-boned and tall for her age, lanky as a boy, with a pale face and short black hair. Her grey eyes were not large, and not at all appealing, but they were set well apart; they were intelligent and frank. She escaped being plain by the skin of her teeth; she would have been plain had her face not been redeemed by a short, straight nose and a beautiful mouth. Somehow her mouth reassured you" (11). The citation, with its insinuated intimacy between author and reader, assures the reader that Joan's appeal is both masculine and feminine. Within the domestic triad in which Joan finds herself, however, she early reacts against her femininity: "They had cut her thick hair during scarlet fever, and Joan refused to allow it to grow again. She invariably found scissors and snipped and snipped, and Mrs. Ogden's resistance broke down at the final act of defiance, when she was discovered hacking at her hair with a pen-knife" (11). In this brief opening passage, Hall already signifies the complex mystery of the boyish girl, at once self-determined and shaped by physical, social, and psychological factors.

As the passages cited above suggest, one basis of the impossibility of lesbian desire has to do with incestuous ties to one's mother. Hall, however, devotes significantly more attention and thought to female friendship as it is figured in Joan's close ties with her tutor, Cambridge-educated Elizabeth Rodney. As they are with the maternal dyad, matters are further complicated by female socioeconomic subordination and by anti-sex attitudes among women, which Hall, in tune with the temper of youthful fashion in the 1920s, regards as destructive. Bourgeois women such as Mrs. Ogden and Mary Olivier's mother attempt to enforce mid-Victorian norms of feminin-ity upon young women in search of autonomy. In revolt is the first genera-tion of New Women. Born for the most part in the 1840s and 1850s, these women founded the single-sex institutions that first provided middle-class women with opportunities for female friendship outside of family settings, communal living, professional development, and service outside the home. "A second generation, born in the 1870s and 1880s . . . took the cause [of women's rights] one step further, demanding political and social changes."[10] They became leaders of the suffragist movement in England in the years leading up to the outbreak of World War I. Following the war, however, members of both groups found themselves abruptly sidestepped by the emergence of yet another generation of young women who rebelled against the "dowdy," "high-minded," female homosocial culture that prevailed at such places as Newnham College. Some rebelled by affirming an interest in boys, marriage, and maternity.[11] Others, women whose sexual interests were in other women or who were bisexual, turned from female-centered to an-drogynous or crossgendered conceptions of aesthetics, gender, and sexuality. Hall, a sometime supporter of female suffrage, was one among this sexually experimental group who were already visible in the early 1910s, that is, be-fore the massive dislocations of World War I, to which the emergence of a lesbian public culture in England is usually attributed.

Regarding this last development, psychoanalysis was behind the curve. It was only in the 1920s that leading male figures within the psychoanalytic movement, such as Freud and Ernest Jones, his leading English disciple, turned their attention to female sexual development. Previously, it had been assimilated to Freud's view of the development of the Oedipus complex in young boys. Freud believed that the first love-object of females was not their mother but their father.[12] Only in his essay "Female Sexuality" (1931; trans. 1932), published seven years after Hall's novel, did he come to recog-nize the importance of what he called "the pre-Oedipus phase in women."[13]

Along with this recognition, he became aware of how the symbiotic relationship between mother and daughter could threaten the individuation and sexuation of young women. In this essay, Freud also gives greater weight than previously to the importance for a young girl of what he calls the masculinity complex, namely, her wish to possess a penis and along with it the benefits enjoyed by children born with one. Freud writes: "To an incredibly late age she clings to the hope of getting a penis some time. That hope becomes her life's aim; and the phantasy of being a man in spite of everything often persists as a formative factor over long periods. This 'masculinity complex' in women can also result in a manifest homosexual choice of object" (229–30).

These shifts in Freud's thinking resulted from pressures both external and internal to psychoanalysis: on the one hand, the sort of social development in which Hall was participating; and on the other hand, the need felt by both Freud and Jones to respond to the increasing significance of female analysts and the case studies they were reporting. During the 1920s, such analysts as Helene Deutsch and Jeanne Lampl-de Groot (both mentioned by Freud, 21: 226–27), Melanie Klein, and Joan Riviere drew attention to the lack of a specific theory of female sexuality in the psychoanalytic canon and began to remedy that lack. Likewise, the growing importance of lesbian public cultures after World War I necessitated analytic and theoretical work. For example, when Jones published his essay on female sexuality in 1927, he reported that "the immediate stimulus to the investigation on which the present paper is mainly based was provided by the unusual experience, a couple of years ago, of having to analyse at the same time five cases of manifest homosexuality in women. The analyses were all deep ones and lasted from three to five years; they have been completed in three of the cases and carried to a far stage in the other two."[14] In other words, Jones was working intensively with female homosexual and bisexual patients at the time when Hall's novel appeared. Similarly, the exponential jump in the public exposure of female homosexuality that resulted from the trial of Hall's publisher, Jonathan Cape, at the time of publication of *The Well of Loneliness* provides part of the setting in which Freud determined that this topic was one on which he needed to weigh in.

Both lesbian visibility and female psychoanalytic practice put male analysts on the defensive regarding their overemphasis on the penis. Jones concedes as much at the beginning of his essay when he acknowledges Karen Horney's complaint that a "bias" in favor of attention to male primary sexual characteristics has resulted in deformations in psychoanalytic theory of early female development. However, in words that indicate how focused on biological difference he continued to be, Jones writes: "There is a healthy suspicion growing that men analysts have been led to adopt an unduly phallo-centric view of the problems in question, the importance of the female organs being correspondingly underestimated" (459). He continues with a snide remark about female fixation on the penis: "Women have on their side contributed to the general mystification by their secretive attitude towards their own genitals and by displaying a hardly disguised preference for interest in the male organ" (459). Perhaps the most interesting implication of the increasing importance attached to the female masculinity complex is the fact that it underscored the importance of bisexuality in females (Freud, 227), while greatly complicating the question of girls' "normal" (230) development toward heterosexuality. Indeed, Freud remarks that "the feminine form of the Oedipus complex . . . is all too often not surmounted by the female at all" (230).

Emphasis on the female masculinity complex resulted in yet another departure within psychoanalytic theory during the 1920s, namely, the emergence of the concept of "womanliness as a masquerade." In her 1929 essay of this title, Riviere argues that the pursuit of masculine ambitions by women is often accompanied by a compensatory masquerade of conventional womanliness. This notion widens the scope of the masculinity complex well beyond the question of the origin of female same-sex desire, since any woman with interests that go beyond the performance of traditional female gender roles might be said to exhibit signs of an unresolved masculinity complex.

Riviere's essay is based on the case study of an American woman, a successful lecturer, who compensated for her competitiveness with men both by flirtatious behavior with older male colleagues and by excelling in the skills of wifely homemaking and female mentorship. Riviere argues that both the seductive behavior and the practice of womanly virtues were motivated by the woman's unconscious anxiety that she would be punished by her father for usurping his prerogatives. The case led Riviere to an insight that undermines the very notion of constitutive gender:

> Womanliness . . . could be assumed and worn as a mask, both to hide the possession of masculinity and to avert the reprisals expected if she was found to possess it—much as a thief will turn out his pockets and

ask to be searched to prove that he has not the stolen goods. The reader may now ask how I define womanliness or where I draw the line between genuine womanliness and the "masquerade." My suggestion is not, however, that there is any such difference; whether radical or superficial, they are the same thing. The capacity for womanliness was there in this woman—and one might even say it exists in the most completely homosexual woman—but owing to her conflicts it did not represent her main development and was used far more as a device for avoiding anxiety than as a primary mode of sexual enjoyment.[15]

If Riviere is correct and womanliness is in this sense a masquerade, then the predominance of heterosexuality in women begins to look like a phantasm. There is no essential distinction to be drawn between a successful female professional and the alternately dreaded and ridiculed figure of the "mannish" lesbian. Riviere's case study bears out this contention. She reports of her patient: "Once, while for a period her husband had had a love-affair with another woman, she had detected a very intense identification with him in regard to the rival woman. It is striking that she had had no homosexual experiences (since before puberty with a younger sister); but it appeared during analysis that this lack was compensated for by frequent homosexual dreams with intense orgasm" (39).

Riviere's radical perception of the indeterminacy of gender had troubling implications for male analysts. As will become evident below in my discussion of Hall's portrayal of Joan's younger sister, Milly, Hall registers the complexity of female psychology in relation not only to the mother-daughter dyad and the female masculinity complex but also to the practice of womanliness as a masquerade. Under the force of these concerns, the notion that either gender *or* sexuality can be determined by primary sexual characteristics yields to an awareness of the psychological *and* social factors that shape biological females.

By attending to relationships in time, Hall avoids what in retrospect appear to be three of the leading weaknesses within male psychoanalytic theory of female sexuality in the 1920s. The first is to take early childhood relations with one's parents, particularly one's father, as the structural template of the adult psyche. Although there is an oedipal component to Joan's incestuous involvement with her mother, nonetheless the unconscious internalization of her relation with her mother is more important than her antagonistic rivalry with her father. Second, the dynamics of the nuclear family do not suffice to account for Joan's failed promise. Hall again parts from psychoanalytic theory and case studies in her emphasis on how other factors, both external and relational, in this case, a double bind within female friendship, limit Joan's ability to achieve a necessary degree of personal autonomy. A third weakness of psychoanalytic theory that Hall avoids is the relentless biological determinism of Jones's and Freud's writing. Freud, with his frequent references to "bisexuality" as an aspect of "the innate disposition of human beings" (227–28), likely would reject this criticism. Despite disclaimers, however, the importance attached to the penis and to penis-envy grounds male psychoanalysis in the presence or absence of two bodily organs: the penis and the vagina (Jones, 464–65).

The main action of the novel involves the struggle between Elizabeth and Mrs. Ogden over Joan. One aspect has to do with Joan's desire for emotionally and intellectually rewarding work and financial independence. After Joan at age fifteen witnesses Elizabeth seriously hurt in an accident, she decides that she would like to become a doctor. Her father is shocked that she would consider pursuing "an unsexing, indecent profession for a woman"; her mother rejects this path as both "masculine" and vulgar: "There are things that a gentleman can do and things he cannot; no gentleman can enter the medical profession" (110). The other aspect of the conflict is personal. In different ways, both Mrs. Ogden and Elizabeth seek to possess Joan.[16]

At his wife's instigation (she does not want her children to attend school with "the offspring of the local tradespeople" [17]), the Colonel has made what both parents eventually see to be a mistaken decision to hire Elizabeth as private tutor for their daughters. At the time, Elizabeth is twenty-six. Born in 1863, she belongs to a generation that falls between the pioneering women born in the 1840s and 1850s and the generation born in the 1870s and 1880s that agitated to win civil, social, and political rights for women. Elizabeth is a member of the first generation of women to enroll in the new foundations for women at Cambridge. Girton College had been founded in 1869 and Newnham in 1871. In 1881, women were permitted for the first time to take the tripos examinations, although they were still denied degrees (Vicinus, 126). Elizabeth, who "had done well at Cambridge," presumably passed the exams: "There were posts open to her." But the jobs didn't pay well. Faced with the option of "life on a pittance" (42) in London or accepting an offer to live with her much older brother, Ralph, at their deceased uncle's home in Seabourne, she chooses the latter. She recognizes, however, that she has chosen a dead end.

Her predicament reflects a number of limitations faced by young middle-class women of the time. One was what Sir Almoth Wright, Professor of Experimental Pathology at the University of London, regarded as the surplus of women arising from the fact that more female than male infants were born in England. In *Feminism*, a suffragist pamphlet of 1912, Sinclair quotes Wright's complaint that " 'the recruiting field for the militant suffragists is the half-million of our excess female population,' the half-million of the unmated."[17] Wright believed that the ranks of feminists were swelled by the sexually "FRUSTRATED" and "THE INCOMPLETE. . . . One side of their nature has undergone atrophy, with the result that they have lost touch with their living fellow men and women" (16).[18] Similar attitudes infected male psychoanalysis. Jones, for example, describes as one of two dominant types among female homosexuals "those who retain their interest in men, but who set their hearts on being accepted by men as one of themselves. To this group belongs the familiar type of women who ceaselessly complain of the unfairness of women's lot and their unjust ill-treatment by men" (467).[19]

The number of women receiving higher education continued to be small. For example, at Girton in 1897, 109 women were enrolled, and at Newnham, 166. Employment opportunities were also limited. As late as 1901, fewer than half of spinsters over forty-five were gainfully employed. Of those who were employed, "slightly over 12 percent . . . were in middle-class jobs," mainly in teaching and nursing. In 1901, when Joan is twenty-four, there were only twenty female physicians in England; ten years later there were sixty.[20] Given Joan's parents' opposition to her becoming a doctor, the figures indicate how extremely unlikely it is that her ambitions will ever be fulfilled. Likewise, it becomes easier to understand why Elizabeth permits herself to be sucked into life in a dull town with a brother twenty years older than herself and whom she scarcely knows. Vicinus writes: "From 1871 to 1893 Girton, Newnham, Somerville [at Oxford], Royal Holloway, and Alexandra College (Dublin) had matriculated a total of 1,486 students; 680 became teachers, 208 married, and 11 entered medicine. Over half the students at Newnham had become teachers, but the college also had the highest percentage who had married. Education was not an opening up of wider opportunities, . . . but a narrow staircase leading to more education as an ill-paid—but respected—teacher" (177).

In view of these statistics, it is surprising that Joan's initial interest is in becoming a doctor rather than a nurse. Despite the challenges, however, Hall makes Joan's aspiration seem both normal and appropriate. And by representing her within the genre of the bildungsroman, Hall pulls the reader along. The implied expectation that the reader will see the process of the protagonist's successful self-fashioning plays against continual reminders of the odds against Joan's survival, much less her triumph.[21] Similarly, although economics alone could account for Elizabeth's decision to come to Seabourne, she offers too many explanations for her decision. It is as though she is trying to rationalize behavior that is in fact overdetermined.[22] Elizabeth's lapse into domesticity and financial dependence runs counter to the self-conscious ideology of the women's colleges, as does her later decision to marry a man she does not love but who offers her wealth and position in the colonies. Remember that in the decades in question fewer than 20 percent of female matriculants at the new women's colleges chose marriage as a career. Elizabeth is an exception to the rule. She fails to heed Caroline Emilia Stephen's warning to students at Newnham: "One thing which all who live alone certainly need is the power—mainly I believe imaginative—to outline their own lives. And by this I mean the power of marking out distinctly the channels into which one's energies should flow, and for which they should be reserved. People are but too ready to make demands on time and strength not obviously appropriated; and without a distinct outline in one's own mind it is doubly hard not to yield to such demands."[23]

Like Joan, but in different ways, Elizabeth is not a conventional young woman. She too is a gender-crosser, though her style differs from that of Joan, who, even at age thirteen sees her as a figure of crossgendered energy: "Joan was thinking: 'She looks like a tree. Why haven't I noticed before how exactly like a tree she is; it must be the green dress. But her eyes are like water, all greeny and shadowy and deep looking—a tree near a pool, that's what she's like, a tall tree. A beech tree? No, that is too spready, a larch tree, that's Elizabeth; a larch tree just greening over'" (34). Even as a prepubescent girl, Joan imagines Elizabeth in terms recognizable as both phallic and vaginal. And on ordinary days, this Daphne-like figure, capable, disciplined, and ascetic, dresses in tailored clothes.

Later, Joan associates this double-gendering with both male virility and female fecundity. One day when Elizabeth is in town with the girls, she is seriously burnt in an unsuccessful attempt to save the life of a serving woman who rushes into the street with her clothes afire. Joan accompanies Elizabeth home after she receives initial treatment for severe burns to her hands. When they arrive, the young general servant at the house panics, and Joan realizes that she will have to help Elizabeth to bed. In Elizabeth's bedroom, a surprise awaits the girl: "The room was very austere in its cold whiteness; it was like Elizabeth and yet it was not like Elizabeth; like the outward Elizabeth perhaps, but was it like the real Elizabeth? Then her eyes fell upon a great tangle of autumn flowers, standing in a bright blue jar on the chest of drawers; something in the strength and virility of their colouring seemed to gibe and taunt the prim little room; they were there as a protest, or so the girl felt. . . . Elizabeth . . . smiled as she followed the direction of Joan's eyes. 'A part of me loves them, needs them,' she said" (99). Conservative feminists of the Victorian period plus many of the celibate, independently living members of the first generation of New Women advocated social purity: that is, male sexual self-control, monogamy, and infrequent sexual intercourse.[24] The austerity of Elizabeth's room suggests an aversion to male-female sexual contact. The flowers, however, suggest that Elizabeth is by no means averse to a double-gendered desire.

Elizabeth and Joan's friendship takes the form of a "rave," the type of friendship that Vicinus suggests characterized relationships between mentors and protégés in the collegiate residences and private schools for girls established and staffed by New Women.[25] Raves were embodied, emotional, even passionate relationships but not explicitly sexual. New Women defined their public missions in terms of the purity, compassion, and maternal instinct that characterized them as women. Sexuality was something beastly, to be associated with male desire and vaginal coitus.[26] Joan gives a glimpse of this outlook later in the novel when she uses the word *beastly* (160) to characterize her sister's affair with a young tradesman.[27] Raves focused on the moral and intellectual fashioning of the student. Discipline and self-discipline were of the essence, with worshipful subordination on one side and loving direction on the other.

Defined at the outset as asexual friendships, the institution of the rave inhibited the possible development of a sexual tie as the younger member approached adulthood and a more nearly equal relation with her superior. The possibility hovers tantalizingly on the horizon of Joan's relationship with her tutor. When Elizabeth's injuries, for example, reduce her to dependence on Joan, Joan reacts with a pleasurable sensation: she "felt that in this new-found intimacy something was lost and something gained. Never again could Elizabeth represent authority in her pupil's eyes; that aspect of their relationship was lost for ever. . . . But in its place there was something else, something infinitely more intimate and interesting" (100).

For years, Elizabeth fantasizes about living with Joan in a flat in London. Unfortunately, New Woman social relations leave Elizabeth in a state of false consciousness about the full implications of her wish. Construing the plan exclusively in terms of a collaborative enterprise to help Joan achieve the aim of becoming a physician, Elizabeth declares to her:

> "Listen. I want you to work as we are doing until you come of age, then I want you to go to Cambridge, as I've often told you, but after that—I want you to make a home with me."
>
> "Elizabeth!"
>
> "Yes. I have a little money put by, not very much, but enough, and I want you to come to London and live there with me. We could jog along somehow; I'd get a job while you studied at the hospital; we'd have a little flat together, and be free and very happy. I've wanted to say this to you for some time and to-day somehow it's all come out; it had to get said sooner of later. Joan, I can't stand Seabourne for many years, and yet as long as you're here I can't get away. . . . How long will you make me stay here, Joan, . . . when we might get free and hustle along with life, when we might be purposeful and tired and happy because we mean something?" (131–32)

The eruption of Elizabeth's desperation speaks to an otherwise unsayable need. Joan, responding, agrees to the proposal, but the warmth of her attachment to Elizabeth is frustrated and befuddled by Elizabeth's insistence on representing their attraction as sexless.

The younger woman, however, is open to taking another view. One of the key moments within Hall's oeuvre is the passage at the end of Book 2 of *The Well of Loneliness* where the protagonist, Stephen Gordon, finds a term for her sense of herself as a masculine woman while reading Richard von Krafft-Ebing's *Psychopathia Sexualis*. A similar occasion arises in *The Unlit Lamp* a few minutes before Elizabeth asks Joan to live with her. In this case, too, a medical textbook provides the opportunity for the two women to make the same sort of discovery that Stephen does. But Elizabeth's recoil against the possibility that there might be something abnormal

about their closeness prohibits either woman from recognizing their relation in a new way. Instead, as they are working together one day, Elizabeth
bursts out:

> I'm trying to take a scientific interest in the disgusting organs of our
> disgusting bodies, to learn how and why they act, or rather how and
> why they don't act, to read patiently and sympathetically about a lot of
> abnormal freaks, who as far as I can see ought all to be shut up in a
> lunatic asylum, to understand and condone the physical and mental
> impulses of hysterics, and I'm doing this all out of scientific interest!
> Scientific interest! That's why I'm slaving as I never slaved at Cam-
> bridge—out of pure scientific interest! Well, I tell you, you're wrong! I
> don't like medical books and I particularly dislike neurotic people, but
> it's been enough for me that you do like all this, that you feel that you
> want to be a doctor and make good in that way. It's not out of scientific
> interest that I've done it, Joan; it's because of you and your career, it's
> because I am mad for you to have a future—I've been so from the first,
> I think— . . . ," she paused. (130)

Elizabeth's unwillingness to think about her own desires in relation to sexology, her body hatred, and her aversion to sexual touch could not be
expressed more clearly than in this passage. It discloses why the offer of a
room shared with Elizabeth is not an outcome with which Joan will be able
to live. Also as clear is Elizabeth's lack of intellectual curiosity, indeed, her
contempt for a certain kind of intellectual desire. This willful limitation of
her selfhood is just as deadly to the prospect that she and Joan might spend
their future together.

Later, at the moment of crisis in the novel, when Joan at twenty-four
has one last chance to leave for London with Elizabeth, the younger woman
recognizes how unconventional the step is. She realizes that if she were
leaving home to marry a male friend, such as Richard Benson, her mother
would not object to her departure. It is because Joan is going to live as a
single woman with a female that her mother opposes the move; hence,
Elizabeth and Joan

> *must* swim against the current; it was ridiculous, preposterous that be-
> cause she did not marry she should be forced to live a crippled exis-
> tence. What real difference could it possibly make to her mother's

loneliness if her daughter shared a flat with Elizabeth instead of with a husband? No difference at all, except in precedent. Then it was only by submitting to precedent that you could be free? What she was proposing seemed cruel now, even to herself; and why? Because it was not softened and toned down by precedent, not wreathed in romance as the world understood romance. "Good God!" she thought bitterly, "can there be no development of individuality in this world without hurting oneself or someone else?" She clenched her fists. "I don't care, I don't care! I've a right to my life, and I shall go in August. I defy precedent. I'm Joan Ogden, a law unto myself, and I mean to prove it." (247–48)

Joan's desire for a life of her own is compromised by the paradoxical sense that she can be "free" only if she remains subservient to her mother.

This double bind is compounded in the relationship with Elizabeth, who offers to support Joan's personal and professional growth but only on the condition that they take a flat together in London. There is a further double bind insofar as Elizabeth speaks clearly about the full extent of her love—and demands—of Joan too late in the game (190–91). With Elizabeth's intellectual, emotional, and sexual support, Joan might have succeeded as did other female couples. But the structure of the pair's relationship in terms of an asexual romantic friendship dictates that Joan will miss the opportunity that Elizabeth seems to be holding open to her. To this reality, one may add Joan (and Hall's) judgment that female intimacy required a social form as public and normal as marriage if women were to be able to achieve personal and professional fulfillment together. This social transformation would have enabled Elizabeth, personally and publicly, to realize the character of her desire.

One approaches then the conviction so important in *The Well of Loneliness* of the need for the institution of female same-sex marriage. Radical though this insight is, however, in Joan's attractive, musically talented sister, Milly, who dies at a young age of tuberculosis, Hall presents gender and sexuality in a yet more radical way. Hall represents gendered and sexual difference in Joan as though they are inherent aspects of selfhood. In psychoanalytic terms, this proposition makes sense in terms of Freud's concept of the bodily ego.[28] Much more challenging both to psychoanalysis and to "centuries of custom, centuries of precedent" (*Unlit Lamp*, 247), is the concept of womanliness as masquerade. Milly is as ambitious as Joan and probably a lot more envious of the penis, but she knows "feminine" ways

of achieving these goals: first, in the narcissistic display of concert performance, her chosen field, and, second, in her ability to please men. At home,
Milly is her father's favorite. Later, when she learns that her father has
squandered in a bad investment the money bequeathed to her and her
sister, she embarks on a rash affair with a young admirer. She abruptly
drops him after Joan ensures that she will still be able to fulfill her dream
of entering the Royal College of Music. Milly's femininity is anything but
natural. Rather, it is calculated, in behavior that she learns from her father,
to enable her to get what she wants in a world in which daughters seem
otherwise to be caught in subjection.

Unlike her sister, Milly actually does manage to leave Seabourne to
study in London. In one of the rare glimpses provided by Hall into the lives
of female subjects of same-sex desire at the time, when Elizabeth and Joan
visit Milly at the Royal College, they find her living among a circle of music
students that includes a talented young singer, Harriet Nelson, and her
infatuated "youthful admirers" (192). One of them, Rosie Wilmot, later
becomes hysterically jealous because Harriet takes an interest in Joan.
When Joan subsequently returns to London to retrieve her sister, who is
being sent home because of her failing health, Harriet, ignoring the seriousness of the situation, first teases and then propositions Joan: "Come up and
see me sometimes" (215), she purrs.

In its final section, the novel jumps forward nineteen years to 1920,
when Joan Ogden is forty-three and female subjects of same-sex desire have
not only emerged in public but have succeeded in becoming fashionable.
The passage of time permits Hall to mark the transition to the postwar
period; it also provides an opportunity for her to assess the change in manners. Shortly after arriving with her mother for their annual vacation at a
hotel at Lynton in North Devon, Joan sits alone in the lobby:

> Two young girls with bobbed hair and well-tailored clothes had come
> on to the veranda from the garden.
>
> One of them was in riding-breeches. They sat down with their backs
> to the open window, through which their voices drifted. "Have you
> seen that funny old thing with the short grey hair?"
>
> "Yes, you mean the one at lunch? Wasn't she killing? Why moiré
> ribbon instead of a proper necktie?"
>
> "And why a pearl brooch across her stiff collar?"
>
> "I believe she's what they used to call a 'New woman,'" said the girl
> in breeches, with a low laugh. "Honey, she's a forerunner, that's what

she is, a kind of pioneer that's got left behind. I believe she's the beginning of things like me. Oh! hang it all, I've left my gloves in the garden; come on, we must look for them." And they went down the steps again.

Joan laid down the newspaper and stared after them. Of course they had not known that she was there. "A forerunner, a kind of pioneer that's got left behind." . . . She saw the truth of this all round her, in women of the type that she had once been, that in a way she still was. Active, aggressively intelligent women, not at all self-conscious in their tailor-made clothes, not ashamed of their cropped hair; women who did things well, important things; women who counted and who would go on counting; smart, neatly put together women, looking like well-bred young men. They might still be in the minority and yet they sprang up everywhere; one saw them now even at Seabourne during the summer season. They were particular about their clothes, in their own way; the boots they wore were thick but well cut, their collars immaculate, their ties carefully chosen. But she, Joan Ogden, was the forerunner who had failed, the pioneer who had got left behind, the prophet who had feared his own prophecies. These others had gone forward, some of them released by the war, others who had always been free-lances, and if the world was not quite ready for them yet, if they had to meet criticism and ridicule and opposition, if they were not all as happy as they might be, still they were at least brave, whereas she had been a coward, conquered by circumstances. (284)

Joan is aware of the waste of her potential, an awareness made the more painful as a result of her momentary exposure to how others see her. More painful, too, because of the semi-cruel carelessness of a pair of young women with whom she identifies. The *new* New Women see themselves as the heirs of New Women who were forerunners, pioneers, and prophets. But the young couple also regards these women as having proven themselves unable to overcome the duties required of them as daughters and sisters. They have lacked the courage to dress as women who are the equals of men. And they have not called a female friend on vacation with them "Honey" in public.

The passage signifies in other ways as well. For one thing, it indicates how large a part semiotics played in the lifestyle of young women who competed with men and chose other young women as their intimates.[29] And it indicates the part that money and status played in their boldness. They required advantages in order to play the new parts that they scripted for themselves. Joan responds in these terms. Minutes before closing time, she runs into town to make a purchase of "some stiff collars, the newest pattern . . . and . . . some neckties." On the way back to the hotel, however, she despairs: "Pioneers that got left behind didn't count; they were lost" (285).

If the passage situates Joan as a representative of the generation born in 1880 and the young women as representatives of those born in 1900, where is Hall situated as author of the book in which they appear? Joan is almost exactly the same age as Hall, who was born in 1880. During the years in which she completed the novel and searched for a publisher, Hall was pre-occupied with reinventing herself, with the help of Troubridge, as one of those "women who did things well, important things; women who counted and who would go on counting" (284). In this respect, Hall can be more closely associated with the young couple, whose peers she saw at first hand in the Soho restaurants and night clubs that she and her partner frequented during these years. Hall identified with these women's smartness and ambition. As a woman who had recently won a lawsuit against a man who had accused her of gross immorality with other women, she also shared their boldness.[30]

Asymmetries in the relation between the two young women, however, register a degree of skepticism on Hall's part regarding the stability of Sapphic pair-bonding in the 1920s. For one thing, the young woman in riding breeches refers to the new breed of independent women as "things like me," not us. Her friend evidently has not yet come out; she is likely bisexual, perhaps primarily heterosexual or at least was so until the breeches-wearer came along. Is she in Devon to test the waters? Her cutting remark, spoken where Joan can overhear, likewise has a defensive air—as if the young woman needs to establish her bona fides with her new (?) lover (?) at the expense of a failed older woman. Moreover, while the first woman clearly has spirit, it also seems likely that she has yet to win her spurs as part of the vanguard. There is promise here, but accomplishment waits on a future date.

Richard Benson is an acquaintance of Joan's childhood, who at the time had encouraged Joan's ambitions for a career in medicine. Both youngsters wanted to become doctors, and Richard showed interest in her as a friend, an intellectual equal, and as perhaps exactly the right life-partner for him. As a young woman, Joan was drawn to Richard, but she rejected his proposal of marriage. When she meets him again at the resort after having lost track of him for many years, he renews the proposal; again she rejects it. Benson understands Joan and her predicament well. He seems like an ideal match—except for the fact that he is of the wrong sex. Nonetheless, Hall writes him into the novel in order to show that the competition between men and women does not mean that affection, understanding friendship, and collaboration are impossible between them. His inclusion also demonstrates by contrast why "marriage," so to speak, to Elizabeth is not possible: because although she is of the right sex and may love Joan, she lacks Richard's intellectual curiosity and commitment to public service and because he at least knows the object of his desires.

Benson's presence also helps make a theoretical point. Hall brought to the topic of female sexuality in the 1920s the concept of a masculinity that she calls female "virility" and that she conceptualizes not through the available Freudian models but in terms of a dynamic process that occurs within the phenomenology of engenderment. She would continue to consider the possibilities of female virility in a number of different contexts in her subsequent novels, including the possibility of heterosexual female virility. As for *The Unlit Lamp*, it is the first major accomplishment of her long-wished-for career as a novelist. It fulfilled a promise that she had made to Batten in 1913,[31] when Batten had attempted to forward Hall's prospects by sending her draft short stories to a sympathetic editor. The step led to an invitation from William Heinemann to lunch, at which, Troubridge reports, he told Hall, "You will set to work at once and write me a novel, and when it is finished I will publish it" (41). It took more than a decade for Heinemann's prediction to be fulfilled. When it was, Hall dedicated the novel "To MABEL VERONICA BATTEN in deep affection, gratitude and respect." The term *virility* is significant here as well because the writing of the novel depended on Hall's collaboration with two long-term lovers: first Batten and subsequently Troubridge (69). For Hall, virility, though it is public in character and in this context connotes professional achievement, is also inherent, something of one's core sense of selfhood. Were this perception to be received with full seriousness, female sexuality would need to be completely rethought. Only with the development of the discussion of transgendered and transsexual existence in the final decade of the twentieth century did this fact come into focus.

Hall brings both to feminist and to psychoanalytic discourse of her day a willingness to see sexual desire between women not as a problem but as a necessary promise of modern life. Desire offered a motive both for building committed relations and for grounding middle-class women's efforts to enter the professions. The pro-sex drive of the novel is likewise evident in the title finally chosen for it, at Troubridge's suggestion, as she reports (69). The phrase "the unlit lamp" appears in "The Statue and the Bust," a poem by Robert Browning about two lovers who, for reasons of convenience, delay the consummation of their mutual desire until the possibility of its realization is foreclosed by the death of both. The book's most powerful and lasting concern is not the naturalistic struggle for survival implied in *Octopi*, Hall's first working title for the novel, nor the ironic moralizing of the second, *After Many Days*,[32] but the "sin" of unrealized love and the failure to build a life together.[33] On this point, Hall is in conversation with the young couple on the veranda.

5

Paris and the Culture of Auto/biography in *The Forge*

Biographies deal in myths of origin. In her memoir of Hall, Troubridge reports that the germ of *The Unlit Lamp* occurred to Hall while the two, on vacation at the Lynton Cottage Hotel in North Devon, noticed an elderly woman with her middle-aged "maiden daughter" under circumstances similar to the ones in which a young female couple notice Joan Ogden near the end of the novel.[1] Similarly, biographies of Radclyffe Hall have a single story to tell about the origin of *The Forge* (1924), her first published novel. In 1922, Hall was working to place the manuscript of *The Unlit Lamp*. Editors admired the text but doubted its commercial possibilities. It was suggested that the book might be easier to market were Hall to precede it with a successful attempt at a comic novel.[2] Hall complied, quickly producing the manuscript of *The Forge*, a novel whose story might easily provide material for a drawing-room comedy of the sort that W. Somerset Maugham was writing in the mid-1920s.

As a commercial property, *The Forge* traffics in features of Hall and Troubridge's highly publicized lives together, which it gently mocks in the form of the ménage of Hilary and Susan Brent plus their adorable but naughty dachshund, Sieglinde.[3] Many readers of the novel's first printing knew Hall and Troubridge either as friends or as friends of friends. Whether they noticed the partial anagrams of Hall's surname and Una's forename in those of Hilary and Susan, respectively, these readers would have recognized pressure points in the lives of each that Hall touches upon in the novel. Like Hall, Hilary is struggling to complete his first novel. Like Troubridge, Susan is caught between her responsibilities as the wife of a would-be writer, the luxurious lifestyle that he affords her, and her own unrealized artistic ambitions.

The Forge presented itself to its first readers as a piece of auto/biographical fiction full of references, both substantive and circumstantial, to the life of its author and her partner. Even those who did not know more personal details would have recognized the parallel between the actual and the fictional couple in such items as Hall and Troubridge's standing in the world of prize show dogs.[4] In presenting a partnership between two women under the fictional guise of marriage between a man and a woman, moreover, Hall signaled, as she does more directly in *The Unlit Lamp*, her interest in a crossgendered protagonist. This identification registers on the title page, where Hall drops Marguerite, the forename that she used as author of her books of poetry, and signs herself as "Radclyffe Hall" instead, appropriating her father's first name as her own at the same time that the name's feminine ending signals its bearer's sex. The dedication of the novel, "To UNA with love," signals its role as an anniversary gift, albeit an unusual one, ending as the novel does with Susan chained to her husband and despairing of her art. The particular gender inflection of the couple's relationship also is not obscure. For example, in its coverage of the novel, *People* "took the opportunity (alongside appropriate photographs) to regale its readers with [Hall's] preference for male dress, confiding that she had boasted she did not possess a single frock in her wardrobe" (Baker, 164).

Hall was a pioneer in both crossgendered and lesbian culture insofar as her experience of gender and same-sex partnering provided an example to others. She was also aware of how after World War I a range of new possibilities was opening for female subjects of same-sex desire on a scale scarcely imaginable previously. Her willingness to act on this realization lends her project a democratic character that her in other ways conservative politics does not negate. Moreover, she recognized that as a newly public arrangement the institution of female marriage, including the roles of husband and wife, means and must mean something different for female partners.

At the start, I said that biographers are committed to myths of origin. But the occasion of an act is not its cause, and a cause without an occasion will not be actualized. To seek the causes or better the motives of *The Forge*, one needs to look further. Writing the novel enabled Hall to help map the variety of modern lesbian existence as it crosses with Bohemian and male homosexual manners in the 1920s. Here the experience of Hall and Troubridge in Paris was crucial. In their first decade together, the pair became familiar with the Sapphic culture that had developed there since the turn of the century. Dissident female artists in this environment took a number of different stances regarding the question of female virility. Likewise, they asked themselves how crossgendered experience could be registered in artistically innovative ways. Cross gender was also highly visible in Parisian dance halls and cabaret performance by both male and female artists, not least Barbette, the young female impersonator, high-wire performer, and trapeze artist from the United States.[5]

In Paris the couple knew Colette, a friend of Natalie Clifford Barney and Romaine Brooks, a wealthy American expatriate painter. Another wealthy expatriate American and author, Barney is best known for the salon that she convened for many years at her home on the Rue Jacob.[6] Colette's first marriage ended after she embarked on a highly publicized affair with another married woman. In the aftermath, Colette for a time supported herself as a music-hall performer, occasionally in crossdress.[7] Although she later made a successful marriage to a much younger man, her continuing interest in desire between women animates perhaps her best-known work, *The Pure and the Impure*, a series of reflections on the variable character of sexual desire.

Work by women in Barney's circle continually plays with biographical and autobiographical reference. In this vein, Colette refers to her erotically knowing first-person narrator as "Colette." As with Djuna Barnes's *Ladies Almanack* (1928), Colette's book engages in an implicit dialogue with Hall and Troubridge both as a celebrity couple and more particularly with Hall's account of sexual inversion in *The Well of Loneliness*.[8] Begun in 1930, *The Pure and the Impure* began appearing in part publication in a journal in 1931 but was abruptly terminated by the editor in mid-sentence in the fourth installment. Written in the first person as the voice of "Colette," the chapters offer a series of reflections on the incompatibility of love with desire. Many are written in the form of dialogues between "Colette" and strangers or well-known friends or acquaintances, the identities of whom are lightly masked.

In *The Pure and the Impure*, Colette deliberately resists approaching dissident desire through the lens of modern psychology. Instead she writes in the French tradition of a lover's discourse. At times, she appears to ground desire in a naturalized view of the two sexes. For the narrator of *The Pure and the Impure*, love between women almost always finds itself at a loss in the face of "the supreme deprivation" of a man's "dazzling difference," by which Colette appears to mean his penis (118). Despite subordinating sex between women to sex between a man and a woman, however, Colette shows greater interest in the former. Moreover, in Colette, women— including her autobiographical persona—can be women with a difference. The narrator describes herself as a psychic hermaphrodite with a "masculine streak" (63) that undercuts her occasional efforts to masquerade as a conventional woman: "I am alluding to a genuine mental hermaphroditism which burdens certain highly complex human beings. . . . I happened to be making a particular effort at the time to rid myself of this ambiguity, along with all its flaws and privileges, and to offer them up, still warm, at the feet of a certain man to whom I offered a healthy and quite female body and its perhaps fallacious vocation of servant. But as for the man, he was not taken in, he had detected the masculine streak in my character by some trait of mine I could not identify, and, though tempted, had fled" (62–63).

In *The Pure and the Impure*, Colette suggests something of the variety of female-female desire in Paris. And although she stops short of exploring sexual ties between working-class women, there is no sense that the typologies she explores exhaust the possibilities. Colette associates female gender-crossing with her experience in Paris at the turn of the century. There, "looking as much as possible like a bad boy," she met members of an exclusive coterie of financially independent, politically conservative, socially discreet, gender-crossing aristocratic women. The set—outmoded by 1930—associated their mode of living with a specific politics: namely, the assertion of the right to "personal freedom" (70). Colette notices that the lovers of these women often were either from theater and the music hall or from the servant or other working classes, "rather rude young creatures, insinuating and grasping. Not surprising, this, for these ladies in male attire had, by birth and from infancy, a taste for below-stairs accomplices and comrades in-livery" (73).

In the chapter on Renée Vivien (Pauline Mary Tarn), a young lover whom Barney greatly cherished, Colette describes another type: the turn-of-the-century female "dandy-aesthete," to use Whitney Chadwick's phrase.[9] Vivien, who died a virtual suicide in 1909, was an English heiress who expatriated to Paris, where she modeled herself on the young French decadent, rebel, and poet Arthur Rimbaud. Vivien's female-female erotic poetry is steeped in the tradition of modern male French verse, whose scandalous representations of Sapphic love are suffused with frustrated desire. Paradigmatic in this tradition are the lesbian poems of Charles Baudelaire's *Les Fleurs du Mal.* In "Damned Women," he invokes:

> Virgins, demons, monsters, martyrs, all
> great spirits scornful of reality,
> saints and satyrs in search of the infinite,
> racked with sobs or loud in ecstasy,
>
> You whom my soul has followed to your hell,
> Sisters! I love you as I pity you
> for your bleak sorrows, for your unslaked thirsts,
> and for the love that gorges your great hearts![10]

Nineteenth-century French male modernist Sapphism set the tone for Anglophone explorations of female-female desire in poetry and the visual arts; witness, for example, a painting such as Brooks's *Weeping Venus*, described in detail by Hall in *The Forge.* From a Parisian perspective, already in the first decade of the new century this Anglophone adaptation of French tradition had become démodé. Colette says of her friend Vivien's poetry: "Renée's work inhabits a region of elevated melancholy, in which the *amies*, the female couple, daydream and weep as often as they embrace. Admirably acquainted with our language, broken to the strict rules of French meter, Renée Vivien betrays her foreignness—that is to say, her assimilation of French masterworks relatively late in life—by exuding her Baudelairism in the years 1900–9, which was rather late for us" (96).

Colette explores other styles too: for example, that of the aging, bisexual, French Jewish actress Amalia X and her extroverted, crossdressing rival for women's attention, Lucienne de——. Distancing herself from masculine-style women, Amalia X contends that feminine-style female subjects of same-sex desire can build happy relationships, a view of which "Colette" is

5. Romaine Brooks. *La Venus triste* (*The Weeping Venus*), 1916–17. Musée Sainte-Croix, Poitiers, France. Collection, Musées de la Ville de Poitiers et de la Société des Antiquaires de l'Ouest. Photograph, all rights reserved, Musées de la Ville de Poitiers, Christian Vignaud.

skeptical. Amalia tells her: "A couple of women can live together a long time and be happy. But if one of the two women lets herself behave in the slightest like what I call a pseudo-man, then . . ." "Then the couple becomes unhappy?" "Not necessarily unhappy, but sad. . . ." "You see, when a woman remains a woman, she is a complete human being. She lacks nothing, even insofar as her *amie* is concerned. But if she ever gets it into her head [as occurred to Lucienne] to try to be a man, then she's grotesque" (107).[11]

Colette has to turn from contemporary Paris to another time and place in order to find examples of enduring sexual and emotional relationships between women free of any trace of masculinity. In the single chapter that does not deal with people she knows, Colette reviews the eighteenth-century journal of Lady Eleanor Butler and Miss Sarah Ponsonby, the legendary Ladies of Llangolen. Hall and Troubridge, more likely the latter, drew Colette's attention to this work.[12] In evoking the pair's "sentimental refuge" (115) in Wales, Colette offers a brilliant analysis of female romantic friendship (whether with a sexual component or not), which she describes in terms of the attraction of like to like, a characterization that would be carried forward fifty years later in lesbian-feminist efforts to recapture such ties, most notably in Lillian Faderman's classic study, *Surpassing the Love of Men* (1981).

Brooks figures prominently in the novel in the guise of the modernist painter Venetia Ford, who assumes a seductive role as Susan's artistic mentor. Ford and her work are ringers for Brooks and her paintings. Here biography and autobiography figure differently from what I have thus far described. Hall and Troubridge knew Brooks at the peak of her reputation in both Paris and London during the early 1920s. The knowingness about the expatriate American painter that Hall parades in *The Forge* accrues social and cultural capital to Hall while contributing to the work of mapping that I refer to above. Like Hall, the daughter of a disturbed, self-absorbed, and socially ambitious American woman, Brooks in her painting and photography materialized new possibilities for women with sexual and emotional ties to other women. This aspect of her work was widely recognized at the time.

The introduction of Venetia into the novel complicates its sexual politics, including the auto/biographical politics of Hall's de facto marriage. Since Troubridge and Brooks were also correspondents in the early 1920s and Brooks painted a well-known portrait of her in the year of publication of the novel (see Figure 10), there is also an element of triangulated personal rivalry. Given Hall's highly competitive attitude toward sexual (and here artistic) alter egos, Susan's resistance to Venetia's sexual overtures affords Hall a fictive triumph over Brooks as potential rival for Troubridge's desire, attention, and respect. In addition, Venetia's presence signals a much more specific and complex engagement on Hall's part with a cosmopolitan contemporary culture of female sexual dissidence than the Hilary-Susan narrative would otherwise permit.

In the first quarter of the twentieth century, Ford/Brooks played a major role in articulating new modes of female sexual dissidence in aesthetic, upper-middle, and upper-class Euro-American culture.[13] In her first solo exhibition at the prestigious Galeries Durand-Ruel in Paris in 1910, Brooks exhibited *Azalées Blanches* (*White Azaleas*), a large-scale painting of a female nude that challenged male conventions in the treatment of this subject.

In contrast to the ample curves of Francisco de Goya's *Naked Maja* (ca. 1799–1800) and Édouard Manet's modernizing revision of the female nude

6. Romaine Brooks. *Azalées Blanches* (*White Azaleas*), 1910. Smithsonian American Art Museum. Gift of the artist.

in *Olympia* (1863), Brooks's painting directs erotic attention toward a small-breasted, linear, and angular female body. Brooks, moreover, retains signs of adult female sexuality usually suppressed in high-art renditions of this subject. She writes: "I grasped every occasion no matter how small to assert my independence of views. I refused to accept slavish traditions in art, and, though aware it would shock, I insisted on marking the sex-triangles of all my female nude figures. The traditional depilatory effect shocked me, and I discarded it altogether."[14]

Manet had displaced the subject of the female nude from the usual mythological setting to the interior of a contemporary Parisian brothel, from which the figure gazes directly outward toward the viewer. In contrast, Brooks paints her model with a reserved gaze, directed aside, her head cast in non-naturalistic shadow as it lies propped against a large pillow that functions primarily as an abstract shape. The abstracting and reserving gestures make clear that this body belongs to its bearer, not to someone who can pay for it. At the same time, the subordination of the nude within the tonal range and the formal patterning chosen by the artist demonstrate that the most important presence here is that of the organizing talent. As Joe

Lucchesi observes, it is evident as well that the model was painted within Brooks's own domestic space (77). From the start of her career, Brooks was well known for her approach to interior design, exemplified in the interior of her apartment, which emphasized the blacks, grays, and muted hues that the dandy-aesthete James McNeill Whistler, her fellow expatriate American artist, preferred (Chadwick, 17). The Japanese prints on the wall behind the sofa pay homage to Whistler's use of similar motifs and tonality in his waterscape prints, drawings, and paintings. In male painting, portraits of the female nude within a brothel or the artist's studio suggested sexual access and control on the part of the painter. Female nudes, not to mention erotically charged ones, were not associated with painting by women or with female painters' studios (Lucchesi, 76). Accordingly, in its simultaneous claims to artistic modernity on the one hand and female physicality on the other hand, Brooks's painting blazons forth what Chadwick has described as a new aesthetic of "lesbian spectatorship" (21).

The nudes that Brooks painted following this work further signified the experimental personal relations that she and other members of Barney's circle embarked upon. Shortly after painting *White Azaleas*, for example, Brooks began affairs with the Italian dandy, aesthete, and poet Gabriele d'Annunzio and the Russian-Jewish dancer and actor Ida Rubinstein. Given d'Annunzio's interest in Rubinstein, the relation quickly triangulated, though, according to Brooks at least, Rubinstein did not succumb to the poet.[15] Personal experimentation, moreover, refracted back into and through art since both Brooks and Rubinstein adapted d'Annunzio's vision of the great artist as an exile of the spirit, calumniated by mere mortals. In 1911, d'Annunzio produced in Paris a *Gesamtkunstwerk*, *The Martyrdom of Saint Sebastian*, with a score by Debussy and with Rubinstein cross-dressed in the title role. D'Annunzio's Catholic religiosity is clearly anthropological, with Sebastian cast in the role of Adonis, the mythological figure who recalls beautiful young men (and women) sacrificed in rites of spring within archaic cultures.[16] One source of the lesbian archetype of the sacrificial artist that one finds in the auto/biography and artistic productions of Brooks, Hall, and Troubridge exists in this particular crossing of personal trajectories in the years before and after World War I.[17]

Rubinstein posed for two allegorical nude subjects painted by Brooks in 1911 and 1912, *Le Trajet* (*The Crossing*) and *Femme avec des fleurs* (*Spring*). These works further associate both painter and model with Decadence in the mode of the expressly female Symbolist and decadent aesthetic of Renée

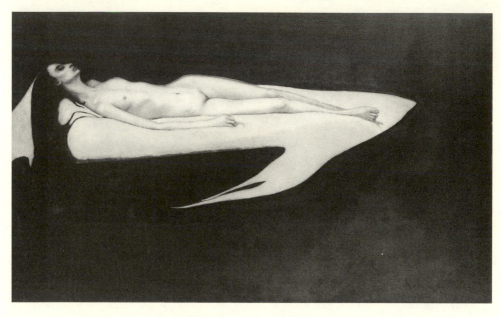

7. Romaine Brooks. *Le Trajet* (*The Crossing*), c. 1911. Smithsonian American Art Museum. Gift of the artist.

Vivien. This melancholic strain within an aesthetic characterized by female-female desire was implicitly religious, focusing on the need to escape from a hampering social and embodied existence. In Vivien, the tendency functions as both symptom and motive of her anorexia and attraction toward an early death.[18] In its self-conscious gynocentrism, however, Vivien's work participates in the utopian tendency within the Decadence, in her case projecting the creation of a new, exclusively female society.[19] Within the context of the Brooks-Rubinstein-d'Annunzio triangle, such images indicate the women's effort to carry d'Annunzio's masculist ideal of solitary genius into new gender and social territory. It should be kept in mind, however, that as the figure Adonis-Sebastian-Rubinstein-d'Annunzio suggests, for both the women and the Italian poet, aesthetic exceptionalism connoted androgyny or psychic hermaphrodeity. D'Annunzio, for example, distinguished between Brooks and his many other female lovers. "You're not," he said, "a woman" (Secrest, 244). But she was not a man either.

During her relationship with Rubinstein, Brooks began a yet more innovative series of private works in photographs of her lover taken in Brooks's studio, possibly in a single session sometime between 1911 and 1912 (Lucchesi, 80).[20] Rubinstein is an active participant, gradually removing her clothes in the face of the camera until she is clothed only in a headband and high, white, laced-up boots (Lucchesi, 81). Brooks photographed herself with portions of the allegorical portraits for which Rubinstein posed in the background.

In a later allegorical painting of Rubinstein, *La Venus triste* (*The Weeping Venus*) (1916–17), painted after their sexual relationship had ended, Brooks emphasizes the losses that she associates with intimacy between women. However, as in the heroic portrait of Rubinstein as a Red Cross nurse that Brooks painted in the opening year of World War I and that eventually won her membership in the French Legion of Honor, the self-abandonment suggested by this work pertains as well to the destruction of European culture, including its Aestheticist and Decadent legacy, in the war.

Whether out of this world a new and better one will emerge remains a major unanswered question within Brooks's aesthetic. In the self-portrait and in other works beginning with the 1914 portrait of Rubinstein, Brooks, in Chadwick's view, entered a new phase of her work, in which she elaborates an aesthetic based on female social, economic, intellectual, and sexual independence. Chadwick isolates two tendencies in these images of "heroic femininity" (14). First are images of women warriors, which eventually coalesce in a figure of the female Amazon, most memorably in *Miss Natalie Barney, "L'Amazone,"* Brooks's 1920 portrait of her friend and lover. The others are portraits of "the crossed-dressed androgynous woman" (31), such as the pianist Renata Borgatti and Elisabeth de Gramont, Duchesse de Clermont-Tonnerre, Brooks's successful rival for Barney's affection (Breeskin, 86).

Brooks's move away from portraiture in favor of pencil and paper in her surreal automatic drawings of the early 1930s indicates both the will to follow inspiration wherever it might lead as well as the relinquishing of public ambitions for her art. Nonetheless, a drawing such as *Breaking Apart* (1930–31), with its three figures that suggest variously a sexual triangle, a psychic splitting, and/or the break-up of a couple, evokes in a new way emotions invested in Brooks's paintings earlier. Beneath the comic surface of Hall's novel as well, one senses high psychic stakes and the stirrings of new erotic and social relations in the postwar period.

Book 1 of *The Forge* focuses on Hilary and Susan's comic misadventures as owners of a large home in rural Devon. The incidents parallel Hall and

8. Romaine Brooks. *La France Croisée* (*The Cross of France*), 1914. Smithsonian American Art Museum. Gift of the artist.

Una's experiences at Chip Chase, the home that Hall purchased for their use outside London in 1919. The couple follow in the footsteps of Hall and Troubridge when they tire of the country and move to a home in central London that proves too small.[21] Dissatisfied with the new house and bored with the smart set that they cultivate after returning to the city, in Book 2,

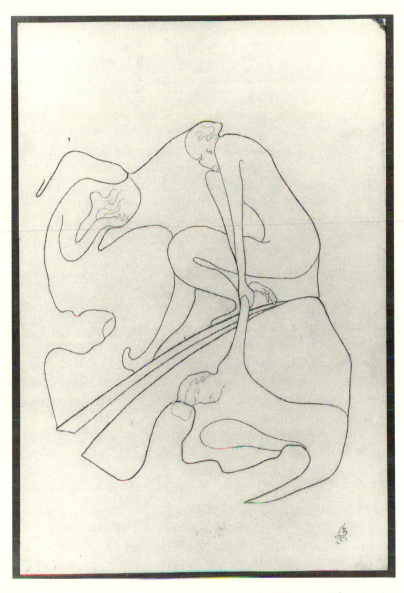

9. Romaine Brooks. *Casse en Deux* (*Breaking Apart*). 1930–34. Smithsonian American Art Museum. Gift of the artist.

Hilary and Susan decide to travel abroad. An extended stay in Paris permits Hall to begin to explore the sexual variety of life there. As often occurs in silent films of the 1920s, an extended cabaret scene permits a break away from the story toward vagaries of desire that more truly represent the interests of the author or filmmaker. In chapter 6, Victor Lumsden, an epicene older friend of Hilary, takes the couple to a fancy dress gala at the Bal Bullier. There, along with other gorgeous birds, what in the 1950s would be called a butch-femme couple enters the novel. Looking at the dance floor from a box in a balcony above, the Brents take in the scene: "Two women passed, dancing together. One of them wore the clothes of a Paris workman, corduroy trousers, and jacket and soft, peaked cap. Around her heavy, handsome throat she had knotted a red bandana. Her partner, a little wisp of a creature, grew tired and they stopped a moment to rest. Then, linking arms, they wandered off in the direction of the garden" (94).[22] Sitting in the next box, Susan notices a striking-looking Venetia Ford.

After being introduced, Susan and Hilary pay a visit to Venetia's studio that shocks Susan out of the torpor of her comfortable if confining bourgeois existence. The discovery that Venetia is the owner of a painting that Susan made in her student days brings back to life her ambition to do serious work. Simultaneously, she becomes aware of her discontent with playing the role of "Hilary's wife" (102). Following a parallel course, though, significantly, without an erotic spur for his restlessness, in Book 3, Hilary first attempts—unsuccessfully—to resume writing his novel, then decides that he needs to be free of domestic ties. At the end of Book 3, he and Susan discover that they share a similar sense of the need to free themselves from their life together. Hilary leaves England for Canada, and Susan leases a studio in Chelsea only to find that a studio of one's own does not an artist make.

The beginning of Book 4 finds Venetia in London, in part presumably to catch up with her new English protégé. Susan has admired Venetia from afar since her student days: "So that was Venetia Ford, the strange, erratic, brilliant genius of whom she had heard so much in the old days at the Slade." Grace Hill, "a fellow-student of hers, had known Venetia Ford in Paris, and the girl had fallen under the spell of this woman's charm, as did most people whom she admitted to her intimacy" (95). Susan has also been long aware that such intimacy tends to be sexual: "The girl had told her of innumerable and very ruthless love affairs, on which it was said that Venetia fed her genius" (96). When Venetia invites Susan into the elaborate boudoir of her London flat, the sexual implication is obvious. And when Venetia is inspired to begin painting, Susan is enlisted to help her find a studio. Once Venetia is ensconced, the seduction proceeds—through the paintbrush.

Venetia grants Susan what she permits few others: namely, the freedom of her studio while she is painting from a female model, presumably nude. Susan registers the scene: "Venetia was like a thing possessed, but all her movements were quiet. You felt the possession rather than saw it, it seemed to permeate the atmosphere. She worked with incredible swiftness and strength, there was never a stroke too much. Wherever her brush met her canvas the effect she desired was produced. No one spoke, the room was intensely still. Sometimes a brush clicked against the palette, the model sighed gently once or twice, but otherwise there was silence. In the midst of this silence Susan slipped away. She did not want to wait for the inevitable moment when Venetia would lay down her palette, she wanted to retain this first impression in all its splendid virility" (229). Susan returns home, then attacks one of her own uncompleted works, "dahlias, a turbulent mass of colour. Quietly and deliberately she picked up a knife and cut the canvas to pieces" (229).

This action is important in Hall's analysis of Susan/Una. Replaying the moment near the end of Wilde's *The Picture of Dorian Gray,* when Dorian uses a knife in an attempt to cut to pieces Basil Hallward's youthful portrait of him, Susan engages in a metaphoric act of *felo-de-se*. Her failure to remain true to the vocation of artist is figured by ambiguous reference to phallic objects: the apparently "good" phallus of the genius, Ford's, rampant Sapphism and virile paintbrush versus the "bad" phallus of Susan's knife, directed with self-disgust against Susan and her half-hearted artistic project. The juxtaposition of the visit to Ford's studio with Susan's behavior in her own suggests a parallel, at once like and unlike, between Freud's notion of the female masculinity complex[23] and what might be called a "virility" complex: a violent sense of inferiority directed by a talented, attractive young woman against herself because she has failed to develop her own virility, both sexually and artistically. In Hall's portrayal, a failed female virility can take the deformed shape of a masculine aggression whose prime object is oneself.[24]

The destructive impact of Susan's exposure to the full force of Venetia's genius is interrupted by a *deus ex machina* in the shape of a letter from Hilary informing Susan that he has decided to return home and wants to see her. Regaining her identification of self with Woman—that is, with her husband's idea of woman, Susan permits herself to be drawn back into her marriage. When Hilary tells Susan that he has been unable to be unfaithful while apart from her, Susan, as Hall puts it, listens "and smiled a little. But her face wore the large and tolerant expression that belongs to the givers of life" (242). Does this phrase suggest that Susan will attempt to lend meaning to her troubled married existence by becoming a mother? The identification of Susan with a naturalizing, even Darwinizing, definition of woman is by no means merely Hilary's. It is undersigned by the narrative voice, which says, Susan "stared at him helplessly. She was not Susan Brent, she was just plain and primitive woman. The stark femininity of all the ages looked out of her eyes into his at that moment" (239). This narrative voice might well be that of the author herself since it was a commonplace of both sexological and psychoanalytic thinking of the day that female sexual inverts were drawn to the sort of women who, if sufficiently attractive, would be desired by heterosexual men. As for what attracts Susan/Una, the description of Venetia's painterly attack specifies that it is a female artist's "virility."

Book 4 is the final and most significant as well as the most tantalizing and unfulfilled book of the novel. In addition to its exploration of female virility, Book 4 is also the one place in Hall's published work where she addresses the challenges posed for her by a self-consciously modernist aesthetic. Ford engages Susan in an extended discussion of the character of modern art. When critics today speak of lesbian Modernism, they usually have in mind the self-consciously experimental writing of such artists as two other expatriate American women in Paris in the 1920s, Djuna Barnes and Gertrude Stein. Brooks's Modernism was of an older kind, based in the nineteenth-century modernity of Manet, Whistler, and Edgar Degas, the last of whom died in 1917. As I mention above, however, Brooks's later Surrealist work indicates that she was prepared to innovate beyond the limits of her allegorical and portrait paintings. When Susan and Venetia meet in London in the final book of the novel, Hall takes the opportunity to explore Brooks's modernist aesthetic, which, it turns out, is surprisingly similar to that of Virginia Woolf. Although Susan, sans Hilary, is now free to paint, her work proves to be, as Venetia bluntly observes, "utterly dead" (216). Susan feels that the reason is a failure of self-expression, but Venetia counters that true art is impersonal, by which she means, as Woolf does, that it escapes the limits of its maker's biography and concerns. For example, in a diary entry of 1920 in which Woolf moves with great excitement toward the idea of writing her next novel in the mode of subjective narration known as indirect free discourse, she poses a question to herself. Can she write in a way that will "provide a wall for the book from oneself" without limiting point of view in the novel to that of a single character, an approach that Woolf finds, "as in Joyce and Richardson, narrowing and restricting"?[25]

For Venetia as for Woolf, impersonal does not mean objective or external. What is objectionable about self-expression in art is egoistic projection, not the consciousness of the artist. Venetia calls this consciousness "spirit," although it might also be termed *idea* as that term is understood within philosophical idealism: namely, the notion that human cognition is always based on the perception and understanding of reality as it is experienced within the mind of a particular individual. In Venetia's words, "It is not the subject of a picture that counts, it's the spirit of the subject that you must paint; and to find the spirit even in a blade of grass one must look with one's entire spirit. Art is the most exacting lover in the world, you can't give too much of yourself. If you don't find fulfilment in painting your flowers you mustn't blame the flowers, blame Susan. You're not really wholeheartedly in love with your art, you can't rise to complete self-abnegation" (216). This view of Brooks/Venetia has a theosophical tenor. Within theosophical thinking, ego, including gender identity and the particularity of individual objects, partakes of an ongoing vitality that exists independently of the mutable forms in which it is glimpsed. Artistic genius is the power of second sight that perceives this sustaining life. Absorption in oneself, another, or material things creates an insuperable obstacle in the path of the would-be artist. The reason for Susan's failure springs from the fact that, as Venetia says, "your allegiance is divided" (217).

For Woolf, the effort to achieve artistic impersonality implied the need to create a new kind of novel, which would no longer be tied to tracking the development of a single protagonist. Hall rarely speaks of Woolf, but *The Forge* refers implicitly to Woolf's experimental fiction, *Jacob's Room*, published a year before Hall wrote her own novel. At the outset, it looks as though *Jacob's Room* will be a bildungsroman, the life story of Jacob Flanders, a young boy to whom we are introduced in the opening chapter. Woolf, however, deliberately disassembles this familiar novelistic form. The Jacob drawn by the novel is never looked at from the inside. As the narrator observes at one piercing moment, "Why are we yet surprised in the window corner by a sudden vision that the young man in the chair is of all things in the world the most real, the most solid, the best known to us—why indeed? For the moment after we know nothing about him. Such is the manner of our seeing. Such the conditions of our love."[26] After Jacob leaves university and moves to London, his personal and working life becomes passive, fragmentary, and aimless. In the meantime, the narrator often leaves Jacob for long stretches as she explores the subjectivities of other Londoners, some of them not even mentioned by name and many of whom Jacob never meets. In its form, the novel plays with the idea that there is no limit or necessity as to which subjectivities a given work of fiction will explore.

In a telling moment within *The Forge*, Hall explores the notion of a novel without action, character, or even protagonist. She does so ironically through the difficulties that Hilary experiences in making the novel he is writing come right.

> The hero, a strong but sensitive man, was also intensely modern; his mentality, complicated by post-war conditions, was contradictory at times. But these very contradictions had originally been intended to bring out the author's skill. Hilary had decided to soar into fame on the strength of this one great character. Recently, however, the hero had struck, and now he refused to be strong; the worst of it was that he was not weak either, he was merely nothing at all. When flogged by his angry creator he lost all semblance of mental balance, and became such an incomprehensible hysteric that to reason with him was impossible. "I ought to dig him out of the book and send him to be psychoanalysed!" thought Hilary, with a flash of bitter humour.
>
> The heroine, who had begun life superbly as a deep-breasted, calm and statuesque woman, was showing a distressing inclination to be Susanish on every occasion. Minor characters either refused to fit in or struggled to usurp too much space. In fact, everyone and everything connected with the book appeared to be enleagued against him. (184–85)

Frustrated by his artistic "sterility," Hilary sets the novel aside.

Hall also flirts with the style of indirect free discourse that Woolf was moving toward. The most significant instance of this approach occurs at the end of Book 2, chapter 6, when Susan returns from the evening at the Bal Bullier. Realizing that her identity has been reduced to the role of wife, Susan regrets having lost contact with Grace Hill and the ambitions they shared while at art school. From this moment, the novel shifts; and—as occurs with the wife in Hilary's ultimately discarded manuscript—Susan becomes the center of interest. As in Woolf's and Hilary's novels, things seem to have a difficult time happening in *The Forge*. It could even be described as a novel in which nothing happens. Obviously bored and frustrated in their marriage and with no work to sustain them, Hilary and Susan are left in much the same position at the end of the novel as at its start. Nor does the knowledge that they consciously decide to stay together make much difference. The same pressures that led to their initial break-up continue to exist.

At the same time, Hall steps back from the ontological and epistemological radicalism of Woolf's novel. For example, Woolf emphasizes the fact that attempts to communicate in language rarely express what is on our minds, what we really feel, or what we really need and wish to communicate. She especially uses personal correspondence to make this point, beginning with a letter that Jacob's mother, a recent widow, is writing to her closest friend, a married man, on the opening page of the novel. In contrast, Hall uses letters twice to shift the course of the novel abruptly. Book 2, and with it the Brents' European tour, is brought to an end when Annie Paget, their house sitter, writes to report that Sieglinde has given birth to puppies after a hitherto unsuspected encounter with a neighbor's pet. And in the penultimate chapter of the novel, Susan's attention switches from Venetia to Hilary when he writes to say that "I have changed very much" (233) and appoints a time to see her.

In a novel focusing on a marriage gone "flat and stale"[27] between two attractive persons in their thirties, adultery is likely to appear on the menu. In *The Forge,* it is the wife, Susan, who comes closest to the act. Such a choice was topical at the time. For example, Maugham's successful West End play of 1926, *The Constant Wife*, focuses on a wronged wife's decision to invert the sexual double standard associated with conventional middle-class propriety. Constance Middleton, the wife of the title, avenges herself upon her unfaithful husband first by going to work to secure her financial self-sufficiency. Then, turning her new economic independence into the ground of a claim to "sexual independence" (84), she leaves to spend six weeks in Italy with a friend who has been in love with her for many years. Faced with the situation, her husband is forced either to accommodate his wife's decision or to lose both Constance and the comforts of home.

Adultery, however, is significant in its absence from Hall's novel. Hall substitutes Sieglinde's misdoings for erotic errancy on the part of her owners. By evading predictable infidelities, Hall is able to affirm marriage—even though the novel is about the impossibility of monogamy. She does so by means of the redundant maxim enunciated at the end of the novel: ties bind us, but life is impossible without them. Hence we agree to continue in relationships that hinder us from achieving our potential as individuals while simultaneously leaving us sexually unfulfilled. Hall's metaphorics of human bondage are repeated both in Maugham and in Colette, whose erotic ethic shapes, while being to a degree betrayed, in Hall's novel. *The Forge*, which echoes the title of Colette's novel *L'Entrave* [The Shackle] (1913) focuses on "Colette's abiding questions: Is there love without complete submission and loss of identity? Is freedom really worth the loneliness that pays for it?"[28] Colette's central insight is the temporary character of love and its incompatibility with desire: hence the title of *The Pure and the Impure*. While love may be pure, it is continually sacrificed to what in one place she calls "the Inexorable" and in another, "the senses" (24, 25). Colette characterizes love as "the pure and burning space that unites, better than the bonds of flesh, two perfect lovers" (28). This unity, however, yields to the desire for sexual mastery.

In one particular, Hall parts company with Colette. Colette sees love as an illusion subverted by desire; Hall sees it as an inescapable psychological reality. As Hilary says,

> Susan, of all the chains in the world the heaviest chain is love; it's so heavy that it almost breaks our hearts, and yet it's the easiest to carry. And because of that it's something deceptive, and we think it isn't there, we go away shouting out loud that we're free; but we've not gone far before we feel its weight, feel its intolerable tug. That's why I'm here, that's what happened to me, the chain grew taut and cut into me. The only way is to keep very close together, a slack chain doesn't hurt so much. . . .
>
> I couldn't get rid of you. I'd left your bodily presence behind, but I'd taken the thought of you with me. I couldn't finish my blessed book, I shall never try to finish it now. (241)

In this presentation, love is desexualized, and desire for the other is psychologized as personal dependence. The shift permits Hall to acknowledge the inescapability, for her, of intimacy between women while relegating to silence the ways in which desire exceeds the bonds of the couple.

Earlier in the book, Hall's description of *The Weeping Venus* indicates her identification of this condition with that of Woman—though by the end of the passage the figure has become crossgendered. Susan sees in the painting "not only the grief of a goddess, but the aching, poignant, exhausting grief of Woman throughout the ages" (106).

> The Venus lay on a sombre couch with a moonlit sky as background. One arm was flung above her head, the other dropped at her side. Susan got the impression of a body languid with too much pleasure, emaciated by too much suffering. Tears fell from under the closed eyelids, and the face seemed to hold the sorrows of all the world. The flesh of the limbs was luminously white; but Susan felt as she looked again that the glow did not come from the moonlight alone, but from something within the figure itself, something hidden, secret, and eternal. In spite of its subject, this picture was holy, and bore a strange likeness of holy things. Had Venetia Ford intended that her "Weeping Venus" should suggest a Pietà? (107)

The paragraph channels into English middlebrow literary culture the insight of Natalie Barney, who in her poem on the same painting, writes,

> Laid out as dead in moonlight shroud
> Beneath a derelict of cloud:
> A double wreckage safe from flight,
> High-caged as grief, in prisoned night—
> Unseeing eyes whose clustering tears
> Tell the pure crystal of her years.—
> No crown of thorns, no wounded side,
> Yet as the God-man crucified,
> Her body expiates the sin
> That love and life with her begin![29]

In her memoir of Hall, Troubridge eagerly lists details of *The Forge* that have correlatives in the couple's life.[30] But she suppresses major matters. For example, the crisis in Hilary and Susan's marriage registers with a new resonance when one learns, not from Troubridge but from her biographer, that Hall and Troubridge nearly broke up while living at Chip Chase.[31] The novel also hints at other complexities. For one thing, Hilary's inability to be unfaithful may comment on Hall's situation during these years. When with Batten, Hall had rebelled against monogamy. And in the 1930s, she would entangle herself, Troubridge, and a younger woman in a triangle that continued until Hall's death in 1943. But in the 1920s, Hall's unresolved guilt over the circumstances of Batten's death seems to have frozen her wandering libido, an effect reinforced by Troubridge's watchful eye.

While Hall may have been bound to Troubridge by love in 1924, she was also chained by the fact that she could not write without her. In the novel, Hall portrays Susan as unable and unwilling to give Hilary the practical assistance and moral support that he needs to write. In the memoir, Troubridge presents the reverse. Although she draws no explicit connection between *The Forge* and her account of her literary collaboration with Hall, Troubridge's extended discussion of this topic immediately follows her remarks on *The Forge*.[32] These pages provide an extended account of her part in Hall's writing. And while the full extent of that contribution never comes quite clear, it is evident that it was highly active. This reality was difficult for the two women to conceptualize since it contradicted their ideology, drawn in part from Brooks and d'Annunzio, of artistic genius as a solitary enterprise, albeit one sustained by occasional sexual liaisons.

Hall recognized that literary collaboration did not suffice to meet Troubridge's artistic and professional needs. Susan's anxiety over having failed to develop her potential as an artist and her guilt about having abandoned her artistic ambitions speak to Hall's sense of Troubridge's similar situation. Likewise, Susan's willingness to be absorbed by Venetia's "genius" repeats Troubridge's lifelong pattern of preferring to play satellite to a partner whose public role she could absorb herself into: first, her husband's position in the British Navy; subsequently, Hall's work as a writer and activist; and, after Hall's death, the remarkable talent and eventual international career of the young Italian bass Nicola Rossi-Lemeni (Baker, 355). Unlike Susan, however, Troubridge found other outlets. For example, she became one of Colette's best translators.[33]

These observations suggest how *The Forge* makes sense within the life itinerary of Hall and Troubridge. They also confirm the role that Philippe Lejeune, the theorist of autobiography, sees as that of the reader of autobiographical fiction. According to Lejeune, the view commonly expressed by writers that the novel is truer than autobiography is based on the assumption that fiction is in fact autobiographical: "The reader is thus invited to read novels not only as *fictions* referring to a truth of 'human nature,' but also as revealing *phantasms* of the individual."[34] Lejeune calls this relation "the phantasmatic pact" between reader, author, and fictional protagonist. In this chapter, I have augmented a reading of this sort with a cultural one. While *The Forge* may have been undertaken to meet the needs of a publisher, Hall took the opportunity to offer in it the fullest example she was to provide of her participation in the lesbian- and/or woman-centered culture that she found in the persons and work of such artists as Barney, Brooks, and Colette. In *The Forge*, auto/biographical fiction works as culture, opening English readers to the gynocentric project going forward in Paris and claiming space for a new mode of female writing.

6

Una Troubridge and Gender Performativity in *A Saturday Life*

This chapter begins and ends with a discussion of the reflexive relationship between Hall's next novel, *A Saturday Life* (1925), and emergent lesbian public culture. Beginning with a discussion of personal agency within the project of modernist self-fashioning, the chapter moves outward to consider how the novel is mediated by an unfolding culture of sexual dissidence: namely, the emergence of Noël Coward as a presence in West End theater in the early 1920s; the continuing impact of Colette's outspoken experiments in sexual self-figuration; and, finally, the material provided by a series of unpublished memoir-like essays written by Hall's partner, Una Troubridge. The trajectory of Hall's fictional biography of Sidonia Shore in *A Saturday Life* lines up with that of young Troubridge. Key aspects of Troubridge's life—the various arts in which she trained, her rejection of male mentors, her ambivalence about her failure to develop fully her potential as an artist, her bisexuality, her ambivalence about being a mother, and her highly self-conscious sense of gender performance—provide the novel with its thematics. The end of the chapter returns to the question of agency through an account of the reception of Hall's novel by a Sapphic readership.

As an adolescent student of art, Troubridge had been fascinated by gender masquerade both in West End theater and in her own experimental approach to dress. A self-blazoned female masculinity characterizes a number of contemporary visual representations, most notably Romaine Brooks's sympathetic but observant 1924 portrait. Brooks appears to have felt a close identification with the younger woman if one is to judge by the close relationship in pose, tonality, and gender-inflection between Brooks' self-portrait of a year earlier and the approach that she chose to take to Troubridge. Even the gesture of Brooks's gloved left hand resembles the torsion of Troubridge's bared right hand, firmly gripping with one finger a prize dachshund by the collar. Troubridge's challenging gaze, directed straight at the observer and monocled no less, declares her "out" inversion while her elongated slenderness suggests the tense sense of vulnerability that accompanies her bravado. At the same time, the eyebrow, arched in concern, and the pursed but slightly askew line of the lips suggests that the performance is not free of care.

Brooks imagines Troubridge as part of a couple, whose other half is slyly signified by the pair of dachshunds before her. The upturned gaze of the one that she holds onto suggests the control that she managed to exercise over Hall for nearly twenty years, while the other dog's lifted gaze, directed toward an object beyond the edge of the picture plane, suggests that Hall has not yet been completely subdued. Troubridge appears more directly as part of a couple in one of the plates prepared by Beresford Egan for *The Sink of Solitude*, a satirical pamphlet published in 1928 at the height of the controversy over *The Well of Loneliness*. In its title, *Similier Similibus*, the work invokes the notion of the attraction of like to like that was crucial to the telepathic model of Sapphic pair-bonding.[1] In this case, Egan satirizes a well-known 1927 photographic studio double portrait of Hall and Troubridge.[2] Hall stands, "unlit cigarette and monocle"[3] in hand, with gaze directed to the left beyond the edge of the photograph. She is dressed in a stock, upturned white collar, patterned smoking jacket, and straight skirt. Troubridge plays the part of a high femme. Her flowing, patterned dress spreads across a leopard skin laid on a divan as she sits, with gaze turned inward, facing away from Hall.

Egan, however, does not see a butch-femme couple in this pair. Rather, he sees two very different kinds of female masculinity. Reversing the position of the two women, Egan places "Hall" reclining on cushions and facing upward toward "Troubridge," who stands. Their linkage as a couple is

10. Romaine Brooks. *Una, Lady Troubridge*, 1924. Smithsonian American Art Museum. Gift of the artist.

11. Romaine Brooks. *Self-Portrait*, 1932. Smithsonian American Art Museum. Gift of the artist.

12. *Radclyffe Hall and Una Troubridge,* detail, 1927. Hulton Getty/Liaison Agency.

graphed by the arabesque line that joins their two outstretched cigarettes. (Troubridge has no cigarette in the photograph.) Hall's is a middle-aged boy/man/woman's face. The white shirt has become a flowing blouse. The stock too flows. And the side view of the trim thigh is attractive. The S-curve of "Troubridge's" jacket and tight skirt likewise suggests femininity, but her exaggerated bosom resembles a breastplate for Brünnhilde, a prosthetic substitute for female primary sexual characteristics. And her arms

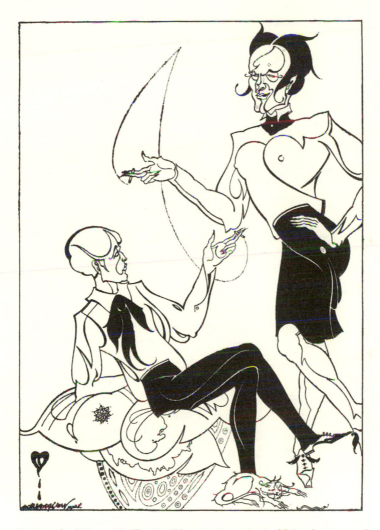

13. Beresford Egan. *Similier Similibus*. In Percy Reginald Stephensen et al.,
The Sink of Solitude. London: Hermes, 1928.

akimbo stance is anything but feminine. The face bears the mask of a
middle-aged male. Egan's reversal of the two women's positions and his
inversions suggest a difference between Hall's so to speak natural perversion and her partner's highly manipulated combination of conflicting semiotic signs. In psychoanalytic terms, Egan's "Troubridge" may be read as
an allegorical figure of Freud's concept of the female masculinity complex

discussed in Chapter 4 while "Hall" might figure what Hall regarded as female virility. Both Brooks's sympathetic fascination with Troubridge's masculinity and Egan's implicit negativity about Troubridge's performance of femininity are worth keeping in mind in reading this chapter, which emphasizes the reflections on performance and performativity that living with Troubridge prompted for Hall.

Hall wrote *A Saturday Life* at a time when her partnership with Troubridge appeared to be flourishing and when Hall was enjoying commercial and critical success as an author while surrounded by a friendly circle of literary collaborators. Talented female couples participated with Troubridge and Audrey Heath, Hall's literary agent, in "red-penciling" the manuscript of the novel.[4] Readers owe to this cooperation the economy of the book and its blithely Sapphic ending. One such pair was Rachel Barrett and her lover, Ida Wylie, a successful writer of fiction. Wylie was an outspoken feminist, suffragette, and Sapphist. Another friend was the novelist Vere Hutchinson. She and her partner, the illustrator Dorothy ("Budge") Burroughes-Burroughes, also lent a hand.[5] This mutually supportive environment accounts for the casual feminism of the novel and its direction from Sapphic perspectives.

During the period when Hall was writing the novel and preparing it for publication, Noël Coward was enjoying his first great success as a playwright and actor in London with *The Vortex* (1924), a *succès du scandale*.[6] Teddie Gerard, who replaced Gertrude Lawrence in the London run of Coward's earlier review, *London Calling!* (1923), was a close friend of Hall and Troubridge at the time.[7] The social exhilaration attending a string of contemporaneous early theatrical successes by Coward that starred acquaintances of Hall such as Tallulah Bankhead likewise contributes to the insouciant tenor of the novel.[8] The absence of plot, the shortage of conventional action, and the emphasis on dialogue share features of Coward's approach in early hits such as *Hay Fever* (1925).

As a Sapphic fiction, *A Saturday Life* has an oblique but powerful referent in the figure of Colette.[9] "Sido," Sidonia's nickname in the novel, was Colette's pet name for her mother. And "Mummy," Sidonia's epithet for her own mother, indexes the appearance of Colette in the guise of a revivified mummy in *Rêve d'Égypte*, a key moment both in the self-invention of Colette as an artistic celebrity and in the formation of early twentieth-century Sapphic public culture.

A Saturday Life focuses on the relations between three women: Sidonia; her mother, Lady Shore; and Frances Reide, a "happily unmarried," middle-aged woman who plays the role of mentor to the other two.[10] Although Mozartian in tone, the novel is shadowed by troubling suggestions of maternal indifference; by the implication of incestuous desire in Sidonia and her mother's triangulated emotional bonds with Frances; by feminine and feminist recoil against heterosexual marriage; and by repeatedly expressed concerns about how women's ambitions, capabilities, and education are shaped by men. The most prominent formal feature of the novel is Hall's use of the theosophical machinery of the "Saturday life" to structure the fictional biography of Sidonia. Readers of *The Well of Loneliness* tend to associate Hall with naturalistic conceptions of gender and sexuality. Naturalism, however, is only one component in Hall's outlook. In *A Saturday Life*, invocation of the theory of reincarnation provides her with a way to project the very different idea of gender and sexuality as performative. Sidonia's continual variability is key to her appeal. Nonetheless, while Hall portrays in Sidonia an ever-changing protagonist, basic questions concerning the conditions of personal agency hover around her performativity.

In the novel, performativity often looks like caprice or willfulness. These aspects of Sidonia's personality are contextualized in two conflicting ways. On the one hand, she is continually subjected to complaints by others that her behavior is egoistical. For example, Einar Jensen, her most influential artistic mentor, complains that her talent as a sculptor is limited by "in the end one sin, just only one sin—Self" (148). On the other hand, Jensen recognizes a contrary quality in her work, "genius": "To me it seems so strange that your work is what it is. Where do you get genius, all shut up as you are?" (148). Genius in this sense means what it does in the work of Frederic Myers, whose views helped motivate Hall's early efforts as a poet. To Myers, genius means the ability of the artist to draw upon unconscious mental processes in her work, a process that he also regards as analogous with the openness of the psyche to communications from the spirits of the deceased.[11] In a moral register, this permeability counters Sidonia's pride and self-love; in this way, openness to otherness enables performativity. But this capability exists in tension and conflict with Sidonia's ego-driven impulses and behavior.

The preoccupation with genius implies difficult questions about aesthetic form and agency. If the abrupt changes in direction that characterize Sidonia's early life result from the incursion of other selves into her ego, to what extent can she be said to be responsible for her actions or, indeed, to be capable of choice? And, without choice, what shape can fictional narrative in the form of biography take?—only the naturalistic one, powerfully traced by Hall in her first completed novel, *The Unlit Lamp*. Naturalism is never far from the lives portrayed in *A Saturday Life*, but Hall makes use of Theosophy to avoid producing a naturalist text.

As we will see later in the chapter when we consider readers' responses to the novel, the question of choice is an important one for a novel whose composition and circulation work to fashion a lesbian public culture. If, in the words of the correspondence of one reader, Grace Spencer, with Hall, her novels demonstrate that it is necessary to "act," what does *action* mean when the very possibility of self-directed action is put in question by the theosophical premise of *A Saturday Life*? Hall answers this question within the framework of popular speculative psychology. Female solidarity is enacted by means of telepathy, a belief in unmediated thinking with and as another that was axiomatic across the spectrum of such psychology, including Freudian psychoanalysis.[12] From this vantage, the chief value, personal and political, instanced by the novel is its performance of transparent communicability.

Sidonia's eccentric path can be understood in both psychological and sociological terms. Her inability to persevere in her artistic pursuits can be assigned to her upbringing as the spoiled child of a deceased father and a detached mother. Sidonia's willfulness in adolescence and early adulthood can likewise be attributed to her status as a trust-fund child, who comes into "a thousand a year, perhaps more," at the age of twenty-one.[13] And her inclination to believe in reincarnation is doubtless influenced by her parents' absorption in Egyptology. The novel itself poses, ironically and lightly but persistently, the possibility of understanding the action in terms of theosophical myth. The latter mode of explanation might account for the formal incongruities of the narrative. First of all, Sidonia, like the representations of vacant modern men that I describe in the preceding chapter, is undefined as a character. In this respect, the novel lacks action in the Aristotelian sense. Instead, from early childhood, Sidonia is successively possessed by a number of different artistic affinities and aspirations. For example, we first see her as a young child improvising a Greek dance. Her next phase is as a Classical pianist; next, she shows the aptitudes of a Renaissance or Rodinesque modeler of wax and clay, and, finally, she undergoes vocal training after learning that she has "a wonderful voice, a fine dramatic soprano" (185). With no prior training, Sidonia performs with virtuosity in all of these ways. However, in each instance, her passion and skill fade as quickly as they begin. In this way, the text experiments with the characterless, actionless form of the modern novel.[14]

Near the end of the novel, Frances finds "a queer old book one day in a second-hand bookshop" in Florence that seems to be "a kind of simple treatise on the different theories held in the East regarding re-incarnation" (212, 213). Glancing through it, she is surprised to find a chapter that appears to address Sidonia's situation:

> According to an Eastern tradition, whose origin is lost in antiquity, there are certain spirits who incarnate seven times only on Earth. The seventh incarnation of such a spirit is known as "The Final Path," but among those in the West who hold this theory it is sometime referred to as "The Saturday Life."
>
> People who are living a "Saturday Life" are said to have no new experiences, but to spend it entirely in a last rehearsal of experiences previously gained. They are said to exhibit remarkable talent for a number of different things; but since they have many memories to revive, they can never concentrate for long on one. (213)

Sidonia is both excited and relieved since, if valid, the theory, in her words, "would explain *me!*" (214). It would also relieve the guilt that she feels for having let down Jensen. Were this "theory" (215) to be true, it would also negate questions of individual agency, responsibility, and cause and effect for the "Saturday Lifer." In that case, as Frances says, Sidonia "would be something very like a convict, chained to . . . [her] previous experiences" (215). The end point of this notion of the interfusion of diverse egos is the same as that of the single individual caught in the toils of modern life in the novel of literary naturalism as criticized by such literary modernists as Virginia Woolf.[15] In both cases, fictional biography is the effect of something else, of the manifestation of prior selves in the present personality in one view, of sociobiological law in the other. Both approaches, the metaphysical and the materialistic, negate personal agency.

Readers today are likely to respond to the myth of a Saturday life with skepticism. It is worth keeping in mind, however, that Hall was attempting to formulate an understanding of psychology in vernacular terms for a female readership in the face of male authority and, in particular, of Freud's attempt to offer an exclusively oedipal analysis of female homosexuality.[16] At the same time, many of the axioms that she derived from her years of psychical research are shared with those from psychoanalysis.[17] For example, Freud too rejected the identification of the ego with the concept of the cogito. Two years before the publication of Hall's book, he wrote, "The character of the ego is a precipitate of abandoned object-cathexes and . . . it contains the history of those object-choices."[18] Both Hall and Freud believed in spectral inhabitants of the psyche.

Hall attempts to resolve the conundrum of agency by means of the modern—and modernist—theory of aesthetic impersonality that she had worked out in her preceding novel, *The Forge*.[19] For the painter, Venetia Ford, in that novel, subject and object in art and life are joined by their share in what Ford calls "spirit," something that grounds all forms of existence[20]—hence too the potential transparency of the relationship between art and its producer or between one mind and another. Just as Hall in 1906 had dedicated her first book of poetry to "MY INSPIRATION," she dedicates the new novel "to Myself" [*sic*], namely, to a self that is permeable to the experience of others. The reliance on the concept of telepathy in *A Saturday Life* likewise echoes the epigraph to the earlier work:

I know that through the waves of air,
Some part of all I feel for you,
Must surely travel swift and true,
Towards the heart for which I care
So dumbly, and before it lay
The words my lips shall never say.[21]

The myth of a Saturday life is only the most explicit form that theosophical thinking takes in the novel. Hall repeatedly turns to theosophical temporality in structuring the novel. For example, at the beginning of the novel, she uses theosophical suggestion in order to provide a Sapphic frame for the action. In this way, Theosophy, as in the lines of poetry quoted above, provides a structure for female-female desire. As I mention in Chapter 1, in addition to *The Forgotten Island* (1915), an imitation of Katherine Bradley and Edith Cooper's late Victorian literary impersonation of Sappho in *Long Ago* (1889), Hall in other poetry frequently fashions a Sapphic pastoral landscape. Writing under the pseudonym of Michael Field, Bradley and Cooper developed a phenomenology of woman's desire that is both homo- and hetero-erotic.[22] Hall adapts this structure in organizing her own novel, which begins in an equivocal Sapphic register, continues through Sidonia's adolescent fixation on Frances, then detours into a heterosexual episode before coming to a point of rest at the end of the novel by reestablishing Sidonia's tie with Frances on a more intimate and adult basis.

The novel begins with Hall's usual introduction of a slim-hipped, young heroine, in this case one whose untutored grace as a classical dancer "suggested something perfect in freedom, that belonged to the youth of the world" (10). Encouraged by Frances, Lady Shore accedes to Sidonia's wish to study dancing. As it happens, the Rose Valery School for dance that she attends is run by the spinster daughter of a clergyman, who indulges herself in the delusion that—like Sappho—she once lived as a courtesan and teacher of dance in ancient Greece. Valery lives in a third-floor flat in Fulham, decorated to look like a Grecian interior. In her account, Hall underscores the materialism of late Victorian popular belief in reincarnation. Valery's fantasy depends on the doubtful authenticity of a Greek lamp, which allegedly has triggered her memory of an earlier life: "'I *am* a Greek reincarnation,' she said doubtfully; 'I feel that I simply must be!'" (35). Valery's reliance on this material sign touches on the obsessive preoccupation within psychical research, including Hall's own, for physical evidence of the continuing existence of human personality after death. The text recognizes that such convictions are driven by subjective need—and this motive Hall rejects.

If the individual psyche does in fact manifest itself in selves that exist in various times and places, then these variations are liable to occur to or even to possess (220), in Frances's word, the present self. None of these selves are effects of her majesty, Ms. Ego. The multilived self is impersonal. For Hall, the notion of this variable selfhood is supplemented by the notion of material disability just as, in the early poem, "The Scar," she attributes her creativity as an artist to the "deep wound" of sexual inversion.[23] The idea that genius depends upon wounds, psychic and physical, is not uncommon, both in nineteenth-century Romanticism and in psychoanalytically inflected modern criticism, such as Edmund Wilson's use of Philoctetes as a type of the artist in *The Wound and the Bow* (1941). Feminist ideology of the early twentieth century endorsed the Freudian notion of activist and artistic sublimation.[24] Hall further links this complex of ideas with Theosophy and the possibility that the crossgendered bodily ego may be perfected as another self in a future incarnation.

Hall mythologizes herself as artist in the person of Jensen, whose work is by his own account "inferior" (149). Blocked in the creation of his art, he also suffers from the physical deformity of a crooked back, which he hopes he may be relieved of in a future life. Conversing with Sidonia, he says:

"What will happen when I die? Shall my back grow straight, you think?
That is what I ask the books—that, and other things."

"Then you believe in an after life?"

"Oh, yes, but I am certain."

"Why, mon maître?"

"I cannot tell you; myself has told myself." (149)

This "myself" is the same condition of selfhood to which Hall dedicates her novel.

In England in 1925, a well-known instance of short-lived versatility in an artist of apparent genius existed in Lord Berners, an avant-garde composer and ambivalent homosexual. Berners produced his final major work, a camp ballet entitled *The Triumph of Neptune,* to a scenario by Sir Sacheverell Sitwell, for Diaghilev's Ballets Russes in 1926, with choreography provided by the twenty-two-year-old George Balanchine. In February 1925, Virginia Woolf comments in her diary on how Berners described himself to her: "One day he wrote two [three actually and it is not clear they were his first] marches for fun. Stravinsky saw them, thought them good, and they were published. So he was accepted as a serious musician with only four lessons from [Sir Donald] Tovey in counterpoint. He had an astonishing facility. He could write things that sounded alright. Suddenly, last year, all his pleasure in it went. He met a painter, asked him how you paint; bought 'hogsheads'—(meant hogs' bristles) and canvas and copied an Italian picture, brilliantly, consummately, says Clive Bell. Has the same facility there: but it will come to nothing, he said, like the other."[25] Coward focuses on a similar flaw in Nicky Lancaster, the young male lead played by Coward in *The Vortex.*[26] Nicky is a classical pianist.[27] In Act 1, Helen and her friend "Pawnie," "an elderly maiden gentleman,"[28] anticipating the young man's arrival home after a year of study in Paris, discuss the progress—or lack thereof—that he has made while away. Pawnie complains that Nicky's playing is "erratic—one or two things perfect, but he's slovenly." Helen replies: "He only takes things seriously in spurts" (99).

In the play, Coward emphasizes sexual and gender fluidity in a trio of young characters. Later in the act, Nicky returns to his parents' home, followed shortly by his new fiancée, Bunty Mainwaring, "more attractive than pretty in a boyish sort of way" (122). Upon arriving, Bunty encounters an old flame, Tom Veryan,[29] young, athletic, and currently involved in an affair with Nicky's mother, Florence, a famous but fading beauty. Bunty's former attachment immediately throws cold water on the notion of her marrying Nicky:

> Tom: It seems so funny you being in love with that sort of chap.
> Bunty: What do you mean by "that sort of chap"?
> Tom: Oh—I don't know, that type seems so unlike you.
> Bunty: Type?
> Tom: Yes, you know—up in the air—effeminate.
> Bunty: You're more bucolic than you used to be, Tom.
> Tom: Here, I say . . . (127–28)

Perhaps Tom in the past has been not quite as straight as he now presents himself to be. Regardless, he succeeds in touching a nerve since Bunty has already told Nicky that he suffers from "hysteria" and "temperament" (125); meeting Tom, she tells him that her fiancé suffers from "nerves" (127).

Act 2 finds the characters translated to Florence's country home for a soggy summer weekend. On Saturday, Tom and Bunty rendezvous privately and renew their relationship. Characteristically, this key action, rather than being dramatized, is casually disclosed in conversation with Tom at the end of the act. Bunty, who in Paris had briefly broken from her philistine background, returns to normalcy now that she is in London and Tom has reappeared. Breaking off her engagement, Bunty echoes Tom's words when she says to Nick: "Well, we're not very suited to one another are we?" (146). To Tom, she observes that he and she are "reverting to type, don't you see?" (154).

With Florence and Nicky both abandoned by their lovers, Coward is in position to fashion a self-consciously modern psychoanalytic set piece in an Act 3 bedroom scene in which Nicky challenges his mother at long last to recognize the destructive effects of her narcissism. He argues that only in this way will it be possible for either of them to change; only in this way does he have any prospect of achieving an adult sexuality.[30] In *A Saturday Life*, the suggestion of incest is touched on intensely but with humor. In adolescence, Sidonia becomes passionately attached to Frances, her mentor at this stage of her life. Like Sappho's pupils, however, Sidonia moves on to marriage and maternity. The novel ends with the birth of her first son on Christmas Day. His given name will be Noel (319), an homage to the young playwright, who was born on December 16, 1899.

Sidonia's desire for a middle-aged woman is complicated by triangulation with Frances's doting regard for Sidonia's mother. At age seventeen, Sidonia tells Frances: "If you were a man I'd marry you" (104):

> "I ask you to kiss me and you won't!" she said furiously. "Oh, you! You're all mother's! Mother this, mother that! God! I'm sick of it! Don't I count at all?" She was childish now, stamping her foot. "What does mother need? Just a mummy, that's all; but I need someone real, I need *you*! Why can't I have you? Aren't I younger than mother? Aren't I attractive? Don't I interest you enough? Frances"—she began to speak softly now—"Frances, look at me! Don't you love me? Frances, *won't* you be my friend? All, *all* my friend? I don't want to marry anyone, I tell you; I just want to work and have you, all of you. Frances, mother would never miss you." (105)

The mummy referred to in the passage is the major archaeological find of Sidonia's father, Sir Godfrey, which, unfortunately, he may have misidentified. The word also signifies in another way: Sidonia implies that her mother wants Frances to be "a mummy," that is, a passive and asexual object to be possessed. In contrast, Sidonia desires an older woman as lover.

Lady Shore's penchant for a mummy obliquely references the mummy best known to Sapphists of Hall's generation: the one played by Colette in *Rêve d'Égypte*, a pantomime for two characters performed for one night only at the Moulin Rouge on January 3, 1907. Estranged from her husband, Colette took the role of a beautiful young mummy. Her protector and lover at the time, the crossdressing marquise, Mathilde de Morny, performed as the archaeologist who restores the mummy to life with a kiss, at which point Colette "comes back to life in a jeweled bra, slowly and seductively unwinds her transparent wrappings, and at the climax of the dance, passionately embraces the archeologist."[31] The performance caused a sensation, less because of the kiss exchanged between two women, since, as Michael Lucey points out, advertisements and articles in the press before the premiere capitalized on Sapphic titillation, than because the Moulin Rouge broke a taboo by reproducing the arms of the de Morny family in publicizing the performance. In protest, an aristocratic claque disrupted the premiere. But when the police ordered that a male actor replace the marquise at the second performance, another disturbance broke out as the audience clamored for de Morny's appearance.[32] Not intimidated, later that year, Colette appeared successfully in another pantomime, *La Chair*, in which she gained further notoriety in a scene in which an angry lover stripped off Colette's shift, thereby exposing her left breast.[33]

Implicit reference to *Rêve d'Égypte* in *A Saturday Life* suggests the power of crossgendered female-female desire, which motivates the main relationships in the novel while remaining confined within respectable contexts. Reference to the Colette–de Morny liaison suggests something of the subliminal character of Frances's appeal, at once masculine and feminine, maternal and phallic, to both Sidonia and her mother. Colette understood de Morny's gender-transgressive behavior primarily in psychoanalytic terms. She believed that de Morny's masculinity developed in response to her beloved mother's attraction to her faithless husband. To Colette, de Morny's femininity enacted the maternal devotion to young females that her mother had flamboyantly denied her. De Morny's phallicized sexuality expressed not masculine aggressiveness but feminine solicitude. As Colette recalls, "If the rocking of your arms doesn't suffice to calm me, your mouth will become fiercer, your hands more amorous, and you will grant me sensual pleasure like a form of succor, like a sovereign exorcism of the demons within me: fever, rage, uncertainty. . . . You will give me pleasure bending over me, your eyes full of maternal anxiety, you who seeks in your impassioned friend the child that you don't have" (quoted in Thurman, 160).

The framing of the novel with reference to the encrypted knowledge of the East is ambivalent. On the one hand, it provides a powerful cultural framework for the concept of reincarnation. Lady Shore and Sir Godfrey first meet Frances in Egypt, and it is Frances who finds the book of ancient wisdom at a stall in Florence. On the other hand, Sidonia's parents have fallen victim to the past: Lady Shore and "her frail, somewhat small Sir Godfrey, with his retrogressive yet adventurous mind, had turned, as it were by common consent, to the past for romance and freedom. They had sought among the ruins of a dead civilisation for the beauty they missed sub-consciously in their own" (12). Tellingly, Lady Shore remains captive throughout the novel to the task of producing her husband's biography.

When, in the final section of the book, Sidonia in her early twenties meets David, her future husband, she finds that he elicits a very different response than had Frances. After watching him play superbly at a polo match, Sidonia reflects: "She had found old Frances quite exciting, but that had been ages ago. In any case, none of those emotions had been the same; their quality had been different. What she had felt this afternoon was more humble yet more exalted; it had seemed to thrust her down and down, and then to sweep her triumphantly upwards" (247). The power that May Sinclair calls Freudian libido or "the Life-Force, the Will-to-live and to-make-live,"[34] quickly issues in marriage and then childbirth. As Sidonia declares to a dismayed Frances: "I've had no life until now. . . . David . . . *is* my career! The trouble is you've never been in love" (252, 253).

In *A Saturday Life*, however, maternity provides no reliable basis for female femininity. Not a gender naturalist, Frances warns Sidonia that her interest in marriage and family, far from revealing to her the meaning of womanhood, will likely prove to be yet one more passing phase. There are repeated reminders in the novel of Lady Shore's unsuitability as a mother, a deficiency that it is left to Frances to compensate for. During Sidonia's stay in Italy in her early twenties, however, she has seen a very different model of motherhood—and femininity—in the person of Liza Ferrari, the fecund, beautiful wife of Sidonia's vocal teacher. Going to stay at the Ferrari villa outside Florence, Sidonia abandons herself to what seems to be the altogether natural existence of the Ferrari household. Of Liza herself, Sidonia says: "She's like Ceres the Mother, she ought to have a sheaf of corn. I believe if she went out and smiled at the garden things would begin to bloom" (176–77). Perhaps it is her summer idyll with the Ferraris that gives Sidonia the idea of becoming a mother, since, before she meets them, she shows no interest in the opposite sex. Indeed, when David seeks Lady Shore's permission to propose to her daughter, she replies: "My dear young man, of course you may propose, but I don't think Sidonia likes men. She's got her career—" (249).

Young David, a Colonel Bogey in the making, believes that the career of "marriage" (250) will suit Sidonia just fine. But Hall suggests the fragility of marriage in her description of the wedding: "It was really a great and desperate adventure dressed up in ridiculous clothes; an adventure of the body, but also of the soul, an adventure concerning the ages that had gone, the ages that were yet to come" (263). The service itself is "all very neat, very British, very proper, in spite of the vicar's exhortations. It was all very like the cut of David's coat, irreproachable, expensive and good" (262). Cutting across this propriety, however, "through the stained glass windows came the sun, throwing shifting, harlequin patterns across the carpet in the chancel" (262). Harlequin, of course, is a figure of fun, folly, masquerade, and deception. "Harlequin patterns" suggest both the psychological perspectivism that undercuts the official meanings of public occasions and the vagaries of human desire that place lifelong commitments at hazard.

Frances's own psychic intimations involve masculine recollections of love for a mother and child:

> Pictures, quiet pictures vaguely tinged with sadness, hidden away in the deeps of Frances, drifting across her mind all unbidden, bringing a smile that was somehow not quite a smile to her hard-bitten, whimsical mouth. Pictures of things seen and half forgotten—sometimes of things imagined. Pictures of rooms looking out on old gardens; pictures of gardens folded up in twilight; pictures of evenings beside a pleasant log-fire; pictures of nights filled with soft, contented breathing; pictures of a woman with a child at her breast. Frances would smile and wonder where they came from, these pictures that belonged to somewhere and someone that had nothing to do with Frances Reide. Would wonder at the strength of the diaphanous things to stir in her a feeling of longing, a sudden discontent with . . . [her] little house in Young Street, a sudden rather fierce resentment against life, a vague, uncomprehending pity for herself, a desire to lift up her voice in protest and ask, "Why? Why? Why?"
>
> But Frances was not a dreamer, nor was she introspective, by choice at all events. (99–100)

In this passage, Frances has an experience of second sight that could explain her double gender to herself and, under other circumstances, enable her fully to live her female masculinity. Hall recalls the passage at the end of the novel, when Frances is with Sidonia and her new baby: "Frances' eyes filled with difficult tears, not because of Sidonia's 'Saturday Life,' but because of her beauty, lying there—a woman with a child at her breast" (319). As the narrator observes, however, Frances chooses *not* to see what otherwise she possibly might see. This double bind explains Frances's melancholy as it also explains her ability to love both Sidonia and her mother. Indeed, in the pages that describe how Frances and Lady Shore come to share their lives after Sidonia's marriage, Frances finds contentment and something close to happiness.

In the final words of the novel, Sidonia tells Frances that she believes her days of changeability are now over: "'I think it's over—I'm in my last act now, Frances.' She stared at the top of the baby's head. 'There can never be anything after him; he's an end in himself, he's *the* end. I've a feeling that it's always ended like this. And, you know, he was born on a Saturday too, the last day of the week'" (319). Florence demurs, suggesting that

Sidonia call him "Monday" instead. She remembers that already at age seven Sidonia showed a streak of pagan self-affirmation comparable with that of Colette. Inadvertently provoking a scandal, Sidonia had carried her naked dancing from home to Miss Valery's school.

Appositely, in *Les Vrilles de la vigne*, an early collection of vignettes, Colette says: "I want to do as I please. . . . I want to perform in pantomimes, even plays. I want to dance naked if a leotard bothers me or mars my figure." These, though, are the words of Colette as quoted by her dog, Toby-Chien, in "imaginary conversation" with her cat Kiki-la-Doucette. The citation offers one example of Colette's continual formal inventiveness in citing her "I" in quotation marks, a practice that Lucey suggests is "part of a project of impersonation—a project of taking up a person" that she uses in this and other books to permit her to assume "same-sex sexualities" and other differences for herself while remaining free to resituate herself in other vignettes. Colette's approach in *Les Vrilles* (a slang term for female subjects of same-sex desire)[35] is to "assign" minority sexualities "to a particular first-person figuration rather than" to assume them "in any definitive way." Key here, even more than sexual rebelliousness, is the insistence on individual choice, made present in the text by continual experiments in pronominal "self-figuration" (Lucey, 94, 100, 98). In her performances as dancer, painter, artist, Sapphic ephebe, married woman, and mother of a newborn infant, Sidonia too continually refigures herself. It is likely this project, broaching but likewise eluding specific sexual identification of the self, that captivated the novel's Sapphic readers.

In addition to Coward and Colette, Troubridge is another self-consciously experimental figure shaping *A Saturday Life*. The adaptation of material from Troubridge's unpublished essays in structuring the narrative complicates the novel generically by drawing it into the sphere of fictional biography. *Such Was Life* constitutes a kind of personal memoir in the form of short essays by Troubridge—a generic twist that recalls Colette's use of the same genre in structuring *Les Vrilles*. The title page of the typescript bears the following dedication: "FOR JOHN, Who made me write them."[36] Subsequently retitled *I Remember*, Troubridge added further topical essays to expand the series.[37]

Hall uses material from the essays in a number of different ways. For example, details of Sidonia's experience at dancing school recall aspects of Troubridge's account of her own school in "The Dancing." Like Sidonia, Troubridge in youth aspired to become an artist; like Sidonia too, her attention shifted from medium to medium. For example, at the early age of thirteen she passed "the stiff entrance examination"[38] and entered the Royal College of Art. Troubridge developed significant talent as a sculptor, most notably seen in a bust from the life of the bisexual, gender-crossing Russian dancer Vaslav Nijinsky, in the role of Debussy's faun.[39] In the novel, Sidonia eventually drops without explanation her work as a sculptor in order to pursue vocal lessons. Later in the same year in which she sculpted Nijinsky, Troubridge, a mezzo-soprano, debuted as a salon singer in a recital on Malta, where her husband was stationed (Ormrod, 30). Pleased with her reception, for the next several years, she "continued to nurture dreams of an operatic career" (54), another ambition shared with Sidonia and likewise relinquished.

The borrowing of such details is in itself incidental. There are, however, significant matters that Hall parses in the novel, one of them being Troubridge's disposable heterosexuality. One might almost read these essays without noticing that Troubridge had married, given birth to, and raised a child. In "Clothes," for example, she mentions in passing that she had "chosen for my husband a man old enough to be my father."[40] And in "Hero Worship," she writes, "It was after I had seen Mr. Fred Terry nineteen times in the *Scarlet Pimpernel*, and had wished my sixteen-year-old self nineteen times in the enviable position of Miss Julia Nielson as Lady Balkeney that I met Captain Troubridge, and married him, chiefly, it must be admitted, because I discerned in his snow-white hair and rather Terryish cast of countenance a likeness to the beloved and for ever unattainable Scarlet Pimpernel of my dreams."[41] The emphatic sense in the novel that there is no direct connection between being a mother and being suitable to play the role of one correlates with Troubridge's equivocal attitude toward the upbringing of her daughter, Andrea. Likewise, Sidonia's repeated acts of rebellion against male authority-figures in the world of art, especially Jensen, whom Hall models on Edouard Lanteri, Professor of Sculpture and Modelling at the Royal College of Art, points to a double bind faced by Troubridge and other promising young women between their own skills and aptitudes as artists and the efforts of gifted male instructors to shape them. In a long passage in "My Teachers," Troubridge writes of her and Lanteri's mutual dedication but also of her decision to drop him: "He did not live to be an old man or even to lose his striking and unusual good looks. . . . He died of influenza while I was still quite a young woman, but he lived long enough for me to disappoint him. He lived until I had added yet one more to his many disillusions. He lived to see me throw overboard with complete indifference the talent that he had nurtured and on which he had built such high and unselfish hopes."[42]

Although the essays that constitute *I Remember* are not chronologically continuous, two biographical emphases occur, both of which Hall draws on in *A Saturday Life*. The first is Troubridge's strong sense of sexual and gender performativity, which emerges in the essays on theater and dress, the latter of which she regarded as a mode of "playacting."[43] Photographs of Troubridge in the biographies show her attired in many different ways, often suggesting an element of gender-crossing, boyish, masculine, or butch. She regarded all of these modes, including high-style feminine, as forms of "masquerade."[44] These texts, however, also provide fragments of a very different life story, one of intermittent surges of female same-sex desire in the protagonist that can be pieced together so as to read *I Remember* as a coming-out narrative. For example, immediately before the passage describing her relationship to Lanteri is another, relating how Una developed a crush on an older girl in one of her art classes; this passage offers the first hint of Troubridge's attraction to other females.[45] The juxtaposition of these two passages suggests that it was perhaps this other desire that disinclined Troubridge from submitting to the role of Galatea to Lanteri's Pygmalion.

In contrast to *A Saturday Life*, which freely explores its protagonist's attractions, both same-sex and opposite, Troubridge denigrates heterosexual marriage and family while defensively effacing the decade-plus that she passed married to a man. In contrast, *I Remember* ends in the recreation of marriage and family in the realized friendship of her second and true marriage with Hall. In the final essay, "Christmasses" [*sic*], the feasts to be contrasted are those spent in the "Tyranny of Kinship" at the home of her sister-in-law versus "Christmas together with the dearest friend of all."[46] The typescript ends with Troubridge and Hall on Christmas stopping at a People's Restaurant in a distant part of London—where they were joined at table by "three strangers," all solitary. When one began to weep over his meal, Troubridge reached under the table to the hand of "Radclyffe Hall" for comfort in face of "the worst of all" Christmases, "Christmas Alone" (9, 10). The account is condescending to Hall's fellow diners and falsely humorous. Inadvertently, however, the incident may indicate what Troubridge feared most: isolation, penury, and the loss of her friend all together. This is the sole passage in *I Remember* where her friend's name, Radclyffe Hall, is given—handwritten into the typescript atop the crossed out phrase "the friend."

Hall's novel breaks off with an indeterminate, implicitly Sapphic ending. When Frances visits Sidonia and the baby, also at Christmas, Sidonia's

14. *A Saturday Life.* Notebook no. 1, cover. Radclyffe Hall collection, 8.3. Harry Ransom Humanities Research Center, University of Texas, Austin, Texas.

every comment to David is dismissive, irritable, or rude, hinting that Sidonia's adult heterosexual phase may be running its course. The last page of the novel finds Sidonia and Frances's close connection restored, only now the female couple has been endowed with a child to raise. The casualness of the ending is characteristic of Hall's general approach, whose tone is likewise suggested by a notebook that she chose for use in writing the novel. The notebook is a child's school exercise book, with a bright red cover and a drawing of a boy in a Buster Brown collar and a girl in a frock. The pair stand on either side of a globe, topped with a sailing ship and supported at bottom by a Tudor rose.[47] The iconography identifies the pair as young British subjects. On the inside of the cover, verso, are affectionate caricatures of Frances Reide and Sidonia.[48] In the drawing, Hall makes three attempts at Sidonia's profile. One is like a profile in a print by Hogarth or Rowlandson; another, with downturned mouth, suggests Sidonia's frustration and puzzlement as she is deserted in turn by each of her artistic inspirations. In the third and most defined profile, her eye is indicated by a cross (+), suggesting her blindness both to the future and to herself.

Above the drawings appears a handwritten sentence: "When he reads her poetry he doesn't know who she is because she has tried to submerge her personality:—But she knows Mark is the reader—."[49] In the completed novel, the adult Sidonia does not write poetry, and there is no character named Mark. Sidonia's effort to "submerge her personality" in her writing brings to mind Hall's modern ideal of aesthetic impersonality, though it also suggests other ways of looking at Sidonia from spiritualist or theosophical points of view. In her artistic vagaries and tendencies to pick up, then drop,

15. *A Saturday Life*. Notebook no. 1, inside cover, verso. Radclyffe Hall collection, 8.3. Harry Ransom Humanities Research Center, University of Texas, Austin, Texas.

friends and intimates, Sidonia perhaps channels other selves (or personalities) as a medium might in a trance. In a theosophical view, perhaps her present self is possessed for a time by other selves that she has been at other times and places. Sidonia's capacity for second sight, however, is much weaker than Frances's. Insofar as Sidonia shares characteristics with Troubridge, Hall may be commenting on her partner as a person of fluid and uncertain selfhood, gender, and genius. Ambiguous herself, in the quotation Sidonia makes a point of being ambiguous in her writing. As will become clear in a moment, the mysterious "Mark" referenced here resembles Troubridge in her function as literary collaborator, a role in which she submerged her personality in the joint performance of Hall's literary genius.

Finally, the sentence suggests a practice of double writing. One is for a potential reader who will be unable to see beyond the mask of impersonality in the poetic text; the second writing, however, is directed to a reader who is envisaged, even *mark*ed, in the text. This double direction can be associated with another sentence, this one scrawled in a flyleaf of the notebook in Box 8, Folder 2. Scribbled in pencil, it precedes the final chapter of Hall's incomplete novel, *The Cunningham Code*, but appears to date from the time of composition of *A Saturday Life*: "Let us tread delicately through the morass of ambiguity, lest they presume to understand us!"[50] This sentence comments on the way in which highly naturalized notions of selfhood, sexuality, and gender are casually but continually undercut in the novel. "They" signifies a world indifferent or hostile to "us," that is, to Hall and Troubridge, to the sexually flexible Sidonia, and to a celibate invert such as Reide.

Leaving aside for now the question of autobiographical reference, who is the "Mark" who will read Sidonia's poetry? Hall provides an answer to this question in the outline of Sidonia's life after marriage written on the first page, recto, of the notebook in folder 3. Readers of the novel have wondered what happens to Sidonia after the birth of her baby and the reestablishment of her friendship with Frances. The outline gives the ages at which Sidonia pursues her various crazes.[51] It also reports that Sidonia's husband and child both die in 1917, killed in World War I. The following year Sidonia joins an ambulance unit on the front. Sidonia marries a second time to a man named Mark, "who helps her at arms [*sic*] length" in her writing (her "inspiration" is "not good enough") until a son is born. In the two final lines on the page, Hall writes a direction to herself: "Leave her—," a good idea since the action indicated in the outline is now repeating itself. Hall risks falling into her chief shortcoming as a novelist, namely, the tendency to write her novels in the form of fictional biographies with protagonists whose life stories have long, unaccentuated middles followed by abrupt endings. It is likely that Heath, Troubridge, and the manuscript's other readers suggested to Hall that she end it where she did. The resulting suspension of the action works perfectly, bringing back into balance the Frances-Sidonia relationship, which provides the novel's main affective thread. It also provides an ending at once radical and traditional, even Victorian, with its establishment of a domestic triad of two women and son.[52]

The feminine/feminist/Sapphic politics of Hall's novel, shaped by the women who helped her fashion the book, communicated with immediacy to receptive readers, among them Grace Spencer. Cline speaks of Spencer as one of a group of women who began writing fan mail to Hall following the critical and commercial success of her next novel, *Adam's Breed* (1926).[53] Spencer found it easy to locate herself affectively in the tie between Hall's boyish female heroines and the celibate middle-aged women who could fall in love with one of them. In one of her letters, Spencer cites characters from three of Hall's pre-*Well* novels: Joan Ogden the protagonist of *The Unlit Lamp*, who sacrifices her desires for independence, work as a professional, and life with Elizabeth Rodney to the selfish demands of her mother;[54] Sidonia Shore and Frances Reide; and Gian-Luca, the feminine man, too sensitive to survive in a postwar world, who is the questing protagonist of *Adam's Breed*. Spencer wrote to Hall:

> May a friend of Joan, & Frances, & Gian-Luca write to thank you, even at this late hour, for all that your books have meant to her since the "Unlit Lamp" was first published?
>
> They are old friends now; they have been read & re-read, but always with an uneasy sense of a debt unpaid—a great gift for which I have never thanked the giver. You must have had so many grateful letters, & I have hesitated to add to their number. . . .
>
> The reading of each book left me all aglow with appreciation, & criticisms, & questions as to the ultimate destiny of certain characters—; bitter deprecation of Joan's final self-immolation—(did her crushed & defeated personality ever revive again?)—doubts of the placid life of motherhood in which you leave Sidonia—surely only another of many succeeding & fresh adventures of her temperament? Above all, *great* delight in Frances. Frances should be the patron saint of all us happily unmarried women!—wise, gallant, full of that detached and dry humour which can transform life and keep alive the spirit of adventure.[55]

Spencer sounds like a celibate female homosexual with an observantly skeptical view of the heterosexual institution of marriage.

The lesbian subtext becomes more evident in the next paragraph, in part vectored through a passion for the protection of animals, in this case the blind pit ponies of the British coal-mining industry, thought of whom distresses Gian-Luca in his final days wandering in the New Forest:

> We cannot have enough of such books as the "Saturday Life"—That delicate & discerning humour which you can give is so rare in modern literature, and so badly needed. Humour & imagination—isn't lack of imagination at the root of all that cruelty of which you write in "Adam's Breed"? One can scarcely bear to read—it has haunted me continually, especially perhaps in the case of the pit ponies—; but how can one help? Grief over such wrongs is mere waste unless one can *act*, and yet I fear only the great tide of public opinion can alter things. Surely it will come, one day; but how one longs to hasten it by personal effort. Your pen will do great service; but what can the rest of us do?[56]

Hall's novels bring the question of the fate of her crossgendered protagonists very much to Spencer's attention. Spencer realizes that what is in question is the need to "*act*"—although in the letter the question gets displaced onto Hall's interventions on behalf of the ponies.[57] Spencer laments that, not being a writer or public speaker as Hall is, she herself can do nothing. The letter points in two directions: toward the facilitation of Hall as an activist and consciousness-raiser and Spencer's hope, implicit as well in the ending of *A Saturday Life*, that women will be able to live beyond marriage and motherhood as currently defined, indeed will learn fully to express their love of one another. For a reader like Spencer, the greatest attribute of Hall's novel was its communicability. This cognitive and affective immediacy brought into focus the very topic about which Hall's novel is persistently ambiguous: namely, the capacity for misfit individuals to achieve both a shared intimacy and a capacity to change the world in which they live.

7

Catholicism, *Adam's Breed*, and the Sacred *Well*

The following two chapters focus in whole or in part on *The Well of Loneliness*. In Chapter 8, I consider how the topic of female same-sex marriage emerged as a focus of discussion in litigation attending publication of the novel. Further, I extend the discussion to other writing—male and female, public and private—at the time, which indicates that Hall's effort was part of a wider attempt by homosexuals between the world wars to invent appropriate interpersonal forms for homosexual existence. The present chapter approaches *The Well of Loneliness* as a sacred text. The religious character of the novel has connections with the issues addressed in Chapter 8: for example, the Roman Catholic Church's condemnation of divorce determined Troubridge and Hall's endorsement of female monogamy, as did the perception within the Church of the character of marriage as a sacrament. Nonetheless, the two approaches proceed along different lines. Chapter 7 begins with a brief discussion of how the attraction of male and female Aesthetes to Catholicism helped Hall find her own way there. More broadly, I place homosexual conversions to Roman Catholicism within the context of a tacit struggle to modernize the pastoral practice of the Church in the light of contemporary science. Before turning to *The Well of Loneliness*, I also consider another sacrament, Holy Communion, as it is figured within *Adam's Breed*, the most explicitly Catholic of Hall's novels and the one whose publication immediately preceded that of *The Well*.[1]

In recent years, a number of young scholars have argued that Catholic theology, iconography, ritual, and devotion provided a space in which late Victorian and early modernist sexual dissidents could imagine themselves, so to speak, into existence.[2] This religious discourse of sexual difference stands in complex, ambivalent, often resistant relationship to sexological discourse. Chronologically, it can precede, parallel, dialogue with, and contest the truths of emergent sexology. In this chapter, it will be seen in all these relations. The religious material is both Anglo- and Roman Catholic, in part Marian, in part focused on the Passion, Crucifixion, death, and Resurrection of Jesus Christ. The cup into which, in some illustrations, his blood is caught is also the chalice of the celebration of the Communion of the Mass. In orthodox Roman Catholic belief, the sacrament of the Holy Eucharist depends on the paradoxical belief that matter can be transformed into something else while retaining its ordinary appearance. This paradox is central as well to romantic love: the notion that what is bodily, even insistently so, can signify transcendence.

The masterpiece of this literature is *De Profundis*, Oscar Wilde's letter from prison. Readers today know the work in bifurcated form. It begins with a long screed in the form of a letter to Lord Alfred Douglas, the young companion and lover who drew Wilde toward and then over the brink into public scandal.[3] In the second half, the writer fashions a portrait of himself as a Christlike icon of the Romantic artist. In order to avoid prosecution for libel in 1905, the editor of the first edition excised the portions of the work that link it directly with Douglas. Hall likely read this version at the time of publication since its conflation of sexual dissidence, social nonconformity, artistic self-assertion, and a highly personal identification with Christ complemented her own psychology. Likewise, a letter, posthumously published in 1908, in which Wilde includes an apology for the work, accords with Hall's attitude in her poetry of that date. In the letter, Wilde writes: "I do not defend my conduct, I explain it."[4]

A generation later, Wilde was still functioning as an alter ego of Hall. On the eve of publication of *The Well of Loneliness*, she had Troubridge reread Wilde's work to her. Interestingly, Baker reports that Troubridge read the first half of the work, which did not become generally available in English until publication in full in 1949 following Douglas's death.[5] If Baker is correct, Troubridge must have been reading either from a transcription of the extensive reporting of *The Times* on this part of the typescript when it was read aloud as part of a libel trial in London in April 1913 or from one of the sixteen complete copies of the work published in the United States later that year for copyright purposes (Wilde, 94). In the latter case, access to this material indicates that Hall enjoyed entrée to Wilde's circle a generation after his death. In *De Profundis*, Catholic rhetoric exists within a composite discourse, at once religious, sexual, and aesthetic. Wilde celebrates the crucified Christ as the supreme example of the artist.

In London in the late nineteenth century and among circles of Oxford graduates and undergraduates, the rejection of marriage as a prescribed duty and the affirmation of emotional and at times sexual relations between males often coexisted with religious devotion—with an attraction to the perverse gorgeousness that these men found in Roman Catholic display, manifest, for example, in the baroque modernity of the Brompton Oratory or in a number of High Anglican congregations in London.[6] This correlation did not escape the attention of authorities within either church. In addition to tension and conflict, however, the situation also called for a measure of tolerance, especially within Anglo-Catholicism. For example, John Bloxam, who wrote a notorious fictional apology for pederastic love while an undergraduate at Oxford in the 1890s, nonetheless was accepted into the Anglican priesthood.[7] Hall herself became a devout albeit at times embattled Roman Catholic. And Wilde, who in youth was undecided as to whether to travel to Rome or to Greece, became a deathbed convert to Roman Catholicism. Both Wilde and Hall were devoted to the figure of Christ *in extremis*.[8] This absorption in the Passion of Christ suggests yet one more ground for the linkage between religion and sexual dissidence. The suffering of Christ provides a context for experiencing, troping, and narrativizing the negativities, psychic and social, that accompanied nonconformity for these individuals.

Wilde and Hall were linked in their heretical response to traditional moral and religious condemnations of sexual and emotional ties between members of the same sex.[9] In this stance, important resources were available in the life and writing of John Henry Newman and, later, the Jesuit theologian George Tyrrell. As converts, both provided a bridge between Anglicanism and Roman Catholicism. Newman's "perversion" to Catholicism in 1845 provoked scandal at Oxford and more largely in England, but his promotion to the rank of cardinal in 1879 and his role as the leading anglophone Catholic intellectual helped make Roman Catholicism respectable, even fashionable. Newman's long, intense, but celibate friendship with a fellow priest, Ambrose St. John (the two men are buried in the same grave), likewise served to make him a memorable figure to such individuals as Wilde and Hall.[10] In 1876, one year after St. John's death, Newman wrote in a note to the executors of his will: "I wish, with all my heart, to be buried in Fr Ambrose St John's grave—and I give this as my last, my imperative will" (Bray, 291). The instruction was published in 1893.

The Church's teachings on sexual morality became entangled in the second half of the nineteenth century with its condemnation of what it called Modernism: that is, the application of reason and, in particular, the methods of modern science in areas of faith, doctrine, and moral teaching. Newman was inclined to resist overreaching by the Vatican on matters having to do with what he refers to as "Nature." In response to the publication of the *Syllabus of Errors* and other anti-liberal, anti-modernist papal documents of the 1860s, for example, he wrote: "The Pope, who comes of Revelation, has no jurisdiction over Nature."[11] In a late nineteenth-century context, in which same-sex desire became a major topic of scientific inquiry, Newman's view had important implications for the position of subjects of same-sex desire. Later in the century, the research of such pioneering sexologists as Richard von Krafft-Ebing caused them to call into question the traditional view that sexual and emotional ties between members of the same sex were unnatural.[12] In other words, the very meaning of the terms *nature* and *human nature* were in flux in scientific thought by 1890.

The conversions of Wilde and Hall to Roman Catholicism owe a great deal to the special character that Newman imparted to English Catholicism. In particular, in responding to Prime Minister William Gladstone's contention in a pamphlet of 1874 that extensions of papal authority threatened to undermine British citizenship, Newman brought to bear an acknowledgedly Protestant conviction of the primacy of human conscience in ordinary matters. Newman conceptualizes conscience as "the voice of God in the nature and heart of man, as distinct from the voice of Revelation"; conscience functions as "the internal witness of both the existence and the law of God" (128). As for natural law, Newman defines it as the "ethical" relation of God to himself, that is, the dynamic play of "the attributes of justice, truth, wisdom, sanctity, benevolence, and mercy" in the divine mind (127). In a presentation of conscience that echoes Coleridge's description of primary imagination in chapter 13 of *Biographia Literaria*, Newman describes conscience as recognizing and practicing these relations within the human mind. In this way, Newman draws the experience of God into human interiority in complex, subtle, and intimate fashion.

Drawing on the medieval theologian Thomas Aquinas, Newman argues that judgments of conscience pertain to the here and now (*hic et nunc*), a sphere in which the pope is not infallible (134). The citizen's ultimate responsibility is neither to religious nor to secular authority but to individual conscience (129). One owes "obedience" (127) to one's conscience, even when doing so puts one at odds with papal teaching on particular matters: "Conscience being a practical dictate, a collision is possible between it and the Pope's authority only when the Pope legislates, or gives particular orders, and the like. But a Pope is not infallible in his laws, nor in his commands, nor in his acts of state, nor in his administration, nor in his public policy" (134). Quoting another Catholic theologian, Newman argues that even in specific reference to religion, a heretic is justified in maintaining his belief "as long as he judges his sect to be more or equally deserving of belief" as the Church (137). Newman's outspoken defense of conscience strengthened the will of sexual heretics while persuading them that there might be room for them within the Church.[13] At the same time, Newman's endorsement of "reserve," his term for tact exercised to avoid scandalizing those less knowing,[14] suggested a style of deportment to be adopted by sexual inverts among the faithful.

The Modernism debate within Roman Catholicism intersects with the question of sexual inversion in the moral theology of George Tyrrell, born nineteen years before Hall and converted to Catholicism the year before her birth. Tyrrell's insistence on the evolution of dogma and the moral teaching of the Church led to his dismissal from the Jesuits in 1905. His view that Catholic belief develops in the individual and shared lives of members of the Church Militant opens a window onto the dual practice of intimacy and faith that Hall and her partners chose to undertake: "To believe in the living historical Catholic community means to believe that by its corporate life and labour it is slowly realizing the ideas and ends in whose service it was founded; that through many fluctuations and errors, . . . it is gradually shaping itself into a more efficient institution for the spiritual and moral development of individuals and societies; that by its continuity and extension it is the collective subject of a vast experience of good and evil, truth and fallacy, and of a slow but sure process of reflection on the same."[15]

In 1907, Tyrrell was excommunicated from the Church as a result of publishing two articles criticizing *Pascendi dominici gregis* (1907), an encyclical of Pope Pius X, in which the pope condemned modernist tendencies within the Church. Before Tyrrell's dismissal, both in work published for limited circulation and in private correspondence with Marc Andre Raffalovich, a Roman Catholic convert from Judaism who had written an important apology on behalf of celibate male homosexuality,[16] Tyrrell argued that same-sex love and attraction do not differ in character from marital love and that both are natural to the species. Tyrrell viewed marriage not through the biological lens of reproduction but through the cultural and philosophical prism of "friendship," a term traditionally more prominent in consideration of same- rather than opposite-sex relations. Of the love of a "human being for a human being" that constitutes the marital tie, Tyrrell wrote, "That an almost similar affection may exist between those of the same sex is obvious. . . . [Even] in its lowest form it is not sexual or unnatural."[17]

Thus far I have emphasized Hall's connection with male tradition, but her Catholic experiment finds another modernist point of reference in the life and work of women, in particular the poetic duo of Katherine Bradley and Edith Cooper, who wrote under the name of Michael Field, and the feminist anthropologist Jane Harrison and Hope Mirrlees, her student and eventual life partner.[18] When Bradley and Cooper converted to Roman Catholicism in 1907, they chose to become celibate; but in the sensual devotional poetry that they subsequently published, they conflate Dionysus, whom they had celebrated in their previous pagan phase, with Christ, their new hero, in tropes of bloody sacrifice and communion. As Camille Cauti has observed, this convergence of Classical with Christian iconology makes their late devotional poetry Decadent. Field's aesthetic "conversion," however, also has a basis in Victorian science in the couple's familiarity with the exploration of fertility rituals in James Frazer's *The Golden Bough* (1890). While Frazer's study in comparative mythography is secular and rationalizing in character, the atavistic sacrifice of a young male divinity did not necessarily negate the sacred character of Christ's Passion, death, and Resurrection. Cooper, for example, writes, "Fraser's [*sic*] book prepared my mind for this pure subsuming of sacrificed divinities under the one divine sacrifice."[19] This sacrifice, moreover, is equally that of a "human being for a human being." In considering the abandonment of self that one encounters in all three of the main protagonists of Hall's religious novels, it is worth keeping in mind that the creatural and the divine meet for her in these acts of self-loss.

In the Victorian period, renewed interest in medieval Catholicism provided men and women with a body-centered, gender-crossing rhetoric of ecstasis and conversion that moved far beyond conventional ideas of gender and sexual roles.[20] At the turn of the twentieth century, the gender-crossing aspects of Marian and Christic devotion are further accentuated by the association of both figures with the Eniautos-Daimon or year spirit.[21] Field's devotional poetry is often more erotic than their earlier work, while their Christ is highly feminized, the wound in his side a fertile flower. In one poem, Mary is seen as even more important than Christ since she is his generator.

"I, if I be lifted up,
Will draw all men unto me!"
Mary did not thus agree—
Mary opened a flower-cup.

Mary doth herself uplift—
And God looketh on His rose,
As the lovely leaves unclose,
Lo, God giveth unto sinners shrift.[22]

In such aggrandizement, one senses reference to the Great Goddess, mother of Dionysus.[23] During World War I, Harrison was scandalized by the retreat of Cambridge academics into a Protestant patriotic jingoism. She riposted in a short essay in the *Classical Review*, in which she identified John the Baptist with the Winter daimon and Salome with the Spring daimon. The article provoked a reaction.[24] As in Field and Frazer, moreover, the daimon could be crossgendered. In the essay, Harrison references from Russian folk mythology Yarilo, "the Spring-god, or goddess," a figure "of shifting sex—like so many daimons."[25]

Wilde's Classical ideal combines individual self-harmony, faculties, expressions, and a balance of physical, mental, and emotional needs, with social harmony based on economic justice. The ideal was articulated primarily in "Art,"[26] the leading type being the idealized male nude of Greek sculpture, a form emphasizing physical beauty, organic life, and symmetrical form. At Oxford, however, debate existed about the character of Greek aesthetics. For example, Walter Pater and A. C. Swinburne, who celebrated both Apollo and Dionysus, were aware of the place of violence, pain, and sacrifice in Greek religion.[27] Had they read Nietzsche, they would have agreed with him about the tragic character of Greek culture, and they would have agreed with his comment that "we are to regard the state of individuation as the origin and primal cause of all suffering, as something objectionable in itself."[28] Objectionable, but also necessary.

In Greek sculpture, social and self-harmony is imaged in an intact bodily contour. In the Christian image of Christ's Passion and Crucifixion, the body is violated by wounds and the loss of bodily fluids: blood, water, sweat, and tears. As Mary Douglas has argued, the emission of bodily fluids signifies impurity, pollution, a threat to personal and social integrity.[29] The abjected body of Christ becomes the preferred trope of the romantic cultural ideal that Wilde presents in *De Profundis*. Wilde comments that "we can discern in Christ that close union of personality with perfection which forms the real distinction between the classical and romantic movement in life."[30] *Personality* is a technical term in Wilde that refers to the multiform possibilities of individual development. In other words, personality is the principle of individuation within human beings. It can also be described as the motivating force of speciation. The word *perfection* refers to Christ's divinity. The combination of the two refers to the Christian doctrine of the Incarnation, the belief that Christ incarnates in his body both a human being and God. "Before his time there had been gods and men, and, feeling through the mysticism of sympathy that in himself each had been made incarnate, he calls himself the Son of the one or the Son of the other, according to his mood" (166). Unlike the Greek ideal, however, the image of this composite human/divine being is dis-integral, the body dissolving into fluids in the sight of the devout. The unification of human with divine being in Christ combines the most humble and material aspects of existence with the most transcendent. The attempt to achieve such a union is bound to include disequilibrium, incongruity, possibly the grotesque, pain, suffering, and death. Another way of describing the difference between the two ideals is to say that one operates within the terms of beauty, the other within those of the sublime. There is no harmonious way of incorporating human with divine existence. Or, rather, although artists make such an attempt in images of the Resurrected Christ, these are not the images preferred by Wilde.

Writing *De Profundis*, Wilde describes "the coronation ceremony of sorrow, one of the most wonderful things in the whole of recorded time:

the crucifixion of the Innocent One before the eyes of his mother and of the disciple whom he loved" (167). The image of the Crucifixion appealed to sexual dissidents in part through the force of sublimation, in part through the resistance to sublimation afforded by this grisly subject. In February 1999, I visited an exhibition at the Metropolitan Museum of New York entitled *Mirror of the Medieval World*. In it appeared a remarkable illumination of the Crucifixion taken from a medieval Missal. This image suggested to me the existence of a bodily drama, at once sacred and profane, of significance to sexual dissidents. Originally the image appeared before the Canon of the Mass, the part of the service during which the priest, in words of Christ taken from the Gospel, consecrates bread and wine as the body and blood of Christ. Just as Wilde in *De Profundis* moves the discussion of Christ from religious into aesthetic terms, the medieval illustrator turns the Crucifixion into a triumph of style, at once aristocratic and artistic, with its cursive elegance and calligraphic elongation and emptying out of the human body. Christ is portrayed in a seemingly impossible position, arm and midriff lifting up in defiance of gravity and torso twisted sideways or back to front as though Christ were seated on a block hidden by drapery, the feet as if *en pointe*. Both Mary and John, in attendance, are androgynous, their biological difference suppressed, and the body decorporealized except for the wavy hair of all three figures and the bodily fluids draining from Christ. The tacit reference to maternal lactation in the blood spurting from the wound in Christ's side crossgenders body and human relationship.[31] These departures from a strict asymmetry of gender are one sign of the dissident appeal of the image. The trio of Mary, John the Evangelist, and Christ could not be more customary in sacred art. And yet all three are removed from the domestic ideology dominant in nineteenth-century England. All three are virgins, though the woman gave birth in the Spirit, an often female-identified figure in medieval and Victorian devotional writing.[32] And Christ and John are passionate albeit chaste lovers. The little book that John holds, sign of the Gospel and the Book of Revelation that he will write, signifies the ability of the lover/artist to textualize this experience, converting it into word and image.

Most significant about this image, however, is the relation between the wounded body that dominates the illustration and the minuscule male half-nude at the bottom, who lifts a chalice to receive the saving drops. This emaciated figure represents Adam, the old Adam, that is. Risen from the dead, he sits in an open sarcophagus, his burial winding sheet fallen below

16. *The Crucifixion*. Leaf from a missal: frontispiece for the Canon of the Mass, French, thirteenth century, c. 1270–90. Metropolitan Museum of Art. Bequest of Thomas W. Lamont, by exchange, 1981 (1981.322). Photograph, all rights reserved, The Metropolitan Museum of Art.

his waist. Above him is the magnified body of Christ, whose saving blood, dripping into the chalice, promises to restore Adam to life and bodily vigor. In Catholic preaching, the large figure is Christ, the New Adam. The exchange of bodily fluids refers to Holy Communion, in which, according to the Anglo- and Roman Catholic doctrine of transubstantiation, the communicant ingests the body and blood of Christ. In a sexualized discourse, this exchange signifies the dream that the exchange of bodily fluids in sexual communion can redeem the body. At the same time, the vulnerability of both bodies signifies the loss that accompanies desire. The image calls the viewer to passionate transcendence while simultaneously insisting on the insufficiency of the human body and psyche.

Hall's first religious novel, *Adam's Breed* (1926), invites reading in terms of Frazer's myth of the sacrifice of the daimon to the Mother Goddess. Although virtually ignored in commentary on the novel, Teresa Boselli, one of its two lead characters, is the book's most memorable figure.[33] In terms of sexual typologies, she is a hybrid, displaying at various times heterosexual, bisexual, lesbian, stone-butch, and asexual characteristics. More successful at business than her husband, Fabio, she is toughly masculine, even masculist. She might well be termed an Amazon—a word drawn from Sapphic culture of 1920s Paris—passionate but virginal and cold to males after having lost her maidenhood to one. But she exceeds the limits of the types of which the Amazon constitutes one figure.

Critical attention focuses on Teresa's orphaned grandson, Gian-Luca, a lost soul, who, despite his gifts, ambition, and imaginative capability, is fated to meet a solitary end at age thirty-four. He is born illegitimate after Teresa's daughter, Olga, is abandoned by her first lover while working for an American family in Italy. Teresa, who loves Olga passionately, rejects Gian-Luca as "alien flesh" because his fair hair and light-colored eyes remind her of what she assumes to be his Anglo-Saxon father.[34] Nonetheless, her grandson's need, conscious and unconscious, for mother-love attaches fiercely to her: "He had realized, without knowing how, that Nonna . . . hated his hair. He lay and pondered these things, bewildered, and his heart felt afraid because of its love. It was dreadful to love a goddess like Nonna—a goddess who hated your hair" (32). Stylistically often inert, with a patronizing masculine narrator, and weighted with a plotless sequence of set-piece scenes, the novel has its weaknesses. Precisely its silences, however—for example, about the actual identity of the boy's father—draw the reader forward to the young man's ultimate sacrifice. But what is the logic

17. Michelangelo Merisi da Caravaggio, *The Supper at Emmaus,* c. 1605. Pinacoteca di Brera, Milan. Photo: Erich Lessing/Art Resource, New York.

of sacrifice in this novel? And is it Christian or pagan? The implicit logic of Frazer and Harrison's work converts the drama of Christ's end into pagan ritual.[35] In contrast, Hall sacramentalizes Gian-Luca's death.

Although Hall at times associates Gian-Luca with Christ, his forenames suggest that he stands more in the relation of disciple or prophet of the Messiah—like the evangelist Luke or John, the disciple whom Jesus loved, or even the John the Baptist who attracted Harrison's attention.[36] Hall approaches the anthropological topic of anthropophagy by means of the sacrament of Holy Communion, initiated by Christ at the Last Supper when he broke bread and gave it to his disciples. Here again a work of religious art comes to mind, in this case, Caravaggio's *The Supper at Emmaus* (c. 1605; Brera, Milan), shown in the exhibition *Caravaggio: The Final Years* at the National Gallery in London in spring 2005. When I saw the image shortly after reading Hall's novel for the first time, Caravaggio's visual meditation immediately suggested to me the telos of the novel in a mystical touch.[37]

The immediate reference of the scene is to the account in the gospel of Luke of the meeting of two of Christ's disciples with a stranger on the road to Emmaus on the third day after Jesus's death. When the two men invite their new acquaintance to join them for supper, he reveals his identity to them by repeating Jesus's action at the Last Supper: "And it came to pass when he reclined at table with them, that he took the bread and blessed and broke and began handing it to them. And their eyes were opened, and they recognized him; and he vanished from their sight" (Luke 24: 30–31). The painting replays the moment in which, in Roman Catholic belief, Christ instituted both the Holy Eucharist—the becoming-present of himself to his followers under the outward appearances of bread and wine—and Holy Communion, in which the priest at Mass, acting in the place of Christ, transforms bread and wine into the body and blood of Christ, to be consumed by the faithful.

Caravaggio sees this transaction in terms of service, literally, waiting on table. At the apex of the group of figures is the innkeeper, the provider of food and lodging for the body, who stands "perplexed" as he watches the stranger's actions.[38] He stands outside the ken of the sacred. Next to him is "his wrinkled wife, who has already bowed her head in prayer, the first person in the room to understand who their mysterious guest must be." In her hands, she holds the meal's main course, a rack of lamb, "the sacrificial animal of Passover and Easter."[39] At the same moment, Christ demonstrates a mystical service as, having broken the bread, he extends his right hand in blessing. The two seated disciples, Cleophas and another, nameless in the Gospel, react. The one to the right, often taken to be Luke,[40] grasps the edge of the table with both hands. As he does so, his right hand brushes Christ's hand, "lit by the glow of divinity. In that touch, or near touch, Caravaggio has concentrated all the fervor of a burning heart and distilled the essence of Christianity as the meeting of God and man."[41]

A second-generation Anglo-Italian, Gian-Luca lives in a small Italian community centered in Old Compton Street, Soho, where his grandparents run Casa Boselli, a salumeria. As a boy, Gian-Luca helps out there. At age fourteen, his grandfather apprentices him to the owner of a local restaurant, the Capo di Monte. Gian-Luca is glad to go: "Perhaps I can serve well." The narrator comments: "He already had great confidence in his own ability to serve" (94).[42] His employer soon discovers that "Gian-Luca possessed that rarest of all gifts, the instinct for perfect service" (118). He goes on to become a waiter at the Doric, a leading London restaurant. When World

War I begins, he is promoted to head-waiter as Italian members of the staff
return to join the Italian army. Deeply disappointed that his illegitimacy
bars him from service with his "brothers" (215) in the Italian army, he is
disappointed yet again when, after being conscripted into the British Army,
he is denied his wish to fight in the lines and is assigned instead to the Army
Service Corps. There he finds himself "working as a sergeant in charge of
an Officers' Mess somewhere far back at the Base" (227). When he returns
to his post at the Doric following the war, he does so with unexplained
"indifference" (250). Ditto his marriage to Maddalena Trevi, a beautiful
but simple young Italian immigrant, who "did not stir his passion" (180).

Adam's Breed is one among a number of contemporary novels that
focus on young men who survive the war physically but without the will to
live.[43] As a character in a 1921 short story by Hugh Walpole observes of
one veteran, "Her discovery quite simply was that he did not exist; that he
was dead, that 'there was nobody there.' "[44] Gian-Luca's family and friends
perceive something similar in him but find themselves incapable of assisting
him. And when his disorientation can no longer be ignored and the owner
of the Doric sends him to his own doctor to be examined, the physician
fails to make the connection with Gian-Luca's war service, presumably because he had not seen action. Nonetheless, already early in the war, doctors
had argued in the British medical journal *The Lancet* that a nervous condition could result not only from being exposed to the sounds of "high explo-
sives or participation in an offensive" but to "being a witness" to the
horrors of war. And as another author wrote, "In medicine there is a neu-
tral zone, a no-man's land, a regnum protisticum, which really defies definition. This nebulous zone shelters many among the sad examples of
nervous trouble sent home from the front."[45] Gian-Luca's condition arises,
on the one hand, from being deprived of the male homosocial intimacy
that Santanu Das and others have explored in accounts of service at the
front, coupled with his work in literally feeding the war machine. In this
role, Gian-Luca was highly aware that a large proportion of the young officers for whom he provided sustenance would shortly be killed or seriously
wounded in action. As it is, he is told that his "depression . . . was simply
the outcome of weakness" (295). The doctor prescribes a vacation and a
pharmaceutical placebo. "Above all," Gian-Luca is told, "he must not
worry" (296).

The climax of his service as a waiter arrives shortly after his return,
when Ugo Doria, an Aestheticist and Decadent poet who recalls Gabriele

D'Annunzio, makes a reservation to eat at the restaurant. An avid reader
since early boyhood who had once cherished hopes of becoming a poet,
Gian-Luca is a fervent admirer of Doria's great early poem, "Gioia della
Luce." Without calling upon a traditional religious belief, for Gian-Luca,
the poem evokes the world of "a saint, a peak of pure whiteness, a lake in
the heart of the mountains" (171). When Gian-Luca decides that he himself
will wait upon the poet, other members of the staff are shocked and disap-
proving: head-waiters do not wait on table. But when an infatuated Doria
arrives with "Milady," "little and lovely," a familiar guest at the restaurant
and "as greedy in passion as in food" (261), Gian-Luca is completely disil-
lusioned. That night at home he burns all of his copies of Doria's works.

Following this fiasco, Gian-Luca is no longer able to motivate himself
to work or to maintain the façade of his domestic life. One day, while on
leave from his position at the Doric and walking aimlessly through the
streets of the city, he encounters a match-seller with her young son. The
boy is blinded, possibly deliberately in order to prompt the pity—and do-
nations—of passersby. "The closed lids were shrunken and flat and disfig-
ured—so woe-begone somehow, they looked, those closed lids, in spite of
. . . [the boy's] quiet expression. And Gian-Luca, who cared not at all for
children, must gaze and gaze at this child as though he were suddenly suffering with him, as though in some curious way he belonged to those woe-
begone, sightless eyes" (282). In this moment of involuntary identification,
Gian-Luca abruptly accesses a lifetime of suppressed pain. He pours the
money in his pockets into the match-seller's tray. She pushes the boy
toward him in hopes of yet more reward, but he turns and flees: "Away
and away from suffering and affliction, and the great, blind sadness of the
world. And even as he ran something ran beside him, he could feel it close
at his elbow. A quiet, persistent, intangible presence—the great, blind sadness of the world" (283).

Mindful of the doctor's recommendation, Maddalena takes her husband to Italy for the first time; but much though he loves the countryside,
the casual cruelty of its inhabitants toward birds and domestic animals
repels him. When the couple returns to London, he quits his job and, having made arrangements for the support of Maddalena, leaves to become a
homeless pilgrim. He makes his way to the New Forest, where he lives
alone, attempting, as he writes his wife, to "try to find God" (343). Exposed
to the elements, he weakens and dies alone.

In the *Supper at Emmaus*, the disciple Luke's hand touches or nearly touches the highlighted left hand of the stranger who has broken the bread and extends his right hand over it. It is this touch for which Gian-Luca hungers. He comes closest to it in the sensitivity to the suffering of others that overtakes his life. Luke writes, "Their eyes were held, that they should not recognize him" (Luke 24:16). The purpose of the scene at Emmaus is to open the eyes of the disciples so that they can recognize the actuality of Christ's Passion, death, and Resurrection. Equally important is recognition of the repetition of Christ's act in instituting the Holy Eucharist. In Holy Communion, the act is repeated again, this time by someone who is simply a human being, the priest, but also by the communicants—like Luke—who receive Christ's sacrifice.

Before his death, Gian-Luca experiences his own Emmaus vision:

> Then, as though a mist had been swept from his vision, he seemed to see clearly for the first time in his life, and seeing the darkness, yet perceived a great glory, shining steadily through that darkness. He was conscious of a vast and indomitable purpose to which all things would ultimately bow; he himself, Gian-Luca, was a part of that purpose as was everything else on this struggling earth—and at that supreme moment he must cry out to God:
>
> "I have found You; You are here in my heart!" (376–77)

In this way, Gian-Luca experiences the Real Presence.

In a following paragraph that may communicate Gian-Luca's thoughts or the narrator's, Hall writes, "The path of the world was the path of His sorrow, and the sorrow of God was the hope of the world, for to suffer with God was to share in the joy of His ultimate triumph over sorrow" (377). These words are the most Christian, Catholic, and orthodox in Hall's fiction. It is worth bearing in mind, moreover, that hers is a Catholicism consonant with the radical humanism that, as I mentioned in Chapter 1, she was able simultaneously to inhabit. Jane Harrison, another humanist, expresses an insight very close to that experienced by Gian-Luca. The word that signals this sensitivity is one of her favorites: *touch*. At the end of "Heresy and Humanity," Harrison argues that "only in a civilized anarchy, we some of us feel, can the individual come to his [*sic*] full right and function." In turn, individual freedom of thought enlarges the meaning of species-being. However, this enlargement depends equally strongly upon "that new emotional imagination, joint offspring of head and heart which is begotten of enlarged sympathies and a more sensitive habit of feeling" toward "the claims of other individual lives that touch our own" (Harrison, 40, 39, 41). As for Gian-Luca, this openness depends not upon receiving or giving love, of which he is bereft, but upon recognizing that the "pain" of others "is our pain" (41).

Hall was enamored of Christ on the cross. After *The Well of Loneliness* was judged to be legally obscene, she followed with another novel, originally entitled *The Carpenter's Son*. In it, the male protagonist hallucinates the sight of a crucified man when he receives Communion. Later, in sympathetic identification with Christ on the cross, he begins to experience stigmata. Hall did so while writing the novel. "Red stains" appeared on her hands, which had to be bandaged (Souhami, 261). Hall's identification with Christ on the cross was in place already in the early 1890s, at the same time she began to see herself as an artist as well as to flirt, fall in love with, and pursue some of the young female singers who studied voice with her stepfather (Souhami, 22).[46] The public destruction of Wilde in 1895 provided a clamorous off-stage accompaniment to the disorderly domestic scene of Hall's home. Years later, as the date of publication of *The Well of Loneliness* approached and Troubridge read to Hall *The Ballad of Reading Gaol* and *De Profundis*, Hall reaffirmed her identification with the Wilde who had been publicly shamed as he stood on a railway platform to await transfer to Reading prison.[47] In the Romantic aesthetic of Wilde and Hall, human perfection, unachieved in pleasure, arrives through sorrow. In the words of a Wilde who praises impurity and adulteration, "just as the body absorbs things of all kinds, things common and unclean no less than those that the priest or a vision has cleansed, and converts them into swiftness or strength, into the play of beautiful muscles and the moulding of fair flesh, into the curves and colours of the hair, the lids, the eye; so the soul in its turn has its nutritive functions also, and can transform into noble moods of thought and passions of high import what in itself is base, cruel, and degrading; nay, more, may find in these its most august modes of assertion, and can often reveal itself most perfectly through what was intended to desecrate or destroy" (156).

Wilde's image recalls the intactness of a Greek marble sculpture of a young male ephebe. But Hall's identification with the Mary of the Pietà introduces an additional factor, both relational and doubly gendered, in

Mary's embrace of the deceased Christ. The strong identification of the female devotee with the body of the crucified Christ and the figuration of this compassion as a metaphor of love between women were internalized within Anglo-Catholic female poetry, devotion, and communal practice. Anglo-Catholic Victorian women used the sacrament of the Eucharist and the passion of Christ to signify desire between women.[48] Frederick Roden, for example, references Eliza Keary's poem "Christine and Mary," whose two speakers' names appear to refer to those of Christina Rossetti and her beloved sister, Maria, who made her final profession of vows as an Anglican nun in 1875. Published in 1874, one year after the high-water mark of Victorian homoerotic Classicism, both male and Sapphic, in Pater's *Studies in the History of the Renaissance* and in the same year as Newman's defense of conscience, Christine's final words describe a painting of Christ's passion on the convent wall:

> . . . the royal brow
> Weighted with anguish; th'absorbing eyes
> Hungry with selfless love.[49]

In Rossetti's poem "Goblin Market," Lizzie, who in the poem's religious allegory partakes of the nature of both Mary *and* Christ, saves her fallen sister, Laura, by first permitting the goblin men to abuse her and by then inviting her sister to suck their juices from her bruised body:

> Eat me, drink me, love me;
> Laura, make much of me;
> For your sake I have braved the glen
> And had to do with goblin merchant men.[50]

Roden comments that "Laura's redemptive eating, drinking, and loving of her sister merges sensual and spiritual gratification in a eucharistic meal."[51] He further observes that a "spiritual female *communitas*," whether evoked between two women who literally were sisters or among the members of an Anglican sisterhood, provided a sanctioned but nonetheless telling alternative to the Victorian ideal of the middle-class married couple.[52]

Images of Christ's crucifixion suggest that the body of the God-man, even as it saves, is not restored to wholeness. It remains the wounded,

bleeding body of a dying man/woman, of a lover too.[53] This sexual/reli-
gious/aesthetic image testifies to the inescapable temporality of human existence; to the vulnerability of the body, to the psychic incompleteness of
human relationships,[54] as well as to the damaging constraints of heteronor-
mative existence. In her fiction, Hall represents love between sexual dissidents as both absolutely necessary and a near impossibility, a paradox
enacted, in a fashion distressing to generations of readers when, at the end
of *The Well of Loneliness*, Stephen Gordon forces her lover, Mary Llewellyn,
to leave her. In the Christological narrative of the novel, this abandonment
is as necessary as was Christ's abandonment by his disciples at Calvary. It
has to occur so that the full devastation of the Passion can be experienced.
Only then will recuperation be possible.

The Well of Loneliness is a new Gospel, written by Hall, to affirm the
saving power of love based in dissident desire.[55] As such, it is a testament
both of faith and doubt, like Ernest Renan's *Vie de Jésus*, which Wilde
admiringly referred to as "the gracious fifth gospel, the gospel according to
St. Thomas, one might call it" (168). (St. Thomas is, of course, the patron
saint of doubters.) *The Well of Loneliness* is also Hall's Apocalypse, to use
the Roman Catholic title of the final book of the Bible. The call for justice
characteristic of the genre is in her case the demand of sexual inverts for
what she refers to as the "right to our existence."[56] This call has been a
source of scandal to some readers, who see in it a continuing subjection on
the part of Stephen (and Hall) to an oppressive masculinist deity. Hall's
Trinity, however, is a bit unusual, including as it does a queer Christ and
Mary and a feminine Holy Spirit. The epiphany of a countless number of
inverts, present, past, and future, experienced by Stephen at the end of the
novel is a phenomenon drawn from religiously heterodox, that is, from
Spiritualist experience. Finally, more significant than the term *God* is the
rhetorical space the word occupies in the genre of apocalypse as the name
of the principle called upon in the name of justice. Equally apt is the writer's
reflexive sense of justice and other terms, such as *life*, the term in whose
name, according to Michel Foucault, the normalizing social order of modernity has been challenged in an ever-proliferating series of demands for
new rights. "The 'right' to life, to one's body, to health, to happiness, to
the satisfaction of needs, and beyond all the oppression or 'alienations,' the
'right' to rediscover what one is and all that one can be, this 'right'—which
the classical juridical system was utterly incapable of comprehending—was
the political response to all these new procedures of power which did not

derive, either, from the traditional right of sovereignty."[57] According to this argument, sexology itself drives Stephen's call for justice.

After Mary's departure, in the final paragraphs of the novel, Stephen (the name is that of the first Christian martyr) experiences a vision of her unhappy friends, including the suicide, Jamie, "with a neat little hole in her side." In words drawing on Gospel accounts of the Crucifixion, an infinity of sexual inverts demand that Stephen become the agent of their salvation. Accepting identification with both Mary and Christ, Stephen gives virgin birth to the communicants of this new Church Militant: "They possessed her. Her barren womb became fruitful—it ached with its fearful and sterile burden. It ached with the fierce yet helpless children who would clamour in vain for their right to salvation. They would turn first to God, and then to the world, and then to her. They would cry out accusing: 'We have asked for bread; will you give us a stone? Answer us: will you give us a stone? You, God, in Whom we, the outcast, believe; you, world, into which we are pitilessly born; you, Stephen, who drained our cup to the dregs—we have asked for bread; will you give us a stone?'" (476). Here the communion chalice reverts to the cup that Jesus prayed might pass from him in the Garden of Gethsemane (Matthew 26:39).

In the final paragraphs, the language becomes that of the Apocalypse. The words are intensely disturbing: "And now there was only one voice, one demand; her own voice into which those millions had entered. A voice like the awful, deep rolling of thunder; a demand like the gathering together of great waters. A terrifying voice that made her ears throb, that made her brain throb, that shook her very entrails, until she must stagger and all but fall beneath this appalling burden of sound that strangled her in its will to be uttered" (447). This moment refers to a particular sort of Spiritualist experience—in which an individual with psychic powers may be seen by others to be accompanied by a host of spirits of the living, the dead, and the as yet unborn.

Among this group are not only deceased female friends from Paris but also a host of male sexual inverts:

> Aye, and those lost and terrible brothers, . . . they were here, and they also were calling: "Stephen, Stephen, speak with your God and ask Him why He has left us forsaken!" She could see their marred and reproach-ful faces with the haunted, melancholy eyes of the invert—eyes that had looked too long on a world that lacked all pity and all understanding:

"Stephen, Stephen, speak with your God and ask Him why he has left us forsaken!" And these terrible ones started pointing at her with their shaking, white-skinned, effeminate fingers: "You and your kind have stolen our birthright; you have taken our strength and given us your weakness!" They were pointing at her with white shaking fingers. (446)

At moments like these, readers are often repelled, seeing the text of the novel as altogether dominated by the rhetoric of late Victorian sexology. I see something else—namely, the return to Hall and to dissident culture of the moment in 1895 when Wilde became the very type of the modern pervert, homosexual and effeminate. Inscribed on the male homosexuals of Hall's novel, in particular on the playwright Jonathan Brockett, the type of the male sexual invert is in part a stereotype. The attack of male inverts on Stephen reenacts the violent imposition of the identity of sexual invert upon Wilde at the time of the trials. The attack refers externally to the aggression of what both Wilde and Hall call "the world." It refers as well to an aggression turned by inverts upon one another. And it refers to a psychic splitting of the subjects of sexual inversion: of Wilde, Stephen Gordon, and implicitly of Hall herself.

In response, Hall becomes at once this collective voice and the voice of Christ on the Cross. She cries: "God, . . . we believe; we have told You we believe. . . . We have not denied You, then rise up and defend us. Acknowledge us, oh God, before the whole world. Give us also the right to our existence" (447). At this point, God is a very different deity from the one who presides over the marriage of Stephen's obnoxious childhood friend, Violet Antrim. The "you" is reflexive, referring both to dissident existence and to the existence of individual psyches. The violence borne home from outside originates also among and within subjects of sexual inversion. This recognition is in a way the most searing allegation lodged by Stephen against their tormentors. Their assailants have set in motion a continual series of destructive acts in the lives of those who are the objects of their violence. Escape from traumatic repetition depends not only on the cease of prosecution by "the world" but also from a transformation of individual and group life among sexual dissidents. Hall recognizes this transformation as a process simultaneously divinizing and profane.

The "coming out" narrative of modern homosexual identity is in form a conversion narrative and a narrative of one's calling to a special vocation. In this context, the ending of the novel is Gordon/Hall's "coming out" and, as such, an affront both to respectable opinion and to the chic ambisexuality of Bloomsbury. Hall's writing secularizes by sexualizing the Catholic discourse within which she writes. In this archetypal but charged and difficult moment in the history of modern sexualities, the ending of the novel does not simply, as I put it earlier, open imaginative spaces for sexual dissidence in the face of sexological definition. On the one hand, it insists that such spaces be habitable, an ethical demand that is at once utopian and practical and that participates in the variously apocalyptic writing of male and female sexual dissidents after 1860. The moment is likewise one of return to other discourses: to the anarchist rhetoric of Wilde's essay on socialism and the letter from prison and to the rhetoric in which such sexologists as Havelock Ellis and Sigmund Freud naturalize and thereby tend to validate same-sex desire. By demanding that God conform his will to that of sexual inverts, Stephen's call is heterodox, blasphemous; and her presentation of herself and other sexual inverts as implicitly divine martyrs is idolatrous. The note of revolt leads outside Roman Catholicism. On the other hand, blasphemy exists within the Church. Witness, for example, the Christ of Wilde, Renan, and the Gospels, who speaks as a Jew against the Judaic law and its official spokespersons. Blasphemous *and* idolatrous, Stephen Gordon and Radclyffe Hall operate simultaneously inside and outside a Catholic rhetoric of sexual dissidence that continues today to shape queer subjectivities, both religious and secular.

Shifting into the genre of apocalypse, past, present, and future time become simultaneous at the end of Hall's novel. Further, the permeability of Stephen's ego at the end undoes the stabilization of character that is one of the most important ideological effects of novelistic realism. At the same time, one finds correlatives for this ending in a number of modernist classics: James Joyce's *Portrait of the Artist as a Young Man*, D. H. Lawrence's *The Rainbow*, and E. M. Forster's *Maurice*, whose male couple escapes into the greenwood at the end of the novel. Hall's experimentalism differs, however, from that of Joyce, Lawrence, and Forster insofar as apocalypse in *The Well of Loneliness* is assertively linked to the mystery of Christ's saving passion. As I have argued, the restaging of this drama within the lives of sexual inverts challenges the moral dicta of the Church at the same time that it projects sexual dissidents onto a cosmic stage where the pursuit of justice requires that life be waged to and at the very edge of annihilation.

8

The Well of Loneliness as an Activist Text

The call to action that a reader like Grace Spencer heard in Hall's early novels is amplified in *The Well of Loneliness*. In that novel, Hall focuses on the question of what spatial and temporal forms are necessary to enable the public existence of sexual inverts.[1] Hall believed the answer to lie in the extension of the civil and religious institution of marriage to female couples. At the time, many Sapphists disagreed with her. For their part, the prosecutors of Hall's publisher singled out the novel's advocacy of same-sex marriage as one of its most objectionable features. Moreover, while the degree of exclusivity implicit in marriage seems clear within the novel, it proved scarcely so in Hall's personal life. To her partner, Troubridge, monogamy was the only proper form of female marriage; but in the decade following publication of the novel, Hall would find this option not livable. The issue was not only a personal one. The question of the elasticity of the bonds of same-sex marriage was a matter of ongoing concern both to heterosexuals and to subjects of same-sex desire.

In recent years, powerful attention has been paid to the tendency in the nineteenth century for female intimates to understand their relations with one another in marital terms. Martha Vicinus writes definitively on this topic in her study of female partners, *Intimate Friends: Women Who Loved Women, 1778–1928*. More recently, Sharon Marcus has canvassed the same topic in *Between Women*. Marcus argues that Vicinus's book remains within the template of 1970s lesbian-feminist analyses of female same-sex friendship and single pair-bonding.[2] But a feature that distinguishes Vicinus's approach from lesbian-feminist ones is her attention to the high value placed on female masculinity in many of the couples that she considers.

Vicinus and the women she discusses regard same-sex relations primarily in domestic terms—marital, familial, and friendly. Like Alan Bray in *The Friend*, they see friendship as existing both outside and inside existing networks of domestic ties.[3] The view of these terms is highly mobile. This tendency is evident, for example, in the opening section of "Part III, Cross-Age and Crossed Love." Although Vicinus classes these relations in terms of a metaphor of "mother-daughter love," she also describes all five of the "daughters" as masculine women, a term derived not from domesticity but from the incipient discourse of modern sexology.[4] For example, Vicinus speaks of the novelist Eliza Lynn Linton as "playing with gender inversion, changeling fantasies, insanity, and fiery passion" (111) in her fictions. Ethel Smyth, who both as a young woman and again later enjoyed playing the role of daughter to an older maternal beloved, also had a long relationship with a man, Harry Brewster (83–84). Vicinus stretches the governing maternal metaphor by describing Smyth's relation with Brewster as one of "male mother–tomboy daughter" love (132). A Victorian feminist and leading antivivisectionist, Frances Power Cobbe, combined terms of religious devotion, domestic life, and friendship when at the end of her autobiography, she wrote: "God has given me two priceless benedictions in life;—[in] my youth a perfect Mother, in my later years a perfect Friend."[5] Edith Simcox, a feminist and trade union activist, believed "married love and passionate friendship" to be the most desirable forms of love between two adults but was prepared to accept as second best the "strange," one might say masochistic, "pleasure" of her unrequited love for George Eliot (123). Marcus is correct in pointing out that Vicinus refers to these investments as lesbian, but given the variety of terms subsumed under this rubric, Vicinus's usage is more like that of "Sapphic" to refer to subjects of female same-sex desire in the early decades of the twentieth century than the current reference of the word *lesbian* to the subject of a particular sexual identity. The tendency of *Intimate Friends* is not toward ontological specification but to an ever-enlarging sense of the varieties of human desire.[6]

In contrast, Marcus's *Between Women* tends to normalize female same-sex desire. She argues persuasively, using both autobiographical materials and novels, that female friendship functioned within the period as one of the main props (and advantages) of middle-class marriage. She also contends that female marriage was quite acceptable in the view of middle-class Victorians. Marcus states the latter view provocatively, but it is not an unusual perspective among writers on Hall. With regard to Hall's early infatuation with the future singer Agnes Nicholls, for example, Sally Cline says, "Certain restrictions . . . were placed on these friendships. Should two women . . . wish to pursue their attachment by forming an established ménage, they had to remember three caveats: first, that if an eligible male appeared he must not be discouraged but must be integrated alongside the women's friendship; secondly, that two women in love were not expected to try and find employment to support their relationship; thirdly, that as such a relationship was not perceived [Marcus might say not declared] by the outside world as erotic, the two women concerned must take great care not to indicate that it was. Given these restrictions, intimate, exclusive, discreetly erotic relations between white middle and upper class women were perceived as 'normal' and compatible with heterosexuality in Anglo-European culture."[7]

Marcus is confident that female subjects of same-sex desire experienced much less epistemological and ontological pressure regarding their preferences in the early and mid-Victorian period than did such women as Hall later. Marcus distinguishes three kinds of erotic relationships between women in the years before 1880: female friendship, which might or might not have a sexual component (260); female marriage, regarded as acceptable within middle- and upper-class society (203); and "unrequited love between women" (257), such as Simcox's for Eliot. Marcus also defines what she means by Victorian female marriage: "The Victorian middle class defined marriage in terms of shared households, financial support, bequests of wealth and property, the care of the body in life and death, and vows and practices of exclusive commitment and unique spiritual communion" (230). This definition points in a very different direction from Charlotte Cushman's practice, discussed in the Introduction—and, later, Hall's—of what might be referred to as "cousinage," or ensembles of blood relatives, friends, and primarily sexual intimates centered around a charismatic woman—one, moreover, with the sense of responsibility and the financial independence necessary to provide support to the network. Marcus's definition focuses attention on a single couple at the expense of other ties. In this sense, the definition makes of female marriage something private rather than something social and ramifying as it existed in Cushman and young Hall's experience.

Marcus does, however, provide an instance in which the practice of female marriage functioned both as an educative example to leading utilitarian reformers and as a basis from which female feminists could intervene in Victorian debates concerning coverture as the basis of family law and the access of women to divorce. In both male and female friendship tradition, friendship was seen to be based on the principles of equality and autonomy between the participants. The ideology of Victorian female marriage was based in part on an ethic of friendship that such women as Cobbe and her partner, Mary Lloyd, succeeded in demonstrating to the allies with whom they worked to gain passage of the Divorce and Matrimonial Causes Act of 1857 (206–7, 211). In this way, the existence of female marriage contributed to the creation of new options for married women and the eventual removal of coverture in 1891.

In France, in the opening years of the twentieth century, Natalie Barney and Renée Vivien affirmed the superiority of Sapphic ties and culture under the banner of Lesbian exceptionalism.[8] While Hall and Troubridge also subscribed to this doctrine, a distinctive feature of Hall's activism is the fact that she advocates on behalf of the civil and social rights of *all* homosexuals, both male and female.[9] While remaining within the language of sexual inversion—so that it is especially the anomalous situation of the crossgendered subject that is emphasized—the jacket copy of the first edition, likely composed by Hall herself, places the general objective of the book front and center: "'The Well of Loneliness' . . . is concerned with the phenomenon of the masculine woman in all its implications. The novel handles very skillfully a psychological problem which needs to be understood in view of its growing importance. In England hitherto the subject has not been treated frankly outside the region of scientific textbooks, but that its social consequences justify a broader and more general treatment is likely to be the opinion of thoughtful and cultured people."[10] Hall directs her study not only to other sexual inverts but also to the apparently conventionally gendered individuals to whom they are attracted, as well as to a larger group, including vicars, educators, and counselors who, in the years following

World War I, increasingly turned to psychology and psychoanalysis for guidance in advising those who sought their assistance. As Graham Richards points out, members of the caring professions and providers of social services were especially drawn to the new psychology.[11]

In scenes within the novel, such as that of Violet Antrim's wedding, Hall speaks caustically against those, including the members of one's own family, who smugly exclude, denigrate, and/or condemn homosexuals in favor of persons who recognize the need to work with them in creating spaces for intimacy and sociality within normal social existence. Given the commercial and literary success of her most recent novel, Hall had earned the prestige and respect necessary to raise this issue. She could have done so while avoiding direct confrontation with the law by arranging to have the book published in Paris. Frank Harris had done so earlier in the decade when he chose to publish abroad his sexually provocative fictional autobiography, *My Life and Loves* (1922).[12] Hall, however, refused to consider this possibility.

The decision to set the novel within contemporary England upped the ante. So also did the author's decision to play with aspects of her own life in representing that of Stephen Gordon, the sexual invert and successful novelist who is the novel's protagonist. Troubridge seconded this mixing of autobiography with fiction. In her memoir of Hall, she writes, "Many of Stephen Gordon's feelings and reactions, though practically none of her circumstances or experiences, were . . . [Hall's] own."[13] Lovat Dickson, who wrote Hall's biography with Troubridge's encouragement, regarded the novel as a fictional autobiography providing a double portrait of aspects of the pair's de facto marriage.[14] He points out that the passage in the memoir in which Troubridge claims that Hall undertook the novel at her urging echoes Mary Llewellyn's challenge when she demands that Stephen make love to her: "What do I care for all you've told me? What do I care for the world's opinion? What do I care for anything but you, and you just as you are, I love you. . . . Can't you understand that all that I am belongs to you, Stephen?"[15]

Troubridge's account in the memoir of how she helped Hall decide to proceed with the novel despite the persecution that might result is written within a Roman Catholic rhetoric that directly links the religious character of *The Well of Loneliness* to its place within a secular history of expanding rights for lesbian, gay, transgendered, and transsexual subjects. Troubridge sets the origin of the novel within a biographical outline of saintly will, suffering, and implicit martyrdom. She describes Hall as saying, in an echo of Jesus at the time of his Passion, that "the time was ripe" to take a public stand (82). Troubridge also makes even larger claims than Dickson does concerning her status as one of the novel's two prime movers. It was, she says, "my decision" (81) that gave Hall permission to proceed. In accord with the hagiographic pattern noted above, Troubridge ends the passage apocalyptically. The saint's triumph, moreover, is hers as much as it is Hall's. If the Ladies of Llangollen illuminated the early nineteenth century, the ladies of 37 Holland Street will enlighten the twentieth. Together, they will "dwell . . . in the palace of truth" (82). In religious terms, the palace of truth is heaven, God's home, and eternal union in Christ. But truth is also the truth of the couple's devotion to one another, to the Cause, and to God. In "our union and . . . all the years that we had shared a home," Troubridge weds this affective and emotional truth to the truth of sexual identity: "I . . . only wished to be known for what I was" (82), she says. Not who I was but "what I was," namely, a female homosexual. At this moment she assumes a new identity: that of the modern lesbian.

Troubridge declares the moment of birth of this identity to be simultaneous with the point of origin of the novel. She grounds both within the pair's union, which, as exemplary model, also motivates Hall's demand in the novel for women with sexual and emotional ties to other women to have access to marriage and parenthood.[16] In Troubridge and Hall's view, only in this way could the isolation that attended the lives of many inverts or the immersion of some in bar culture in Paris and Soho or the hysterical complexities for others of Sapphic sex at Mediterranean beach spots be remedied. Marriage for inverts would create stable and secure horizons of time and space, at once public and personal, for female same-sex intimacy. The triumphal linkage of pair-bonding, authorship, ideology, and religious ecstasis in Troubridge's account of the origin of the novel suited her to a T. But what of Hall? The suturing of monogamy with artistic achievement and the novel's social "theme" (81) captured Hall within a set of commitments that might not permanently suit. The paragraphs lay out a trajectory for the couple until the very end of their lives. In doing so, the words not only affirm, they also demand.

For the sake of both women, it would have been more apt to read the origin of the novel in the relation that Hall had already built with her readership. After the trials, Hall received hundreds of letters from female readers in which they expressed their gratitude and told her something of their own stories. Had this archive survived, it would today provide invaluable information as to the circumstances in which female subjects of same-sex desire lived in the 1920s. Evident as well would be the relevance to them of the sort of life that Hall wished to make possible for them. Unfortunately, these letters have not been preserved. At the National Library of Canada in Ottawa, however, there exist comparable letters from the year before Hall wrote *The Well of Loneliness*. Troubridge, who functioned as keeper of records, saved them as testimonials of the praise that Hall received as the author of *Adam's Breed*.

Though not incompatible with Troubridge's account in the memoir, analysis of Hall's fan mail nonetheless suggests a very different way of looking at the writing of *The Well*. Viewed in terms of the readerly effects of her previously published fiction, it is clear that Hall was carefully constructing a lesbian public consciousness in her choice of topic and form. As a bildungsroman, the novel worked to refashion the subjectivities of individually isolated readers into persons capable of recognizing their and others' sexual and emotional desires as well as the impediments to actualizing these desires in everyday existence. This work of subjectivity formation similarly pulled the reader, through responsive reading, into Hall's public work of defining a social problem and working toward a solution. For fans of Hall, such as Clarice Jones and Grace Spencer, *The Well of Loneliness* offered a welcome next step in this ongoing project.

Given the probability of a negative reaction to the publication of the novel, Hall took remarkable care to control to the degree possible the public environment in which the book would appear. In part, this effort was complicated by the fact that Martin Secker, one of the publishers she had approached in attempting to place the novel, already had plans under way to publish *Extraordinary Women*, a comic novel by Compton Mackenzie in which he satirizes the Sapphic community on Capri. Mackenzie's novel appeared virtually simultaneously with Hall's.[17] The potential for an embarrassing juxtaposition was realized when, in its issue of August 25, 1928, the *New Statesman* published a full review of Mackenzie's novel under the headline "The Vulgarity of Lesbianism" while relegating Hall's novel to brief mention in an omnibus review by Cyril Connolly.[18] By this editorial sleight of hand, the journal was able to indicate its disapproval of both the female masculinity and the sexual attachments between women foregrounded in *The Well of Loneliness*. In its commentary in the same issue on the events of the week, the *New Statesman* criticized Sir William Joynson-Hicks, the Home Secretary, for having quickly moved to request the publisher of Hall's book to withdraw it; but again the magazine distinguished between its defense of free speech and its distaste for "lesbianism." "The Lesbian cult exists, but it is like those anaerobic bacilli which cannot endure fresh air. A little publicity in the form of such perfectly sincere writing as is to be found in these two books will do far more than any Public Prosecutor can do to eradicate this intrinsically unimportant post-war disease. Suppression can but add to its furtive charms the wholly undeserved glamour of martyrdom."[19]

Hall had attempted to forestall this sort of adverse coverage by offering to underwrite half the costs of advertising the novel. In a letter of June 27, 1928, Cape proposed to spend a total of £300 if Hall were willing to pick up £150 in charges.[20] In a handwritten reply of June 29, Hall tells him that, in response to his letter, she has instructed her agent to send him at once a check for £150. The letter shows that Hall had already learned that *Extraordinary Women* would be forthcoming in August and that she wanted as much as possible to beat Mackenzie to the punch: "You know what the book means to me—in every way—you know as well as I do the exact circumstances we are up against—including C. M. & Secker—& you certainly know very much better than I can do the best and wisest way to defeat our rivals and steer the Well of Loneliness to success." The following lines indicate both how defensive and how militant Hall was as the date of publication approached. This double posture would increase as the book quickly drew both praise and blame: "One thing I do want to make clear to you—I have always despised author's [*sic*] who paid for publicity & thus took an advantage over their poorer brethren—and it is only because of the very exceptional circumstances which have arisen that I thought it on this one occasion only fair to myself, to my book and its courageous publisher to do what I could to help."[21]

Before the publication of the novel on July 27, 1928, Hall was busy lining up reviewers for prompt, prominent notices in the leading English papers.[22] In a letter of August 13 to Gerard Manley Hopkins acknowledging with thanks a note congratulating her upon publication of the novel, Hall responds that she had approached its writing and publication in the spirit of a "propagandist," a word used with favor in one of the book's positive reviews.[23] After commenting on a number of reviews, including what she regarded as Leonard Woolf's "dastardly attack, hitting below the belt with a veng[e]ance,"[24] she concludes by sharing with Hopkins the letters that she is already receiving from throughout the country.

From all over the country are coming letters from unknown people, many are inverts & say so, but many would appear to be normal beings. So far they are letters of praise and not of abuse. The inverts who write all say much the same thing: "Thank you for having broken the silence." That dreadful conspiracy of silence, it seems, has been to them an added humiliation & burden—they have long resented it. These people's letters are often very painful, but so far very restrained and dignified, and I am glad to note this. One woman asked me if toleration of the third sex would ever come, & I replied that Havelock Ellis thought there was a faint light in the darkness, but that it would probably not come in our life time. She wrote back saying "I am just 23—do you think it will be very long?" I could not help visualizing the many stony miles that her feet must tread. I have told you all this because of your letter which makes me know that you are interested in the fortunes of my book. Again I thank you.[25]

The notorious attack on the novel by James Douglas, editor of the *Sunday Express*, appeared on the following Sunday, August 19. Although Michael Baker says that "the storm suddenly broke out of the blue" (222), that is not quite the case. In the Berg Collection, there is a short, handwritten note by Hall, dated August 18, which she brought round to Hopkins's house on Saturday. It includes as enclosure an abstract of an article to appear in the next day's paper:

A BOOK THAT
SHOULD BE
SUPPRESSED.
"I would rather give a healthy boy or a healthy girl a phial of prussic acid than this novel. Poison kills the body, but moral poison kills the soul. This book must at once be withdrawn. . . . I appeal to the Home Secretary to set the law in motion."
A well-known woman writer has published an astounding new novel. It is the first English novel devoted to a particularly hideous aspect of life as it exists among us to-day.

It discusses frankly and vividly a subject so utterly degrading that decent people regard it as an unspeakable horror. Moreover, it attempts to defend and justify the degeneracy with which it deals.

VIGOROUS EXPOSURE

The Editor of the "Sunday Express," in a vigorous exposure of the book in to-morrow's "Sunday Express," demands that it be suppressed by the publisher, the circulating libraries, and if necessary by the Public Prosecutor.

"It is no excuse," he writes, "to say that the novel possesses fine qualities or that its author is an accomplished artist. The answer is that the adroitness and cleverness of the book intensifies its moral danger. If Christianity does not destroy the doctrine that this book preaches, then the doctrine will destroy Christianity together with the civilisation which it has built on the ruins of paganism."

The advertisement indicates how serious Douglas's paper was: namely, not very. Given the popular and sensational tone of the *Sunday Express*, there was little reason to believe that the Conservative government of the day would move to endorse its recommendations.[26] But the appeal to the Home Secretary and the demand that the Public Prosecutor intervene to suppress the unnamed novel sound ominous notes. Claiming Britain's youth to be at risk and invoking degeneration theory, Douglas presses the button of an all-out moral panic.

Behind the scenes, Douglas was already in contact with government officials, and plans were being shaped to launch legal action against the novel's publisher. Without informing Hall, on Monday, August 20, Cape wrote to the Home Secretary to offer to withdraw the novel from sale if he regarded it to be obscene. Baker suggests that Cape believed that Joynson-Hicks would side with him, but the speed with which Cape acted suggests otherwise. On August 22, Joynson-Hicks responded with a letter to Cape demanding that he suppress the book. At this point, Cape was already arranging to have molds taken from the type to be sent to Paris, where he planned to continue printing the book with a partner, the Pegasus Press, for sale on the Continent and by export to England. Hall was angered both by Cape's offer and the Home Secretary's directive. But when Cape on August 22 suggested the plan to continue publication abroad, she reluctantly agreed. In this way, she was maneuvered into supporting Cape's at best devious tactics. On October 4, Customs officials intercepted a large shipment of copies of the novel into England.[27] Both Cape and Leopold Hill, a London bookseller, were charged with violating the Obscene Publications Act of 1857.

Following the November trial and the conclusion of the appeal in December, The *New Statesman* blamed not Cape but Hall both for submitting the original request for an opinion to the Home Office and for subsequently ignoring its spirit by arranging to have copies of the novel imported for sale in England.[28] Cape's actions exposed Hall to criticism and undercut the defense of the book on grounds of both free speech and the restraint with which female homosexuality is treated in the book. When Customs officials inspected the novel in October, they came to the conclusion that it would be very difficult successfully to prosecute the publisher:

> Our examination of the book leaves us in considerable doubt whether the book can properly be regarded as indecent or obscene. The subject is treated seriously and sincerely with restraint in expression and with great literary skill and delicacy. In effect it is an appeal for compassion and understanding and the pitiful tragedy of the story does not seem calculated to arouse sexual emotion or to corrupt morals by encouraging the practice of sexual inversion. If the subject is one that can permissibly be treated at all in a novel, it is difficult to see how it could be treated with more restraint. If on the other hand the subject is to be regarded as inadmissible it will be difficult to know where our censorship is to stop, and questions will at once arise whether similar action must not be taken against other books, particularly Mr. Compton Mackenzie's "Extraordinary Women."[29]

The die, however, had already been cast in a memo to Joynson-Hicks from the Office of the Director of Public Prosecutions on August 21. In the memo, Sir Guy Stephenson concludes, "It is in effect . . . a plea not only for the toleration but for the recognition of sexual perversion amongst women." The view is echoed in the Home Secretary's letter of the next day to Cape: "I am satisfied that . . . [the book] is inherently obscene in that it deals with and supports a depraved practice and that its tendency is [therefore] to corrupt."[30]

The sequence of events suggests how the discussion about the moral character of the book tended to segue into discussion of the moral character of its author. In this respect, the vulnerability that Hall felt at the time of the trials is highly understandable. Stephenson, for example, included a hit at her in his memo: "Incidentally it would appear to be clear that the authoress is herself what I believe is known as a homo-sexualist, or as she prefers to describe it an 'invert.'" Even more offensive than the topic of female homosexuality was the fact that Hall had written an apologia on behalf of the "masculine woman." To many of Hall's readers, her position on behalf of Sapphists, that is, women with sexual and emotional ties with other women, was to the point. Particularly for those who found the novel offensive, however, the description of the subject of female-female desire as a sexual invert was egregious. The prejudice against female masculinity that motivates the legal action against the book becomes even more evident in the argument of Attorney General T. W. H. Inskip at the trial on appeal. Inskip contended that the novel

is, as I submit, propaganda. This very plea, the last sentence [of the novel,] which I have read[,] of an appeal to Almighty God to recognise these people whom he made, is propaganda for the practice which has long been known as Lesbianism—a well-known vice, unnatural, destructive of the moral and physical fibre of the passive persons who indulge in it, the victims of others; and this book is a plea for the active persons who practice this vice. When the book is fairly read—and I have described, I hope, sufficiently accurately the general plot to enable your Lordship to understand and appreciate the passages that have been read—when this book is looked at in its nakedness, I submit it is corrupting and obscene and its publication is a misdemeanour, which is the way in which the Act of 1857 deals with the matter. (Appeal, 30)

If there ever existed internal Home Office memos assessing how objectionable the topic of "Lesbianism" was, these have been cleaned from the record.[31] If one wishes to ascertain the views of aides on the question, one has to look at the Home Office file on *Extraordinary Women*, which came under scrutiny in September and October 1928. In the latter case, the publisher was not in the end prosecuted. The memos in the file indicate the thinking, affects, and political calculations of the players as they broached the possibility of another prosecution on grounds of obscenity. In a memo of October 15 that summarizes the opinion of Sir Chartres Biron, who would preside over *The Well of Loneliness* trial in the following month, an aide writes: "The view which on the whole the Chief Magistrate has formed

. . . is against proceedings. Necessarily in the course of my interview we touched upon '*The Well of Loneliness*,' and there can be no doubt what opinion the Chief Magistrate holds upon that book, which rather extols or at least finds excuses for indulgence in vice, whereas 'Extraordinary Women' draws a most distasteful and detestable picture of practitioners in vice and the degraded condition into which they ultimately fall."[32] The debates between counsel during the trial and appeal often focus on the question of sexual "practices" and their representation in the novel. Because, as Customs correctly observed, there is no explicit sex in the novel, the Attorney General was reduced to arguing that the claim for toleration of female homosexuals amounted to the obscene description of sex acts between them.

Previous commentators have overlooked the importance in the arguments of the place of marriage, both heterosexual and, potentially, between women with sexual and emotional ties to other women. Both J. B. Melville, who spoke on behalf of the defense at both trials, and Inskip emphasize two relationships in the novel. The first is Stephen's unconsummated infatuation with Angela Crossby, whose name overlays Stephen's naïve idealization of this young married woman with suggestions of purity, asexuality, bisexuality, and deviousness. The second is Stephen's extended relationship with Mary Llewellyn, a virginal young woman whom Stephen meets while working with an ambulance corps in France during World War I.

Stephen's involvement with Angela comes to a head when Stephen, promising her love, loyalty, and financial support, urges her to leave her husband. Angela, who has no intention of relinquishing the advantages of marriage, such as she finds them, immediately takes stock and replies, "Could you marry me, Stephen?"[33] This question makes Hall's polemical point that in 1928, a female lover could not offer another woman emotional and financial security in a publicly recognized relationship. Implicitly, if the Stephens of this world are to have a chance at fashioning durable relationships with female partners, change is required that would create civil and religious sanctions in support of such unions.

In the case of Mary, the moment of truth comes near the end of the book when Stephen forces her to leave her for the arms of Martin Hallam, a decent man and Stephen's former suitor, who now reappears in the novel and begins to fall in love with Mary. In Stephen's eyes, Martin can offer Mary things she needs that Stephen cannot provide. Hall writes of Stephen: "Never before had she seen so clearly all that was lacking to Mary Llewellyn, all that would pass from her faltering grasp, perhaps never to return, with the passing of Martin—children, a home that the world would respect, ties of affection that the world would hold sacred, the blessèd security and the peace of being released from the world's persecution. And suddenly Martin appeared to Stephen as a creature endowed with incalculable bounty, having in his hands all those priceless gifts which she, love's mendicant could never offer. Only one gift could she offer to love, to Mary, and that was the gift of Martin" (438–39).

In his defense of the decency of the novel, Melville focuses on these two instances of Stephen's efforts to build a long-term relationship with another woman. Assuming that the novel is directed to a double readership of inverts and the general public, he argues that "the moral" of the book for the first group is this: "People who are born with this misfortune cannot expect [to live except in isolation], and not only cannot expect but should act with charity in their minds" toward those to whom they may be attracted. It is in this way that Melville interprets the novel's title. As for the general reader, "to those at large," the novel "says that there should be toleration and understanding for those who are God's creatures."[34]

Theorists of sexual inversion in contemporary sexology found it difficult to account for the women whom masculine women chose as their love-objects. Some theorists were unable to imagine that women who were not psychically masculine could experience spontaneous sexual attraction to other women.[35] Given the fact that Hall chose to conceptualize the character of Stephen within the terms of sexual-inversion theory, this point of impasse is necessarily imported into the psychology of the character. Stephen experiences continual confusion in assessing the sexual flexibility and capacity for agency of the women to whom she is sexually drawn. In connection with both Angela and Mary, once Stephen recognizes that a long-term relationship is not feasible, she beats a retreat. As Melville mentions in discussing the letter in which Stephen breaks off with Angela, Stephen takes pains to portray Angela as having expressed no desire for her despite their long mutual flirtation. Further, Stephen conceals the fact that Angela is having an affair with Roger Antrim. The effect of these suppressions is to fashion Angela as though she were one of Inskip's "passive persons who indulge in . . . [lesbian intimacy], the victims of others [i.e., of the 'active persons who practice this vice']." In the confrontation that follows her mother's discovery of Stephen's entanglement, she affirms her love for Angela. Stephen expresses this love, however, exclusively in terms of masculine agency and heterosexual marriage: "As my father loved you, I loved. As a man loves a woman, that was how I loved—protectively, like my father. . . . I'd have laid down my life a thousand times over for Angela Crossby. If I could have I'd have married her and brought her home—I wanted to bring her home here to Morton" (204). In contrast, Angela's interest in Stephen is strictly experimental. As I have mentioned, she has no intention of leaving her husband. Moreover, at the same time that she is involved with Stephen, she embarks on the affair with Antrim.

The positioning of the female beloved as incapable of spontaneously experiencing sexual desire for another woman takes on much more serious implications later in the novel when Stephen meets, works, falls in love with, and eventually becomes Mary's full-time partner. As Melville points out during the appeal trial, it is Mary who takes the initiative in opening the sexual phase of the pair's relationship.[36] Nonetheless, and as though forgetting this fact, when Stephen at the end of the novel decides to renounce Mary, she categorizes her as a woman both in the sense of not being capable of exercising sexual agency toward another woman but also in the sense of being biologically and culturally destined to fulfillment in heterosexual marriage and motherhood. In response to the prosecution's allegation of obscenity, Melville emphasizes Stephen's (and Hall's) assertion of a naturalizing definition of womanhood throughout the novel as a sign of the novel's adherence to conventional moral values. This commitment, however, and Stephen's decision to expel Mary contradict the implicit ethic of the novel, which is to affirm women's choice to live with one another as sexual, emotional, and life partners. This ethic requires as a corollary recognition of the capacity and right of individual women to make such a choice.[37]

Stephen has good reasons not to continue the relationship. Because of her obsessive work routine as a writer, she needs a woman, much as Hall needed Troubridge, capable of combining the functions of lover, companion, editor, secretary, organizer, hostess, and domestic manager. In part for reasons of class, however, Mary is not suited to fill these multiple roles. Moreover, because Stephen needs to sequester herself for long periods if she is to write at all, she is ill equipped to attend to Mary's needs. Both the biological sterility of the relationship and the absence of acceptable social outlets for lesbian social life begin to weigh on the relationship. Stephen, however, is incapable of discussing these factors with Mary on an equal basis.

Working from a masculinist perspective on gender much like Stephen's, the narrator comments:

> There comes a time in all passionate attachments when life, real life must be faced once again with its varied and endless obligations, when the lover knows in his innermost heart that the halcyon days are over. He may well regret this prosaic intrusion, yet to him it will usually seem quite natural, so that while loving not one whit the less, he will bend his neck to the yoke of existence. But the woman, for whom love is an end in itself, finds it harder to submit thus calmly. To every devoted and ardent woman there comes this moment of poignant regretting; and struggle she must to hold it at bay. "Not yet, not yet—just a little longer"; until Nature, abhorring her idleness, forces on her the labour of procreation.
>
> But in such relationships as Mary's and Stephen's, Nature must pay for experimenting. (342)

By moving these views of gender out of Stephen's point of view and into that of the narrator, Hall seconds them while at the same time once again asserting Stephen's masculinity. In considering the conservatism of the representation of female gender in this and similar passages, however, one should bear in mind that in the 1920s such views were widely shared, including among some advanced thinkers. In his essay on a case of female homosexuality, for example, Sigmund Freud speaks of his patient as having lost her "womanhood" when she turned to homosexuality.[38] By womanhood, he means heterosexual desire and the desire to bear children.

As I have mentioned, Mary does not in fact lack Sapphic sexual agency. Moreover, the ideal of marriage upheld by Stephen (and the narrator as well) is at odds with the representation of marriage in the novel. Stephen regards her parents' life together as providing the model of an ideal marriage; likewise, throughout the novel, the family estate of Morton epitomizes the values of home for Stephen. But the perfection of her parents' marriage is based on her father's acceptance of her mother's intellectual and moral inferiority. Moreover, the harmony of parents and child, to the extent that it did exist, could be sustained only on the basis of a secret. Although Stephen's father recognized that his daughter was a sexual invert, he could never bring himself to broach this topic to either his wife or his daughter. Heterosexual normalcy could be preserved only by excluding recognition of the fact that Stephen was different. Moreover, the normalcy that existed at Morton was a façade for, as Stephen learns in the confrontation scene, her mother has always felt repelled by her: "All your life I've felt very strangely towards you. . . . I've felt a kind of physical repulsion, a desire not to touch or to be touched by you—a terrible thing for a mother to feel—it has often made me deeply unhappy. I've often felt that I was being unjust, unnatural—but now I know that my instinct was right; it is you who are unnatural, not I" (203). Given the silence, lack of mutual confidence, and tacit cruelty that exists within this family, what basis does it offer as an example for the lives of same-sex couples?[39]

The assertion of women's sexual agency and the implicit demand for public recognition of women's choice of other women as sexual and life partners offended male privilege at the trials. The masculine style of the chief female actor in the novel further exacerbated this offense. The prosecution objected to the scientific naturalism of the novel, for which sexual and emotional ties between women were psychological and social facts no different in character from other such facts. The prosecution also objected to Hall's Pauline call for belief in a God of love rather than the law. But neither these factors nor the novel's call for tolerance rendered the novel unacceptable. What made it obscene was its potential effect on human imagination.

As I have noted earlier, Inskip experienced difficulty in finding offensive descriptions of sexual "practices" in the novel. Instead, the obscenity of the book consisted in its construction of marriage. First of all, Inskip found the book opposed to heterosexual marriage. "It is represented," he argues, "that normal sexual relations are repellent" (Appeal, 10).[40] Next, in the absence of explicitly sexual material, he is thrown back upon arguing that the very suggestion of lesbian marriage is calculated to inflame the imagination of susceptible readers, particularly male and female adolescents: "'Could you marry me, Stephen?' What does that mean. Imagine a young person reading that and coming to the end of the page. Imagine a pure woman or even a young man of adolescence reading it 'Could you marry me, Stephen?' What is the picture conjured up at once? He says 'What do those words mean?' His mind revolves round libidinous thoughts and it depraves him and corrupts him as he conjures up the picture which the writer of this book intends" (Appeal, 14–15). Melville responds quizzically that Angela's question scarcely inflames the imagination: "It is suggested—I do not follow the suggestion—that that will immediately arouse libidinous thoughts in the minds of people who read it. I should have thought, respectfully, that it simply suggests that the position is impossible" (Appeal, 52).

Inskip, however, was in one sense correct in complaining about the imaginative effect of Hall's novel. Her offense was to prompt her readers, especially younger ones, to imagine differently and better than Stephen herself could. The utopian aspect of the novel, despite its trafficking in conservative notions of male and female engenderment, lay in its capacity to challenge its readers to imagine lives and the world differently. The attacks launched on the novel, even the parodies that came from queer sources, such as Djuna Barnes, who mocks Hall and Troubridge's advocacy of same-sex marriage in *Ladies Almanack* (1928), testify to this capability. Marriage itself was to change.

After the frustration and anger but also the excitement and stimulus prompted by the suppression of the novel in England, life quieted for Hall and Troubridge. In the following years, their social lives narrowed as they spent long periods abroad or at Rye in East Sussex. They discovered this picturesque town on August 9, 1928, before Douglas's attack and at a time when *The Well of Loneliness* was selling well and being favorably reviewed. Troubridge wrote in her diary: "John & I called at 6.30, & in car to Rye. Hucksteps Row—to Anne Elsner. We got there for luncheon—all very delightful & we longed for a cottage there. We pottered in Rye, drove to Fairlight & went over an old cottage in Church Square."[41] On the next day, they looked at other vacant cottages before returning to London. The entry for August 10 is one of the rare occasions in the diaries on which Troubridge mentions that John is "happy." The couple's pleasure in Rye and the attendant fantasy of purchasing property and moving there reflected their state of mind in the immediate aftermath of the launch of the novel. In the much different atmosphere of September and October, between consultations with publishers and lawyers, the couple house-hunted in the southeast of England and eventually secured their first home in Rye, the perhaps too aptly named Journey's End.[42]

After they moved to another house, the Black Boy, in 1930, the meaning of Rye gradually changed as it came to signify that their moment in the limelight of London and Paris was passing. In addition, as Cline observes, Hall and Troubridge's relationship was in decline during this period. Hall sexually and emotionally withdrew from Troubridge into preoccupation with the manuscript of her next novel, *The Master of the House* (1932), a text that shows little confidence in the possibility of human communication.[43] Hall's confidence in the stability of long-term relationships between women, moreover, was subverted by upheavals in the lives of a small circle of friends. In nearby Smallhythe, the triangulated domesticity of the writer Christopher St. John (Ellen Terry's daughter), Edy Craig, and the painter Clare "Tony" Atwood was put in crisis when St. John fell in love with a younger married woman named Vita Sackville-West. Sackville-West, for her part, responded to St. John after having already triangulated and nearly ended the "marriage" of two other friends of Hall, Olive Rinder and Evelyn Irons. Hall and Troubridge were kept well informed of the turns in this tangle.[44]

Hall began writing *The Master of the House* on October 14, 1929; she completed it on November 25, 1931. The novel, a devout theosophical fiction and once again a bildungsroman in form, follows the life of Christophe Bénédit, a young Provençal carpenter, who from childhood onward experiences flashbacks to his prior life as the Carpenter of Nazareth. Christophe is another of Hall's inverted protagonists, but libido in this novel is thoroughly sublimated into a sacrificial humanism. A virginal, feminine male, the great love of Christophe's life is his cousin Jan (in terms of the Christian allegory, read John the Baptist). To Hall's chagrin, after a promising start, sales of the novel stalled, and reviews were unfavorable.[45] The novel was her first not to succeed, financially and critically.

Both she and Troubridge remained permanently convinced that it was Hall's "best book" (Troubridge, 73). It is possible, however, that the novel is one that Hall wrote primarily for herself at a time of great unhappiness. Moreover, there are signs that she faced its launch with uncertainty. In contrast to the publication of *The Well of Loneliness*, she deliberately refrained from setting the stage for the appearance of the new work. In a letter penned at the Black Boy on October 10, 1931, she wrote, quite amazingly, to Cape's American office: "I am particularly anxious, in fact I consider it essential, that no synopsis or 'blurb' should be employed in connection with this new book, either in its introduction to booksellers, or in Publishers' advertising, or in Press Publicity of any description, or upon the dust-wrapper of the volume itself." Her reasoning was that she did not want to put off either portion of her double readership, Sapphic and conventional, by describing the contents of the novel. Hall continues: "I think, therefore, that it would be a great mistake to inform members of the public what the nature of my new book is. I wish them to buy or borrow the book on the strength of my literary reputation and to find out for themselves, not only its subject, but also whether or not they like it as a piece of literature."[46] Hall's double retreat to the "literary" in this quotation sounds highly defensive, particularly since the interest in the degeneration of a highly localized community and the presentation of a crossgendered though not sexually inverted protagonist is as evident in *The Master of the House* as it had been in *Adam's Breed*. Succeeding in disappointing the expectations of nearly everyone, the novel diminished both Hall's reputation and the size of her "public."

Writing *The Master of the House* marked a reaction against the cult of celebrity. Hall received far more public support than vilification during and after the 1928 trials, and in the United States the courts held that the book was not obscene. In the letter cited above as well, she reminds her American publishers that *The Well of Loneliness* had gone on to sell over 150,000 copies worldwide. But the legal condemnation of the book in England affronted Hall and Troubridge's sense of entitlement, and an incisive caricature cut a wound that did not heal. Shortly after publication of the novel, a lampoon entitled *The Sink of Solitude* appeared, with a preface by P. R. Stephensen and a set of drawings by the talented young artist Beresford Egan.[47] In one of the illustrations, Egan portrays Hall attired as she was at the trial and nailed to a cross in the position usually reserved for Christ. Across her jumps a Betty Boop female nude. In this double image, Egan exposes the conflated identification within the novel of Christ, Stephen Gordon, and the author as redemptive martyr and victim. At the same time, the nude "votaress of the vulva," to use the phrase of Adrian Woodhouse, desublimates the novel's erotic earnestness.[48] In portraying Hall in her signature sombrero and tailored jacket, moreover, Egan subtly signifies the sexual signification of her high-style attire, which Kathryn Bond Stockton has characterized in terms of "cloth wounds," that is, gender-crossing dress that blazons rather than conceals the shame of gender dysphoria.[49] Shocked and outraged, Hall felt that she must atone for the blasphemous character of the drawing, hence the topic of her new novel, whose protagonist, caught between Allied forces and those of the Turks in Palestine during World War I, is crucified at the end of the novel, a martyr to the futility of war.

The failure of the novel further undermined Hall's relationship with Troubridge. Part of their contract from the start had been Troubridge's

18. Beresford Egan. *St. Stephen*. In Percy Reginald Stephensen et al., *The Sink of Solitude*. London: Hermes, 1928.

undertaking to help Hall achieve her ambitions as a writer. Troubridge, however, had made a serious error of judgment as to the quality of Hall's latest novel. Hall did not overtly blame her partner for the damage sustained as a result of the book, but Troubridge's value was diminished. After the success of *The Well of Loneliness*, Hall ceased to function as a commercial property, a continuing flow of royalties from *The Well* excepted; and she was troubled by continual anxieties as to whether she had lost her touch as a writer. The basis of Troubridge's failure, however, was more personal. Hall had based both *The Forge* and *A Saturday Life* in part on aspects of Troubridge's biography. After *The Well of Loneliness*, Troubridge no longer fired Hall's imagination. Hall needed something—and someone—else. Troubridge chose not to recognize this fact. Instead, from 1934 onward, she criticized Hall's draft fiction as it drew on the sensations and emotions of Hall's affair with a new lover. In a final counter-collaborative act, after Hall's death, Troubridge destroyed the last of the incomplete autobiographical fictions that Hall based on this adulterous relationship.[50]

In 1934, while vacationing in France, Hall met and fell in love with Evguenia Souline, a stateless White Russian émigré working in Paris whom Hall had hired as a nurse when Troubridge fell ill. From then until her death in 1943, Hall attempted to maintain relations with both women. During the 1920s, Hall and Troubridge had presented themselves to the world as a married pair, even as husband and wife.[51] In 1934, Hall found that this self-fashioning together with advocacy of monogamous marriage as the solution to the modern problem of lesbian existence carried with it certain liabilities. The perfect collaboration that, in Troubridge's eyes, had produced Hall's most widely read novel now made itself felt as a curb to Hall's need to begin yet another experiment in the relation between life and writing.

On July 30, after Troubridge was feeling better and Souline had returned to her home in Paris, Hall requested Troubridge's permission to spend time alone with Souline in Paris on the way back to England. Troubridge refused. Instead, she demanded that Hall immediately relinquish her new interest.[52] Troubridge did so in the same terms that she later used in her memoirs to discuss the origin of *The Well of Loneliness*. Since they had undertaken that project together and both been subject to the resulting public obloquy, Hall had no right to be unfaithful. Distraught, Hall wrote to Souline: "She means to keep us apart. I dare not blame her, I do not blame her. . . . When all the world seemed to be against me at the time of the 'Well of Loneliness' persecution, Una stood shoulder to shoulder with me, fighting every inch of that terrific battle. She has given me all of her interest and indeed of her life ever since we made common cause, therefore she has the right to do what she is doing and she will not cede that right" (32).[53] In any event, Troubridge was unable to prevent a sexual intimacy from developing between the pair. But already in this early letter, Hall let Souline know that their relation would always be secondary. The letter continues. After arguing all night, in the morning, Troubridge "reminded me over & over again until I have nearly gone mad, that I have always stood for fidelity in the case of inverted unions, that the eyes of the inverted all over the world are turned towards me, that they look up to me, in a word, that for years now they have respected me because my own union has been faithful and open" (33).[54] Hall had coveted the role of activist. Now she learned the price exacted by her role and her message.

Few members of the international set in which Hall moved advocated same-sex marriage. But before her death in 1916, Mrs. Havelock Ellis, herself a Sapphist, had already argued in a lecture on the social utility of sexual inversion that "all lovely things are possible when Love leads."[55] And evidence, both private and public, exists that the question of fidelity in pair-bonding was a live concern.[56] Francesco Rapazzini makes an important contribution to this discussion in his study of the life of Elisabeth de Gramont, Duchess of Clermont-Tonnerre, the beautiful young woman who became the most significant of Barney's long-term attachments.[57]

Despite the limits imposed by her social status and by marriage to a physically abusive husband, Gramont was a self-declared epicurean, socialist, and patron of advanced art. Intellectually curious, her socializing with Count Robert de Montesquiou, Mathilde de Morny, Colette's mistress, and other members of High Bohemia brought her into contact with the Sapphist writer Lucie Delarue-Mardrus, a sometime lover of Barney, who introduced the two women. In spring 1909, a relationship began that would last until Gramont's death in 1954.

After Barney began a serious affair with Romaine Brooks in fall 1916, Gramont reacted by engaging in a number of affairs of her own, the most significant of which was with Régina Regis de Oliviera, a Brazilian countess and writer. Gramont wrote to Barney: "At the end of the day, you haven't left Mrs. B[rooks] and I take exactly the same attitude. . . . I am a cynical philosopher and for me pleasure is perhaps the only certainty that we have, along with beauty. You are of course beautiful with your new hairstyle à la Brooks—the blond and the brunette—very becoming—and I wonder if it is right to try to separate that which life has brought together" (19). In reply, on June 20, 1918, Barney drew up to present to Gramont a "Marriage Contract stipulated after nine years of life together, joys and worries shared,

19. Romaine Brooks. *Elisabeth de Gramont, duchesse de Clermont-Tonnerre*, 1932. Musée Carnavalet, Paris, France. Photo: Réunion des Musées Nationaux/Art Resource, New York.

20. Romaine Brooks. *Miss Natalie Barney, "L'Amazone,"* 1920. Musée Carnavalet, Paris, France. Photo: Giraudon/Art Resource, New York.

and affairs confessed. For the survival of a bond that we believe—and wish to believe—is unbreakable" (6).

Intent on saving her connection with Gramont, Barney wrote:

> The union, sorely tried by the passing years, failed doubly the faithfulness test in its sixth year, showing us that adultery is inevitable in these relationships where there is no prejudice, no religion other than feelings, no laws other than desire, incapable of vain sacrifices that seem to be the negation of life itself.
>
> We are, however, strong in the knowledge that we can, without delusion or exaggeration, live or die for each other. So much so that while we recognize that one is not sufficient for the other, we are indispensable one for the other. Our love passion—which knew no obstacle, pure, exclusive, devouring, free as fire—has become love love—another sort of beauty, a different purity; mature, patient, pitiful, supple, cruel, logical, human and complex, as is life. (6)

In the second part of the contract, Barney considers the temptation to enter affairs that continually threatened to subvert the pair's "union." In case of inevitable straying, Barney writes, "Since the danger of affairs is ever present and impossible to foresee, one will just have to bring the other back, neither out of revenge, nor to limit the other, but because the union demands it. . . . No other union shall be so strong as this union, nor another joining so tender—nor relationship so lasting" (7).

Barney insists on the primacy of the "union" of two despite the fact of mutual adultery. While this statement is made in a private address, Noël Coward, a new friend and neighbor of Troubridge and Hall in Rye,[58] insists on the same point in the public setting of a hit play in which he starred with Gertrude Lawrence. The action of *Shadow Play* (1935) begins on the night when Vicky and Simon, an estranged married couple, consider filing for a divorce. In case interested parties might miss the point that the questions raised in the play are equally or even more pertinent to same-sex pairings, Coward assigns the couple the surname Gayforth (forthcomingly gay?). At the end of the play, despite their mutual infidelity, Vicky and Simon decide to stay together. Immediately before they do so, Vicky, who is sleeping restlessly after taking one sleeping tablet too many, recalls in a dream what Simon had said to her at a moment of mutual happiness during their honeymoon in Venice:

"Darling—we're here together close as close and it's the beginning—but we're going to be together for a long time—probably all our lives, so we must be careful—I want to reassure you now about later on—about any tricks the future might play on us—I know I love you with all my heart—with every bit of me—it's easy now, because it's summer weather and there isn't a cloud in the sky and we're alone—but there'll be other people presently—we can't live our whole lives on this little island—other people are dangerous—they spoil true love, not consciously because they want to, but because they're themselves—out for all they can get—mischievous—you do see what I mean, don't you?"

When Vicky indicates that she does, Simon continues: "If I'm bad or foolish or unkind, or even unfaithful—just remember this, because this is what really matters—this lovely understanding of each other—it may be a jumping-off place for many future journeys—but however long the journey one's got to come back some time, and this is the white cliffs of Dover—hang on to the white cliffs of Dover."[59]

Coward emphasizes "mischievous" others, who attempt to use sex to destroy love and companionship when they encounter it in the lives of others. Following a nervous collapse in 1926, he noted in a passage that can serve as a gloss of Simon's comment: "People were the danger. People were greedy and predatory, and if you gave them a chance they would steal unscrupulously the heart and soul out of you without really wanting to or even meaning to."[60] Coward makes the point again in the second half of *Present Laughter* (1942), a play whose protagonist, Gary Essendine, he was to tell the BBC in 1972 "is me."[61] "Union" is fated to be disrupted by the envy of others. Nonetheless, in one of his rare uses of metaphor, a patriotic one at that, Coward insists on the need to "hang on to" the memory of actual commitment. Barney, Gramont, and Coward all look for a third option, one that envisages monogamous commitment crossed but not canceled by the likelihood of adultery. The option was necessary in view of the fact that, as Barney points out, their intimate relationships were governed by "no prejudice, no religion other than feelings, no laws other than desire."

In recognizing the experimental character of the ways of life that these individuals and others like them devised, it is important to remember that the solutions they attempted are both individualistic and focused on the primary couple in any particular set of relations. In this respect, when Hall argued on behalf of same-sex monogamy, the activist atmosphere that she promoted, however social and public, was in the service of private lives. In this respect, the new world of lesbian identity that Hall helped bring into existence implied a step back from the complex, open-edged sets of relations that she had constituted in her youth or that Cushman managed over many years. In this respect, the older model of sexual and emotional ties between women resembles to a degree the collective experiments of late twentieth-century lesbian and queer life recorded, for example, by an archivist such as Catherine Opie in her photographic dossier of radical female collectives in the West Adams neighborhood of Los Angeles.[62] Despite the obvious differences between the two ways of life, Victorian and Edwardian "cousinage" has more to do with queer sociality than do the directions set out by Barney, Hall, and Coward between 1918 and 1935, directions pursued at present in the gay and lesbian politics of liberal reform.[63]

9

From Sexual Inversion to Cross Gender in "Miss Ogilvy Finds Herself"

In **The Well of Loneliness,** Hall parsed female same-sex desire through the sexological model of sexual inversion. As I mentioned in the preceding chapter, this choice was strategic. If Hall was to claim public space for the lives of subjects of female same-sex desire, it was necessary that those subjects be recognizable in widely shared, implicitly objective terms. For this purpose, the obvious place to turn was the language of sexology; and in that direction the available terms were *female homosexuality* and *female sexual inversion*, phrases in synonymous use at the time. In choosing such a model, however, Hall subjected herself and those on whose behalf she wrote to the operations of medical biopolitics. To the degree to which the activist objectives of *The Well of Loneliness* succeeded, female subjects of same-sex desire would be normalized as masculine women.

Hall's choice was not only political; it was also personal. From the mid-1920s onward, Hall identified herself as a sexual invert. When she declared her love to Souline in 1934 and Souline responded that she feared that their mutual attraction might be "emotionally wrong," Hall replied: "My dearest child, it is not emotionally wrong for your John. I have never felt an impulse towards a man in all my life, this because I am a congenital invert.

For me to sleep with a man would be 'wrong' because it would be an outrage against nature. Can't you try to understand, to believe that we exist—we people who are not of the so called normal? Where's your medical knowledge—we do exist and believe me you must not think us perverted."[1] Hall's performance of self in this letter demonstrates the naturalization of a new identity—both singular and plural—in the same breath in which she acknowledges that this new identity is "not of the so called normal." To Hall, it was important to emphasize that inversion occurred naturally, that is, congenitally. She claimed that because of this origin, her desires were not inherently immoral or "perverted." Instead the moral character of inverted passion depended upon whether its expression was motivated by friendship: "love without friendship is not love but lust" (47).

While Hall was determined to rivet her desire to a fixed position, the ontological status of the object of that desire remained anything but secure. Proceeding with a tutorial on the varieties of sexual subjectivity, Hall informed Souline that she was bisexual: "Don't you know that an enormous number of people are bi-sexual, capable of falling in love equally with a man or a woman?" (51). Unlike inversion, however, bisexuality did not necessarily name a specific sexual type. It might denote instead indetermination, uncertainty, and unpredictability regarding the direction of one's desires and engagements. In Havelock Ellis's study of female sexual inversion, Ellis had shown himself notoriously unable to provide an organic etiology of the womanly woman's desire for a masculine woman.[2] In the letter, Hall supplemented Ellis's account of feminine women who were the objects of desire of masculine women with the theory of primitive or original bisexuality put forward by Freud in his 1920 essay on female homosexuality.[3] Referring to the work of a medical student at Cambridge to whose research she had recently contributed, she wrote: "I helped a young doctor a little while ago to prepair [sic] his paper for his final medical degree at Cambridge; he maintains that the bi-sexual is the true *normal*" (52).

Hall's commitment to the sexual-inversion model committed her to two contradictory views of sexual formation: one in which it took a precisely defined form and another in which lack of definition was predominant. As I have noted, in doing so, she accurately mirrored an inconsistency within sexological thinking that radically undermined the attempt to suture sexual object-choice with personal identity. There may, however, be yet a further factor in play. The model of relationship that Hall projected onto her connection with Souline suggests that Hall's notion of female masculinity was relational. In Hall's thought and personal experience, it was impossible to think about female sexual inversion apart from the inverted subject's desire for a womanly woman.

At the same time that Hall became officially, so to speak, an invert, she wrote a short story, "Miss Ogilvy Finds Herself," with an inverted female protagonist. Within the story Hall suggests a relational model of sexual identity. In doing so, she suggests something else as well, a notion that Miss Ogilvy experiences her sexual and gendered self in a continual process of transition between the condition of being female and the condition of being male. In other words, Hall emphasizes what a twenty-first-century theorist such as Jay Prosser refers to as "the trope of crossing."[4] In this context, one might say that the old-fashioned (at least to Freud) concept of sexual inversion draws Hall forward to postmodern concepts of transsexual and transgendered identity. In speaking of this impetus in Hall's work, I prefer to use the term *crossgendered* in order to avoid anachronistic usage. It is noteworthy that Prosser's conceptualization of both categories takes place in individual not relational terms, though there is evidence particularly in accounts of transgendered experience that the selfhood of such subjects is at times construed in explicitly relational terms.[5]

First written in 1926 and likely revised for publication in a collection of short stories by Hall that appeared in 1934, "Miss Ogilvy Finds Herself" is situated significantly both before and after the date of publication of *The Well of Loneliness*. Accordingly, Troubridge may be correct in characterizing the short story as the point of departure for the novel.[6] But the story's double temporal relation to the novel also permits a retrospective look that finds in *The Well*'s avowed inversionism license for the exploration of crossgendered existence. Prosser, for example, reads the novel as a fictional transsexual autobiography written before the medical invention of the term.[7]

In the realist first half of the story, Hall shows how service in extreme conditions during World War I makes it possible for Ogilvy to escape for a time the confining limits of her upper-middle-class family and to "come out" as a subject of female same-sex desire. This narrative is abruptly juxtaposed with what Hall refers to as a venture "into the realms of the fantastic."[8] In the second half of the story, the protagonist escapes into a land and seascape, at once primitive and national, in which sexual love between him/herself and another woman, impossible at home, becomes recoverable as a result of returning to a lost "English" paradise. Hall's fantasy is both utopian and dystopian. As characterization, it focuses upon the reality of split subjectivities with attendant unhappiness and lack of fulfillment. At the same time, by successfully traversing with Miss Ogilvy disjunctures of temporality, gender, sex, and culture, Hall moves the reader sympathetic to the character's desires to a here and now that is also an elsewhere at another time.

The generic splitting of the story permits Hall's most outspoken exploration of the modernist–antimodernist dialectic that structures her work. Ogilvy is both a beneficiary and a casualty of modernity. The mass mobilization of populations in wartime that occurs in Western Europe in World War I enables her to escape from a confining domestic existence into a rewarding mental and physical life within civilian medical services at the front. This change likewise enables her for the first time to meet other women like herself and to exercise her masculine selfhood. At the same time, ideological and economic retrenchment after the war aborts this change and shifts her back into the former pattern, which she now finds literally unlivable. For Miss Ogilvy, escape from this mold becomes necessary no matter the price.

This escape is framed within antimodernist terms of return to a primitive, pastoral, indigenously "English" existence. Even the national referent is marked by the modernist/antimodernist caesura. As I discuss in Chapter 1, Hall attempted early to position herself in alliance with the renovation of English music. From about 1910 onward, composers and musicians turned to pre- and early modern musical melodies, harmonies, instrumentation, and folk materials for resources in fashioning musical Modernism in England. In order to create a national style, practitioners adapted the materials of nearly lost and newly reinvented traditions. This turn back in order to move forward resulted in odd temporal dislocations, with the result that what was new could be characterized as simultaneously both primitive and decadent insofar as the return to origins was taking place late in the history of civilization. The crisis that attends this temporal loop is exacerbated in the fantasy portion of Hall's story, whose Neolithic male protagonist is about to be massacred along with his fellow villagers by Bronze Age invaders. The story is the most apocalyptic of Hall's various envisagings of the threat posed to communal existence as a result of technological and other contemporary innovations.

Apologies on behalf of sexual inverts were often framed in terms of eugenics, which Mrs. Havelock Ellis defines as "the study of all agencies, under social control, that may improve or impair the racial qualities of future generations."[9] In these accounts, the chronotypes of evolutionary progress and degeneracy are to the fore. Hall draws upon both. In its second half, the narrative moves backward in time to a moment in prehistoric Britain when a Neolithic community was about to be supplanted by Bronze Age invaders. Hall observes the truths of contemporary paleontology in describing the young warrior whom Miss Ogilvy becomes. He has "sad brown eyes like those of a monkey. . . . His nose was blunt, his jaw somewhat bestial" (26). But he also shows signs of evolution into a higher type: "his mouth, though full-lipped, contradicted his jaw, being very gentle and sweet in expression" (26). In fact, he is superior to most of the people whom Miss Ogilvy knows in twentieth-century England. Moving forward into the past, s/he becomes a composite, in some respects improved, type. This ambivalent realization parallels representations of sexual inversion by such self-consciously sympathetic sexologists as Havelock Ellis. On the one hand, Ellis continually compares sexual inverts with members of savage and primitive races. On the other hand, he argues that inverts are characterized by superior endowments, such as artistic genius and shamanic powers. Inverts are both early and late, primitive but also subject to the degenerative pressures of civilization, and at the same time harbingers of an improved future human existence.[10]

In a prefatory note to the 1934 volume, Hall refers to Ogilvy as a "sexual invert," but she also complicates the sexological picture. In a general discussion of the definition of human existence, Michel Foucault has discussed several ways in which impermissible thoughts may nonetheless be uttered. He describes the last of these as follows: "It consists of subjecting an utterance, which appears to conform to the accepted code, to another code whose key is contained within that same utterance so that this utterance becomes divided within itself. It says what it says, but it adds a silent surplus that quietly enunciates what it says and according to which code it says what it says."[11] The representation of Miss Ogilvy as a masculinized woman corresponds to the code of third-sex theory. As it turns out, defined and defining herself in this way, she is incapable of becoming a sexual actant. And yet the climax of the story is the moment when s/he *is able* to experience bliss with another woman. The affirmation of sexual intimacy between two women provides the second code at work within the story. It is the story's "silent surplus," its motivating ethic. Implicit is the need to go beyond the contradictory and disabling terms of sexological theory.

In the account of Ogilvy's wartime experiences that opens the story, Hall in effect argues that war service enabled many female subjects of same-sex desire to leave home, find suitable work, and gain economic independence. As a result, they were able to find each other and themselves. Again, in the "Author's Forenote," Hall memorializes "the noble and selfless work done by hundreds of sexually inverted women during the Great War." At the same time, the story is shadowed by reflections on loss, mourning, and melancholy prompted by World War I. Like other writers, such as Virginia Woolf, Hall responds to the fissures opened by World War I by imagining a patriotism before the imperial kind that can become available as a possibility in a post-imperial future. "Miss Ogilvy Finds Herself" is at one with Woolf's *Three Guineas* (1938) in the opposition of both writers to marriage as a career for women, in their grief over the death of young men in war, and in their disdain for the conversion of the land and seascape of England into private holdings.[12]

Hall turns to fantasy and aspects of dream-narrative to represent the central action of the story, Ogilvy's transformation into a heroic but doomed young fighter. In doing so, Hall articulates psychoanalytic insights within a theosophical armature. Theosophy provides a vernacular mode of speculative psychology whereby Hall attempts to explain her perception of the possibilities, including bodily, of becoming other.[13] Theosophists were especially aware of constraints of gender, sexuality, and race, which some were willing to challenge. Ellis, for example, remarks that Madame Blavatsky was "either homosexual or bisexual" (197). The aura of sexual nonconformity that surrounded her and close associates, such as the Anglican clergyman Charles Webster Leadbetter, drew attacks upon the group. In this light, it is not surprising that *Lucifer*, the English theosophical magazine, condemned the behavior of Oscar Wilde. Despite efforts to maintain the respectability of the movement and its leaders, however, theosophist teachings on gender and, implicitly, sexuality continued to be rich and contradictory. Theosophical mythology of reincarnation envisaged the self as moving through a series of, in turn, increasingly masculine or feminine physical existences at different times and in different places. These changes were used to explain the phenomena of sexual inversion. Experience as a subject of both genders was necessary to the perfection of the self, which joined aspects of what Freud refers to as the bodily ego with what theosophists called "a True or Higher Self that stood beyond and before the only temporarily sexed and gendered self of this particular incarnation—the 'I' that was always watching and analyzing its present vehicle was much more than could ever be expressed on the 'lower planes.' "[14]

Theosophical axioms shape the representation of Miss Ogilvy. Her transformation into a primitive warrior makes sense in terms of the view that "reincarnation" could "provide a sense of a different—and somehow more true or authentic—identity drawn from one's past" (Dixon, 428). The transgendered, implicitly feminist aspects of this identity had already been sounded in 1905 when a certain "W.F.K." wrote in the *Theosophical Review* that suffragettes reincarnated "racial Viking tendencies."[15] The concept of the Higher Self also helps account for the fact that Miss Ogilvy continues to be Miss Ogilvy even when she no longer remembers her twentieth-century existence as well as when she has become a Neolithic "he." The sense of ontology involved is counter to any singular notion of what being might mean.

Beginning as a study of changes in English manners stemming from the war years, in its course, "Miss Ogilvy Finds Herself" turns into a primitivist fantasy. Hall marks this shift in terms of a split in the consciousness of the protagonist: "She thought that she lay there struggling to reason, that her eyes were closed in the painful effort, and that as she closed them she continued to puff the inevitable cigarette. At least that was what she thought at one moment—the next, she was out in a sunset evening, and a large red sun was sinking slowly to the rim of a distant sea" (24). The space indicated by the dash is apocalyptic, by which I mean that it registers a complete change in the spatio-temporal organization of the subject. Even before that moment, two shes are registered: in theosophical terms, the I of the Higher Self that thinks into being, physically prostrate and "struggling to reason." On the left side of the dash, Miss Ogilvy is the former successful commander of a Red Cross ambulance unit on the French front. The salient word is "former." Before the war, Ogilvy had played the role of spinster daughter in an upper-middle-class family. After her father dies, she becomes responsible for managing the affairs of her ailing mother and two "neurotic" (9) younger sisters. A shortage of manpower as a result of exorbitant casualties gives Miss Ogilvy an opportunity to leave home for London. There she forms a motorized ambulance unit and successfully lobbies for permission to move her equipment and nurses to the front lines. On the right side of the dash, Miss Ogilvy, while on a solitary visit to an unspoiled island off the coast of Devon, is transported into a prehistoric past.

She forgets her dismal twentieth-century existence and briefly enjoys life as the capable and tender Stone Age lover of a beautiful young "woman" (26).

Hall's story begins with the end of the war, the disbanding of the unit, and the forced return of Ogilvy to peacetime unemployment. Driven to despair by blank existence in a Surrey village, Miss Ogilvy, on a desperate whim, leaves for the island. The apocalypse of World War I—which Hall sees to have been both devastating and liberating—stands in causal relation to the apocalyptic metadiscourse in which the hybrid fiction is set. The setting sun and archaic beauty of the island are enmeshed in a discursive topography that signifies nation and empire. In an apocalyptic register, the sunset implies the end of the British Empire consequent upon the reduced status of Great Britain after the war. Although the passage cited emphasizes phenomenological aspects of life ("moment," duration), Hall's primary emphasis is ontological—a point she makes clear in the sentence that follows: "Miss Ogilvy knew that she was herself, that is to say she was conscious of her being, and yet she was not Miss Ogilvy at all, nor had she a memory of her" (56). Ogilvy's demand entails a transformation of being that requires the loss of defining aspects of consciousness such as memory. The effacement of her memory is a means used by Hall to resist psychoanalytic recuperation of the significance of the story. Without access to memory, Freudian psychoanalysis cannot provide a metonymic account of Miss Ogilvy's consciousness through the analysis of dreams, symptomatic actions, and so forth. Instead, Ogilvy's desire to become otherwise becomes imaginable only within the terms of another, transgendered, even transsexual existence. Moving in the opposite direction in the second half of the story, Hall mimes Freudian analysis through Ogilvy's anamnesis. Remembering her earlier existence simultaneously with recognizing the disappearance of her memory as Miss Ogilvy, Ogilvy is able to emphasize that her love of a woman is "perfectly natural" (24).

In addition to theosophy, Hall draws upon sexological description in representing "the difficulties" of Miss Ogilvy's "nature" (8). For one thing, there is that cigarette. Ellis writes in his classic description of the modern lesbian, "In the habits not only is there frequently a pronounced taste for smoking cigarettes, often found in quite feminine women, but also a decided taste and toleration for cigars."[16] In other details too, Hall follows Ellis's typology. For example, she notes Ogilvy's "tall, awkward body with its queer look of strength" (3). But sexology provides only one discursive frame for the passage. The social changes brought about by the war create the conditions in which it becomes possible and necessary for Miss Ogilvy to demand *another existence.*

Hall shows how the changes in women's roles necessitated by the war effort in effect produced a new form of sexual identity, single and collective, for women who, before the war, had been forced either to live celibate lives or to accept subjection within the family. This modern identity is termed *lesbian.* In the present context, lesbian existence, though characterized by Ogilvy in terms of female masculinity, is not so much the discursive effect of sexual-inversion theory as the result of social and technological change. But she is also a throwback to the heroic Dorians (ancient Greek soldiers with male lovers) whom Edward Carpenter describes in *The Intermediate Sex* (1908). The members of "that glorious Unit" (Hall, 4) display the "hardihood and courage" of those whom Carpenter prophesies will build up "new forms of society, new orders of thought, and new institutions of human solidarity."[17] Hall adapts Carpenter's ideal, in context male, to lesbian subjects. She observes that when Ogilvy went to London during the war, for the first time she realized that she was not the only odd woman at large: "In London she had found herself quite at her ease, for many another of her kind was in London doing excellent work for the nation. It was really surprising how many cropped heads had suddenly appeared as it were out of space; how many Miss Ogilvies, losing their shyness, had come forward asserting their right to serve, asserting their claim to attention" (11–12). After the war, the arena of this heroic effort is removed, and a quiet struggle ensues as determined efforts are made to circumscribe women once more within the private sphere. Ogilvy experiences "complete frustration" (6) as she is pushed back into domestic existence.

Although enlisted in the service of "the nation," Hall makes clear that Ogilvy's unit maintained a distance between itself and the war effort. First of all, the Red Cross service was nonbelligerent; second, Ogilvy puts herself and her cohorts in the service not of the British field command but of their French allies. In this way, Ogilvy accentuates the humanity of her service, not its identification with government objectives. This sort of independence was noticed. Nor was it all that was noticed. Three years after the war, for the first time in British history, an attempt to outlaw lesbian sexual practices was made in Parliament. The amendment, which reads as follows, attempted to extend to women involved in sexual activity with other women the same sanctions that had been levied against Oscar Wilde in

1895: "Any act of gross indecency between female persons shall be a misdemeanor and punishable in the same manner as any such act committed by male persons under section 11 of the Criminal Law Amendment Act 1885."[18] Although the amendment was passed, the bill to which it was attached failed to clear the House. These are *not* the terms upon which the Miss Ogilvies of World War I wished to achieve equality with men before the law. The destruction of nascent lesbian existence experienced by Miss Ogilvy is directly related to the efforts made to intimidate female subjects of same-sex desire and to exclude middle-class women from well-paid managerial and professional work. Hall contends that this process intensified after the war despite, in part because of, legal steps taken at the time to emancipate women. In *Three Guineas,* Woolf observes, in a rhetoric at once materialist, sardonic, and apocalyptic, the opening of the professions to women by act of Parliament in 1919. She likewise demonstrates how modest the economic advances opened for women proved in actuality to be. Similarly, the achievement of partial enfranchisement for women in 1918 did not preclude efforts to return them to the world of "the private house."[19]

The threat of extinction hovers over the idyll that Ogilvy experiences after her metempsychosis as an ancient Briton. Just what or whom, however, is threatened with extinction? Is it young men, whether like Wilfred Owen they resisted the seductions of war or whether they rushed to their deaths? Is it, by analogy, the British Empire in decline? Does the second half of the story begin a work of mourning for the loss of national greatness? Is it the anachronistic world of Victorian domestic values—uncomfortably lodged in the woman with whom the Briton is in love? Is it the sexual subjectivity that marks Ogilvy as a split subject: a self-suppressing, middle-aged, middle-class spinster and, in another incarnation, a man who can take a woman as Miss Ogilvy, shamefully, cannot? Is it the late Victorian sexology, summed in the name of Ellis, that Hall needed in order to give scientific sanction to *The Well of Loneliness*? The answer to all these questions is yes.

When Miss Ogilvy arrives, she meets the owner of the island, Mrs. Nanceskivel, who shows her the partial remains of the skeleton of a late Stone Age man, dug up on the island and now kept in a cupboard in the scullery because she does not want the island to become the site of an archaeological dig. "'Look, miss, he was killed,' she remarked rather proudly, 'and they tell me that the axe that killed him was bronze'" (21–22).

The indignity to which the fragments are subject angers Ogilvy. For Ogilvy (and Hall) *Mrs.* Nanceskivel is typical of those married women whom Woolf describes in *Three Guineas* as the economic and ideological captives (and upholders) of the "patriarchal" order (64). "And now Miss Ogilvy was swept by another emotion that was even more strange and more devastating: such a grief as she had not conceived could exist; a terrible unassuageable grief, without hope, without respite, without palliation, so that with something akin to despair she touched the long gash in the skull. Then her eyes, that had never wept since her childhood, filled slowly with large, hot, difficult, tears. She must blink very hard, then close her eyelids, turn away from the lamp" (22–23). Miss Ogilvy takes leaves of her hostess and goes upstairs. Mourning the profanation of the man's remains, she also mourns the loss of potential capabilities of agency within herself. In recognizing loss, she approaches at-one-ment with the deceased. Then the moment of metempsychosis occurs.

After struggling, alone on her bed, with "reason," she wakes as another subject, evidently although not definitively the warrior whose remains she has just grieved. "She pictured herself as immensely tall; she was feeling immensely tall at that moment. As a matter of fact she was five feet eight which, however, was quite a considerable height when compared to her fellow-tribesmen. She was wearing a single garment of pelts which came to her knees and left her arms sleeveless. Her arms and her legs, which were closely tattooed with blue zig-zag lines, were extremely hairy" (25). Moments later, she recognizes that she is a "young man" (26). As such, she experiences a romantic interlude. As the sun sets, the "pretty" young woman at the young man's side bestows upon him her virgin love: "All of me is for you and none other. For you this body has ripened" (26). The pair retires to the same cave, the sight of which had jarred Ogilvy's recollection as she arrived on the island. They make love. Although the fact is not stated, the text implies that on this very night the young man will be killed. Presumably, his "wife" will be taken captive and enslaved.

Ogilvy achieves romantic union with another person only when the gift of an attractive younger woman's love enables her to cross from the liminal state of she/he ("Her arms and legs . . . were extremely hairy") into her identification as a "young man," warrior, de facto husband. The pronoun shift from she to he is bridged by the passage in which her/his "little companion" both defines herself as feminine ("pretty," she calls herself) and declares her love for the warrior. Ogilvy simultaneously marvels "because of her beauty" (25), an unmixed pleasure that Miss Ogilvy never permitted herself to enjoy.

Ogilvy can fully respond to another female only if she is able to identify her as woman and finds that identification to be accepted: "'You . . . woman,' he murmured contentedly, and the sound seemed to come from the depths of his being" (26). To be desirable, the female object of desire has to be positioned as a particular subject. In this context, the English word *woman* like the French word *femme* and the German word *Frau* engenders the female as *wife*. The subject is the familiar Victorian one of the angel of the house—the figure that Woolf tells us it is necessary for the modern female writer to kill.[20] Defined in terms of "Love" (32), her name in Neolithic language carries a number of meanings that are more resonant with Victorian bourgeois ideology than with prehistoric existence. The narrator remarks that the warrior's "speech was slow and lacking in words when it came to expressing a vital emotion, so one word must suffice and this he now spoke, and the word that he spoke had a number of meanings. It meant: 'Little spring of exceedingly pure water.' It meant: 'Hut of peace for a man after battle.' It meant: 'Ripe red berry sweet to the taste.' It meant 'Happy small home of future generations.' All these things he must try to express by a word, and because of their loving she understood him" (26–27). These meanings conflate in a single term the concepts of feminine and natural purity, sexual enjoyment and its naturalness, plus the values of home, family, and community. This combination coheres within the terms of the subjectivity of the former Miss Ogilvy, a capable woman of conservative views, who happened to be sexually and emotionally drawn to other women. These values, however, can be experienced in unified fashion by Ogilvy only if she becomes completely other, a he. In Miss Ogilvy's transformation, moving from one side of the hyphen to the other requires no work; it just happens. Nothing in Miss Ogilvy's everyday existence, however, is easy. And the prehistoric Britain to which s/he arrives is marked by tensions and threatened with violence. The resistance of actuality to desire is signified in the threat of attack on the village by the newcomers. Unlike the warrior, whose weapons are of stone, the interlopers carry weapons of bronze. Although they are nominally "friends" of the natives, the warrior fears them. His Cassandra-like warnings of imminent disaster have made him persona non grata with the woman's father, who is the head of the

village. Accordingly, the love of the couple is threatened both by an unaware patriarchal authority within the village and by the superiority of newcomers.

Hall's passionate identification with young soldiers helps explain why
Miss Ogilvy, when transformed, becomes a young warrior. Like Hall too,
at the outbreak of war, Ogilvy declares: "If only I were a man!" (10; Baker,
54–55). At the start of World War I, Hall was caught up in war fever; but,
in "Miss Ogilvy Finds Herself," something else is at work: the love and guilt
of author and character in face of the deaths of young soldiers. The intensity
of Ogilvy's unacknowledged mourning shows in the fact that she is found
dead the morning after metempsychosis occurs. As Freud says, loved "objects . . . are . . . in a sense taken into our ego." In the face of mortality,
"libido clings to its objects and will not renounce those that are lost even
when a substitute lies ready to hand. Such then is mourning."[21] Ogilvy's
crossgendered identification enables her to mourn both the loss of the possibility of her own sexual and emotional fulfillment and the losses sustained
by the young men whose wounds she tended in wartime.

At the end of "Miss Ogilvy Finds Herself," Miss Ogilvy is found the
next morning, seated in front of the cave in which her other self has found
bliss. "She was dead, with her hands thrust deep into her pockets" (34).
The position of her hands, a typical gesture, indicates her inability ever to
arrive at the moment when she would actually touch one of the women
whom she loved. Earlier, Mrs. Nanceskivel pointed out to her the mark of
the gash on the ancient man's skull. The scarred skull in the story suggests
the diacritical marking of Ogilvy as a split subject: schizophrenic, in Luce
Irigaray's term, as a result of her disidentification from her roles as woman;
caught in mourning; sundered in the classification of herself as a man/
woman; split in ethnic, national, and racial terms as a traditional English
woman whose moment of emancipation had occurred within the terms of
mass mobilization and technological advance.[22]

Marking this split, Hall's story too is generically divided. But this aesthetic utterance says more than even an "expert" could, were he available
for forensic analysis. Retrospectively predicting the end of the theory of
sexual inversion upon which it is in part modeled, Hall's story glimpses the
approaching end of the oppressive institutions whose traces characterize
third-sex theory. The story looks backward to a time before the denial of
sexual alterity; it looks ahead to a time, after death, loss, and mourning,
when a different imagination of sexual and emotional ties, including those

of transsexual subjects and those who call themselves he-shes, would make other lives possible.

As I have mentioned, Miss Ogilvy's split subjectivity resonates in a number of registers: in that of woman defined as wife; in that of the lesbian as modern sexual subject, relegated simultaneously to invisibility and, as Hall learned after the publication of *The Well of Loneliness*, to contumely. The phantasmatic conversion of Ogilvy from female to male lends itself to a postmodern transsexual reading. Her comment "If only I were a man!" suggests that she may be transsexual before the fact. Ogilvy's contrary-to-fact wish, however, acknowledges that her actual body is female. And this recognition is consistent with the possibility that what she expresses here is recognition of her existence as crossgendered. This possibility is further underwritten if we consider the direction of her desire in the story as not to the wish to become man but rather to actualize in her own bodily ego the relation of male to female that is figured metaphorically in the union of the tender male warrior with the brave young woman who will become his wife for one night only. What Ogilvy may desire is an entry into manhood that would unlock her affectively and sexually and, through finding sexual love, enable her to reclaim her own estranged female embodiment. If so, then, in her own fictional terms and relying on the languages of sex and psychology that existed at the time, what Hall envisages for her readers is the existence of a fully enabled he-she. In that case too, Hall invites readers of the twenty-first century to consider crossgendered existence not in terms of individual but of relational identity.

10

After Economic Man

"The Rest Cure—1932"

The fates of Miss Ogilvy and other protagonists of the short stories included in Hall's 1934 collection are marked by their experience of World War I. This much is also true of Charles Duffell, the protagonist of "The Rest Cure—1932." As someone who played the role of a leading industrialist during the war, Duffell's consciousness is very much an effect of that conflict. As with Ogilvy, Hall is interested in knowing whether he can survive the war. This question is specifically directed toward Duffell's masculine engenderment. In Hall's analysis, the coherence of Duffell's masculine bodily ego is based upon his identification with male power and authority in economic and genealogical relations that exclude the possibility of a rapprochement with women. Duffell's isolation is exacerbated by an even more striking absence of significant ties with male equals or subordinates, despite his position as the moving force within his company. Duffell has neither female lovers nor male friends.

The question with which the war leaves Duffell is rather like the question that the next war would present to Noël Coward and others of his generation. At a lunch early in 1946, Coward was asked "whether he could be said to have survived the war." Crisply he replied, "Like Mother

Goddam, I shall always survive."[1] At White Cliffs, a house overlooking the
sea at Dover, which he had recently leased, however, Coward discovered
that survival was indeed in question. During World War II, Coward had
been both a leading propagandist on behalf of the British Navy and a widely
traveled entertainer of members of British and Commonwealth armed services.[2] On January 29, he wrote in his diary:

> A heavy sea, but bright sunshine. After breakfast I started thinking . . .
> [about an upcoming show,] but could not concentrate. After a while I
> began reading Roald Dahl's short stories about flying and war experi-
> ences. Then suddenly I found out what was wrong. These stories pierced
> the layers of my consciousness and stirred up the very deep feelings I
> had during the war and have since, almost deliberately, been in danger
> of losing. If I forget these feelings or allow them to be obscured because
> they are uncomfortable, I shall be lost. . . . Something click[ed] in my
> mind and brought back the things I knew so clearly during the war; not
> all the time, but at moments in hospitals and Messes and ships. I must
> hang on to those moments or I shall not have survived the war. (50)

In contrast, Duffell remains unknowing of "the layers" of his "consciousness" and "the very deep feelings" stirred by the war.

Considering the state of mind of this character led Hall to the most self-
conscious analysis of the ego that occurs in her fiction. Charles Duffell is a
subject of suppressed cross gender. In the story, to exist in this condition is
to find existence intolerable. He is also someone whose selfhood has been
bound over to a highly regimented subscription to doing what is expected
of him. As the date "1932" signifies, the story engages public contexts, in
particular, the historical one of the consequences of the stock market crash
of 1929. A conservative critique of the modern market economy structures
the first major psychic movement in the story: namely, Duffell's abandonment of his constituted self. The consequent opening to an ecstatic but
pragmatically impossible sense of cross gender occurs in the story's final
movement.

Hall understands this turn in terms of the pantheistic ontology that she
had expressed earlier in her poetry and in *The Well of Loneliness*. Feminist
philosophy of the decade of World War I provides the intellectual and ethical ground for the representation of Duffell's transition. In "The New Mysticism" of May Sinclair, the story finds a metaphysical basis for Hall's

conviction that complex engenderment and the need for sexual and emotional intimacy are integral to the life of the self in the world. Sinclair's phrase refers to her eclectic synthesis of Western philosophy and Buddhist thought. Defending what she describes as the position of "pantheistic Monism,"[3] Sinclair writes, "The metaphysical argument . . . supposes one infinite and absolute Spirit manifesting itself in many forms to many finite spirits. It supposes the selves of the many finite spirits to receive and to maintain their reality in and through one infinite Self as truly as their organisms received and maintained their life through Its appearance as one Life-Force" (334). As the use of the pronoun "Its" indicates, this "Self" is not anthropomorphic. It is also not synonymous with the "Life-Force." Paradoxically, however, it is a form of both conscious and unconscious existence.[4]

After October 1929, Hall remained a wealthy woman, though on a reduced scale. The suffering brought on by the ensuing economic depression did not prompt her even at this time to question the extreme inequality of the distribution of wealth and property in the United Kingdom. Politically, she remained a quietist. But the economic shock and its aftermath did remind her of the fictional character of the rational and self-interested "I" on whose existence the theory of classical political economy depends. Hall also recognized the isolating and ultimately destructive capabilities of egoistic illusions of ambition, accomplishment, wealth, and power. As a successful steel manufacturer, Duffell made a major contribution to the British effort during World War I. The economic downturn that occurred shortly after the war, however, breached his confidence in the secular trinity of nation-state, empire, and international finance. For Duffell, the postwar order entailed looming bankruptcy for his firm. Losing his bearings on a trip to New York, the world's new financial capital, he decides to take a plunge: "That delirious orgy of speculation. . . . The germs of the illness so thick in the air that only to breathe was to catch the infection—he had caught it at once, yes, and caught it badly. Looking back it appeared incredible that a staid and experienced man of affairs should have hoped thus to add vast sums to his fortune, yet so it had been, he had hoped for just that, he had hoped to pump golden blood into Duffells."[5] The market hysteria to which Duffell succumbs accentuates his aloneness even further. It is difficult to be other-regarding in the midst of a financial bubble.

Three years later, the economy has collapsed; and Duffell's company is about to do so as well. Simultaneously, he breaks down. Like Coward in his moment of truth, Duffell is overcome with an unbearable "anguish to know himself alive" (181). Unlike Coward, however, Duffell has exited the war with no "moments" of knowledge of alterity "in hospitals and Messes and ships"—or in factories, in Duffell's case—to cling to. Further, given this absence, he lacks awareness even of the need to "hang on to" something other than the I. He knows only that he has in fact nothing to hang onto. To compensate, he fantasizes about the possibility of escape in stasis: " If only one need not see, need not hear, need not be conscious of movement and sound; if only a man could lie absolutely still in a universe of invulnerable stillness" (186). In this way, one might hope to escape the "anguish" of knowing oneself to be alive. Undergoing a loss of affect that he mistakenly reads as a transformation of the self that can restore him to "a conviction of power," Duffell experiences a delusory "Godlike and omnipotent sense of detachment." He asks:

> What is Charles Duffell? The purest illusion. That's the reason why none of this need go on, why Charles Duffell himself need not go on . . . so easy, as he never really existed! IT was born and tradition labeled IT: "Man." IT might have been labeled anything else. IT might have been labeled: "Tree," for instance. And he looked up, and said, "I see men as trees, walking." Undoubtedly, very significant words. . . . or IT might have been given no label at all, in which case IT could have controlled ITS own fate. Labels should never be tacked on to Life, they are in the nature of a challenge to God—God assures me that he objects to labels. (187–88)

In this passage, Duffell seems to experience an intimation of the Buddhist state of Nirvâna. In Buddhism, the assertion of ego, either in the individual human being or in the name of the species, is an act of phantasmatic projection. Duffell sums this error in the misplaced confidence of human beings in their capacity to name themselves and other things, a process inevitably of misrecognition.

In Sinclair's account of Buddhism, the world of material objects is merely apparent; what is real is the "Life-force" that drives the process of individuation within this world of appearances. For Sinclair, the "God" from which the Life-Force emanates is singular, "One," but not a personality. In a discussion near the end of *A Defence of Idealism* that throws light on Duffell's dilemma, she lists a number of the metaphysical axioms that block the experience of Nirvâna or "Extinction" (329), namely, death to attachment both to material objects and to the intellectual arrogance of metaphysical speculation. Unfortunately, despite Duffell's will to revert from an "I" to an "IT," he continues to act on the basis of a number of these beliefs—for one, the axiom that "I have not a self," which he states in the third person in the passage quoted above. Until the end of the story, he persists in two others: "By myself I am conscious of myself"; and "By myself I am conscious of my not-self" (331). A number of further errors characterize Duffell's position as well. One is his continuing attachment to a world of objects, a defect that will prove to be both enigmatic and crucial at the end of the story. Another is the careless indulgence in speculation in the passage quoted above, an exercise that in Buddhist terms needs to be corrected by meditation if one is to learn how to distinguish appearances from actualities.

Having pooh-poohed the suggestion of his doctor that he take a rest cure, Duffell unconsciously prescribes one for himself. Following an ellipsis in the text, he next appears on board a train bound for Penzance. When it stops at "a wayside station" (191), however, he abruptly gets off. After checking in at a local hotel, he embarks on a number of walks, each aimed at enabling him to overcome the pain of being alive by identifying first with horses in a pasture, second with a tree, and finally with a stone. "One thing was quite clear," he theorizes, "the organism was solely responsible for all suffering, and the higher the organism the more nerves wherewith to apprehend and perceive, therefore better go down in the scale of creation. The lower one got the less one perceived" (196). Despite his efforts to will himself to become an animal, plant, or stone, however, Duffell never ceases to be an "I" and is therefore unable to achieve either the stasis he seeks or Nirvâna, "the utter extinction of the self as such" (Sinclair, 329).

His excursion a failure, Duffell experiences what mystics call the dark night of the soul: "'Oh, my God!' cried Mr. Duffell, 'oh, Christ Jesus . . . what am I doing in this place?' At that moment Mr. Duffell knew the meaning of hell, then the darkness descended again like a curtain" (199). "When next he spoke he did so to a stone that his fingers were tapping automatically: 'I believe you're the nearest thing to extinction, the farthest away from the Life-force,' he told it, 'in you there surely can't be much Life—at all events not enough Life to count, and that being so you don't see and don't hear. You're nerveless and quite unconscious of movement. As you'll still be a stone in Eternity, you've got less to dread through being eternal. You're naked and hard and insensitive'" (199–200).

Duffell is discomfited after a laborer reports seeing him to a policeman, who calls an ambulance. When the attendant approaches, Duffell reports that he is another of the "dead" stones lying in the field (200). But the attendant contradicts him: "Well, now, I don't know about stones being dead. I've cracked open a stone and found a crystal; if that don't show life, then I'll eat my hat! It must take a bit of doing to form those crystals. To my way of thinking a stone's full of life" (201). Unable to escape evidence of "life" at work, even in a stone, Duffell snaps into a psychotic rage and attacks the man. "Another attendant rushed up, and together they over-powered and bound Mr. Duffell" (201). Buddhism negates what appears to be life but isn't; it does not negate the Life-Force nor its source as Duffell attempts to do.

Duffell's extremity figures the failure of the soul to recognize the existence of God, a God that in Hall's short story identifies the "Christ Jesus" of Roman Catholic faith with the "Absolute" (Sinclair, 289) that sustains all existence. The evidence of the latter exists in the contemplative practice that Duffell does *not* undertake. What connection do this ability and Duffell's predicament have with the engenderment of the self? Hall offers a clue in the problem of naming. When Duffell experiences his first realization of the fictitious character of the ego, he associates this failure with the hubris of naming, an act that he identifies with norms of class and status. The capture of the infant Duffell by his name destines him to a life of false effort and values. "A name is a frightful thing to possess, from the first it imposes an intolerable bondage, the bondage of traditions attached to that name. I inherited the Duffell traditions. I endured with patience because I believed that I was a person called Charles Edward Duffell who was the head of a firm known as Duffell & Son, a firm of almost unique importance. Illusion again—just the purest illusion. What is personality after all but a monstrous mass-conception? And what, for that matter, is Duffell & Son but the monstrous conception of a certain George Duffell who was labeled in 1829, and who passed his chains on to his unhappy descendants?" (188). In the passage, Duffell's problematic engenderment is presented as an effect of conscious genealogy in its insistence on the construction of his masculinity as phallocentric. The double crisis, both his and the economy's, with which the story opens involves a specifically psychic crisis arising from the attempt to affix gender univocally to a particular concept of self.

Just as Hall represents mystical apprehension in the mode of negation, so also do gender and sexuality impinge primarily in the negative. Cline refers to Duffell as "a particularly profound portrait within Radclyffe Hall's gallery of characters who inhabit an introspective, isolated world alienated from love, cut off from friendship."[6] At the outset, we are told, "Those years that had followed his father's death, how calm they had been; calm, successful years during which he had decided never to marry, had decided that a wife would be in the way of a man already wedded to business" (182). Duffell is both masculinist and not very sexuate, physically and affectively deadened. Sex, if he has it, is limited to contact with prostitutes (185), a reconstitution of intimacy in terms of the cash nexus. In his crisis, signs of estrangement from nature occur. The stone he attempts to fix in his embrace at the end of the story is oddly double-gendered. His words phallicize it. But the stones on the moor are breast-like, "round, smooth stones" (199). And then there is the attempted intimacy of Duffell's stripping himself. "The blighter's stark naked!" (200), as the laborer tells the policeman. By the time the attendant arrives, Duffell is convinced that he has become a stone.

Both the narration and Duffell gender the inert object of desire as both masculine and feminine, as an "it" become a "you" that encases Duffell's queer, suppressed engenderment. "'Up there on the moor,' says the laborer to the cop: 'he's all humped together, it's awful queer, and he is kind of curled round—never saw such a thing'" (200). The energies of life vector randomly in ever-shifting fields of force that humans label masculine or feminine, male or female. But nature knows no such fixed limits. Sinclair hints at the sense of existence from which Duffell finds himself cut off:

Every generalization of physical science, and every correlation of physical laws, amounts to a plain statement that within the range of the generalization the order of things is one. The law of conservation of energy is nothing if not a confession that, as far as the physical world goes, incorrigible multiplicity and difference do not obtain. It would even seem that, ultimately, the entire physical world is definable in terms of energy. And if the ultimate constitution of matter is invisible, imponderable, impalpable to any sense (its density disappeared long ago); if all the grossness, all the heaviness and hardness, all the intractable lumpiness of matter, all its so-called material qualities are not to be found in it, but only in our consciousness of it, we need no longer juggle with terms that are so interchangeable. The realist and idealist are both agreed that there is no physical It behind those qualities. And unless we are satisfied that he is right in contending that they exist, "on their own," we may as well say straight out that these two worlds, anyhow, are one; and that the ultimate reality of "matter" is spiritual energy. (292)

Much better known than Sinclair's forays into mystical experience were those of Evelyn Underhill, who popularized the topic in numerous books written in the first decades of the twentieth century. Although Underhill was not highly sexuate, her Roman Catholic spiritual adviser thought her to be primarily attracted to other women. In her best-known work, *Mysticism: A Study in the Nature and Development of Man's Spiritual Consciousness* (1911), she is preoccupied with the relationship between sexual and mystical desire. As Joy Dixon points out, through succeeding editions of this work and others, Underhill repeatedly defends the integrity of mystical experience, usually Catholic, against allegations by a Decadent such as Arthur Symons and psychologists, such as Ellis and Freud, that mystical experience could be understood as a masked or sublimated form of sexual desire, directed especially to the figure of the wounded, bleeding Christ.[7] Sinclair too was concerned about the tendency to reduce religious feeling to sexual feeling: "Now it is quite clear that in the classics of Mysticism we are dealing not only with a peculiar kind of experience, but with a peculiar kind of genius. And, again, having made all allowance for the influence of 'mystical ill-health,' the lover of literature must protest against the grossness of the interpretations that have been brought to these texts. The writings of the great mystics are not *all* charged with 'unsublimated libido'" (285). For her part, Sinclair focuses on the sublimation of libido in religious ecstasy, in which she finds an upward movement of both the species and the individual spirit. But Hall doesn't need to sublimate sexual desire in order to find it holy. Her spirituality is highly naturalist. And, as in the case of two earlier Roman Catholic converts, Katharine Bradley and Edith Cooper, pagan desire and Christian mix freely in Hall's writing.[8] "The Rest Cure—1932" glances only briefly in the direction of desire for the body of the suffering Christ, but the appeal of mystical absorption, experienced in negation by Duffell, blocked by the continuing assertion of ego, retains its force for Hall.

In this discussion I have emphasized the negativity of Duffell's access to mystical experience, but there are suggestions in the story that he is also able to access liminally the state of "ecstasy of contemplation" (330) that Sinclair suggests may occur following the awareness of one's nonexistence.

Duffell's embrace of nudity and his identification with both hard gemlike stone and its rounded, breast-like shapes suggest an opening, in extremis, to the dynamic polarities of gendered existence. For Duffell, such glimpses are incompatible with normal social life; nonetheless, his limited but intense grasp of them is worth the sacrifice required. In "The Rest Cure— 1932," the landscape of the West Country becomes the vehicle by which Duffell embraces an alterity whose transformative effects upon psychology and social existence continue to be played out.

11

Oneself as The Other

Hall, Evguenia Souline, and the Final Writing

The final chapter of this book focuses on three sets of writing, each of which is premised on Hall's involvement with Evguenia Souline: Hall's letters to Souline, published for the first time more than half a century after Hall's death; the incomplete manuscripts of *Emblem Hurlstone*, a novel that Hall undertook during the period of suspense after she and Souline had met but before they became lovers; and the typescript and printed versions of *The Sixth Beatitude* (1936). Hall repeatedly assured Souline that she provided the inspiration for both novels. But the letters also include the only meta-commentary on her approach to the writer's work that Hall has left us. She offers insight into the various roles that she believed auto/biography plays in the work of a novelist. She also provides insights into a philosophy of Greek desire grounded in Sappho's lyric utterance. Likewise, Hall reflects upon the connections between romantic passion and her sense of the unification of existence in mystical experience.

In this late work, Hall continues to expand her sense of crossgendered experience, both her own and that of others. *The Sixth Beatitude* includes new experiments in cross gender, for example in the "faithful friendship"

of Watercrease-Bill and Jumping-Jimmie, the sole portrait of a male homosexual couple to appear in her novels. She emphasizes female virility, a
concept foregrounded in *The Well of Loneliness* but signs of which can be
found as early as the manuscript of *Michael West*. But now female virility
is perceived to be variable in relation to sexual object-choice. Hannah Bullen, the female protagonist and Souline-figure of *The Sixth Beatitude,* is a
highly sexuate single mother strongly attracted to manly men.

Emblem Hurlstone

Hall met Souline at the spa of Bagnoles de l'Orne in Normandy in July
1934. She had been hired from Paris to nurse Troubridge, who was suffering from an attack of enteritis.[1] Una recovered, and Souline was soon back
in Paris. Hall, however, was falling in love. By the time that Hall and Troubridge reached the northern Italian resort town of Sirmione on July 31, Hall
was determined to see Souline again when she and Troubridge returned to
England at the end of their vacation. When Troubridge refused Hall permission to visit Souline alone in Paris, Hall reluctantly permitted her partner to accompany her but left her cooling her heels alone at their hotel
while Hall was elsewhere becoming Souline's lover. About this encounter,
Hall later wrote to Souline: "No one but me has the right to touch you. I
took your virginity, do you hear? I taught you all you know about love. You
belong to me body & soul, and I claim you."[2]

In Sirmione, Hall's sexual frustration found release in writing as she
began work on the manuscript of a new novel, *Emblem Hurlstone*. Hurlstone, the protagonist, is a scholar and successful popularizer of classical
Greek culture. Traumatized by his mother's painful final illness and finding
himself blocked as a writer after her death, Emblem sells the family home
and departs for Venice, where he has arranged to meet a pedantic German
scholar. Traveling by rail through northern Italy, he glimpses the town of
Alcione (Sirmione) across Lake Garda and on a whim decides to stop there.

Ambivalent about her reputation as the author of a scandalous best
seller, Hall in a letter to Souline referred to the new work as "a perfectly
normal love story—thanks be" (88). Nonetheless, there are hints of sexual
abnormality. For instance, though nominally heterosexual, Hurlstone, repelled by the prospect of marriage with its accompanying sexual demands,
is celibate. Continuing in her letter, Hall notes without elaborating that
the manuscript reflects her interest in "abnormal psychology" (89). The

21. Holograph inscription by Radclyffe Hall to Evguenia Souline. Half-title page. *The Master of the House.* Harry Ransom Humanities Research Center, University of Texas, Austin, Texas.

location of Alcione/Sirmione likewise touches on this preoccupation since, as Hall points out in chapter 2, Sirmione was the home of Catullus, "a pagan poet," well known as a translator of Sappho and a lover of women and boys.[3] Also significant is the implicit analogy drawn by Hall between Hurlstone and Johann Winckelmann, a classical Greek archaeologist who became the chief critical theorist of "Anacreontism" within late eighteenth-century Neoclassicism. This aesthetic favored references to erotic themes in Greek mythology over the strenuous subjects associated with Republican Rome. The tendency is named after Anacreon, an early Greek lyric and pastoral poet often linked with his contemporary, Sappho. Cicero said of him what might have been said of both poets: "The poetry of Anacreon deals solely with love." His vogue lasted well into the nineteenth century with such poets as Gautier and Baudelaire both writing verses in his honor. Winckelmann's particular contribution was to elevate the ephebic male youth of classical Greek sculpture, vase drawing, and poetry "to the apogee of male beauty," indeed as the apogee of beauty in general.[4] His sculptural ideal was the androgynous youth, sometimes female but usually male. In his criticism and in the contemporary art that it influenced, gender and sexuality shift with opposite-sex, male same-sex, and male age-differentiated desire all being signified in gentle polymorphosis.[5]

In Alcione, Hurlstone accepts an invitation to stay at the lakeside villa of a new acquaintance, Paolo, a young Italian doctor and lover of the classics, who quickly becomes devoted to him. The intensifying relationship is steered in a conventional direction after Hurlstone meets Paolo's wife, Felia, a Polish refugee.[6] "Normal" desire clicks in, though there is nothing normal about the intensity of the obsession to which Hurlstone quickly surrenders himself. The remainder of the text deals with his predatory pursuit of the young woman, whose own desires remain masked until nearly the point at which the manuscript breaks off. What Hall had in mind for the couple is not specified except for an enigmatic remark in a letter of December 1, 1934, to Souline: "I knew what my people would do, and when they would end it, and how they would end it."[7] Likely, the couple "would" commit adultery, which they would subsequently renounce out of regard for Paolo. "How they would end it" sounds ominous but most probably by Hurlstone deciding to leave town.

Hall describes Hurlstone's first view of Alcione in a crossed-out paragraph that conjures it as a sort of beautiful mirage rising from the surface of the lake.[8] As such, it becomes another of those places of fulfilled desire, somewhere out of this world, referenced by Baudelaire in *Les Fleurs du Mal* (1857).[9] Hursltone's consciously unmotivated stopover speaks to Hall's view of the character of sexual desire as unconsciously driven. Hurlstone "just happens" to be drawn to Alcione much as Paolo "just happens" to be attracted to him and Hurlstone "just happens" to be attracted to Paolo's wife.[10] For Hall, such apparent misdirections switch her characters out of the dead routines of ordinary existence and thereby open the possibility of personal transformation.

The manuscript of *Emblem Hurlstone* ends shortly after Felia confesses her love for Emblem: "She . . . realized to the utmost his weakness, and sout [*sic*] to fall back upon her own strength, only to find that this also was weakness. . . . For nothing was strong in them now . . . but . . . their love, . . . and the terrible and . . .urgent need that they felt to see each other, to hear each other, to be able to touch each other's hands— . . . , only that, to be able to touch each others [*sic*] hands. Anything, . . . so long as they two were not . . . parted."[11] It makes sense that the manuscript cease here since, as Hall says in the letter, the question on her mind when the story came to her was whether Souline would respond to Hall's desire. Once Hall received a positive answer in Paris in September, the manuscript had served its psychic purpose and Hall left it unfinished. Souline's secret (and, for Hall, that of eternal Woman) had been unveiled.

Emblem and Felia share an adulterous desire that must be sacrificed in the name of loyalty to the husband whose idealism Felia admires but for whom she feels no sexual attraction. Felia's marital status and Emblem's friendship for Paolo block the pair from becoming lovers in an impasse resembling that which occurs in the popular film *Casablanca* (1942).[12] In the stand-off, the subject-positioning of Felia-as-Souline/Woman shifts from one reflecting Hall's obsessive desire and uncertainty to the subject-position to which Troubridge called Hall, namely, that of the mate who would choose not to violate her marriage vows. The novel could not be finished for two reasons: a) because Emblem/Hall later in 1934 received a positive response from Souline/Felia; and b) because Hall, the celebrity activist, was unwilling publicly to expose and thereby to affirm her infidelity. The marriage vow needed to be maintained—even after it had been decisively broken in Paris in September and in Souline's passionate sojourn with Hall in England two months later. Nonetheless, the manuscript served its psychic purpose in delivering to Hall a Felia/Souline corresponding with Hall's needs at a time when matters were in doubt.

Redirected Desire

Even though Hall would eventually announce that she was abandoning *Emblem Hurlstone* in order to undertake a new novel, she remained convinced that Souline was revitalizing her work. In an important letter, dated significantly Easter 1935, Hall writes: "As you know, before I met you I was dry—as dry as bones—then I fell in love and that stirred the fluid again, that awoke me, energised me, made me come alive—and I began writing" (121).[13] She acknowledges, however, that *Emblem Hurlstone* had turned out to be not "the right book" (121). Instead, she had begun another, eventually titled *The Sixth Beatitude*, that was completed in October 1935 and published the following year. "Darling, I am working as though possessed—and so I am possessed by inspiration—thanks be. But darling, I have a great surprise for you—it is not the book about Sirmione, no, it is quite another book and quite another story. This is a story that I have had in my mind for a long, long time; it is about the very poor, the very poor of this Sussex. You see, having lived among them I know them inside out, and the book is my best work—yes it is that. For some years this book has been nagging at me, and now it has taken me completely" (120).

The new book was to chart the decline and extinction of yet another traditional community in the face of modern life. Crofts Lane, the locus of the lower working-class types described in the novel, is based on Hall's experience of Hucksteps Row, a lane of slum housing near her home, the Forecastle, in Rye.[14] The major event that occurs during the year traversed in the novel is the announcement that the row of half-timbered, Elizabethan cottages is to be razed and the impoverished inhabitants moved to newly built Council houses facing the railway line. In December, the process is accelerated when a fire sweeping through the lane during a gale destroys the cottages.

An analogue to Hall's approach to this community may be found in Michael Powell's 1937 film, *The Edge of the World*, which explores the removal of Highlanders from the isle of St. Kilda in the Outer Hebrides. The film begins with the following title:

> The slow shadow of Death is falling
> upon the Outer Isles of Scotland.
> This is the story of one of them—and
> of all of them.[15]

Powell and other ethnographic filmmakers of the 1920s and 1930s found a "clean, primitive honesty"[16] in the remote communities where they filmed. Hall emphasizes not only the spontaneous vitality of her characters but also what she sees to be their biological, social, and cultural degeneracy, characteristics troped in the novel in terms of the "gipsy" blood that taints the members of Bullen family.[17] While the unself-conscious racialism and classism of Hall's portrayal of the people of Crofts Lane is impossible to ignore or excuse, she also details objective grounds of their immiseration: inadequate income and job opportunities, low wages for long hours of labor, unsafe working conditions, inadequate access to medical care, dependence on the dole, the humiliation of being forced into the Union house, and the reliance of entire families on the Old Age Pension as their sole source of income. She also sees positive aspects of lower working-class life, in particular, in domestic and communal solidarity. And there can be no doubt of Hall's compassion, condescending though it sometimes is.

Hannah Bullen's labor as a maid-of-all-work supports her extended family. Like a number of protagonists in other novels by Hall, Hannah is an attractive, sexuate woman with a slender, boyish physicality. Out of the ordinary for Hall, however, in this novel the sexual desire of the boy-woman is directed not toward other women but toward men. In addition to Hannah, the chief presence in the novel is Romney Marsh, a leading feature of the landscape of East Sussex. In keeping with the naturalism and simplification of narrative form in the novel, Hall structures the chapters in terms of the months of a single calendar year. Hannah finds pleasure and a reason for existence in the familiar world of marsh, sea, sailing ships, wind and tides, and lunar and seasonal cycles that surround her. At the same time, she is shamed by the feckless poverty of her family and by her own out-of-wedlock motherhood. The mother of two young daughters at the start of the novel, during its course, she becomes pregnant yet again. Because of her reverence for life, she is unwilling to consider an abortion. As a result, by year's end she faces the certain loss of her job at the home of the local vicar and the consequent financial desperation of her family, including the possible loss of her children to state care.

If Hall was pleased with the normal sexuality of the protagonists of *Emblem Hurlstone*, she must have been even more so with Hannah and her lover, a local gardener and male of bullish physicality named Michael Paine. Troubridge certainly was.[18] Hall's publisher appears to have seen the novel in similar fashion. The cover design and text of the wrapper ignore the novel's transgressive and sexual force. Instead, the book is presented as a heterosexual romance directed to female readers. On the cover appears a drawing of a high-waisted, slender, young rural woman, with wash basket in hand and clothes flying in the wind on a makeshift clothesline. She looks across the marsh, in which a river serpentines its way to the sea.

The publisher has done everything possible to make the book seem safe, high minded, and a bit dull. Except for the title, selected at Troubridge's suggestion, he also plays down the novel's mythic resonances: classical, Christian, and Wagnerian. The text on the wrapper further positions the novel in the descriptive, rural/naturalist/radical mode of Thomas Hardy and late Victorian humanist dissidence generally.

> *Blessed are the pure in heart, for they shall see God.* This, the sixth beatitude of the Scriptures, must indeed embrace Hannah Bullen, the woman whose thirty-first year Radclyffe Hall describes in this new novel. For she assuredly was as pure in heart as she was honest of mind, simple of speech and straight of limb. . . .
>
> . . . Thus Hannah Bullen rises from the pages of this book as the very spirit of the Romney Marsh, a living monument of that English life which has wrested a living from its green stretches this thousand years.

"Thus" is a non sequitur.

Only when the reader arrives at a passage in the novel where Hall identifies Hannah with "the life-force" does one realizes that the novel is not operating as a mode of moral discourse. Defending Hannah against her hardworking, respectable, upwardly mobile brother, Hall writes: "He saw Hannah as a loose-living, shameless woman, who had taken her pleasure where she could find it; nor did he perceive that her gravest faults were one with her highest and noblest virtues; that the life-force, be it ardent enough, may flow into many and divers channels, so that her fine generosity, her will to work, her will to endure, her will to indulge the desires of her flesh, her will to be fruitful, her will to mother were all one and the same—the outcome of that force that she could not control because it lay far beyond the range of her poor understanding" (*SB*, 44).

The sole signals in the jacket blurb of Hall's unconventional take on Hannah's desire occur in the description of her as straight-limbed and in the phallicism of the verb "rises." In these allusions to what I will later term Hannah's female virility, Hall uses opposite-sex sexual desire to interweave

22. Jacket cover. *The Sixth Beatitude.* Harry Ransom Humanities Research Center, University of Texas, Austin, Texas.

male virility, female fecundity, and same-sex desire in ways that undermine the novel's heterosexual publicity. In its unfolding, Hall's novel will negate common-sense gender distinctions.

Thinking Sex and Gender Otherwise

The chapters of *The Sixth Beatitude* are named after the months of the year, but in some instances more than one chapter bears the name of a particular month. For instance, the novel opens with three chapters entitled "January." At the end of the third of these, Hall introduces two old men, Watercrease-Bill and Jumping-Jimmie. Although the two have no connection with the main action of the novel, Hall emphasizes them by placing their inset story at the end of the novel's first movement. "A queer couple," who "passed their days in an almost complete isolation," the pair are virtual chthonic guardians of the lane, near whose entrance they live in a "tumble-down shed . . . , not fit for pigs."[19] No one can remember when Bill and Jimmie first came to live there, and despite contradictory rumors, no one knows where they came from: "They themselves said never a word that could throw the least light on their previous history. Precisely how they lived was a puzzle, for apart from the old-age pension they had nothing" (*SB*, 32–33). The narrator provides one hint that the dwellers of Crofts Lane ignore: "They spoke as men speak in far better conditions, they had not a trace of the Sussex accent" (34).

When introduced, Jumping-Jimmie, so-called because of his St. Vitus's Dance, is suffering from the cold, lice, and hunger. Arguing with Bill over their meager dinner, he laments: "I wish I were dead." Watercrease-Bill responds anxiously: "'Oh, come on, I'm sorry I nagged,' he told him; 'it's the cold, it always gets on my nerves—blessed are they who live in the tropics! Come on, don't sulk, I've apologised and no one can do more than that, now can they?' Very neatly he divided the fish from the bone, then he covered a thick slice of bread with dripping: 'Eat,' he coaxed, 'eat your supper to please me, Jim.' And he fed his despondent friend with his fingers, thrusting the food deftly into his mouth as occasion offered between the twitchings" (35).

In March, Jimmie dies and Bill, removed to a Union house, fasts to death. In describing Jimmie's death, Hall comes closest to adopting the tone of public rhetorical address that one hears often in *The Well of Loneliness*. The narrator, however, also witnesses Jim's death from Bill's vantage. The lines suggest that the lives of the two men have been shaped since youth by a sexual scandal that ostracized them from work and family. The passage also suggests that their transgression has been not only sexual but gendered. Both—or at least one—have been "womanish."

> Death was smoothing the lines out of Jimmie's face and rubbing the distortions of age from his features, so that Bill saw him as he had been in the earliest years of their faithful friendship. Saw his nose with its delicately formed nostrils and its aquiline bridge; saw his heavy eyelids; saw his mouth, rather full in the underlip, rather womanish-weak and inclined to be wilful. At least Bill fancied that he saw these things—and who shall presume to say that he did not?
>
> Death was wiping the work stains from Jimmie's hands, so that they looked very white and useless. His almond-shaped nails were no longer torn, they had grown, or so it appeared to Bill. Very beautiful hands they appeared to Bill—and who shall presume to say that they were not?
>
> Death was gradually straightening Jimmie's limbs. He seemed a long man, lying there on his pallet. A long, slim, elegant man he seemed, or rather that was how Bill now saw him; a long, slim, and finely proportioned man—and who shall presume to say that he was not? (*SB*, 62)

Hall often associates the psychic isolation of male homosexuals with a compensatory overinvestment in physical beauty. For example, Hurlstone, the sexually ambiguous, middle-class professional, betrays this feeling-complex. Here, however, Hall shows how an emphasis on the beauty of the upper-class male body can become something else as a result of pair-bonding of long duration in the midst of punitive deprivation and ultimate loss. Representations of effeminate men in Hall's novels tend to be highly ambivalent. In this passage, however, a "womanish" character is redeemed by commitment and sacrifice.

Transgressive engenderment is something that Jimmie and Bill share with the novel's female protagonist. Hall marks it in the first of several verbally similar descriptions that occur in the novel. Hannah is described as "tall: her body suggested a branch denuded of leaves, it was stark and strong. The beauty of her body lay in this strength which gave it a kind of gaunt dignity. The dignity of toil—that was what you felt about Hannah, that was why you looked at her twice: at her large gnarled hands that held with precision, at her large sure feet that trod masterfully, at her grey stead-fast eyes that saw life as it was, and seeing life neither feared nor despised it" (*SB*, 2). The typescript of the novel in the National Archives of Canada includes few emendations. One that does appear, however, is highly sig-nificant. In chapter 9, "May," Hannah meets Michael Paine for a possible lover's assignation. As with Bill, Hall enters Hannah's subjectivity: "He smelt good, she thought. He smelt of the earth that still clung to his clothes and discoloured his hands; she could feel the dried earth embedded in the furrows at the back of his neck where her own hands clasped him, and she knew that his skin had been roughened by it. A proper man, lusty and masterful; a man claiming his birthright, that was what he was. She could understand this, it seemed natural to her—she herself had been one who had claimed her birthright. It was good, very good to stand close to a man, to feel his strength, his vitality. . . . She herself had been one who had claimed her birthright."[20] In the typescript, Hall crosses out the word *vital-ity* and writes in the word *virility*. The substitution is a key one, revealing her sense that virility, in men and women, is synonymous with life itself.[21]

The novel affords a more ambiguous instance of gender-crossing in an incident involving Hannah's favored young daughter, Ermie. In August, Michael's mother-in-law, Mrs. Osborne, arrives to care for her daughter, who has failed to regain her strength after the birth of her third child. Mrs. Osborne, who decides to rent the one good cottage standing in Crofts Lane, quickly registers her disapproval of the other inhabitants, particularly the Bullens. She is especially cruel to Hannah, with whose illegitimate children Mrs. Osborne forbids her grandchildren to play. When Ermie, confused and hurt, one day asks her mother why young Walt has been forbidden to play with her, Hannah, bursts out: " 'Cause she's a bloody bitch!" (*SB*, 143). Later Ermie and Sid, a neighbor's child, get into mischief:

> That evening, when Ermie was feeling more cheerful, she went off by herself in search of Sid who usually had a nice bit of chalk by him. And she borrowed his chalk, after which she and Sid crept round to Mrs. Osborne's side wall. And more out of fun than resentment Ermie drew a grotesquely hideous face under which she printed in large, crooked type:
> "This bloody bich is Mrs. Osbin."

"Yer aren't spelt bitch proper, yer aren't," Sid told her. "Now I'm going to write somethin' what's worse than bitch—it's somethin' as our old cat's always doin'."

A fearful upheaval there was the next morning. (*SB*, 143–44)

But the neighbors stand by the children.

The incident turns on the question of the maternal function of females. Mrs. Osborne condemns Hannah because she has sex—and bears children—out of wedlock. In this respect, it is Hannah who is a bitch. But Mrs. Osborne is a bitch in the more significant sense of failing properly to nurture her young ones. Her daughter is sickly as are her grandchildren. The likelihood that Mrs. Osborne has been a neglectful parent is reinforced by the fact that when Mrs. Paine falls ill with double pneumonia and Mrs. Osborne is called to help her, she "put a young niece of hers in charge [of the children]; a scatter-brained girl. Hannah didn't trust her" (*SB*, 254). On the night of the disastrous fire, the children are placed in danger because the girl has left them alone at home while she has gone off to "the pictures" (*SB*, 259). Hannah, responding instinctively, dies trying to rescue the children from the flames. Indirectly, Mrs. Osborne is responsible both for endangering her grandchildren and for Hannah's death.

This vignette also functions in an auto/biographical register. Ermie publicly protests against the mistreatment that she and her mother have received from Mrs. Osborne. The incident speaks to Hall's protective identification with daughters and abused young girls; it also speaks to her self-identification as such a daughter. As though Ermie's action were an image in a dream, individual figures signify severally. In her letters to Souline of the time, Hall frequently refers to Souline as *her* child. At the same time, Hall regarded herself as an object of abuse at the hands of her own mother. As cat/bitch/witch/substituted mother/bad mother, Mrs. Osborne parallels Hall's own mother. Likewise, the misspelled word, *bich,* calls to mind Hall's dyslexia. Curious in this series of superimposed rhetorical figures is Ermie's alliance with a young member of the opposite sex. Sid supplies the chalk with which Ermie draws and writes. Such alliances are rare in Hall's life or fiction. And when one is attempted, the woman in question usually resists support from a male. In terms of Hall's thinking about crossed gender in this novel, Sid as sidekick suggests an attempt by Hall to integrate opposite-sex relations and paternal potency with the experience of female gender-crossing.[22] Ermie/Sid functions in effect as a composite figure of the he-she. As I have suggested, however, the composite also draws Sid into a web of phantasmatic female relations, both fictional and autobiographical. Experimenting, Hall works along both lines in the novel. Finally, the public character of Ermie's protest against females put at a disadvantage echoes Hall's characteristic posture as an activist. In *The Sixth Beatitude*, she defends Ermie and Hannah as she had earlier defended both herself and "my own poor kind" (33).[23]

Autobiographical Registration: The Self as Other

The preceding paragraph exemplifies the license involved in auto/biographical recontextualizations of fictional material. Literary texts are subject to conscious control, although Hall's ideology of literary production, which finds a powerful analogy in unconscious communication "coming through very fast" (*Your John*, 121), provides a historical basis for the kind of reading I have suggested. As we will see in this section, Hall was highly aware of the shifting boundary between conscious and unconscious meaning in her work. Indeed, as a psychologist, she may be at her best in tracing this wavering border. Nonetheless, for the literary critic or biographer such readings are necessarily speculative. They do, however, have a heuristic value, and they are pertinent to the political project of Hall's work and more generally of later feminist and queer critique. In this instance, the reading offered above reinforces the need to protest against abuse—of children, of daughters, of transgressive women (in the novel, out-of-wedlock or alcoholic mothers), of gender-transgressive individuals, of members of sexual minorities, including feminine males, and, in this novel, of the economically impoverished. Responding to an early letter in which Souline commented that Hall writes about outsiders, Hall connects this identification with her own self-identification as a he-she: "My work and why is it that the people [*sic*] I write of are so very often lonely people? Are they? I think that perhaps you may be right. I greatly feel the loneliness of the soul—nearly every soul is more or less lonely. Then again: I have been called the writer of 'misfits.' And it may be that being myself a 'misfit,' for as you know, beloved, I am a born invert, it may be that I *am* a writer of 'misfits' in one form or another—I think I understand them—their joys & their sorrows, indeed I know I do, and all the misfits of this world are lonely, being conscious that they differ from the rank and file" (78).

In a series of letters written to Souline, Hall takes a number of different positions as to how autobiographical *Emblem Hurlstone* and *The Sixth Beatitude* are. In a letter written on October 29, 1935, while "some of the old cottages" in Hucksteps Row were being torn down, she responds to a question from Souline by flatly denying that her fiction is autobiographical: "I never write my own life—I could not, though my own life often gives me ideas which are used up in a different set of circumstances. This must surely be so with all authors" (137). The actual situation, however, is more complex. First of all, as the letters indicate, Hall's autobiographical "I" cannot be defined in terms of a single gender. Rather, hers is a continually varying performance of gender. At one point, she regrets the physiological limits that prevent her from inseminating Souline: "Had I been a man I would have given you a child" (97). But at another she speaks in the idiom of the male lover: "You belong to me and don't you forget it. . . . I took your virginity" (140); "I kneel down and worship you my most blessed woman—you who for my sake became a woman" (71). More frequently, however, Hall casts their relationship in terms of the dyad of mother-child or mother-daughter; she addresses Souline as "Beloved child" (87), "beloved child of my body, beloved child and woman in one" (121). Earlier, Hall describes their connection as procreative: they have given birth to a child, namely, the manuscript of *Emblem Hurlstone*: "Our child is sleeping for the moment; its trouble lies in the cutting of its third tooth. In other words while I have re-written that Chapter III and like it much better, I am still not perfectly content" (85).

In contrast to the presentation of her own engenderment, Hall attempts to fix Souline as singularly feminine. She even identifies her with the New Stone Age woman that Miss Ogilvy dreams of in "Miss Ogilvy Finds Herself." This primitive woman presumably is all natural. But New Stone Age man names her woman in the language of poetry. Hall does so likewise: "As the man of the stone-age says to his mate in . . . 'Miss Ogilvy' so I say to you: 'Hut of peace for a man after battle'" (81). Hall believes that early language was metaphoric; likewise, Souline's womanliness is a metaphoric construction. But Hall also believes that a woman becomes a woman by being initiated into sexual love—as she has taught Souline to love. Referring again to their first lovemaking in Paris, Hall writes, "You . . . for my sake became a woman" (71). And when Souline expresses fear that in having succumbed sexually to another woman she has revealed herself to be abnormal, Hall, rejecting the idea, tells Souline to say to herself: "I'm a normal woman, and when my John loves me my response is normal—my body loves John and John gives it joy—and will give it that joy many, many times" (69). Normal women, however, as the sexologists and Hall believed, experience sexual attraction primarily to men. From the beginning of the relationship, then, Hall feared that Souline would betray her with a man. Hence, even when Hall prefers to think of gender as single, doing so provokes immediate distrust of the other and lack of confidence in Hall's own gendered hybridity.

The unstable performative and rhetorical engenderment registered by the "I" of the love letters indicates that even in genres that may appear to be straightforwardly autobiographical, a text in the "I" may be no simple thing. The ontological and epistemological uncertainty attending gender, moreover, is trumped by uncontrolled psychological projection. Over and over again, Hall claims that she and Souline are one. "I feel as though I were you, as though I had lost my innocence to love, as you lost yours, my Soulina. I felt that first day [in Paris] when I came to your room as nervous [*sic*] and shy as a boy of 16" (100). And later, "I am so much yours that I am no longer myself" (107). You are "my other heart" (138), the "heart of my innermost being" (120), "*my* body" (109). "My body (your body) is as soar [*sic*] as a boil" (115); "You and I are one flesh, one Spirit" (130). To this conflation of self and other is added the admixture of manifestations of the self in other times and places: "It may be that we two have met before—I think I believe in re-incarnation" (82).

Hall explicitly addresses the question of the relation between autobiography and fiction in an unpublished letter of December 1, 1934. In the letter, she discloses that the idea for *Emblem Hurlstone* came to her on the way from France to Sirmione shortly after she and Souline had met for the first time in July but before they became lovers. Hall suggests that the content of fiction is based in the autobiographical experience of the writer, in particular in his/her "suffering," but in achieved art, the personal element is sublimated "quite critically and calmly."[24] In this way, subjectivity becomes objectivity.

Other parts of the letter, however, offer a very different view of artistic composition. First of all, the condition of anxiety in which Hall habitually writes is at odds with the claim that the manuscript is being written "quite critically and calmly": "Last night I worked very late again—until 1. am, and this morning I have worked with my typist, and I am tired as always when a big spell of work has taken me in hand—thats [*sic*] how I do it, big chunks at a time & little sleep while the storm[']s at its heights [*sic*]. 'Not good for my Johnnie's health?' you will say—I know, darling, but its [*sic*] hopeless [*sic*] to try to repress me, I must write and write when the spirit moves me—its [*sic*] like that that all my books have been written." Later in the letter, she describes *Emblem Hurlstone* as the collaborative result of their lovemaking:

> I know this book to be one of my best, you see we have had a mental child you & I—a kind of mental—imaculate [*sic*]—conception. This book is entirely the result of our love, the result of its joy and its desperation. I conceived the story that terrible night when I was in the train on my way to Sermione [*sic*], and while I was in torment during the summer I found the details flooding into my mind. I *felt* the awfulness of unfulfilled love—The awfulness of longing, the awfulness of living. Then it was that I knew what my people would do, and when they would end it, and how they would end it. Now, thank God, I have you and so I can write—I can use my own suffering quite critically and calmly becuase [*sic*] the worst suffering is over and done with—out of ourselves I will make a book, I am making a good one for you, Soulina.

The passage suggests the question, if the writing of fiction is auto/biographical, whose auto/biography is being written here: Hall's, Souline's, or both?

The Sixth Beatitude has been admired for its descriptions of the landscape of the southeast of England. In a letter written a few days after Souline had left the Forecastle to return to France at the end of her first intimate vacation with Hall, Hall sent her a description of Romney Marsh, which they had walked across just a few days earlier: "I walked across the marsh to Lesam Hill, and up Lesam Hill & home by the road that leads through the old Land Gate. . . . Over everything was an English blue sky, very pale and pure, and that queer strong light that one only seems to get on Romney Marsh—a kind of other-worldly light, strong & yet soft, & so beautiful, Soulina" (79–80). The perception is suffused with memory of the other, of walking together, of making love together. How is one to classify auto/biographical registration here? No one term, no single temporality will do. "Soulina—but its beauty, indeed all beauty these days, is almost too painful to be endured when you are not near to share it with me. And so I walked on full of thoughts of you—full of regrets that you could not have see[n] the loveliness that I saw this morning, but full also of the determination that you shall see it, my beloved" (*Your John*, 80). The letter offers an example of autobiographical writing as an attempt to describe the experience of actuality with another whom one loves and as the other might be able to experience it. Although there is necessarily an element of projection, the text is not solipsistic but relational. In it, autobiographical writing becomes plural.

In chapter 7, "April," spring arrives, and Hannah, still disturbed at the death of Jimmie, feels "the physical urge that is part of living" (*SB*, 75). Hall's extended description of Romney Marsh at lambing time along with the immediately following description of Hannah offer instances of how the reverie that Hall experienced walking across the marsh in November can be reshaped as fiction:[25]

> A heron made his magnificent progress: heavy powerful wings beating with dignity, slender powerful legs stretched out stiffly behind him. In a little while he would have reached his goal, a certain wide dyke that provided good fishing. Plovers circled and screamed above their young; moor-hens paddled in and out of the rushes; larks dropped like plummets then soared up and up, seeming to shatter themselves with singing; while the thorn trees that grew at the edge of the Marsh were so heavy with blossom that their boughs were hidden.
>
> Life, everywhere life, and the will to give life. Nests in the trees, in the grass, in the hedges; the warm lambing-pens with their rush-thatched sides, awaiting those cumbrous-bellied ewes who, their time being near, might lamb that evening. Life, everywhere life now on Romney Marsh—on the whole length and breadth of Romney Marsh. Life in the air and life on the soil; life coupling and striving under the soil, and in the mud banks that bordered the dykes, and in the water that flowed between them. (*SB*, 78–79)

The text continues directly into a description of Hannah that echoes the reader's introduction to her in chapter 1 (*SB*, 79). In this passage as in the preceding paragraphs describing the marsh, both it and Hannah are permeated by Hall's intensely physical sense of her new lover. Hannah is herself *and* Woman *and* Souline. Equally important, Hannah incorporates the confident virility that Hall rekindled by contact with Souline. Hannah's "thin, muscular thighs" express the same energy that the narrator evokes in "the slender powerful legs stretched out stiffly behind" the heron (*SB*,

79). Hannah, in one register, functions in the passage as a rhetorical figure of the vitalized double engenderment that Hall experienced in sex. In another, Hannah in fiction and Souline in liaison empower Hall as mother— mother to Souline and mother to the texts that she attempted to birth during the first year of the relationship. As she wrote in December, while still working on *Emblem Hurlstone*, "That my meeting with you and all I suffered before we became everything to each other inspired the book there is no doubt whatever. You woke me up and the process was very painful indeed, and out of the pain this book was born" (*Your John*, 89).

Sapphic Mythmaking

If one seeks something in these texts that is not autobiographically suffused, it will be found in aspects that, while no less personal, realize what is personal in terms of multiple and overlaid Sapphic mythmaking. Sapphism in this context refers not only to female-female desire but also to dissident engenderment, not so much the female masculinities of later twentieth- and early twenty-first-century activism but the particular styles of feminine virility espoused in *Emblem Hurlstone* and *The Sixth Beatitude*. As the quotation at the end of section IV indicates, this virility was expressly painful; but the pain was a source of great joy—because it was perceived to be coextensive with the very sense of being alive.

In the final book of *The Well of Loneliness*, Valérie Seymour advises Stephen Gordon that instead of attempting absurd conciliations with conventional religion, Sapphists need to create a metaphorics, mythology, and metaphysics of their own: "It was quite true that inverts were often religious, but church-going in them was a form of weakness; they must be a religion unto themselves if they felt that they really needed religion."[26] In *The Sixth Beatitude*, Hall joins the effort of fashioning a Sapphic mythography that women in Paris, such as Natalie Barney, had pursued since 1900.

The text of the novel is conceived as a prose poem, with a limited vocabulary, rhythmic, repetitive, motivic, and patterned. First is the organization of the chapters in terms of the months of the year, beginning with Hannah's thirtieth birthday on New Year's Day and ending with her death exactly one year later. Second is Hall's imitation of the form of Greek tragedy with the women of the lane serving as chorus and Hannah as heroic protagonist driven by fate. Third is Hall's adaptation of the figure of Brünnhilde from

Wagner's Ring Cycle. Fourth is the novel's reliance on formal elements of fairy tale, including the long tale of sacrificial female love that Hannah tells Ermie early in the novel. Fifth is Hall's heterodox association of Hannah's maternal love with that of the Virgin Mary.

The mythmaking focuses in the first instance on Hannah, who like Brünnhilde is pure, ardent, transgressive, and endowed with heroic qualities, both masculine and feminine. In Wagner, Brünnhilde is a warrior-maiden, prepared to violate the prescriptions of male power in Wotan in order to protect Sieglinde, the heroic Siegmund's wife and sister, and their son Siegfried from Wotan's judgment. Hannah, despite her irregular sexual life, is her family's provider, defender, and protector. As *genius loci* of Crofts Lane and the marsh it overlooks, Hannah is both daughter of the earth—as Brünnhilde is of Erda in Wagner's libretto—and the embodiment of natural vitality, figured repeatedly through the novel by her fascination with fire. In the apocalypse with which the novel ends, she sacrifices herself in the flames of Mrs. Osborne's home in order to save the lives of two children and an infant while the cottages of Crofts Lane burn to the ground.

The fairy tale is in part confessional, in part an apology or defense by Hannah of her choices, in part instruction and a gift to her daughter. In Hannah's primary desire to be cleansed, she acknowledges her shame to her illegitimate child. But in the magical landscape that Hannah describes, she communicates to her daughter the strength and beauty of her love for her daughter's sailor father, a very young man who had arrived in port one spring along with a shipload of timber from Scandinavia.

The metaphorics of Hannah's tale is drawn in turn from the first description of Ermie in chapter 1. Again, Hall works in terms of a double gendering. On the one hand, Hannah's intense, quasi-incestuous relationship with her daughter is thoroughly feminine; on the other, Hannah identifies her daughter's uncanny, spritelike temperament with her Nordic father, the Siegfriedlike young Scandinavian, innocent, naïve, passionate, highly imaginative, and absorbed in the forest landscapes of his childhood. "Sometimes he had told her fabulous stories; half in jest, half in earnest, he had told her of fairies. And legends he had told her, legends conceived in the hearts and the minds of his own Norse people. . . . And Hannah had listened attentively, smiling while not always understanding, yet queerly happy because this man was awakening in her work-benumbed soul its first timid realisation of beauty" (*SB*, 10, 11).

And there are intimations of a Marian, Christian narrative in the old ballad sung by the carolers who walk through the lane on Christmas Eve.[27] Like Christ at the time of his birth, Hannah's children soon will be depending upon strangers for their protection:

> Mary the Mother, sat rocking her child:
> "Now who will be kind to my little Jesus?"
> The beasts gathered round and their eyes were mild
> As they rested on Mary the undefiled,
> On Mary the Mother who rocked her child:
> "Now, who will be kind to my little Jesus?" (*SB*, 251)

But, as in Wagner, Christian mythography is subordinated to pagan. At the end of *Götterdämmerung*, Brünnhilde, having despaired at the death of her lover, Siegfried, prepares to throw herself upon his funeral pyre:

> I shall share that pure, holy flame
>   with the hero;
> we both shall blaze in the fire.[28]

The stage direction reads, "She . . . leaps with a single bound into the blazing pyre" (*Ring*, 328). At the end of *The Sixth Beatitude*, Hall writes: "Hannah Bullen leapt forward. She leapt like a flame. Her body was lighted up by the flames. Her body was a thing to marvel at. It was purpose personified. It was action. Her mind was empty of all but one thought that beat like a hammer upon her brain: Ermie—it was Ermie she was going to save, because Ermie was every child in the world, and every child in the world was Ermie" (*SB*, 259–60).

Masochistic Jouissance

The Sixth Beatitude articulates philosophical Sapphism in the form of an extended meditation on the character of eros. The novel insists upon human desire, despite its recalcitrance, as a self-validating phenomenon. It need not attend to the exigencies of the other; it need not do good and avoid evil; it requires simply to be. At the end of her career, Hall returns to the amoral world of primitive Greek pastoral that she had embraced in her early poetry—poetry that insists on the primacy of blind attraction/repulsion over attempts to impose conventional morality on the movements of desire.[29] Sappho's translator, Anne Carson, points out that the first Greek lyric poet is the inventor of the term *glukupikron*, translated as "sweetbitter," to describe the experience of desire. In Fragment 130, Sappho writes: "Eros once again limb-loosener whirls me / Sweetbitter, impossible to fight off, creature stealing up."[30] Desire happens. In Sappho's phenomenology, it is a mysterious factor, external to the self, whose advent issues in masochistic jouissance. Such pleasure in pain is neither moralized nor understood in medical terms as perverse; rather, it is an epiphenomenon of the tripartite structure of desire: first the pleasure or delight of experiencing attraction to something or someone other; second, the perception of a third term that inhibits or limits that pleasure. The third term checks pleasure—and that check is experienced as pain. Phenomenologically, the three aspects may be experienced virtually simultaneously. Because of the inescapable character and immediacy with which pain is experienced, it provides as great a source of pleasure as does the initial pleasure itself. Beyond the experience of the sensation of pleasure/pain, at an intellectual level the check prompts awareness of psychic self-division, a temporal differentiation of states of desire, and a reinforced sense of the inescapable separateness between subject and object of desire.[31]

To Hall's mind, this structure of experience is both an aspect and a driver of "the life-force." As such, the experience is by definition beyond good and evil. To be alive is to be subject to this force, which is not subject to the operations of human judgment. In the metaphorics of Greek verse, desire is blind to the human beings through whom it courses; conversely, individuals are blind to the forces that move them in surprising and unanticipated fashion. Desire understood in this way constitutes what the Greeks—and Hall—recognize as destiny or fate. In Hall's version of Greek tragedy, it is Hannah's susceptibility to this force that ennobles her existence at the same time that it determines her death. In the letters, Hall invites Souline into this play of sensation:

Evguenia—beloved—my life, my all, write quickly, and give me some peace until you come. I want you—I am all on fire with longing, I'm crazy to feel you in my arms—to feel your body against my mouth, to hear you cry out with the pain of passion. Oh, my God—its [*sic*] not safe to play with me just now. Suffer—suffer—why not? Don't I have to suffer? I wanted to spare you and not write of these things, but now I have no more the desire to spare you. There are times when I could cut my body to pieces because of the longing thats [sic] in it for you. Times when my nerves are tortured with longing. Times when I cannot sleep for longing. As I write this I don't know what to do with myself for the craving I feel to have your hand on me, your body pressed hard, hard against my own, your mouth on my mouth. I could kiss you till you bled—I could tear you to pieces Evguenia. (*Your John*, 140–41)

Souline's rather literal objections to this sort of demand compelled Hall to attempt to parse the inescapable admixture of pain in their pleasure. Responding, Hall was required not simply to express desire but to attempt to articulate an understanding of the operations of desire at a meta-level. "Love is a strange thing," she writes; "it intensifies all beauty, turns joy into pain, and pain into joy—if the pain is endured for the sake of the beloved" (*Your John*, 129). A few days before Souline joined Hall for the summer of 1935, Hall asks:

You ask me why our love is so intense? That I cannot say, my honey-sweet—some force in us both that having come to life is doubled in strength because we are lovers? It may be so. But falling in love and loving is one of this world's greatest mysteries. We meet hundreds of people & then comes the *one* person and the thing has happened and nothing can stop it and nothing can ever undo it. But the pain of such love—that makes you ask why? I think because all great emotions are one. This is hard to explain but I know what I mean. The circle meets in all great emotions—its [sic] a part of the curious Oneness that I feel—that I tried to write of in The Master of the House, and probably wrote of extremely badly because its [sic] a thing that lies just beyond the conscious mind—its [sic] always just out of reach, yet its [sic] there—in us, of us, and all around us. The placid, contented and pain-less love is not love at all as you & I know love. (*Your John*, 131)

Like Hannah's, Hall's desire is transgressive, anarchic, even nihilistic. Against it, social conventions don't count. Troubridge certainly felt its annihilating force. In February 1943, Souline visited the ailing Hall, who had sought rural refuge from wartime London in Lynton, where she was living in seclusion with Troubridge. Upset as usual when Souline was on the scene, Troubridge was cast back upon bitter memories of the days she had spent alone in Paris in September 1934, when Hall and Souline first became intimate. In a passage crossed out in Troubridge's Day Book, she writes: "In a way I am relieved that I *can rest* while the woman is here, & know that John is doing what she wishes, and yet, I suppose because of the memory of those dreadful and desolate days in Paris when the clock crawled round, hour after hour while I tried to kill time & drug my misery with walking, reading, patience, anything & everything, the memory of when John's one thought was to find *all* her relaxation & pleasure away from me, I still feel a sick little sadness when, as soon as this heartless & worthless woman comes over the horizon, I feel that John wants to know me safe & well, but *not there*; that when I *am* there her pleasure is spoiled."[32] In Troubridge's words, one hears nemesis at work: the destructive desire of another that one's own transgressive desire can release.

And what, Troubridge might have asked, of marriage? Logical contradictions aside, Hall continued to affirm same-sex marriage in *The Sixth Beatitude*, which she observes in the union to the death of Watercrease-Bill and Jumping-Jimmie. After Bill slips away in his sleep, Hall concludes, "These then were the only claims to distinction of Watercrease-Bill and Jumping-Jimmie: they had lived in a verminous shed in Crofts Lane for more years than the Rother folk could remember; they had loved each other for better or for worse, in sickness and in health to the end and beyond, and their epitaph had been composed by children: 'Watercrease-Bill went up the 'ill to fetch a pail of water. / 'E tumbled down and broke 'is crown and Jim come tumblin' after!'" (*SB*, 67, 66) Hall continues to emphasize loyalty. Marriage too can express desire heedless of cost. But Hall finds in it no promise of happiness.

Published in spring 1936, by summer *The Sixth Beatitude* had sold over six thousand copies in England and two thousand in the United States. While the U.S. numbers were disappointing, sales of the novel in the United Kingdom compared favorably with those of Hall's early novels. Nonetheless, Hall once again judged the publication of a new novel to be a commercial failure. Having published what proved to be an international best seller in *The Well of Loneliness*, she was unwilling to recede to a more modest celebrity. And yet the desire to be a best-selling author was unsuited to her actual ambitions, which were to write for her people while continuing to be well regarded as an author of literary fiction. In that light, a more suitable aim would have been to attempt to achieve something like the commercial and critical success of *Adam's Breed*, which had sold close to 9,500 copies in its first four months of publication in the United Kingdom. In its "poetic intensity" and strong emphasis on self-sacrifice, *The Sixth Beatitude* closely resembles the earlier novel.[33] For general readers who had admired *Adam's Breed*, however, the mingling of these features with the portrayal of a heterosexual but crossgendered female protagonist may have been disorienting. As for Hall's sizable Sapphic readership, those familiar with Hall and Troubridge are likely to have recognized the ways in which Sapphic romance shaped the materials of the novel. As Troubridge's biographer, Richard Ormrod, observes, "The Rye novel, originally called *Hannah*, . . . was heavily imbued with aspects of . . . [the] relationship with Souline."[34] Those in the know accordingly may have found the emphasis on Hannah's heterosexuality to be puzzling at best. At the same time, Hall's Sapphic readership would have been better positioned to embrace the affirmation of transgressive desire in the novel had its author not been attempting simultaneously to maintain a public façade of monogamy. If anything makes this novel, it is passion. But Hall believed that her position in lesbian public culture required that she continue to exemplify a life of chastity. As a result, she sent mixed signals to both components of her readership.

In late 1936, Hall began working on her final, unfinished novel, *The Shoemaker of Merano*, while the triangle shared an unhappy, enforced vacation together at Merano in the north of Italy. Again, Hall attempted to refigure in fiction the complex of emotions in which she was caught. After her death in 1943, Troubridge destroyed the manuscript in order, as she said, to fulfill a promise to Hall:

> The true reason for the destruction of the book was a simple one: she had, during the closing years of her life, been very deeply hurt by someone and when she knew that her days were numbered she had forgiven both the injury and the person concerned. But she felt that into the writing of that book she had almost unconsciously allowed the intrusion of a measure of her personal suffering and natural resentment and, as she said when she told me to destroy it: "It isn't forgiveness if one leaves a record that might be recognized and give pain . . . ."
>
> I know she regretted the sacrifice of her work; no one knew better than she how good it was and no one knew better what it had cost her.

But she was in no doubt as to what she wished; I gave her my promise, and after her death I lost no time in carrying out that promise.[35]

The shift between quoting her partner and assuring the reader that "I know" her view of the matter opens a space between reportage and projection on Troubridge's part. From Troubridge's vantage as Hall's longtime literary collaborator, who better than she would know "how good" the manuscript to be destroyed was? Who was better positioned to take in the "cost" of the relationship with Souline—even if Hall should choose not to voice this price? The final act of Troubridge's literary collaboration with Hall occurs in Troubridge's memoirs as she writes Hall's demand that the manuscript testifying to her infidelity be destroyed. The penultimate act was to arrange to have prepared for her dying partner's signature a brief will, rescinding the bequest of half her property to Souline.[36]

In its final working out, the triangulated relationship between Hall, Troubridge, and Souline failed to conform to any of the three social forms of female same-sex relations discussed in this book: Hall and Troubridge's public position as proponents of life-long, single pair-bonding; the option of marriage with exceptions, on behalf of which Barney and Coward argued; and the quasi-domestic Victorian and Edwardian form in which a circle of "belongings" gathered around a particular woman. While it is not necessary to look further than the particular personalities and histories involved to account for this fact, it is also the case that the very fact of the call for public recognition of female monogamy transformed the norms that had governed earlier forms of female marriage while complicating twentieth-century efforts to articulate non–strictly monogamous forms of female union. This effect may be one reason why, at the time of publication of *The Well of Loneliness* and subsequently, radical subjects of female same-sex desire have reacted negatively to the sexual politics of the book. One may anticipate that tensions will continue to exist between female monogamy and other forms of sexual relationship between and among women in the twenty-first century even as the practice of legal female same-sex marriage continues to expand.

Part of Radclyffe Hall's writing is known only by its absence. One regrets the conflagration of *The Shoemaker of Merano*. *The Sixth Beatitude* had been an important indicator of continuing growth on the part of Hall. In writing it, she found that she did not need the form of the bildungsroman to show how her characters have become what they are. The narrative functions economically with an emphasis on the sort of "pattern," the absence of which Leonard Woolf had complained of in *The Well of Loneliness*.[37] In the novel, Hall embraces her own fate as a "misfit" writing about other misfits. She provides a powerful, highly sympathetic portrait of a male homosexual couple faithful until death, despite the persecution that they have endured.[38] And her sense of the multiform character of crossgendered existence expands to include the effeminate Jimmie, the nurturing Bill, and the plebeian Amazon, Hannah. Hall once again shows herself to be a gifted nature writer with a strong religious sense in her evocation of Romney Marsh. Finally, she offers a direct, nonmoralizing take on the necessities of desire in human life and the unforgiving world in which it is set.

In the letters to Souline written between 1934 and 1943, Hall gave her "kind," as she termed them, a new creed, one very different from the program of monogamous marriage proposed in *The Well of Loneliness*. In all three sets of texts discussed in this chapter, Hall affirmed the body in its needs and the impulses of the heart as justification in their own right. She turned from the Christic rhetoric of "the intolerable load" (33) that must be borne to a classical emphasis on the overpowering force of passion that derives from Sappho's poetry. For many years, this Sapphic doctrine remained private to a degree, quoted by such biographers as Richard Ormrod and Michael Baker in their books, but published in extenso only in 1997. Hall's final Sapphic doctrine is, however, consistent with the Aestheticist Epicureanism of her first published work. Moreover, the focus on extreme, self-lacerating pain that one finds in the letters and the embrace of martyrdom and a self-consuming love of the other in *The Sixth Beatitude* both carry strong, if heterodox, overtones of the central mystery of Christianity. In this respect, Beresford Egan's *St. Stephen*, however irreverent, caught a real paradox at the center of the writing of Radclyffe Hall.

NOTES

Preface

1. Michael Baker, *Our Three Selves*, 43–44.

2. Barbara Low's *Psycho-Analysis* (1920) is a good example of the type.

3. Sigmund Freud, "The Psychogenesis of Homosexuality in the Case of a Woman," in *Complete Works*, 170–72.

4. The theory of sexual inversion attempts to explain same-sex desire in terms of the formula *anima muliebris virili corpore inclusa*, the soul of a woman enclosed in the body of a man, and vice versa (Christopher Craft, *Another Kind of Love*, 162).

5. See Judith Halberstam, *Female Masculinity*, 75–110; and Jay Prosser, *Second Skins*, 135–69.

6. Ellis Hanson, *Decadence and Catholicism*; Frederick S. Roden, *Same-Sex Desire in Victorian Religious Culture*; Roden et al., *Catholic Figures, Queer Narratives*; Patrick O'Malley, *Catholicism, Sexual Deviance, and Victorian Gothic Culture*.

7. Sally Cline, *Radclyffe Hall*, 30.

8. "Psychical Research," 4.

9. For a classic study of female teacher-student, mentor-protégé relations, see Martha Vicinus, *Independent Women* (1985). Vicinus revises her view of female same-sex intimacy in *Intimate Friends* (2004). In *Between Women*, Sharon Marcus has argued the normalcy of female friendships earlier in the nineteenth century. For my response to Marcus, see "Friendship, Marriage, and *Between Women*."

10. Francesco Rapazzini, "Elisabeth de Gramont, Natalie Barney's 'Eternal Mate,'" 7.

11. Noël Coward, *Tonight at 8:30*, 175.

Introduction

1. In contrast, consider Michael Warner, *Publics and Counterpublics.*

2. Laura Doan and Jay Prosser, *Palatable Poison,* 87.

3. James Strachey, Freud's translator and commentator (of *Standard Edition of the Complete Psychological Works*), remarks of the phrase: "The ego is ultimately derived from bodily sensations." Regarding the bodily ego, I follow Prosser's correction of Judith Butler's misreading of Freud's use of the term. Freud believed that the ego necessarily included an awareness of physical embodiment. See Jay Prosser, *Second Skins,* 40–41—hereafter cited in notes and text as Prosser.

4. Eve Kosofsky Sedgwick, *Tendencies,* xii; Prosser, 21.

5. In the following pages, I frequently refer to Hall as crossgendered or gender-crossing. I do so in order to distinguish her position from that of those who now refer to themselves as transgendered. Transgendered identification currently functions as a term of minority identification. Hall has much in common with contemporary trans-gendered individuals, but she doesn't present the queer sense of gender described in this paragraph as constituting a particular individual and group identity.

6. Benjamin Harshav, *Language in Time of Revolution,* 53–54.

7. See Harry Oosterhuis, *Stepchildren of Nature.*

8. Neil McKenna, *Secret Life of Oscar Wilde,* xii—hereafter cited in notes as Mc-Kenna.

9. Julia Markus, *Across an Untried Sea* (hereafter cited in text and notes as Mar-kus). On Bernhardt as artist, celebrity, and sexual bohemian, see Carol Ockman and Kenneth E. Silver, *Sarah Bernhardt: The Art of High Drama.*

10. Richard Ellmann, *Oscar Wilde,* 112–13.

11. Joy Dixon, " 'Love Is a Sacrament.' "

12. Martha Vicinus does a good deal of this work in *Intimate Friends.* See also Alan Bray, *The Friend.*

13. Cathy Gere, *Knossos and the Prophets of Modernism,* 6.

14. John Updike has observed that most biographies "are really just novels with indexes" (Peter France and William St. Clair, *Mapping Lives,* 8).

15. Philippe Lejeune, *On Autobiography,* ix—hereafter cited in text and notes as Lejeune.

16. A research assistant to Sally Cline, one of Hall's biographers, whom I con-tacted to ask about which hand Hall wrote with, responded that were Hall naturally left-handed, so to speak, at the time when she was young, she likely would have been forced to write with her right hand. If so, this compulsion is likely to have connected the act of writing with a complex psychic element—one which perhaps incited her to rebellious expression in her writing at the same time that the actual process of compo-sition might have been one fraught with struggle and difficulty. Hall's inclination toward left-handedness is also pertinent to her dyslexia since a disproportionate per-centage of dyslexics are left-handed.

17. Lejeune, 27.

18. *Sapphic* is the preferred term for female-female desire in the writing of women who affirm emotional and at times sexual desire between women in the late nineteenth and early twentieth centuries. As the work of Compton Mackenzie indicates, the term also had wide general currency. The reference to such subjects as "lesbian" or "Lesbian" often refers to this usage since Sappho lived on the Greek isle of Lesbos. For Hall, *lesbian* is not a term of choice to refer to a category of sexual identity.

19. Radclyffe Hall, "Forebears and Infancy," ms, Radclyffe Hall collection, Ransom, 22.4. Hereafter referred to in text as Version 1. Inserted pages in the notebook suggest that Hall wrote the draft while researching her final published novel, *The Sixth Beatitude* (1936).

20. Hall, "Forebears and Infancy," holograph ms in the hand of Una Troubridge, Radclyffe Hall collection, Ransom, 22.5. Hereafter referred to in text and notes as Version 3.

21. Lee Edelman, *No Future*, 1–31. See also Judith Halberstam, *In a Queer Time and Place*, 1–21.

22. Hall's prior success as a novelist in fact made possible the publication of *The Well of Loneliness* and the seriousness with which it was received. In this introduction, however, it is as the author of *The Well* that Hall figures.

23. Written in the mid-1930s, after the beginning of Hall's affair with a nurse, Evguenia Souline, the passage functions at the conscious level as an homage to the heroic capabilities of nurses. Unconsciously, the passage plays out the shaping fantasy of Hall's obsessive involvement with Souline, namely, the belief that intimacy with her could save Hall both from what she regarded as the failure of her relationship with Troubridge as well as from writer's block.

24. Radclyffe Hall, *Michael West*, ms, Radclyffe Hall collection, Ransom, 8.1.

25. That is, she never understood Hall's deviation from conventional norms of sex and gender.

26. Hall sees intimacy in terms of chains. The notion is the main thematic element in her first published novel, *The Forge* (1924).

27. On the title page of *Michael West*, Hall signs her name as John Radclyffe (*Michael West*, ms., 8.1). John is the pet name given Hall by Batten. Both Batten and Troubridge found Hall's boyish good looks and manner attractive, and both encouraged her to adopt a masculine style. In this sense, both lovers fostered Hall's female masculinity. The name John, however, also recalls that of her paternal great-grandfather.

Hall's surname was Radclyffe-Hall. She eventually adopted the pen name of Radclyffe Hall, an act that affirms her identification both with the patronymic and with her father, whose given name was Radclyffe.

28. Charles Surface was the young male protagonist of Richard Brinsley Sheridan's classic comedy *A School for Scandal* (1777). In a famous scene at the beginning of Act IV, Charles demonstrates filial loyalty to his uncle and benefactor, Sir Oliver Surface, by refusing to sell a portrait of him.

29. For Solidor, Cahun, and Moore, see Tirza True Latimer, *Women Together/ Women Apart*. For the others, see Chapter 5.

30. Compare Jacques Lacan, *Feminine Sexuality*, 36–38.

31. Diana Souhami, *Trials of Radclyffe Hall*, 69. Subsequent page references to Souhami in the text and notes are to this book.

32. J. Hinshelwood, *Congenital Word Blindness* (London: H. K. Lewis, 1917), p. 40, quoted in *Developmental Psychopathology*, 2nd ed., vol. 3, ed. Dante Cicchetti and Donald J. Cohen (New York: John Wiley and Sons, 2006), 271. For Samuel Orton, see Judith Felson Duchan, "Getting Here: A Short History of Speech Pathology in America," online at http://www.acsu.buffalo.edu/~duchan/history_subpages/samuel orton.html.

33. See, for example, Thomas G. West, *In the Mind's Eye*.

34. "Forebears and Infancy," ms., untitled, Radclyffe Hall collection, Ransom, 22.5. The draft bears no title and seems to be written in part in response to a request for advice to writers. Content is anomalous in relation to the rest of the draft material for this essay. I call this Version 2. Words crossed out in the original are struck through. Words and punctuation in square brackets have been added by myself. Words within curly brackets are additional cancellations within sections already crossed out. I would like to thank Richard Orem, librarian at the Ransom, for proofing and correcting my typescript against the manuscript. The preceding transcription incorporates his suggestions. April 29 and 30, 2003.

35. Sally Cline is the first biographer to recognize the significance of *Michael West* as an autobiographical account of Hall's first twenty years (Cline, *Radclyffe Hall*, 19— hereafter cited in notes as Cline).

The novel has a significant relation to a subgenre of crossgendered, autobiographical bildungsromans by women attracted to women who possessed "manly" virtues but without masculine stylization. See, for example, Deborah T. Meem's discussion of Eliza Lynn Linton's autobiographical novel, *The Autobiography of Christopher Kirkland* (1885) (in "Eliza Lynn Linton and the Rise of Lesbian Consciousness").

36. *Michael West*, 8.1, Ransom.

37. *Michael West*, notebook 2, 7.5, Ransom, ch. 5. Words crossed out in the original are struck through. Words and punctuation in square brackets have been added by myself.

38. Ibid., ch. 6.

39. Charles Dickens's *David Copperfield* exemplifies the narrative type.

40. For a theoretical reflection on the impossibility of autobiographical writing, see Judith Butler, *Giving an Account of Oneself*.

41. Maggie Magee and Diana C. Miller, *Lesbian Lives*, 61–66.

42. Dean Rapp, "Reception of Freud by the British Press"; Graham Richards, "Britain on the Couch."

43. Jean Laplanche and J.-B. Pontalis, *Language of Psycho-Analysis*, 328–29.

44. Kenneth Reinhard et al., *The Neighbor*, 29. See also 28—hereafter cited in notes as Reinhard.

45. Ibid., 31. Reinhard further associates *das Ding* with Lacan's rethinking of the concept of "the real" in the 1960s (30–31).

46. Cline, 12.

47. *Michael West*, 8.1, Ransom.

48. Reinhard, 30–31.

Chapter 1. Reading the Poetry

Note to epigraph: *Sussex Daily News*, March 22, 1913. Cited in Marguerite Radclyffe-Hall, *The Forgotten Island*, 83. Subsequent page references to *The Forgotten Island* appear in the text.

1. Markus, 32–35. Cushman and Stebbins exchanged rings and regarded themselves as married.

2. Michel Foucault, *History of Sexuality, Vol. I*, 106–7.

3. Information in the preceding paragraph is from Baker, *Our Three Selves*, 25–27. Subsequent page references to Baker in text and notes are to this book.

4. Between 1906 and 1915, Hall published five books of poetry. Marguerite Radclyffe-Hall is the name that appears on the title page of these books. In this chapter, she is referred to in text and notes as "Hall," the form of her last name that she used in signing her subsequent published work.

5. Souhami, 51.

6. Baker, 33–34; Cline, 61–62; Souhami, 37–41.

7. Hence too the masculinity of the deity of love in the lines cited above.

8. Cline, 73.

9. See Jessica Douglas-Home, *Violet: The Life and Loves of Violet Gordon Woodhouse*.

10. Cline, 94, 98–99.

11. Anne Carson, *Eros the Bittersweet*, 3. I discuss the term in Chapter 11.

12. *Forgotten Island*, 58.

13. For linkages to other women, such as Violet Hunt and Dolly Diehl, see Cline (55–56) and Souhami (33–34, 43).

14. For the haunting, consider Daphne Du Maurier's short story "Don't Look Now," in *Don't Look Now*, 3–58. My thinking about the ideal of telepathic communication owes a good deal to conversations with Lysa Lapointe.

15. Other turn of the century writers, such as Vernon Lee and Henry James, were fascinated by questions of personal responsibility in situations in which a ghostly presence seems to incur. Consider Lee's short story "Oke of Okehurst" and Henry James's *The Turn of the Screw* as examples.

16. Sophie Fuller, "Elgar and the Salons," 226, 233.

17. Mark Amory, *Lord Berners*, 67. Alberto Visetti, Hall's stepfather, was also a well-connected voice teacher.

18. Richard Dellamora, "Swinburne, Modern Desire, and the Hellenistic Revival."

19. Lovat Dickson, *Radclyffe Hall at the Well of Loneliness*, 45–46.

20. Frederic W. H. Myers, *Human Personality*, 71.

21. Roger Luckhurst, *Invention of Telepathy*, 269–70.

22. Ibid., 274. See also Freud, "A Note on the Unconscious."

23. Luckhurst, 270.

24. Myers has in mind Max Nordau's attack on all three artists in *Degeneration*. The argument in this paragraph owes a debt to Gere, *Knossos and the Prophets of Modernism*, 6–7.

25. Radclyffe Hall, *The Well of Loneliness*, 208.

26. T. J. Jackson Lears, *No Place of Grace*, xiii. Jackson's book is a study of Antimodernism in American culture between 1880 and 1920. Antimodernism in England shares many features and links with its North American cousin.

27. I attempt to illustrate this distinction in the brief account provided later in the chapter of the antimodernist impulse in new English music in the early years of the century.

28. In addition to her involvement in English music, Woodhouse helped promote national Modernism in new compositions from Spain, France, and the Hungary of Béla Bartók (Douglas-Home, 189).

29. Ibid., 120, 122.

30. See, for example, current discussions of Englishness in the work of Sir Edward Elgar, particularly for the masque *The Crown of India* (Nalini Ghuman, "Elgar and the British Raj"; Deborah Heckert, "Working the Crowd"; Leon Botstein, "Transcending the Enigmas of Biography").

31. Amory, 67 (interpolation mine). Lears has a good deal to say about Roman and Anglo-Catholic Antimodernism (183–215). For the sexual politics of American Antimodernism, an excellent point of reference is Douglass Shand-Tucci, *Boston Bohemia*.

32. Butterworth, who was killed in action during World War I, wrote a song cycle of poems from *A Shropshire Lad*. Another instance occurs in young Herbert Howells's Piano Quartet in A Minor, Op. 21 (1916), an early example of the use of pastoral elements in modern English high musical culture. See the discussion in *Elgar and His World* (66). Howells used a financial award received in recognition of this work, strongly affected by losses experienced in World War I, to edit Tudor and Elizabethan music.

33. The affair with Hoare began in May or June 1913. Cline discusses it best (91–106).

34. The similarity was recognized at the time. See *Forgotten Island*, 78.

35. Walter Pater, *Plato and Platonism*, 90–91. Cited by Stephano-Maria Evangelista, "Narcissism and Romantic Reflections in Pater's *Plato and Platonism*," 6.

36. A. E. Housman, "Introductory Lecture," in *The Name and Nature of Poetry*, 9–10. The lecture was delivered before the Faculties of Arts and Laws and of Science at University College, London, on October 3, 1892, on the occasion of the appointment of Housman, then thirty-four, as Professor of Latin.

37. Housman, *Name and Nature of Poetry*, 7.

38. Housman, *Shropshire Lad*, 2.

39. Marguerite Radclyffe-Hall, *Songs of Three Counties and Other Poems*, 18.

40. Peter Howarth, "Housman's Dirty Postcards," 766–67.

41. Housman, *Collected Poems*, "Additional Poems," XVIII, 233. The poem was first published in 1937 in Laurence Housman's posthumous memoir of his brother. The echo of the final line of the poem that appears in the final paragraphs of *The Well of Loneliness* suggests that Hall may have read a privately circulated transcript.

42. Ibid.

43. Howarth, 764.

44. "Fruit of the Nispero," XVI (*Poems of the Past and Present*, 115).

45. In lyric no. LVI, for example, Michael Field focuses on a virginal consciousness that Bradley and Cooper associate with integral selfhood. In passion, however, this sense of self gives way to "the strange, / Deep-severing change / That comes to women when / Elected, raised above / All else, they thrill with love, / The love of gods or men" (*Long Ago*, lxxxv). LVI deals with the betrayal of love between two women that occurs after the marriage of both, but for Field, Sapphic sexual passion always implies a fall from virginity into "strange, / Deep-severing change." Far from being regretted, this loss is regarded as necessary for the self to engage the full range of human experience.

46. See also Dellamora, *Friendship's Bonds* (verso of dedication page).

47. Hall, *A Sheaf of Verses*, 108.

48. For more on a doubly sexed Christ, see Chapter 7.

49. Hall, *A Sheaf of Verses*, 38. Souhami reports that on October 2, 1910, Hall, Batten, and George went with "Ladye's sister-in-law, Nelly Hatch, to a concert at the Albert Hall, where Louise Kirkby-Lunn sang Ladye's setting of John's 'Ode to Sappho'" (52).

50. From "Miscellaneous Poems," Part 2 of *Songs of Three Counties*, 43, 44.

51. Robert Buchanan, *Fleshly School of Poetry*.

52. Hall, *Poems of the Past and Present*, 22.

53. Ibid., 22–23.

54. *Songs of Three Counties*, 32.

55. Rosa Bracco, *Merchants of Hope*, 196.

56. See the holograph manuscript of her undelivered public address "Ghosts."

57. Mignon Nevada, letter of June 10, 1918.

58. Ibid.

59. Quoted from a news clipping enclosed in ibid.

60. For Admiral Troubridge's involvement with the far right-wing National Party, see Philip Hoare, *Oscar Wilde's Last Stand*, 144.

61. I say lesbian rather than Sapphic because in Nevada's reaction one senses, I think, an emerging view that such phenomena as the Allan sensation involved an attack on individuals who were beginning to be understood as constituting a particular minority group, defined in terms of the shared same-sex sexual-object choices of its members.

62. Letter from Chappell & Co. Ltd., June 13, 1918. Lovat Dickson Collection, MG30, D237, vol. 4, folder 11.

63. James Harding, *Ivor Novello*, 67.

64. The name is the same as that of the East End actress whom Dorian Gray becomes infatuated with in Wilde's novel *The Picture of Dorian Gray*.

65. To this account could be added a discussion of her first efforts at the writing of fiction: unpublished short stories and an incomplete feminist novel set in the Victorian period, *The Cunningham Code* (Cline, 53).

Chapter 2. Psychic Incorporation

1. Hall, letter to Sir Oliver Lodge, July 2, 1918.

2. See Chapter 1; see also Cline, 91–106.

3. For Myers, see Chapter 1.

4. Cited by Jenny Hazelgrove, *Spiritualism and British Society Between the Wars*, 193.

5. "Feda made herself known to young Leonard one evening when she and two other young women were experimenting with table rapping. After receiving messages from both their deceased mothers, the girls were contacted by a Communicator who gave her name as Feda, and explained that she was an ancestress of mine. She had married my great-great-grandfather. My mother had often told me about an Indian girl who married this ancestor, but you know how bored children are by frequently-repeated family history? —I had not taken much notice at the time. After marrying this native girl, my great-great-grandfather, William Hamilton, was not popular in India, and he made arrangements to bring Feda home to England. On the eve of starting home she gave birth to a son, and died. She was then only thirteen. This was about the year 1800" (Gladys Osborne Leonard, *My Life in Two Worlds*, 29–30)—hereafter cited as Leonard in text and notes.

6. The usage is mine. I do not mean *enactment* as the term is used within psychoanalysis.

7. Leonard, 52.

8. Souhami, xix. I discuss dyslexia and Hall in the Introduction.

9. William James, "Notes on Automatic Writing," 555—hereafter cited in notes as James.

10. Alice Johnson, "On the Automatic Writing of Mrs. Holland," 175. Subsequent page references to Johnson in the text and notes refer to this work.

11. Luckhurst, 70–73.

12. Ibid., 264.

13. James, 551; Johnson, 166.

14. Dixon, *Divine Feminine*, 41–44.

15. Hall and Troubridge, "On a Series of Sittings with Mrs. Osborne Leonard," 340. Subsequent page references to Hall in the text of this chapter, unless otherwise noted, refer to this essay.

16. Laplanche and Pontalis, 455–62.

17. Ormrod, *Una Troubridge*, 52—hereafter cited in text and notes as Ormrod. See also Cline, 116–17.

18. Una, Lady Troubridge, *Life of Radclyffe Hall*, 45. Unless otherwise cited, subsequent page references to Troubridge in the text and notes refer to this book.

19. "Twonnie," is Feda's version of Batten's pet name for Hall, "Johnnie," which Feda found difficult to pronounce. Feda addressed Hall as "Mrs. Twonnie" (344) during the sittings. See also Cline, 66.

20. Because of Hall's psychic investment in the sittings and because she read the oral version of the essay presented to the Society, I refer to the writing as hers; but the proviso about the collaborative character of the paper needs to be kept in mind. The section on Billy, for example, shows involvement by both women.

21. The date Troubridge gives is incorrect.

22. Early in the affair, Hall had warned Troubridge that she was taking it too seriously (46).

23. *Hall v. Lakin*, partial transcript, 8.

24. Sir Oliver J. Lodge, *Raymond or Life and Death*, 6th ed. Page references to Lodge in text and notes refer to this edition.

25. Jacques Derrida, *Archive Fever*, 11.

26. In Freud's "second theory of the psychical apparatus, . . . in the case of psychosis a rupture between ego and reality occurs straight away, leaving the ego under the sway of the id; then, at a second stage—that of the onset of delusions—the ego is supposed to reconstruct a new reality in accordance with the desires of the id" (Laplanche and Pontalis, 372). Laplanche and Pontalis point out the question-begging aspect of this formulation since in it "Freud is obliged to make reality play the part of an actual autonomous force, almost as though it was itself an agency of the psychical apparatus" (372).

27. Cline, 118, 171. Dickson has his doubts: "The prescription which Dr Sachs, the well-known gynaecologist to whom Dr Miller referred Una, gave her is noted down in . . . [her] diary. Medical opinion confirms that this is not for the grave disease of syphilis, but for a gynaecological irregularity. Crichton-Miller would surely have made a thorough physical examination of Una when she became his patient. He said that he could cure her by the use of psychoanalysis and hypnosis. The conclusion to which one is regretfully drawn is that this was a fantasy conjured up by Una's need to justify to herself and her friends her action in leaving the Admiral for Radclyffe Hall" (55n).

28. Joy Dixon, "Sexology and the Occult."

29. Craft, *Another Kind of Love*, 34.

30. Freud, *The Ego and the Id*, cited in Prosser, 40.

31. Prosser, 21–27.

32. Vernon Lee, "Deterioration of Soul," 938. The two women were introduced by the composer Ethel Smyth (Cline, 64). I discuss Lee's essay in "Productive Decadence: 'The Queer Comradeship of Outlawed Thought.'"

33. Cited by Kathy Psomiades, "'Still Burning,'" 24.

Chapter 3. Symbiosis of Publicity and Privacy

1. Jodie Medd provides an exception in a chapter of her 2001 Cornell University doctoral thesis, "Extraordinary Allegations." Unless otherwise noted, subsequent page references in the text and notes to Medd refer to this work.

2. One of these women was Ethel Smyth, a composer and a friend of Mabel Batten. A devotee of Spiritualism, Smyth was delighted to make Hall and Troubridge's acquaintance while golfing (Louise Collis, *Impetuous Heart*, 163–64).

3. Baker, 123.

4. "Psychical Research: The Spirits of the Dead," *The Times*, 4—hereafter cited in the notes as "Psychical Research." Unless otherwise noted, subsequent page references in the text to *The Times* refer to this article. The association of Spiritualism with female hysteria was a familiar one. For example, in Vernon Lee's early novel, *Miss Brown* (1884), Anne Brown becomes fascinated with the Russian cousin of her benefactor, Walter Hamlin. Madame Elaguine, or Sacha, is a talented medium (vol. 2, 232, 233). When Anne introduces her to a young doctor, he immediately diagnoses her as a hysterical subject. But when Anne objects that Sacha is not "subject to . . . fits," he responds, "That's not what *we* mean by hysteria. Hysteria isn't a fit of hysterics; it is a condition of morbid nervous excitability, usually accompanied by a certain loss of will-power. Hysterical subjects are a kind of milder mad men and women; their characters undergo curious modifications. . . . I wonder whether that lady is not a spiritualist,—she looks like it" (Vernon Lee, *Miss Brown*, 2, 254–55).

5. Luckhurst argues that the privileged, philosophical, and scientific backgrounds of the founding members of the Society played a large part in gaining credibility for their interest in mental telepathy and related psychological phenomena.

6. Lodge, viii.

7. Douglas Murray, *Bosie*, 169–70.

8. Hoare, 18.

9. Hoare, 18–21.

10. "Psychical Research," 4. Baker, 131, notes that Fox-Pitt was Douglas's former brother-in-law.

11. "Psychical Research," 4.

12. Baker, 130.

13. Cline, 140. Developments in mid- to late nineteenth-century technology—the telegraph, the telephone, new uses of electricity—suggested by analogy the possibility that one could communicate with the consciousness of another directly and immediately. See Pamela Thurschwell, *Literature, Technology, and Magical Thinking*, 12–13, 25.

14. Published in November 1916, the volume went through six printings in two months.

15. "More important than talking is to get things through with his own people, and to give absolute evidence" (Lodge, 159).

16. Baker, 54, 93.

17. See also Nicky Hallett: "Lesbian masculine identification, afforded in new ways in the early twentieth century, was one means to authorship" (*Lesbian Lives*, 80).

18. Medd argues the centrality of lesbian scandal to the culture of literary Modernism in "Extraordinary Allegations."

19. Bart Schultz, "Truth and Its Consequences," 23. The argument in this paragraph is drawn from Schultz's important essay.

20. Ibid., 26–27.

21. Ormrod, 103.

22. These factors are especially evident in the parliamentary debate surrounding attempts to define lesbian "gross indecency" in 1921 (Medd, 100–22).

23. See Medd, "Cult of the Clitoris," 25–26, 47 n39.

24. Jeffrey Weeks, *Coming Out*, 106; see also Medd, 100–22. The amendment reads as follows: "Any act of gross indecency between female persons shall be a misdemeanor and punishable in the same manner as any such act committed by male persons under section 11 of the Criminal Law Amendment Act 1885" (cited in Sheila Jeffreys, *The Spinster and Her Enemies*, 113)—hereafter cited as Jeffreys in text and notes.

25. The phrase recurs in the agitation against *The Well of Loneliness* in 1928.

26. "Psychical Research," 4.

27. Hoare, 66.

28. It is an index of the success she achieved that Rebecca West at the end of the decade would describe her as "a personality whom most of us like and admire. . . . She has all the virtues of the English aristocratic type, courage, self-restraint, steadfastness, and a very fine intelligence" (Laura Doan, *Fashioning Sapphism*, 182).

29. The emphasis was on appearance. Billing had a mistress, and Douglas continued to be sexually interested in young men.

30. Hoare, 218.

31. Ibid., 110. "Old Squiffy" is Margot's husband, Prime Minister Asquith, who had appointed Ross president of the Imperial War Museum.

32. Ibid., 99, 140.

33. "Psychical Research," 4.

34. Hoare, 125, 123n. He incorrectly identifies Hope as Troubridge's sister-in-law.

35. Jeffreys, 104.

36. Sharon Marcus, *Between Women*; Martha Vicinus, *Intimate Friends*.

37. See Fred Roden's discussions of this important intervention: "Introduction: The Catholic Modernist Crisis, Queer Modern Catholicisms," and "Michael Field, John Gray, and Marc-Andre Raffalovich: Reinventing Romantic Friendship in Modernity," in *Catholic Figures, Queer Narratives*, ed. Lowell Gallagher, Frederick S. Roden, and Patricia Juliana Smith, 1–18, 57–68.

38. Oscar Wilde, *Complete Short Fiction*, 270 n60.

39. Nicky Hallett, *Lesbian Lives*, 43.

40. Ibid., 44.

41. Baker, 130–131.

42. Troubridge, "The *Modus Operandi* in So-Called Mediumistic Trance."

43. Cited by Doan, 186.

Chapter 4. *The Unlit Lamp*

1. "Female sexuality" is not an ideal phrase; I use it in this chapter because Freud chose it as the title of an influential 1931 essay.

2. Laplanche and Pontalis, 302–4, 308–11.

3. For Hall's interest in the crossgendered bildungsroman, see the Introduction, note 36.

4. Cline, 160—hereafter cited in notes and text as Cline.

5. Sinclair's novels show a preoccupation with this problem. See Terry Phillips, "Battling with the Angel."

6. See Patricia Juliana Smith's discussion of the novel in *Lesbian Panic*, 18–37—hereafter cited as Smith in text and notes.

7. I discuss Hall's psychical research in Chapters 2 and 3.

8. Claudia Stillman Franks offers a naturalist reading of the novel in *Beyond "The Well of Loneliness,"* 47–59.

9. Hall, *The Unlit Lamp*, 122–23. Subsequent page references to this edition of the novel are included in the text and notes.

10. Vicinus, *Independent Women*, 7. Unless otherwise cited, subsequent page references to Vicinus in the text and notes refer to this book.

11. Ibid., 147–48. Vicinus points out that youthful rebellion against the conservative style of the generation of 1840 to 1860 was already growing in the years immediately before the war. This late Edwardian and Georgian mood has connections with attempts at the time to resuscitate the reputation of Oscar Wilde and the cultural heritage of late Victorian Aestheticism and the Decadence as well. See Chapter 3. Consider as well Carroll Smith-Rosenberg, "Body Politic," 116, 120. Marcus's recent normalizing account of female friendship in *Between Women* focuses on friendship writing for the most part earlier than that discussed by Vicinus in *Intimate Friends*. As

a result, Marcus does not consider aestheticist material from the mid-1860s onward that suggests the sexualizing of female friendship.

12. Freud, "Some Psychological Consequences of the Anatomical Distinction Between the Sexes," *Complete Works*, 19: 244.

13. Freud, "Female Sexuality," *Complete Works*, 21: 226. Subsequent page references to this essay appear in the text.

14. Ernest Jones, "Early Development of Female Sexuality," 459—hereafter cited in text and notes as Jones.

15. Joan Riviere, "Womanliness as a Masquerade," 38. Subsequent page references to the essay appear in the text.

16. Regarding Elizabeth's desire, see pp. 190–91.

17. May Sinclair, *Feminism*, 16. Subsequent page references to this work appear in the text.

18. Capitals are Sinclair's.

19. See also pp. 469–70.

20. Vicinus, 27, 28, 29.

21. For the implications of the genre for lesbian and other female protagonists, see Elizabeth Abel et al., *The Voyage In*.

22. The key chapter in this respect is chapter 6.

23. Cited in Vicinus, 37.

24. See Jeffreys.

25. Information on raves in this paragraph is from Vicinus, 187–210.

26. See Psomiades, " 'Still Burning,' " 21–41.

27. Joan finds the status transgression to be just as disturbing as the sexual one.

28. See the Introduction.

29. A boyish look and elements of male attire characterized both heterosexual and homosexual styles among fashionable women in the 1920s. See Doan's authoritative study, *Fashioning Sapphism*.

30. The case is discussed in detail in Chapter 3.

31. Troubridge, *Life of Radclyffe Hall*, 41. Subsequent page references to Troubridge in the text refer to this work.

32. Cline, 147, 182. See also *The Unlit Lamp*, 42–43.

33. Robert Browning, "The Statue and the Bust," in *Poetry*, 148.

Chapter 5. Paris and the Culture of Auto/biography in *The Forge*

1. Troubridge, *Life of Radclyffe Hall*, 69.

2. Baker, 156–57.

3. Troubridge reports that Sieglinde was based on "Thora the Fairest of Women, a red dachshund bitch of matchless beauty" (64) that Hall gave her.

4. Souhami republishes an illustration of Hall, Troubridge, and half a dozen dachshunds, which originally appeared in *The Queen*, August 23, 1923 (*Trials of Radclyffe Hall*, facing p. 330).

5. For Sapphism and cross gender in Parisian cabaret culture, see Latimer, *Women Together/ Women Apart*. Barbette became a theatrical phenomenon in England and on the Continent, particularly in Paris, in 1923 and 1924. In 1924, while appearing at the London Palladium, Barbette "was found engaged in sexual activity with another man. His contract was cancelled and he was never able to obtain a work permit for England again."

In a novel and play that she cowrote and in the early talkie, *Murder!* (1930), Clemence Dane, along with Alfred Hitchcock, plays off Barbette's celebrity and notoriety in fashioning the effeminate killer, Handel Fane (played by Esmé Percy), a cross-dressing trapeze artist. In the film, Fane murders a young woman who threatens to reveal the fact that he is a half-caste. The police, in the course of their investigation, watch a farce from backstage in which Fane, also an actor, crossdresses first as a woman and subsequently as an English bobby. See Donald Spoto, *The Art of Alfred Hitchcock*, 29–30. Biographical information on Barbette is drawn from en.wikipedia.org/wiki/Barbette_(performer).

Hall had a long, mutually appreciative but also competitive relationship with Dane, a longtime friend of Noël Coward as well as a successful novelist and author of plays in her own right, including *A Regiment of Women* (1917). Hall was disappointed when Dane declined an invitation to dramatize *The Well of Loneliness* for the stage. See Cline, 64, 147, 213, 235, and 277.

6. Barney appears in the novel in the guise of Rosamund Randolph, the "tall, fair woman dressed in white," who greets the Brents when they visit Ford's Paris studio in Book 2, chapter 8 (*The Forge*, 107).

7. Of this phase of her youth, Colette writes: "I was not long deluded by those photographs that show me wearing a stiff mannish collar, necktie, short jacket over a straight skirt, a lighted cigarette between two fingers" (68). Page references in the notes and text to Colette are to Colette, *The Pure and the Impure*.

8. Colette corresponded with Hall and Troubridge at the time of publication of *The Well*. See Judith Thurman, *Secrets of the Flesh*, 386–87—hereafter cited in notes as Thurman.

9. Whitney Chadwick, *Amazons in the Drawing Room*, 17—hereafter cited in notes and text as Chadwick.

10. Charles Baudelaire, *Les Fleurs du Mal*, 130.

11. For Amalia, the woman who "is a complete human being" is also virile, sexually "the equal of a man" (107).

12. Thurman, 389, 549 n38.

13. Information on Brooks's career is drawn from Chadwick; Joe Lucchesi, "'Apparition in a Black Flowing Cloak,'"—hereafter cited in notes as Lucchesi; and Adelyn D. Breeskin's pioneering exhibition catalog *Romaine Brooks: "Thief of Souls"*—hereafter cited in the text as Breeskin.

14. Cited in Lucchesi, 76.

15. Lucchesi quotes Brooks's unpublished autobiography, 79. See also Meryle Secrest, *Between Me and Life*, 244—hereafter cited in notes as Secrest.

16. Gabriele D'Annunzio, *Le martyre de saint Sebastien*, 55–72.

17. In her memoir of Hall, Troubridge gives inordinate space to the efforts she made to arrange a meeting between Hall and d'Annunzio in Italy in the 1930s (118–25).

18. Karla Jay, *The Amazon and the Page*, 19–20—hereafter cited in notes as Jay.

19. Jay, chapter 3, "Gynocentricity," 36–60. On Decadent utopianism, see Dellamora, "Productive Decadence," 1–18.

20. These works were not included in either of the retrospectives of Brooks's work mounted since 1971.

21. Troubridge, *Life of Radclyffe Hall*, 69.

22. The passage includes a sexological touch. In his chapter on female sexual inversion, Havelock Ellis argues that masculine women often find lovers among undersexed, relatively unattractive but otherwise normal women. See Ellis, "Sexual Inversion in Women," 222.

23. I discuss Freud's concept of the female masculinity complex in Chapter 4.

24. My use of the phrase "female virility" needs to be distinguished from queer cultural analyses in which *virility* is used as a negative term of value. See, for example, Carla Freccero, "Carnivorous Virility, or Becoming-Dog."

25. Cited in Smith, 40.

26. Virginia Woolf, *Jacob's Room*, 78.

27. W. Somerset Maugham, *The Constant Wife*, 81.

28. Thurman, introduction to Colette, *Gigi, Julie de Carneilhan, Chance Acquaintances*, xiv.

29. Quoted in Secrest, 413.

30. She also mentions her and her partner's friendships with Colette, Barney, and Brooks, whom she describes as "the painter of memorable canvases" (83).

31. Ormrod, 137. By recording this information in her diary, which she later put in the hands of her literary executor, Troubridge set the stage for the eventual revelation of this fact.

32. Troubridge, *Life of Radclyffe Hall*, 69–76.

33. Thurman, 386. Troubridge was also the first translator of Colette's fiction into English (Baker, 194).

34. Lejeune, 27. See the discussion of Lejeune in the Introduction.

Chapter 6. Una Troubridge and Gender Performativity in *A Saturday Life*

1. Percy Reginald Stephensen et al., *The Sink of Solitude*.

2. For a detailed discussion of the image, see Doan, 185–86. Doan reproduces the photograph (fig. 13, following 94).

3. Ibid., 185.

4. Cline, 186.

5. Ibid., 172–73.

6. Later, Coward would draw on Hall's relationship with Batten and Troubridge in his Spiritualist farce, *Blithe Spirit* (1941). See the discussion in Terry Castle, *Noël Coward and Radclyffe Hall*, 82–95 (hereafter cited in notes as Castle).

7. Ibid., 20–21.

8. Baker, 164; Castle, 19, 20–21.

9. For Hall and Troubridge's friendship with Colette, see Chapter 5.

10. Grace Spencer, letter to Radclyffe Hall, January 23, 1927—hereafter cited in notes as Spencer letter to Hall, unless otherwise indicated.

11. See the discussion of Myers in Chapter 1.

12. See Luckhurst, 270–76.

13. Hall, *A Saturday Life*, 99. Subsequent page references to this edition appear in the text.

14. Hall broaches this problem directly in *The Forge*. See my discussion in Chapter 5, which contextualizes the problem in relation to Woolf's recently published novel, *Jacob's Room* (1922). The specific phenomenon of the emptiness of the modern upper-middle-class male is foregrounded in both novels.

15. Woolf, "Mr. Bennett and Mrs. Brown."

16. Freud, "The Psychogenesis of Homosexuality in the Case of a Woman." Originally published in German in 1920, the essay was published in English translation by Barbara Low and R. Gabler in 1920 and 1924.

17. I discuss the relation between her thinking and Freud's in the 1920s both in the Preface and in Chapter 4.

18. Suzanne Raitt, *May Sinclair*, 135, 170–71.

19. Hall, *The Forge*, 216. See the discussion of artistic impersonality in Chapter 5.

20. Within psychical research, this something was believed literally to be the ether, an electromagnetic medium through which brain waves were transmitted (Luckhurst, 87–88).

21. Hall, *'Twixt Earth and Stars*, 7.

22. See my discussion in "The Sapphic Culture of Michael Field and Radclyffe Hall."

23. Hall, *A Sheaf of Verses*, 108.

24. See May Sinclair, *Feminism*; also Dellamora, "Female Adolescence in May Sinclair's *Mary Olivier*."

25. Cited in Amory, 102. Lord Berners, Woolf, and Coward inhabited a small world: for example, *London Calling!* "included the controversial satirical sketch 'The Swiss Family Whittlebot,' which roused the enmity of the three Sitwells, and ignited flames of recrimination and self-advertisement, fanned on both sides, that continued to smoulder for years to come" (Noël Coward, *Plays: One*, 2). Subsequent references to Coward in text and notes refer to this volume.

26. As with Hall in *The Forge*, Coward plays on characteristics possibly shared between himself and the character he plays.

27. On the homosexual connotations of classical piano playing, see Kevin Kopelson, *Beethoven's Kiss*.

28. Coward, 97. "Pawnie" = Pansy? Nonce?

29. His name suggests a number of meanings. Tom = a Tom? (Florence has a habit of taking flings with young men), a tomcat? Also short for tomboy, slang for a boyish, young female subject of same-sex desire. Veryan = very young? varying? sexually flexible?

30. Nicky's defective pianism and "temperament," a term frequently associated with artists and homosexuality, suggest that homosexuality may be a more appropriate telos for him than the heterosexuality that he has diffidently reached for with "Bunty," a nickname suitable for a female sporting type.

31. Thurman, *Secrets of the Flesh*, 171—hereafter cited in notes as Thurman.

32. Lucey, *Never Say I*, 110—hereafter cited as Lucey in text and notes.

33. Thurman, 182.

34. Sinclair, *A Defence of Idealism*, 8.

35. The term specifically refers "to those upper-class women and courtesans whose sexual tourism brings them to places in which they might find working-class women to pick up" (Lucey, 92).

36. Troubridge, *Such Was Life*. Date of composition not known but likely the early mid-1920s.

37. Troubridge continued to toy with typescripts of essays collected under this title as late as 1962.

38. Ormrod, 13.

39. Troubridge, "Nijinsky, 1913," in *Such Was Life*. The faun is a frequently visited figure in Sapphic writing and sculpture of the nineteenth century. Colette's first significant appearance on stage was in the role of a faun (Thurman, 163–64). Troubridge's sculptural investigation of Nijinsky took place at a time when she was in analysis as a result of symptoms associated with underlying incompatibilities in her marriage. She began her studies of Nijinsky a few days after an *"epoch making visit"* to her analyst, Dr. Hugh Crichton-Miller on January 23, 1913. According to Troubridge's biographer, "It may well be that Miller had discussed 'inversion' with her and that she had gained spontaneous insight into her own latent nature" (Ormrod, 52).

40. Troubridge, "Clothes," in *I Remember*, 3.10, 5.

41. Troubridge, "Hero Worship," in *I Remember*, 3.9, 5.

42. Troubridge, "My Teachers," in *I Remember*, 3.9, 6–7.

43. Troubridge, "Clothes," 3.10, 5.

44. Ibid., 5, 6.

45. Troubridge, "My Teachers," 3.9, 5.

46. Troubridge, "Christmasses" [*sic*], in *I Remember*," 3.10, 6.

47. *A Saturday Life*, notebook no. 1, cover, 8.3, Ransom.

48. Ibid., inside cover, verso.

49. Ibid.

50. *A Saturday Life,* notebook, inside cover, verso, 8.2.

51. According to the outline, Sidonia is born in 1887, the same year in which Troubridge was born.

52. Female Victorian writers who today might be termed heterosexual frequently indicated their sexual ambivalence about male-female sex by creating domestic situations involving two women and a child. A leading example is the Italian idyll of Aurora Leigh and Marian Earle that occurs at the beginning of Book VIII of Elizabeth Barrett's *Aurora Leigh* or of Margaret Oliphant's posthumously published short story, "A Story of a Wedding Tour." See Elizabeth Barrett Browning, *Aurora Leigh,* 261–62; Glennis Stephenson, *Nineteenth-Century Stories by Women,* 403–27.

53. Cline, 218, 393 n47.

54. Spencer, letter to Radclyffe Hall, January 30, 1927. Spencer speaks of Mrs. Ogden as a "vampire mother."

55. Spencer letter to Hall, January 23, 1927.

56. Ibid.

57. Animal-rights protection has long been of special interest to subjects of female-female desire. Consider, for example, the work of Frances Power Cobbe, a leading Victorian feminist, in this area (Susan Hamilton, "Still Lives" and "Pets and Scientific Subjects").

Chapter 7. Catholicism, *Adam's Breed,* and the Sacred *Well*

1. For Hall's interest in this novel in portraying life within a working-class, immigrant, Roman Catholic community, see my comments in the Preface.

2. I have in mind Stephen Arata, Ellis Hanson, Richard Kaye, Patrick O'Malley, Richard Rambuss, and Frederick S. Roden. Douglass Shand-Tucci also speaks to the point. Patricia Juliana Smith was an excellent collocutor in developing the argument of the paper on which this chapter is in part based.

3. In the aftermath of *The Well of Loneliness* trials, Douglas was pathetically eager to meet Hall and Troubridge (Baker, 284–85).

4. Oscar Wilde, *De Profundis and Other Writings,* 92—hereafter cited in notes and text as Wilde.

5. Baker, 207; Wilde, 5.

6. David Hilliard, "Unenglish and Unmanly."

7. John Bloxam, "The Priest and the Acolyte." See Ellis Hanson, *Decadence and Catholicism,* 310–11; and Brian Reade, *Sexual Heretics,* 47.

8. Souhami reports that as an adolescent Hall hung "a large wooden crucifix" on her bedroom wall (22).

9. Neither Hall nor Troubridge disclosed the sexual character of their relationship to their confessors. To do so would have been to subject themselves to the Church's view of the sinful character of their tie. Wilde's deathbed conversion came at a moment for him when sexual ties to other men were literally no longer possible.

10. Bray, *The Friend*, 289–90.

11. John Henry Newman, "A Letter Addressed to His Grace, the Duke of Norfolk," 133. The statement is quoted in an article by Garry Wills, "High Fidelity," 40. Subsequent page references to Newman in the text refer to this work.

12. See Harry Oosterhuis, *Stepchildren of Nature*.

13. In summer 1875, Wilde, traveling in Italy, sent Newman a copy of a new poem, "Rome Unvisited," in which Wilde refers to the pope as "the only God-appointed King." On his first visit to Rome in 1877, Wilde was granted an audience with Pius IX, who hoped he would convert to Roman Catholicism (Richard Ellmann, *Oscar Wilde*, 55, 70—hereafter cited in notes as Ellmann).

14. Newman's practice prompted Charles Kingsley's notorious broadside: *What, Then, Does Dr. Newman Mean?* in which Kingsley writes: "So far from thinking truth for its own sake to be no virtue, he considers it a virtue so lofty, as to be unattainable by man, who must therefore, in certain cases, take up with what-it-is-no-more-than-a-hyperbole-to-call lies; and who, if he should be so lucky as to get any truth into his possession, will be wise in 'economizing' the same, and 'dividing it,' so giving away a bit here and a bit there, lest he should waste so precious a possession" (Newman, *Apologia Pro Vita Sua*, 334). For more on the principle of reserve in relation to religious belief, see Patrick R. O'Malley, "Epistemology of the Cloister."

15. Frederick S. Roden, "Introduction: The Catholic Modernist Crisis," 2—hereafter cited in notes as "Crisis."

16. Raffalovich and John Gray, who became a priest in the Roman Catholic Church, fashioned their own particular form of celibate marriage. See Roden, "Michael Field, John Gray, and Marc-Andre Raffalovich."

17. "Crisis," 4, 5; quoted from George Tyrrell, *Notes on the Catholic Doctrine of Purity* (1897), "printed at a Jesuit press 'For Private Circulation'" and prefaced "by a letter from the Jesuit provincial at the time, Fr. Francis Scoles, addressed to Superiors" (4).

18. Ruth Vanita, "'Uncovenanted Joys.'" Vanita argues that Mirrlees, in her modernist novel *Madeleine: One of Love's Jansenists* (1919), portrays the *Précieuses*, members of the circle of bluestockings around the seventeenth-century French novelist Madeleine de Scudery, as protagonists in a communal Sapphic tragedy that parallels the experience of their contemporaries, the Jansenists, a heretical Roman Catholic group (89–91). Mirrlees's linkage of sexual with religious heterodoxy makes her novel cognate with Hall's *The Well of Loneliness*. By the same author, see also "Tragic Love and the Ungendered Heart."

On the importance of heresy, see "Heresy and Humanity," Jane Harrison's inaugural lecture for the Cambridge Society of Heretics (1909), published in Jane Ellen

Harrison, *Alpha and Omega*, 27–41. In the essay, Harrison writes: "The gist of heresy is free personal choice in act, and specially in thought" (28). Subsequent page references to Harrison in the notes, unless otherwise noted, are to this essay. See also Shanyn Fiske, *Heretical Hellenism*, 1–3—hereafter cited in notes as Fiske.

19. Camille Cauti, "Michael Field's Pagan Catholicism," 181; quotation on 184.

20. Roden, *Same-Sex Desire in Victorian Religious Culture*. Page references to this work are cited as Roden, *Same-Sex Desire in Victorian Religious Culture*, in the text and notes.

21. On Harrison's account of the Eniautos-Daimon, see Fiske, 167–68.

22. Cited in Cauti, 187. Cauti cites Vanita's discussion of this poem in *Sappho and the Virgin Mary*, 133–34.

23. See Gere's discussion of Harrison's resuscitation of "the original Great Goddess" (*Knossos and the Prophets of Modernism*, 89–91).

24. Fiske, 167–173.

25. Harrison, "The Head of John the Baptist," 218.

26. "The Soul of Man under Socialism" (1891), in Wilde, *The Artist as Critic*, 289.

27. Dellamora, *Masculine Desire*, chapters 5, 9 et passim.

28. Cited in Herbert Muschamp, "The Dionysian Drama of Today's Design," 41.

29. Mary Douglas, *Purity and Danger*.

30. Wilde, 165. On Wilde and Christ, see John Albert, "The Christ of Oscar Wilde," and Stephen Arata, "Oscar Wilde and Jesus Christ."

31. Richard Rambuss, *Closet Devotions*, 36–37; Karma Lochrie, "Mystical Acts, Queer Tendencies," 187–88.

32. Thanks to Patricia Smith, in conversation, in Los Angeles, July 1999. On the Holy Spirit, see Roden, "Same-Sex Desire in Victorian Religious Culture," 126, 164 n13.

33. Although the critical literature focuses primarily on Gian-Luca, the novel begins and ends with his grandmother. In the final paragraphs, Hall signals as her primary concern Teresa's inability to acknowledge, even to herself, her love for her grandson.

34. Hall, *Adam's Breed*, 91. Subsequent page references to the novel appear in the text.

35. See James George Frazer, *The Golden Bough*, Book 3, chapter 5, 666–76.

36. At fifteen, Gian-Luca also attracts the attention of a sexually ambiguous young bohemian, who flirts with the boy in Wildean fashion. He also invites Gian-Luca to pose as "a sort of John the Baptist" (120) for an artist friend. There is a Caravaggesque connection here in view of the painter's numerous, strongly homoerotic images of adolescent John the Baptists. Gian-Luca rejects the young man's overtures in a way that suggests that Gian-Luca will refuse conscious awareness of homoerotic desire. Of the protagonists of Hall's three religious novels, he is the only one who lacks a strong, not to say passionate, same-sex attachment. In *Adam's Breed*, the great passion of Teresa's life is for her daughter, Olga.

37. The painting is in a sense a contemporary of Hall. Lionello Venturi identified it as a work by Caravaggio in 1912. Its authenticity was questioned by M. Marangoni in 1922–23 and by H. Voss in 1924, but today the authenticity of the work is "universally acknowledged" (*Age of Caravaggio*, 308).

38. Ingrid D. Rowland, "The Battle of Light with Darkness," 10. Unless otherwise noted, references to Rowland in the notes refer to this article.

39. Ibid.

40. *Age of Caravaggio*, 271.

41. Rowland, 10. For additional commentaries on the painting, see *Caravaggio: The Final Years*, 100–103; *Age of Caravaggio*, 306–10, 271–76; and John Gash, *Caravaggio*, 80. In another essay, Rowland points out that in the desperate final years of his life, Caravaggio became more and more interested in touch, both in painterly action and in viewer's sensation. Caravaggio, Rowland writes, tests "the capacities of slick oil on rough canvas to awaken . . . the whole range of our sense of touch" ("Radiant, Angry Caravaggio," 10).

42. The standard article on the novel focuses on this term within a context of "chivalric masculinity and English nationalism" (Claire Buck, "'Still Some Obstinate Emotion Remains,'" 193).

43. For the most explicit reference to the impact on Gian-Luca of mass casualties on the Western Front, see p. 369.

44. Hugh Walpole, "Nobody," 257.

45. Santanu Das, *Touch and Intimacy in First World War Literature*, quotations on 195.

46. According to Troubridge, Visetti made "improper advances" to Hall (Souhami, 19).

47. Ellmann, 465; Souhami, 186.

48. Roden, *Same-Sex Desire in Victorian Religious Culture*, chapters 2 and 3.

49. Quoted in ibid. 79. See also Shand-Tucci, *Art of Scandal*, 223. Ruth Vanita first became aware of the Sapphic interpretation of Marian desire in Victorian male Aestheticism as a result of reading Walter Pater's essay on Leonardo da Vinci in this volume (*Sappho and the Virgin Mary*, 1, 62–82).

50. Lines 471–74; quoted in Roden, *Same-Sex Desire in Victorian Religious Culture*, 44.

51. Roden, *Same-Sex Desire in Victorian Religious Culture*, 44.

52. Roden, "Same-Sex Desire in Victorian Religious Culture," 231.

53. A woman because, metaphorically, the body lactates; metaphorically too, a male lover, since semen is milky in color.

54. See Christopher Lane, *Burdens of Intimacy*.

55. Ed Madden has also made this point in "*Well of Loneliness*," 164.

56. Hall, *The Well of Loneliness*, 447. Subsequent page references to the novel occur in the text. I discuss the demand for justice as an aspect of the genre of apocalypse in "Tony Kushner and the 'Not Yet' of Gay Existence."

57. Foucault, *History of Sexuality*, 145.

Chapter 8. *The Well of Loneliness* as an Activist Text

1. For a consideration of the topic in updated terms, see Halberstam, *In a Queer Time and Place*, 1–21.

2. Marcus, 11.

3. Bray emphasizes that the essential aspect of friendship is that it is a form of "voluntary kinship" (*The Friend*, 104), that is, a close relationship that exists independently of blood ties. He also points out, however, that strong friendships were often pulled into the system of alliance by means of marriage to the sister or another female relation of one's friend.

4. Vicinus, *Intimate Friends*, 113, 111. Subsequent page references to Vicinus in the text and notes refer to this book unless otherwise noted.

5. Cited in Vicinus, 113.

6. A case in point is provided in Vicinus's essay on the romantic triangle that developed between Katharine Bradley, Edith Cooper, and young Bernard Berenson ("'Sister Souls': Bernard Berenson and Michael Field").

7. Cline, 41–42.

8. Karla Jay, *The Amazon and the Page*, 51–52, 121–25; Shari Benstock, *Women of the Left Bank*. Capitalized, *Lesbian* at this date signifies adherents of the ancient Greek poet and lover of women, Sappho, who conducted a school for unmarried young women on the isle of Lesbos.

9. Both Havelock Ellis and Sigmund Freud use the term *homosexual* to refer both to those whom Hall, following Ellis and Richard von Krafft-Ebing, refers to as sexual inverts as well as, more generally, to subjects of same-sex desire.

10. Cited in the transcript of the trial on appeal of Jonathan Cape, publisher of *The Well of Loneliness*, and Leopold Hill, Friday, December 14, 1928, 7. Subsequent page references to the transcript are referred to as Appeal in the text and notes.

11. Graham Richards, "Britain on the Couch."

12. Dickson, 139.

13. Troubridge, *Life and Death of Radclyffe Hall*, 103.

14. Dickson, 138.

15. Quoted in ibid., 133.

16. In point of fact, Andrea, Troubridge's daughter by marriage, often seemed to be regarded by Troubridge and Hall as an incidental fact whose impact on their life together was to be minimized to the greatest degree possible.

17. Dickson, 142.

18. *New Statesman*, August 25, 1928, 614–15.

19. Ibid., 602.

20. Jonathan Cape, letter to Radclyffe Hall, June 27, 1928.

21. Radclyffe Hall letter to Jonathan Cape and Harrison-Smith, Inc., June 29, 1928.

22. Baker, 208, 209.

23. Hall, letter to Gerard Manley Hopkins. Quotations in the following two paragraphs refer to the same letter.

24. Reprinted in part in Doan and Prosser, 52–54.

25. Hall, letter to Gerard Manley Hopkins, August 13, 1928.

26. *The New Statesman* makes this point (September 1, 1928, 636).

27. Information in the paragraph is from Baker, 226–28, 232.

28. HO144/22547; *The New Statesman*, November 24, 1928. Hall set the record straight in a letter from her solicitor that appeared in the issue of December 1.

29. HO144/22547. [memo of October 9].

30. Ibid.

31. Doan, ix.

32. HO45/15727.

33. Hall, *The Well of Loneliness*, 149. Subsequent page references to the novel appear in the text.

34. J. B. Melville, *Speech*, 12. Unless otherwise noted, citations from Melville in the text refer to this document.

35. In recent years, this perception has become widely shared. See, for example, Latimer's discussion of Havelock Ellis on this point in *Women Together/Women Apart*, 90–92.

36. Appeal, 59.

37. Within the context of *The Well of Loneliness* as a myth of heroic sacrifice, Stephen's treatment of Mary may be regarded as a test of the faith of the beloved in the couple's love. Mary fails this test and in that way vindicates Stephen's position in Book 5. Cf. Ruth Vanita: "Stephen's pretended infidelity [with Valerie Seymour] is a test that Mary fails" ("Tragic Love and the Ungendered Heart," 147). In other words, Mary chooses to renounce her love for Stephen.

38. Freud, "The Psychogenesis of a Case of Homosexuality in a Woman," *Complete Works*, 18:157.

39. Heather Love comments on Hall's implicit subversion of her idealization of Morton (*Feeling Backward*, 108–14).

40. The immediate reference is to young Stephen's feeling of revulsion when she unexpectedly receives a proposal of marriage from Martin Hallam early in the novel. In context in Inskip's argument, however, it sounds as though Hall rejects the institution of heterosexual marriage. In rebuttal, Melville points out the highly idealizing representations of the marriage of Williams, the old groom at Morton, and his wife and the marriage of Stephen's servant, Adèle, to Jean late in the novel (chapter 49).

41. Troubridge, diary, August 9, 1928.

42. Ibid., October 25, 1928.

43. Cline, 286–308.

44. Ibid., 291–92, 303–305. Much earlier, St. John had been in love with Violet Gwynne. Shortly before her marriage to Gordon Woodhouse, St. John wrote him a letter of warning: "I can talk to you unreservedly about her. I feel in a hundred

ways now that she loves you—but not a bit as most women love men" (Douglas-Home, 35).

45. See Baker, 276–78.

46. Hall, letter to Jonathan Cape and Harrison-Smith Inc.

47. On Egan, see Adrian Woodhouse, *Beresford Egan.*

48. Email message to the author, August 20, 2010.

49. Kathryn Bond Stockton, "Cloth Wounds," 53–54.

50. Cline, 377.

51. Vicinus, 9.

52. Hall, *Your John: The Love Letters of Radclyffe Hall*, 32. Subsequent page references to the letters appear in the text.

53. Minor emendations based on the manuscript of this letter at the Ransom Center have been incorporated into the text.

54. "Open" to the public, that is, not to other partners.

55. Mrs. Havelock Ellis, *New Horizon in Love and Life*, 68.

56. In her essay "Semi-Detached Marriage," Mrs. Ellis supported the principle of open marriage (23–31).

57. Information regarding Gramont and Barney is from Francesco Rapazzini, "Elisabeth de Gramont, Natalie Barney's 'Eternal Mate.'" Page references to Gramont and Barney in the following paragraphs refer to this article. See also Rapazzini, *Elisabeth de Gramont: Avant-Gardiste.*

58. Cline, 252, 258, 295.

59. Coward, *Tonight at 8:30*, 175.

60. John Lahr, *Coward the Playwright*, 36.

61. Ibid., 34. Coward took the role of Essendine in the original production.

62. *Catherine Opie*, v–vi, viii, x.

63. Regarding himself, Coward appears to have preferred the earlier model. Graham Payn, his lover and life partner, observes that Coward collected around himself a small group, comprised mainly of women, who constituted his "family." Coward involved and depended upon members of this group in both his professional and personal life (Graham Payn, *My Life with Noël Coward*, 223).

Chapter 9. From Sexual Inversion to Cross Gender in "Miss Ogilvy Finds Herself"

1. Hall, *Your John*, 50–51. Subsequent page references to the letters appear in the text.

2. Ellis, "Sexual Inversion in Women," 222.

3. The essay was published both in German and in English in the same year, the translation provided by Barbara Low, a leading mediator in England of Freudian psychoanalysis. See Freud, *Complete Works*, 18:146.

4. Prosser, 21.

5. Consider, for example, the letter to "Dear Theresa" that begins Leslie Feinberg's *Stone Butch Blues*, 5–12.

6. Baker, 188–89.

7. Prosser, ch. 4. See also Heather Love, *Feeling Backward*, 116–19, 181 n6.

8. Hall, Author's Forenote, *Miss Ogilvy Finds Herself*. Subsequent page references to this book appear in the text.

9. Mrs. Ellis, 55.

10. Similarly, in *Degeneration*, Max Nordau sees the nineteenth-century artists and philosophers whom he condemns as simultaneously atavistic and decadent.

11. Foucault, "Madness, the Absence of Work," 294.

12. Claire Buck provides an excellent analysis of problematic aspects of the attempt by writers such as Hall and Woolf to recuperate "Englishness" in face of the demands of the twentieth-century imperial nation-state, including its regressive gender politics ("'Still Some Obstinate Emotion Remains'").

13. Dixon, "Sexology and the Occult," 430.

14. Dixon, 416, 419, 431, 422, 423, 430.

15. Dixon, 433 n91; cf. Vicinus, *Independent Women*, 260.

16. Jeffreys, 106.

17. Edward Carpenter, *Selected Writings*, 1:217.

18. Cited in Jeffreys, 113.

19. Virginia Woolf, *Three Guineas*, 15.

20. Virginia Woolf, *Women and Writing*, 58–60.

21. Freud is commenting on responses to the outbreak of World War I (Freud, *Complete Works*, 14:306).

22. Barbara Godard, "Luce Irigaray," 368.

Chapter 10. After Economic Man

1. Coward, *Diaries*, 47.

2. Coward's drama of a naval shipwreck, *In Which We Serve*, won the Oscar for best picture in 1942. Coward produced, codirected, scripted, and provided the musical score for this film.

3. Sinclair, *A Defence of Idealism*, 240–89, 337. Subsequent page references to this work appear in the text and notes. Hall likely knew Sinclair's book firsthand since it appeared at the height of Hall's interest in speculative psychology. Sinclair's ongoing experiments in these years in modernist feminist fiction, her familiarity with psychoanalytic concepts of sublimation and the unconscious, and her unique position in England as a woman writing serious texts in philosophy commended her work to Hall's attention. Although Hall became a personal friend only in the 1920s, she may have met her early in the new century at the home of her literary and possibly intimate

friend, Violet Hunt. See Cline, *Radclyffe Hall*, 55–57, 101. I am indebted to Suzanne Raitt's analysis of Sinclair's philosophical idealism in *May Sinclair*.

4. Sinclair argues analogically that, just as a dreamer is able to observe projections of herself in the personages of a dream, so also a universal consciousness may be able to subsume all other existent consciousnesses. See Sinclair, 334–39.

5. Radclyffe Hall, "The Rest Cure—1932," in *"Miss Ogilvy Finds Herself"*. Subsequent page references to the story appear in the text.

6. Cline, *Radclyffe Hall*, 7.

7. Information on Underhill in this paragraph is drawn from Dixon, "Dark Ecstasies." Used with permission.

8. On the combination of Roman Catholicism with pagan naturalism in Michael Field's poetry, see Chapters 1 and 8.

Chapter 11. Oneself as The Other

1. Troubridge, *Life and Death of Radclyffe Hall*, 115.

2. Hall, letter of November 3, 1935, *Your John*, 140. Subsequent references to Hall in this chapter refer to this work, unless otherwise noted.

3. Hall, *Emblem Hurlstone*, notebook 1.

4. Abigail Solomon-Godeau, *Male Trouble*, 103. Subsequent references to Anacreontism in the text refer to this work, pp. 102–16.

5. Emblem's appointment in Venice parodies the famous meeting that Winckelmann was scheduled to have with the young writer Wolfgang von Goethe. Unfortunately, however, turning back en route, Winckelmann met his death at Trieste, where he was murdered by a stranger, Francesco Arcangeli. Traditionally, this death has been read as the result of a sexual tryst gone awry. Walter Pater recounts the story in *Studies in the History of the Renaissance* (1873); see the discussion of Winckelmann in Dellamora, *Masculine Desire*, 109–16. For a study of the relationship between Hellenistic culture and the invention of modern sexualities, see my essay, "Greek Desire and Modern Sexualities."

6. Cline, 320n.

7. In Hall to Souline, Letters, Harry Ransom Humanities Research Center, University of Texas, Austin, Texas.

8. Hall, *Emblem Hurlstone*, notebook 1.

9. For example, the poem, "Invitation to the Voyage."

10. This pattern of triangulated desire is familiar from Eve Kosofsky Sedgwick's discussion of male homosocial desire in *Between Men*. Hall presents it with a knowing, psychoanalytic edge.

11. *Emblem Hurlstone*, large notebook. The page has been struck through with a single line in blue. Ellipses in the quotation are mine, indicating crossed-out words in the manuscript.

12. In *Casablanca*, Rick Blaine (Humphrey Bogart) must forgo renewing his affair with Ilsa Lund (Ingrid Bergman) because of her loyalty to her husband, Victor Laszlo (Paul Henreid), a fugitive Czech Resistance leader long sought by the Nazis.

13. Quotation modified in accordance with the original manuscript.

14. Ormrod, 215.

15. Michael Powell, *Edge of the World*, 325—hereafter cited in notes as Powell. In contrast to the remoteness of these islands off the northwestern tip of Scotland, Hall explores the catastrophe of what might be termed the near exotic.

16. C. A. Lejeune, cited in the introduction to Powell, xiii.

17. Hall, *The Sixth Beatitude*, 3, 85—hereafter cited in text and notes as *SB*.

18. Souhami, 308.

19. *SB*, 65, 32, 31.

20. *The Sixth Beatitude*, typescript, 97–98; also *SB*, 1936, 91–92.

21. The novel draws on May Sinclair's suggestion that women have a special relation to what Sinclair calls "the Life-Force" (*Feminism*, 30–31). Hall proposes that this relation is compatible with the transgression of conventional norms of sex and gender. I discuss Sinclair in Chapters 1 and 10.

22. The potent father in the novel is the unnamed young sailor who is Ermie's father.

23. In context, the phrase refers to Sapphists. Hall uses it in the letter of July 31, 1934, in which she gave Souline the bad, though to be anticipated, news that Troubridge intended to squelch the affair before it began. The citation has been modified to accord with the manuscript.

24. The suggestion is a commonplace in commentary by Sinclair and other English writers who were writing under Freud's influence. See Low, *Psycho-Analysis*, 91–93.

25. The parallel to spring lambing in Powell's book is the August sheep running (231). Both Hall and Powell work these scenes into the dramatic structure of their respective works, Hall by juxtaposition and Powell, who intercuts the community ritual with the secret rendezvous of the film's young lovers, by montage: "The Run has now a definite purpose. It changes the tempo at the proper moment, it creates unique atmosphere, it provides a shield for the meeting of the lovers, by its contrast of busy action with complete calm. It is no longer only [ethnographic,] pictorial and instructive, it is dramatic—and a necessary part of the film" (234).

26. Hall, *The Well of Loneliness* (A), 470.

27. On Mary as a model for subjects of female same-sex desire, see Vanita, *Sappho and the Virgin Mary*, 14–36.

28. Richard Wagner, *Ring of the Nibelung*, 325.

29. Technically speaking, Greek pastoral is late, that is, a product of Hellenistic culture; but to Hall it was "primitive."A good example of the "sweetbitter" eros that Hall found in Sappho's verse may be found in Hall's "Ode to Sappho" in *A Sheaf of Verses*, 36–38. I discuss the poem in Chapter 1.

30. Anne Carson, *Eros the Bittersweet*, 3—hereafter cited in notes as Carson.

31. The argument in these two paragraphs follows Carson, 7–10.

32. Troubridge, Day Book, entry for February 26, 1943.

33. Baker, 316, 182, 183, 186.

34. Ormrod, 236.

35. Troubridge, *Life of Radclyffe Hall*, 171–72.

36. Cline, 369–70; Souhami, 381–83.

37. Doan and Prosser, 54.

38. This representation contradicts Troubridge's claim that "John had never been in any doubt that *The Well of Loneliness* contained all that she had to say on . . . [the] subject [of sexual inversion]; that she had never for a moment contemplated . . . any return to that aspect of nature" (Troubridge, *Life of Radclyffe Hall*, 171).

BIBLIOGRAPHY

Abel, Elizabeth, Marianne Hirsch, and Elizabeth Langland. *The Voyage In: Fictions of Female Development*. Hanover, N.H.: University Press of New England, 1983.

The Age of Caravaggio. New York: Metropolitan Museum of Art, 1985.

Albert, John. "The Christ of Oscar Wilde." In *Critical Essays on Oscar Wilde*, ed. Regenia Gagnier, 242–57. New York: G. K. Hall, 1991.

Amory, Mark. *Lord Berners: The Last Eccentric*. London: Pimlico, 1999.

Arata, Stephen. "Oscar Wilde and Jesus Christ." Paper presented at "The New Wilde Criticism: Aesthetics, Politics, Sexuality," William Andrews Clark Library, Los Angeles, Calif., April 10, 1999.

Baker, Michael. *Our Three Selves: A Life of Radclyffe Hall*. London: GMP, 1985.

Barker, Juliet R. V. *The Brontës: Selected Poems*. London: J. M. Dent & Sons, 1991.

Baudelaire, Charles. *Les Fleurs du Mal*. Trans. Richard Howard and illus. Michael Mazur. Boston: David R. Godine, 1982.

Benstock, Shari. *Women of the Left Bank: Paris 1900–1940*. Austin: University of Texas Press, 1986.

Bloxam, John. "The Priest and the Acolyte." In *Sexual Heretics: Male Homosexuality in English Literature from 1850 to 1900*, ed. and introd. Brian Reade, 349–60. New York: Coward-McCann, 1970.

Botstein, Leon. "Transcending the Enigmas of Biography: The Cultural Context of Sir Edward Elgar's Career." In *Edward Elgar and His World*, ed. Byron Adams, 365–405. Princeton, N.J.: Princeton University Press, 2007.

Bracco, Rosa Maria. *Merchants of Hope: British Middlebrow Writers and the First World War, 1919–1939*. Providence, R.I.: Berg, 1993.

Bray, Alan. *The Friend*. Chicago: University of Chicago Press, 2003.

Breeskin, Adelyn D. *Romaine Brooks: "Thief of Souls."* Washington, D.C.: Smithsonian Institution Press, 1971.

Bristow, Joseph. "'A Complex Multiform Creature': Wilde's Sexual Identities." In *The Cambridge Companion to Oscar Wilde*, ed. Peter Raby, 195–218. Cambridge: Cambridge University Press, 1997.

———. "Michael Field's Lyrical Aestheticism: *Underneath the Bough.*" In *Michael Field and Their World*, ed. Margaret D. Stetz and Cheryl A. Wilson, 49–62. High Wycombe, U.K.: Rivendale Press, 2007.

Browning, Elizabeth Barrett. *Aurora Leigh.* Ed. Kerry McSweeney. New York: Oxford University Press, 1998.

Browning, Robert. *Poetry.* Ed. James F. Loucks. New York: W. W. Norton, 1979.

Buchanan, Robert. *The Fleshly School of Poetry and Other Phenomena of the Day.* 1872. Reprint, New York: AMS Press, 1975.

Buck, Claire. "'Still Some Obstinate Emotion Remains': Radclyffe Hall and the Meanings of Service." In *Women's Fiction and the Great War*, ed. Suzanne Raitt and Trudi Tate, 174–96. Oxford: Clarendon Press, 1997.

Butler, Judith. *Giving an Account of Oneself.* New York: Fordham University Press, 2005.

Cape, Jonathan. Letter to Radclyffe Hall, June 27, 1928. Lovat Dickson Collection, MG30, D237. 4.18. National Archives of Canada, Ottawa, Ontario.

Caravaggio: The Final Years. [Naples:] Electa Napoli, 2005.

Carpenter, Edward. *Selected Writings: Volume One: Sex.* With an introduction by Noël Greig. London: GMP, 1984.

Carson, Anne. *Eros the Bittersweet: An Essay.* Princeton, N.J.: Princeton University Press, 1985.

———. *If Not, Winter: Fragments of Sappho.* New York: Alfred A. Knopf, 2002.

Castle, Terry. *Noël Coward and Radclyffe Hall: Kindred Spirits.* New York: Columbia University Press, 1996.

Catherine Opie. Ed. Stephanie Emerson. Los Angeles: Museum of Contemporary Art, 1997.

Cauti, Camille. "Michael Field's Pagan Catholicism." In *Michael Field and Their World*, ed. Margaret D. Stetz and Cheryl A. Wilson, 181–89. High Wycombe, U.K.: Rivendale Press, 2007.

Chadwick, Whitney. *Amazons in the Drawing Room: The Art of Romaine Brooks.* With an essay by Joe Lucchesi. Berkeley: University of California Press, 2000.

Cline, Sally. *Radclyffe Hall: A Woman Called John.* New York: Overlook Press, 1998.

Colette. *The Pure and the Impure.* Trans. Herma Briffault and intro. Judith Thurman. New York: New York Review Books, 2000.

Collis, Louise. *Impetuous Heart: The Story of Ethel Smyth.* London: William Kimber, 1984.

Connor, Steven. "The Machine in the Ghost: Spiritualism, Technology, and the 'Direct Voice.'" In *Ghosts: Deconstruction, Psychoanalysis, History*, ed. Peter Buse and Andrew Stott, 203–25. New York: St. Martin's, 1999.

Coward, Noël. *Diaries.* Ed. Graham Payn and Sheridan Morley. Boston: Little, Brown, 1982.

————. *Plays: One*. London: Eyre Methuen, 1979.

————. *Tonight at 8:30*. New York: Sun Dial Press, 1936.

Craft, Christopher. *Another Kind of Love: Male Homosexual Desire in English Discourse, 1850–1920*. Berkeley: University of California Press, 1994.

D'Annunzio, Gabriele. *Le martyre de saint Sebastien; mystère en cinq actes*. Music by Claude Debussy. Transcription by André Caplet. English version by Hermann Klein. Paris: Editions Durand, 1914.

Das, Santanu. *Touch and Intimacy in First World War Literature*. Cambridge: Cambridge University Press, 2005.

De Lauretis, Teresa. *The Practice of Love: Lesbian Sexuality and Perverse Desire*. Bloomington: Indiana University Press, 1994.

Dellamora, Richard. "Female Adolescence in May Sinclair's *Mary Olivier* and the Construction of a Dialectic Between Victorian and Modern." *Nineteenth Century Studies*, 20 (2006): 171–82.

————. "Friendship, Marriage, and *Between Women*." *Victorian Studies* 50.1 (Autumn 2007): 67–74.

————. *Friendship's Bonds: Democracy and the Novel in Victorian England*. Philadelphia: University of Pennsylvania Press, 2004.

————. "Greek Desire and Modern Sexualities." In *Imagination and Logos: Essays on C. P. Cavafy*, ed. Pangiotis Roilos, 121–42. Cambridge: Harvard University Press, 2010.

————. *Masculine Desire: The Sexual Politics of Victorian Aestheticism*. Chapel Hill: University of North Carolina Press, 1990.

————. "Productive Decadence: 'The Queer Comradeship of Outlawed Thought': Vernon Lee, Max Nordau, and Oscar Wilde." *New Literary History* 35 (Autumn 2004): 1–18.

————. "The Sapphic Culture of Michael Field and Radclyffe Hall." In *Michael Field and Their World*, ed. Margaret D. Stetz and Cheryl A. Wilson, 127–36. High Wycombe, U.K.: Rivendale Press, 2007.

————. "Swinburne, Modern Desire, and the Hellenistic Revival." Paper presented at "Swinburne: A Centenary Conference," Institute of English Studies, University of London, July 11, 2009.

————. "Tony Kushner and the 'Not Yet' of Gay Existence." *Journal of American Drama and Theatre* 9 (Fall 1997): 73–101.

Derrida, Jacques. *Archive Fever: A Freudian Impression*. Trans. Eric Prenowitz. Chicago: University of Chicago Press, 1996.

Dickson, Lovat. *Radclyffe Hall at the Well of Loneliness: A Sapphic Chronicle*. Toronto: Collins, 1975.

Director of Public Prosecutions v. Jonathan Cape and Leopold Hill. Transcript. County of London Sessions. Friday, December 14, 1928. Lovat Dickson Collection, MG30, D237. 5.10. National Archives of Canada, Ottawa, Ontario.

Dixon, Joy. "'Dark Ecstasies': Sex, Mysticism, and Psychology in Early Twentieth Century England." Unpublished paper.

———. *Divine Feminine: Theosophy and Feminism in England*. Baltimore: Johns Hopkins University Press, 2001.

———. "'Love Is a Sacrament That Should Be Taken Kneeling': Sexuality, Religion, and the Troubled History of 'Secularization.'" Annual meeting, Victorian Studies Association of Ontario, University of Toronto, April 29, 2006.

———. "Sexology and the Occult: Sexuality and Subjectivity in Theosophy's New Age." *Journal of the History of Sexuality* 7 (1997): 409–33.

Doan, Laura. *Fashioning Sapphism: The Origins of a Modern English Lesbian Culture*. New York: Columbia University Press, 2001.

Doan, Laura, and Jay Prosser, eds. *Palatable Poison: Critical Perspectives on* The Well of Loneliness *Past and Present*. New York: Columbia University Press, 2001.

Douglas, Mary. *Purity and Danger: An Analysis of Concepts of Pollution and Taboo*. 1966. Reprint, Harmondsworth, U.K.: Penguin, 1970.

Douglas-Home, Jessica. *Violet: The Life and Loves of Violet Gordon Woodhouse*. New York: Farrar, Straus & Giroux, 1997.

Du Maurier, Daphne. *Don't Look Now: Stories*. Intro. Patrick McGrath. New York: New York Review Books, 2008.

Edelman, Lee. *No Future: Queer Theory and the Death Drive*. Durham, N.C.: Duke University Press, 2004.

Elgar and His World. Annandale-on-Hudson, N.Y.: Bard College, 2007.

Ellis, Havelock. "Sexual Inversion in Women." In *Studies in the Psychology of Sex*. Volume 2. *Part One: Sexual Selection in Man; Part Two. Sexual Inversion*, 195–263. 1910. Reprint, New York: Random House, 1936.

Ellis, Mrs. Havelock. *The New Horizon in Love and Life*. Intro. Marguerite Tracy, with a preface by Edward Carpenter. London: A & C Black, 1921.

Ellmann, Richard. *Oscar Wilde*. New York: Penguin, 1987.

Evangelista, Stephano-Maria. "Narcissism and Romantic Reflections in Pater's *Plato and Platonism*." Paper presented at third annual meeting of NAVSA (North American Victorian Studies Association), Charlottesville, Va., October 2, 2005.

Feinberg, Leslie. *Stone Butch Blues, A Novel*. Los Angeles: Alyson Books, 2003.

Field, Michael. *Long Ago*. 1889. Reprint, Portland, Me.: Thomas B. Mosher, 1897.

Fiske, Shanyn. *Heretical Hellenism: Women Writers, Ancient Greece, and the Victorian Popular Imagination*. Athens: Ohio University Press, 2008.

Foucault, Michel. *The History of Sexuality. Volume I: An Introduction*. Trans. Robert Hurley. New York: Vintage, 1980.

———. "Madness, the Absence of Work." *Critical Inquiry* 21 (Winter 1995): 290–98.

France, Peter, and William St. Clair, eds. *Mapping Lives: The Uses of Biography*. Oxford: British Academy, 2002.

Franks, Claudia Stillman. *Beyond* The Well of Loneliness: *The Fiction of Radclyffe Hall*. Avebury, 1982.

Frazer, James George. *The Golden Bough: A Study in Magic and Religion*, ed. Robert Fraser. A new abridgement from the 2nd and 3rd editions. Oxford: Oxford University Press, 2009.

Freccero, Carla. "Carnivorous Virility, or Becoming-Dog." Paper presented at Critical Theory Institute, University of California at Irvine, November 16, 2009.

Freud, Sigmund. "A Note on the Unconscious." *Proceedings of the Society on Psychical Research* 18 (1912): 312–18.

———. *The Standard Edition of the Complete Psychological Works,* trans. and ed. James Strachey in collaboration with Anna Freud. 24 vols. London: Hogarth Press, 1971–74.

Fuller, Sophie. "Elgar and the Salons: The Significance of a Private Musical World." In *Edward Elgar and His World,* ed. Byron Adams, 223–47. Princeton, N.J.: Princeton University Press, 2007.

Gallagher, Lowell; Frederick S. Roden; and Patricia Juliana Smith, eds. *Catholic Figures, Queer Narratives.* New York: Palgrave Macmillan, 2007.

Gash, John. *Caravaggio.* London: Jupiter Books, 1980.

Gere, Cathy. *Knossos and the Prophets of Modernism.* Chicago: University of Chicago Press, 2009.

Ghuman, Nalini. "Elgar and the British Raj: Can the Mughals March?" In *Edward Elgar and His World,* ed. Byron Adams, 249–85. Princeton, N.J.: Princeton University Press, 2007.

Godard, Barbara. "Luce Irigaray." *Encyclopedia of Contemporary Literary Theory,* ed. Irena R. Makaryk. Toronto: University of Toronto Press, 1993.

Halberstam, Judith. *Female Masculinity.* Durham, N.C.: Duke University Press, 1998.

———. *In a Queer Time and Place: Transgender Bodies, Subcultural Lives.* New York: New York University Press, 2005.

Hall, Radclyffe. *Adam's Breed.* Intro. Alison Hennegan. London: Virago, 1985.

———. "Anticedance [*sic*] and Infancy." Draft ms. Radclyffe Hall collection. 22.4. Harry Ransom Humanities Research Center, University of Texas, Austin, Texas.

———. *Emblem Hurlstone.* Ms., notebook 1 (black cover). Radclyffe Hall collection. 3.1. Harry Ransom Humanities Research Center, University of Texas, Austin, Texas.

———. *Emblem Hurlstone.* Ms., large notebook, unpaged. Radclyffe Hall collection. 3.3. Harry Ransom Humanities Research Center, University of Texas, Austin, Texas.

———. "Forebears and Infancy." Draft holograph ms. Radclyffe Hall collection. 22.4. Harry Ransom Humanities Research Center, University of Texas, Austin, Texas. (Version 1)

———. "Forebears and Infancy." Ms, untitled. Radclyffe Hall collection. 22.5. Harry Ransom Humanities Research Center, University of Texas, Austin, Texas. (Version 2)

———. "Forebears and Infancy." Ms (in the hand of Una Troubridge). Radclyffe Hall collection. 22.5. Harry Ransom Humanities Research Center, University of Texas, Austin, Texas. (Version 3)

———. *The Forge.* 1924. Reprint, London: Falcon Press, 1952.

———. [Radclyffe-Hall, Marguerite.] *The Forgotten Island.* London: Chapman & Hall, 1915.

———. "Ghosts." Ms. Radclyffe Hall collection. 18.8. Harry Ransom Humanities Research Center, University of Texas, Austin, Texas.

———. Letter to Jonathan Cape & Harrison-Smith Inc., June 29, 1928. Lovat Dickson Collection, MG30, D237. 4.18. National Archives of Canada, Ottawa, Ontario.

———. Letter to Jonathan Cape & Harrison-Smith Inc., October 10, 1931. Lovat Dickson Collection, MG30, D237. 4.18. National Archives of Canada, Ottawa, Ontario.

———. Letter to Gerard Manley Hopkins, August 13, 1928. The Henry W. and Albert A. Berg Collection of English and American Literature. The New York Public Library, Astor, Lenox and Tilden Foundations.

———. Letter to Sir Oliver Lodge, July 2, 1918. Society for Psychical Research Archives, Mrs. Leonard's Papers, SPR.MS 34, Cambridge University Library.

———. Letter to Winifred Macey, February 15, 1927. Harry Ransom Humanities Research Center, University of Texas, Austin, Texas.

———. Letter to Evguenia Souline, July 31, 1934. Harry Ransom Humanities Research Center, University of Texas, Austin, Texas.

———. Letter to Evguenia Souline, December 1, 1934. Harry Ransom Humanities Research Center, University of Texas, Austin, Texas.

———. *Michael West.* Notebook 2. Radclyffe Hall collection. 7.5. Harry Ransom Humanities Research Center, University of Texas, Austin, Texas.

———. *Michael West.* Ms. Radclyffe Hall collection. 8.1. Harry Ransom Humanities Research Center, University of Texas, Austin, Texas.

———. "Miss Ogilvy Finds Herself." London: William Heinemann, 1934.

———. [Radclyffe-Hall, Marguerite.] *Poems of the Past and Present.* London: Chapman & Hall, 1910.

———. *A Saturday Life.* 1925. Reprint, New York: Jonathan Cape and Harrison Smith, 1930.

———. *A Saturday Life.* Notebook. Radclyffe Hall collection. 8.2. Harry Ransom Humanities Research Center, University of Texas, Austin, Texas.

———. *A Saturday Life.* Notebook no. 1. Radclyffe Hall collection. 8.3. Harry Ransom Humanities Research Center, University of Texas, Austin, Texas.

———. [Radclyffe-Hall, Marguerite.] *A Sheaf of Verses.* London: John and Edward Bumpus, 1908.

———. *The Sixth Beatitude.* London: William Heinemann, 1936.

———. *The Sixth Beatitude.* Typescript. Lovat Dickson Collection, MG30, D237. 5.20. National Archives of Canada, Ottawa, Ontario.

———. [Radclyffe-Hall, Marguerite.] *Songs of Three Counties and Other Poems.* Intro. R. B. Cunninghame-Grahame. London: Chapman & Hall, 1913.

———. [Radclyffe-Hall, Marguerite.] *'Twixt Earth and Stars.* London: John and Edward Bumpus, 1906.

———. *The Unlit Lamp*. New York: Dial Press, 1981.

———. *The Well of Loneliness*. Intro. Alison Hennegan. London: Virago, 1994.

———. *The Well of Loneliness*. Commentary by Havelock Ellis. 1928. Reprint, New York: Blue Ribbon Books, 1937.

———. *Your John: The Love Letters of Radclyffe Hall*. Ed. Joanne Glasgow. New York: New York University Press, 1997.

Hall, Radclyffe, and (Una) Lady Troubridge. "On a Series of Sittings with Mrs. Osborne Leonard." *Proceedings of the Society for Psychical Research* 30 (December 1919): 339–554.

Hall v. Lakin. [Partial transcript.] Assizes Courts. Oxford. Thursday, June 10, 1915.

Hallett, Nicky. *Lesbian Lives: Identity and Auto/Biography in the Twentieth Century*. London: Pluto Press, 1999.

Hamilton, Susan. *Frances Power Cobbe and Victorian Feminism*. London: Palgrave Macmillan, 2003.

———. "Pets and Scientific Subjects: Constructions of the Animal Body in Victorian Anti-Vivisection Periodicals." *Literature and the Body*, ed. Anthony George Purdy, 77–93. Amsterdam: Rodopi, 1992.

———. "Still Lives: Gender and the Literature of the Victorian Vivisection Controversy." *Victorian Review* 17.2 (1991): 21–34.

Hanson, Ellis. *Decadence and Catholicism*. Cambridge, Mass.: Harvard University Press, 1997.

Harding, James. *Ivor Novello*. Pen-y-bont ar Ogwr, Wales: Welsh Academic Press, 1997.

Harrison, Jane Ellen. *Alpha and Omega*. London: Sidgwick & Jackson, 1915.

———. "The Head of John Baptist." *Classical Review* 30:8 (1916): 216–19.

Harshav, Benjamin. *Language in Time of Revolution*. Berkeley: University of California Press, 1993.

Hazelgrove. Jenny. *Spiritualism and British Society Between the Wars*. Manchester: Manchester University Press, 2000.

Heath, Stephen. "Joan Riviere and the Masquerade." In *Formations of Fantasy*, ed. Victor Burgin, James Donald, and Cora Kaplan, 45–61. New York: Routledge, 1986.

Heckert, Deborah. "Working the Crowd: Elgar, Class, and Reformulations of Popular Culture at the Turn of the Twentieth Century." In *Edward Elgar and His World*, ed. Byron Adams, 287–315. Princeton, N.J.: Princeton University Press, 2007.

Henderson, Linda Dalrymple. "Modernism's Quest for Invisible Realities." In *Make It New*, ed. Kurt Heinzelman, 135–39. Austin, Tex.: Harry Ransom Humanities Research Center, 2004.

Hilliard, David. "Unenglish and Unmanly: Anglo-Catholicism and Homosexuality." *Victorian Studies* 25 (1982): 181–210.

Hoare, Philip. *Oscar Wilde's Last Stand: Decadence, Conspiracy, and the Most Outrageous Trial of the Century*. New York: Arcade, 1997.

Home Office. HO 45/15727. [File on Compton Mackenzie, *Extraordinary Women.*] Public Records Office. Richmond, England.

Home Office. HO 144/22547. [File on Radclyffe Hall, *The Well of Loneliness*]. Public Records Office. Richmond, England.

Housman, A. E. *The Collected Poems.* New York: Henry Holt, 1965.

———. *The Name and Nature of Poetry and Other Selected Prose,* ed. John Carter. New York: New Amsterdam, 1961.

———. *A Shropshire Lad.* New York: Dover, 1990.

Howarth, Peter. "Housman's Dirty Postcards: Poetry, Modernism, and Masochism." *PMLA* 124:3 (2009): 764–81.

James, William. "Notes on Automatic Writing." *Proceedings of the American Society for Psychical Research* 1 (1885–1889): 548–64.

Jay, Karla. *The Amazon and the Page: Natalie Clifford Barney and Renée Vivien.* Bloomington: Indiana University Press, 1988.

Jeffreys, Sheila. *The Spinster and Her Enemies: Feminism and Sexuality, 1880–1930.* London: Pandora, 1985.

Johnson, Alice. "On the Automatic Writing of Mrs. Holland." *Proceedings of the Society for Psychical Research* 21 (June 1908): 166–391.

Jones, Ernest. "The Early Development of Female Sexuality." *International Journal of Psycho-Analysis* 8 (October 1927): 459–72.

Kopelson, Kevin. *Beethoven's Kiss: Pianism, Perversion, and the Mastery of Desire.* Stanford, Calif.: Stanford University Press, 1996.

Lacan, Jacques. *Feminine Sexuality: Jacques Lacan and the école freudienne.* Ed. Juliet Mitchell and Jacqueline Rose. Trans. Jacqueline Rose. New York: W. W. Norton, 1985.

Lahr, John. *Coward the Playwright.* Berkeley: University of California Press, 1982.

Lane, Christopher. *The Burdens of Intimacy: Psychoanalysis and Victorian Masculinity.* Chicago: University of Chicago Press, 1999.

Laplanche, Jean, and J.-B. Pontalis. *The Language of Psycho-Analysis.* Trans. Donald Nicholson-Smith and intro. Daniel Lagache. New York: Norton, 1973.

Latimer, Tirza True. *Women Together/Women Apart: Portraits of Lesbian Paris.* New Brunswick, N.J.: Rutgers University Press, 2005.

Lears, T. J. Jackson. *No Place of Grace: Antimodernism and the Transformation of American Culture, 1880–1920.* New York: Pantheon, 1981.

Lee, Vernon. "Deterioration of Soul." *Fortnightly Review,* n.s. 59 (June 1896): 928–43.

———. *"Hauntings" and Other Fantastic Tales.* Ed. Catherine Maxwell and Patricia Pulham. Peterborough, Ont.: Broadview, 2006.

———. *Miss Brown: A Novel.* Vol. 2. Edinburgh: William Blackwood and Sons, 1884.

Lejeune, Philippe. *On Autobiography.* Ed. with a foreword by Paul John Eakin, trans. Katherine Leary. Minneapolis: University of Minnesota Press, 1989.

Leonard, Gladys Osborne. *My Life in Two Worlds.* Foreword by Sir Oliver Lodge. London: Cassell, 1931.

Lochrie, Karma. "Mystical Acts, Queer Tendencies." In *Constructing Medieval Sexuality*, ed. Karma Lochrie, Peggy McCracken, and James A. Schultz, 180–200. Minneapolis: University of Minnesota Press, 1997.

Lodge, Sir Oliver J. *Raymond or Life and Death: With Examples of the Evidence for Survival of Memory and Affection After Death*. 6th edition. London: Methuen, 1916.

Love, Heather. *Feeling Backward: Loss and the Politics of Queer History*. Cambridge, Mass.: Harvard University Press, 2007.

Low, Barbara. *Psycho-Analysis: A Brief Account of the Freudian Theory*. Intro. Ernest Jones. London: George Allen & Unwin, 1920.

Lucchesi, Joe. "'An Apparition in a Black Flowing Cloak': Romaine Brooks's Portraits of Ida Rubinstein." In Whitney Chadwick, *Amazons in the Drawing Room: The Art of Romaine Brooks*, 73–87. Berkeley: University of California Press, 2000.

Lucey, Michael. *The Misfit of the Family: Balzac and the Social Forms of Sexuality*. Durham, N.C.: Duke University Press, 2003.

———. *Never Say I: Sexuality and the First Person in Colette, Gide, and Proust*. Durham, N.C.: Duke University Press, 2006.

Luckhurst, Roger. *The Invention of Telepathy: 1870–1901*. Oxford: Oxford University Press, 2002.

Mackenzie, Compton. *Extraordinary Women: Theme and Variations*. London: Hogarth Press, 1986.

Madden, Ed. "*Well of Loneliness*, or the Gospel According to Radclyffe Hall." In *Reclaiming the Sacred: The Bible in Gay and Lesbian Culture*, ed. Raymond-Jean Frontain, 163–86. New York: Haworth, 1997.

Magee, Maggie, and Diana C. Miller. *Lesbian Lives: Psychoanalytic Narratives Old and New*. Hillsdale, N.J.: Analytic, 1997.

Marcus, Sharon. *Between Women: Friendship, Desire and Marriage in Victorian England*. Princeton, N.J.: Princeton University Press, 2007.

Markus, Julia. *Across an Untried Sea: Discovering Lives Hidden in the Shadow of Convention and Time*. New York: Knopf, 2000.

Maugham, W. Somerset. *The Constant Wife*. Garden City, N.Y.: Doubleday, 1926.

McKenna, Neil. *The Secret Life of Oscar Wilde*. New York: Basic Books, 2005.

Medd, Jodie. "'The Cult of the Clitoris': Anatomy of a National Scandal." *Modernism/ Modernity* 9 (January 2002): 21–49.

———. "Extraordinary Allegations: Scandalous Female Homosexuality and the Culture of Modernism." Ph.D. diss., Cornell University, 2001.

Meem, Deborah T. "Eliza Lynn Linton and the Rise of Lesbian Consciousness." *Journal of the History of Sexuality* 7 (1997): 537–60.

Melville, J. B. *Speech*. Typescript. *Director of Public Prosecutions v. Jonathan Cape and Leopold Hill*. Bow Street Police Court. Friday, November 9, 1928. Lovat Dickson Collection, MG30, D237. 5.8. National Archives of Canada, Ottawa, Ontario.

Mirror of the Medieval World. Catalogue of the exhibition at the Metropolitan Museum of Art, March 9–July 18, 1999. New York: Harry N. Abrams, 1999.

Montgomery-Hyde, H. *The Trials of Oscar Wilde*. New York: Dover, 1973.

Murray, Douglas. *Bosie: A Biography of Lord Alfred Douglas*. New York: Hyperion, 2000.

Muschamp, Herbert. "The Dionysian Drama of Today's Design." *New York Times*, March 26, 2000, Arts, 41.

Myers, Frederic W. H. *Human Personality and Its Survival of Bodily Death*. Intro. Gardner Murphy, volume 1. 1903. Reprint, New York: Arno Press, 1975.

Nevada, Mignon. Letter of June 10, 1918. Lovat Dickson Collection, MG30, D237, vol. 4, folder 11. trans. National Archives of Canada, Ottawa, Ontario.

Newman, John Henry. *Apologia Pro Vita Sua*. Ed. David J. DeLaura. New York: W. W. Norton, 1968.

———. "A Letter Addressed to His Grace, the Duke of Norfolk." In *Newman and Gladstone: The Vatican Decrees*, intro. Alvan S. Ryan. Notre Dame, Ind.: University of Notre Dame Press, 1962.

Ockman, Carol, and Kenneth E. Silver. *Sarah Bernhardt: The Art of High Drama*. New Haven, Conn.: Yale University Press, 2006.

O'Malley, Patrick. *Catholicism, Sexual Deviance, and Victorian Gothic Culture*. Cambridge: Cambridge University Press, 2006.

———. "Epistemology of the Cloister: Victorian England's Queer Catholicism." *GLQ* 15:4 (2009): 535–64.

Oosterhuis, Harry. *Stepchildren of Nature: Krafft-Ebing, Psychiatry, and the Making of Sexual Identity*. Chicago: University of Chicago Press, 2000.

Ormrod, Richard. *Una Troubridge: The Friend of Radclyffe Hall*. London: Jonathan Cape, 1984.

Pater, Walter. *Plato and Platonism: A Series of Lectures*, 1893. Reprint, London: Macmillan, 1910.

———. *Studies in the History of the Renaissance*. London: Macmillan, 1873.

Payn, Graham, with Barry Day. *My Life with Noël Coward*. New York: Applause Books, 1994.

Phillips, Terry. "Battling with the Angel: May Sinclair's Powerful Mothers." In *Image and Power: Women in Fiction in the Twentieth Century*, ed. Sarah Sceats and Gail Cunningham, 128–38. New York: Longman, 1996.

Powell, Michael. *Edge of the World: The Making of a Film*. 1938. Reprint, London: Faber and Faber, 1990.

Primamore, Elizabeth. *The Invention of "Michael Field": A Dandy-Androgyne, Modernism and the Aesthetic World of Katherine Bradley and Edith Cooper*. Ann Arbor, Mich.: ProQuest Information and Learning Company, 2005.

Prins, Yopie. *Victorian Sappho*. Princeton, N.J.: Princeton University Press, 1999.

Prosser, Jay. *Second Skins: The Body Narratives of Transsexuality*. New York: Columbia University Press, 1998.

Psomiades, Kathy. "'Still Burning from This Strangling Embrace': Vernon Lee on Desire and Aesthetics." In *Victorian Sexual Dissidence*, ed. Richard Dellamora, 21–41. Chicago: University of Chicago Press, 1999.

"Psychical Research: The Spirits of the Dead," *The Times*, November 19, 1920, 4.

Raffalovich, Marc André. *Uranisme et Unisexualité: Étude sur Différentes Manifestations de l'Instinct Sexuel*. Bibliothèque de Criminologie. Vol. 15. 1896. Lyons: A. Storck; Paris: Masson, 1896.

Raitt, Suzanne. *May Sinclair: A Modern Victorian*. Oxford: Clarendon Press, 2000.

———. *Vita and Virginia: The Work and Friendship of V. Sackville-West and Virginia Woolf*. Oxford: Clarendon Press, 1993.

Rambuss, Richard. *Closet Devotions*. Durham, N.C.: Duke University Press, 1998.

Rapazzini, Francesco. *Elisabeth de Gramont, Avant-Gardiste*. Paris: Fayard, 2004.

———. "Elisabeth de Gramont, Natalie Barney's 'Eternal Mate.'" Special issue: "Natalie Barney and Her Circle." *South Central Review* 22:3 (Fall 2005): 6–31.

Rapp, Dean. "The Reception of Freud by the British Press: General Interest and Literary Magazines, 1920–1925." *Journal of the History of the Behavioral Sciences* 24 (April 1988): 191–201.

Reade, Brian, ed. *Sexual Heretics: Male Homosexuality in English Literature from 1850 to 1900*. New York: Coward-McCann, 1970.

Reinhard, Kenneth; Eric L. Santer; and Slavoj Zizek. *The Neighbor: Three Inquiries in Political Theology*. Chicago: University of Chicago Press, 2005.

Richards, Graham. "Britain on the Couch: The Popularization of Psychoanalysis in Britain, 1918–1940." *Science in Context* 13 (2000): 183–230.

Riviere, Joan. "Womanliness as a Masquerade." In *Formations of Fantasy*, ed. Victor Burgin, James Donald, and Cora Kaplan, 35–44. New York: Routledge, 1986.

———. *Same-Sex Desire in Victorian Religious Culture*. New York: Palgrave Macmillan, 2002.

Roden, Frederick S. "Introduction: The Catholic Modernist Crisis, Queer Modern Catholicisms." In *Catholic Figures, Queer Narratives*, ed. Lowell Gallagher, Frederick S. Roden, and Patricia Juliana Smith, 1–18. New York: Palgrave Macmillan, 2007.

———. "Michael Field, John Gray, and Marc-Andre Raffalovich: Reinventing Romantic Friendship in Modernity." In *Catholic Figures, Queer Narratives*, ed. Lowell Gallagher, Frederick S. Roden, and Patricia Juliana Smith, 57–68. New York: Palgrave Macmillan, 2007.

———. "Same-Sex Desire in Victorian Religious Culture." Ph.D. diss. New York University, 1999.

———. *Same-Sex Desire in Victorian Religious Culture*. New York: Palgrave Macmillan, 2002.

Roden, Frederick S.; Lowell Gallagher; and Patricia Juliana Smith, eds. *Catholic Figures, Queer Narratives*. New York: Palgrave Macmillan, 2007.

Rowland, Ingrid D. "The Battle of Light with Darkness." *New York Review of Books*, May 12, 2005, 10–13.

———. "Radiant, Angry Caravaggio." *New York Review of Books*, May 27, 2010, 10–14.

Schultz, Bart. "Truth and Its Consequences: The Friendship of Symonds and Henry Sidgwick." In John Pemble, ed., *John Addington Symonds: Culture and the Demon Desire,* 22–45. New York: St. Martin's Press, 2000.

Secrest, Meryle. *Between Me and Life: A Biography of Romaine Brooks.* New York: Doubleday, 1974.

Sedgwick, Eve Kosofsky. *Between Men: English Literature and Male Homosocial Desire.* New York: Columbia University Press, 1985.

———. *Tendencies.* Durham, N.C.: Duke University Press, 1993.

Shand-Tucci, Douglass. *The Art of Scandal: The Life and Times of Isabella Stewart Gardner.* New York: HarperCollins, 1997.

———. *Boston Bohemia, 1881–1900: Ralph Adams Cram: Life and Architecture.* Amherst: University of Massachusetts Press, 1995.

Showalter, Elaine. *A Literature of Their Own: British Women Novelists from Brontë to Lessing.* Princeton, N.J.: Princeton University Press, 1977.

Sinclair, May. *A Defence of Idealism: Some Questions and Conclusions.* New York: Macmillan, 1917.

———. *Feminism.* London: Women Writers' Suffrage League, [1912].

Smith, Patricia Juliana. *Lesbian Panic: Homoeroticism in Modern British Women's Fiction.* New York: Columbia University Press, 1997.

Smith-Rosenberg, Carroll. "The Body Politic." In *Coming to Terms: Feminism, Theory, Politics,* ed. Elizabeth Weed, 101–21. New York: Routledge, 1989.

Solomon-Godeau, Abigail. *Male Trouble: A Crisis in Representation.* London: Thames and Hudson, 1997.

Souhami, Diana. *Gluck, 1895–1978: Her Biography.* Rev. ed. London: Weidenfeld and Nicolson, 2000.

———. *The Trials of Radclyffe Hall.* New York: Doubleday, 1999.

Spencer, Grace S. Letters to Radclyffe Hall. January 23 and 30, 1927. Mss. Lovat Dickson Collection, MG30, D237, 4.9. National Archives of Canada, Ottawa, Ontario.

Spoto, Donald. *The Art of Alfred Hitchcock: Fifty Years of His Motion Pictures.* 2nd edition, rev. New York: Doubleday, 1992.

Stephensen, Percy Reginald, and Beresford Egan, et al. *The Sink of Solitude.* London: Hermes, 1928.

Stephenson, Glennis, ed. *Nineteenth-Century Stories by Women.* Peterborough, Ont.: Broadview, 1993.

Stetz, Margaret D., and Cheryl A. Wilson. *Michael Field and Their World.* High Wycombe, U.K.: Rivendale, 2007.

Stockton, Kathryn Bond. "Cloth Wounds, or When Queers Are Martyred to Clothes: Debasements of a Fabricated Skin." In *Beautiful Bottom, Beautiful Shame: Where "Black" Meets "Queer,"* 39–66. Durham, N.C.: Duke University Press, 2006.

Thurman, Judith. Introduction. In Colette, *Gigi, Julie de Carneilhan, Chance Acquaintances,* vii–xxii. New York: Farrar, Straus and Giroux, 2001.

———. *Secrets of the Flesh: A Life of Colette.* New York: Alfred A. Knopf, 1999.

Thurschwell, Pamela. *Literature, Technology, and Magical Thinking, 1880–1920*. Cambridge: Cambridge University Press, 2001.

Trial on appeal of Jonathan Cape and Leopold Hill, Friday, December 14. 1928. Transcript. Lovat Dickson Collection, MG30, D237. 5.10. National Archives of Canada, Ottawa, Ontario.

Troubridge, Una. Day Book, volume 60, Feb. 6, 1943—June 21, 1943 Radclyffe Hall fonds. 32.4. Harry Ransom Humanities Research Center, University of Texas, Austin, Texas.

———. Diary, 1928. Lovat Dickson Collection, MG30, D237. 2.6. National Archives of Canada, Ottawa, Ontario.

———. *I Remember*. Typescript. Lovat Dickson Collection, MG30, D237. 3.9, 3.10, 3.11. National Archives of Canada, Ottawa, Ontario.

———. *The Life and Death of Radclyffe Hall*. London: Hammond, Hammond, 1961.

———. *The Life of Radclyffe Hall*. New York: Citadel, 1963.

———. [Lady Troubridge.] "The *Modus Operandi* in So-Called Mediumistic Trance." *Proceedings of the Society for Psychical Research* 32 (January 1922): 344–78.

———. *Such Was Life*. Typescript. Lovat Dickson Collection, MG30, D237. 3.8. National Archives of Canada, Ottawa, Ontario.

Tyrrell, George. *Notes on the Catholic Doctrine of Purity*. Roehampton: Manresa Press, 1897.

Underhill, Evelyn. *Mysticism: A Study in the Nature and Development of Man's Spiritual Consciousness*. London: Methuen, 1911.

Vanita, Ruth. *Sappho and the Virgin Mary: Same-Sex Love and the English Literary Imagination*. New York: Columbia University Press, 1996.

———. "Tragic Love and the Ungendered Heart: Readng *The Well of Loneliness* in India and the West." In *Gandhi's Tiger and Sita's Smile: Essays on Gender, Sexuality and Culture*, 136–53. New Delhi: Yoda Press, 2005.

———. "'Uncovenanted Joys': Catholicism, Sapphism, and Cambridge Ritual Theory in Hope Mirrlees' *Madeleine: One of Love's Jansenists*." In *Catholic Figures, Queer Narratives*, ed. Lowell Gallagher, Frederick S. Roden, and Patricia Juliana Smith, 85–96. New York: Palgrave Macmillan, 2007.

Vicinus, Martha. *Independent Women: Work and Community for Single Women, 1850–1920*. Chicago: University of Chicago Press, 1985.

———. *Intimate Friends: Women Who Loved Women, 1778–1928*. Chicago: University of Chicago Press, 2004.

———. "'Sister Souls': Bernard Berenson and Michael Field (Katharine Bradley and Edith Cooper)." *Nineteenth-Century Literature* 60 (December 2005): 326–54.

Wagner, Richard. *The Ring of the Nibelung*. German text with English translation by Andrew Porter. New York: W. W. Norton, 1977.

Walpole, Hugh. "Nobody." In *The Penguin Book of First World War Stories*, ed. Barbara Korte and Anne-Marie Einhaus, 256–77. London: Penguin Books, 2007.

Warner, Michael. *Publics and Counterpublics*. New York: Zone Books, 2002.

Waters, Sarah. *Tipping the Velvet*. London: Virago, 2003.

Weeks, Jeffrey. *Coming Out: Homosexual Politics in Britain, from the Nineteenth Century to the Present*. London: Quartet Books, 1977.

West, Thomas G. *In the Mind's Eye: Visual Thinkers, Gifted People with Learning Difficulties, Computer Images, and the Ironies of Creativity*. Updated edition. Amherst, N.Y.: Prometheus, 1997.

Wilde, Oscar. *The Artist as Critic: Critical Writings of Oscar Wilde*. Ed. Richard Ellmann. New York: Vintage, 1969.

———. *Complete Short Fiction*. Harmondsworth: Penguin, 1994.

———. *De Profundis and Other Writings*. Intro. Hesketh Pearson. London: Penguin Books, 1986.

Wills, Garry. "High Fidelity." *New York Review of Books*, December 5, 2002, 40–43.

Wilson, Edmund. *The Wound and the Bow: Seven Studies in Literature*. London: Methuen, 1961.

Woodhouse, Adrian. *Beresford Egan*. Leyburn: Tartarus, 2005.

Woolf, Virginia. *Jacob's Room*. Intro. David Denby. New York: Signet, 1994.

———. "Mr. Bennett and Mrs. Brown." In *Approaches to the Novel: Materials for a Poetics*, ed. Robert Scholes, 186–206. Rev. ed. San Francisco: Chandler, 1966.

———. *Orlando: A Biography*, New York: Signet, 1960.

———. "Professions for Women." In *The Death of the Moth and Other Essays*, 235–42. New York: Harcourt, Brace, 1942.

———. *Three Guineas*. New York: Harcourt Brace Jovanovich, 1966.

———. *Women and Writing*. Intro. Michèle Barrett. London: Women's Press, 1979.

Wright, Sir Almroth. "Suffrage Fallacies." *The Times*, March 28, 1912, 7–8.

Zorn, Christa. *Vernon Lee: Aesthetics, History, and the Victorian Female Intellectual*. Athens: Ohio University Press, 2003.

INDEX

ACKNOWLEDGMENTS

This book began with an invitation to present a paper on Radclyffe Hall at the conference "Counter Modernisms," organized by Lynne Hapgood and Nancy L. Paxton at Nottingham Trent University (U.K.) in 1996. I am grateful to the conference organizers and, in particular, to Nancy Paxton for having opened the way that led to the present book. A generous multi-year research grant from the Social Sciences and Humanities Research Council of Canada provided the practical means required to undertake archival research on Hall's writing in the United States, Canada, and the United Kingdom along with unpublished writings by Una Troubridge. During this period, the Dean of Graduate Studies and the Office of Research at my home institution, Trent University in Peterborough, Ontario, Canada, provided continual practical and moral support. Conversations with colleagues, undergraduates, and graduate students at Trent over the past decade have enlivened and enriched this study. And summer and sabbatical stays in the departments of English at the University of California at Los Angeles and the University of California at Irvine have provided intellectual and practical resources for chapters researched and written during summers there, beginning in 1998 and continuing to the present.

In undertaking this project, I also received encouragement, support, and at times direction from colleagues and friends, among them Laura Doan, Jack Halberstam, Neville Hoad, Ann Cvetkovich, Kathy Psomiades, Margaret D. Stetz, and Martha Vicinus. To the many listeners who responded to conference papers and invited lectures presented at a number of venues in Canada, the United Kingdom, and the United States, I am also grateful. Their comments and questions have made the resulting book a better one than it otherwise would have been. The work of feminist Aesthetes provides one important point of reference for Hall's early work as a writer. During the period in which I researched and wrote the book, I was able to draw on the critical mass recently achieved in feminist research on a number of these authors (namely, Vernon Lee; Katherine Bradley and Edith Cooper, who wrote under the pen name of Michael Field; and the early modernist May Sinclair). Much of this work was made available at international conferences on Lee at the University of London in June 2003, and on Field at the University of Delaware in February 2004. The occasion of a keynote address delivered at the conference "Decadence, Ancient and Modern," sponsored by the Bristol Institute of Hellenic and Roman Studies at the University of Bristol in Bristol, England, in July 2003, provided me with additional opportunity for thinking Hall, so to speak, within the contexts of late nineteenth-century Decadence and Aestheticism.

I am extremely grateful to Jonathan Lovat Dickson, Literary Executor of the Estate of Radclyffe Hall, and A. M. Heath & Company Ltd. for permission to make use of digitized images for illustrations and to draw on holograph writing and typescripts by Hall and Troubridge in the primary archives at Texas and in Ottawa and for individual letters in the Berg Collection (New York Public Library) and the Cambridge University Library. And I would like to thank Maxine Y. Hunt and Oriol, Lady Bowden, trustees of the Estate of Beresford Egan, for permission to reproduce two images from Egan's suite of six for *The Sink of Solitude*.

I would also like to thank Patrice Fox at the Harry Ransom Humanities Research Center at the University of Texas at Austin for her assistance on many occasions as well as that of Sophie Tellier at the Archives of the National Library in Ottawa, Canada. Librarians at the Public Records Office at Kew and the Colindale Newspaper Library assisted me while researching in England. Closer to home, librarians at the Young Research Library at UCLA and the Pratt Library at Victoria College of the University of Toronto have been helpful on a daily basis. Martha B. Campbell was an excellent host during visits to Austin.

I wish to acknowledge with thanks permission to reproduce in Chapter 8 in revised form a portion of the symposium contribution "Friendship, Marriage, and *Between Women*," which originally appeared in *Victorian Studies*, 50.1 (Autumn 2007): 67–74; in Chapter 7 a portion in revised form of the essay "*The Well of Loneliness* and the Catholic Rhetoric of Sexual

Dissidence," which originally appeared in *Catholic Figures, Queer Narratives*, ed. Lowell Gallagher, Frederick Roden, and Patricia Smith (London: Palgrave Macmillan, 2007), 114–28; and in Chapter 9 a portion in revised form of the essay "Engendering Modernism: The Vernacular Modernism of Radclyffe Hall," in *Outside Modernism: In Pursuit of the English Novel, 1900–1930*, ed. Lynne Hapgood and Nancy L. Paxton (Basingstoke, England: Macmillan, 2000), 85–103.

From the outset, I have enjoyed the strong, patient, and continuing encouragement of Jerry Singerman, Humanities Editor at the University of Pennsylvania Press, and the able assistance of staff at the Press.